The
Wadsworth Guide to Research

The
Wadsworth Guide to Research

Second
Edition

Susan K. Miller-Cochran

North Carolina State University

Rochelle L. Rodrigo

Old Dominion University

WADSWORTH
CENGAGE Learning

Australia • Brazil • Japan • Korea • Mexico • Singapore • Spain • United Kingdom • United States

WADSWORTH
CENGAGE Learning™

The Wadsworth Guide to Research, **Second Edition**
Susan K. Miller-Cochran
Rochelle L. Rodrigo

Publisher: Monica Eckman

Acquiring Sponsoring Editor:
Kate Derrick

Supervising Development
Editor: Leslie Taggart

Development Editor:
Stephanie P. Carpenter

Assistant Editor:
Danielle Warchol

Editorial Assistant:
Marjorie Cross

Media Editor: Cara Douglass-Graff

Brand Manager: Lydia LeStar

Content Project Manager:
Rosemary Winfield

Art Director: Marissa Falco

Manufacturing Planner:
Betsy Donaghey

Rights Acquisition Specialist:
Alexandra Ricciardi

Production Service: Matrix
Productions, Cenveo
Publishing

Text and Cover Designer:
Paul Fry

Cover Image: (c) Laurent Hamels/
Photo Alto/Corbis

Compositor: Cenveo Publisher
Services

For product information and technology assistance, contact us at **Cengage Learning Customer & Sales Support, 1-800-354-9706**.

For permission to use material from this text or product, submit all requests online at **www.cengage.com/permissions**. Further permissions questions can be emailed to **permissionrequest@cengage.com**.

Library of Congress Control Number: 2012950278

ISBN-13: 978-0-495-91287-3

ISBN-10: 0-495-91287-5

Wadsworth
20 Channel Center Street
Boston, MA 02210
USA

Cengage Learning is a leading provider of customized learning solutions with office locations around the globe, including Singapore, the United Kingdom, Australia, Mexico, Brazil, and Japan. Locate your local office at **international.cengage.com/region**.

Cengage Learning products are represented in Canada by Nelson Education, Ltd.

For your course and learning solutions, visit **www.cengage.com**. Purchase any of our products at your local college store or at our preferred online store **www.cengagebrain.com**.

Instructors: Please visit **login.cengage.com** and log in to access instructor-specific resources.

Printed in China
2 3 4 5 16 15 14 13

Contents

chapter five: **Conducting Primary Research 93**

chapter six: **Rhetorically Reading, Tracking, and Evaluating Resources 111**

part 3: Reporting on Research 165

chapter eight: Developing an Argument 167

chapter nine: Selecting and Integrating Evidence 189

chapter ten: Sharing the Results 201

Research. Ick.

Sound familiar?

Nothing sounds more boring to students—more irrelevant to their everyday lives—than research.

And yet we do research every day. We compare gas prices and cell phone plans, make grocery lists, and read movie reviews. We look up music lyrics, class schedules, headlines, weather reports, game scores, personal ads, and newspaper articles. And often we use the information we find to make decisions—and to persuade others to make decisions as well.

So . . . why are students so put off by the idea of doing research?

We are convinced that one of the reasons is because students don't realize that they already do research every day, and they can refine the skills they already have to conduct effective academic research. Research skills are transferable, but students have to understand that the context of their research impacts the kinds of strategies they will find useful and the results that they'll find.

What's more, academic research can be overwhelming. Students are often faced with big end-of-semester research projects, due at the same time as several other projects for different classes, all on topics that they don't know much about and in genres with which they're not yet familiar—yet they feel they must sound as if they are experts on the topics by the time they're finished. Anyone would be intimidated by such a situation, and students often don't know where to start. The short-term solution is generally to put the projects off until the last minute and then try to come up with something the night before they're due.

WHAT'S DIFFERENT ABOUT THIS RESEARCH GUIDE?

This guide approaches research in a unique way—by helping students think about how to look for connections between the research they already do in their personal, academic, and perhaps even professional lives. By breaking research down into a set of smaller strategies that fit together into a research process for students, *The Wadsworth Guide to Research* makes the task of academic research more manageable, relevant, and—believe it or not—even enjoyable. Perhaps most importantly, this guide emphasizes that *context matters*. Research strategies are affected by the rhetorical situations in which we research—the audiences we write to, the topics we write about, the purposes for which we're writing, and the background and perspective of the author who is doing the writing and researching.

Research is a complex process, and it needs to be adapted to the situation surrounding it. Yet the leading texts that teach research-based writing tend to treat the research process as *one* process—a step-by-step plan that will work in any situation—without acknowledging the ways that context influences research or the fact that research takes place in settings outside of academia. This book presents a different approach to research-based writing, one that encourages students to think critically about the situation surrounding a research project and how that context shapes and influences the decisions they make in their research.

Specifically, we ask students to think about how the purpose, audience, topic, and perspective of the author connect and influence the research they conduct:

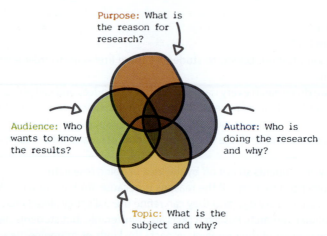

Purpose: What is the reason for research?

Audience: Who wants to know the results?

Author: Who is doing the research and why?

Topic: What is the subject and why?

Figure 1.1   The Rhetorical Situation

The driving philosophy behind this textbook is that all research takes place in a certain place at a certain time, and the context surrounding the research project impacts the process. Successful researchers learn to identify what is important in their research situation and weave those elements into their research process. They also have a variety of different tools at their disposal that they can draw on in order to match their context with the needs of their research project. Research-based writing is about choices, and our goal is to provide students with tools to make effective choices—not to make all of the choices for them.

In addition, this text is based on the premise that research projects take shape in the form of different genres. Therefore, we have included examples of different genres from a variety of disciplines and research contexts to help scaffold students' research processes.

WHAT'S NEW IN THIS EDITION?

The newly revised and expanded DIY (Do-It-Yourself) sections in Parts 1–4 (which replace the Research in Progress sections) provide examples of various genres to emphasize the writing that is done in different academic disciplines and professional contexts. You'll find a greater variety of examples and more robust and integrated support for research projects in this edition.

At the end of each DIY, you'll find a feature designed to help students "Make It with Multiple Media." Each of these sections provides students with an example of a student-designed research project using multimedia to accomplish the goals of that DIY section.

One of the biggest changes in this edition is the addition of Chapter 11, "Understanding Citation Styles Rhetorically." Many instructors struggle with making citation practices interesting and relevant to students. We've integrated the focus on rhetorical context into a discussion of citation styles to help students understand that citation systems are rhetorically constructed and reflect the values and conventions of the academic disciplines that use them. The Part 4 DIY, "Writing a Rhetorical Analysis of Citations," also new to this edition, provides guidance through a variety of writing projects that ask students to think about citation styles from this perspective, such as writing a rhetorical analysis of citation practices.

HOW IS THE GUIDE ORGANIZED?

Are there common steps that most researchers take when working through a research project? Absolutely! The key is that these steps are "common," but not necessarily "identical." Other research textbooks tend to present research as one monolithic process without acknowledging that researchers adapt their approaches and sometimes rearrange the steps depending on the situations they encounter. *The Wadsworth Guide to Research* is organized to walk students through some of the common elements of a research process while allowing them to adapt those steps to the project they are tackling. The various strategies are organized into four sections:

- **Part One: Preparing for Research.** Part One walks students through the process of identifying a topic that they would like to research (usually the most daunting task for students), formulating a research question, and writing a research proposal.

- **Part Two: Conducting Research.** With research, organization is key, and Part Two guides students through the gathering of data and resources that will help them respond to their research question. Having students respond to their own research question gives them a sense of ownership and investment.

- **Part Three: Reporting on Research.** Sending the results of our research out into the world can be intimidating, but it can be less so if we have the right tools and strategies for communicating our message. Part Three guides students through the process of putting research results into an appropriate format so that they can share their research effectively with others to achieve their intended purpose.

- **Part Four: Formatting Your Research.** Research is most effective when it follows expected conventions for a particular rhetorical situation. Part Four helps students use academic citation systems to document their research by explaining these systems from a rhetorical perspective.

As students work through the different sections of the book, the features and activities help them identify the specific rhetorical situation of their own research while also understanding how research is conducted in and adapted to different contexts.

- Chapters 1–11 open with a **Research in Action** scenario that gives students a specific example of how the principles introduced in that chapter might work in a specific rhetorical context.

    Why use this feature? These quick case studies can be used as classroom discussion starters, and they can provide a starting point for having students practice analyzing the context of research.

- The **reflect** activities ask students to think about prior research they've done and the potential connections between current research and research they have already done or are doing in different contexts.

Why use this feature? These activities ask students to explore aspects of the rhetorical situation of their own research project.

- The `write` activities walk students through the steps of actually writing about and drafting a report of their research.

  Why use this feature? These activities break the research process down into manageable pieces for students to tackle one at a time.

- The `techno tip` activities offer suggestions and instructions for how students might use various technological tools in their own research. Even though many students now are familiar with using technology, they likely haven't used technology extensively to conduct effective academic research.

  Why use this feature? The Techno Tips can be a powerful way for students to make connections between what they already know and what they can learn to help strengthen their research practices. Students will learn to use technology for many purposes—from generating ideas to getting organized to finding sources. Even if you or your students don't already know how to utilize these technologies—don't worry! These tips focus on several different web-based applications that students can use at various stages of their research, and they emphasize open source and freeware applications wherever possible.

- Many instructors agree that the most typical research assignments are a research proposal, a review of prior research, and a researched argument. To help students understand the different genres associated with each assignment, as well as what's required of them for these common assignments, the DIY (Do-It-Yourself) sections at the end of each part of the guide summarize and make use of all the skills explained in the prior chapters. The fourth DIY section, focusing on citation styles, helps students understand the importance and complexity of citation systems through common assignment genres like a rhetorical analysis.

  Why use this feature? Each DIY section includes descriptions of different genres that do the "work" of the specific assignment (proposal, review of literature, researched argument, and understanding citation). The chapters also include student examples, showing teacher comments to highlight strengths and weaknesses. The DIY assignments build on each other to walk students through the entire process of developing an extended research project.

- At the end of each DIY section there is a **Make It with Multiple Media** section where students are introduced to a variety of suggestions on how to present their project in a different format or media. Students will be introduced to making presentations, social bookmarking, constructing web sites, and producing videos.

  Why use this feature? Not only have research processes themselves become highly mediated, but the way individuals share research results—both inside and outside the academy—have become highly mediated as well. Asking students to at least think about the rhetorical implications of presenting their research in a different media, if not explicitly having them construct and publish in that media, helps prepare students for work in the information economy of the twenty-first century.

WHY SHOULD YOU USE THIS RESEARCH GUIDE?

Everyone is a researcher. The text used in a class that teaches research-based writing should help students realize that research is a necessary part of their personal, academic, and professional lives and prepare them for the kinds of research they'll need to do. Unfortunately, most research textbooks continue to emphasize only one approach and fail to make research relevant to students. *The Wadsworth Guide to Research* can help you make those connections with your students and prepare them to conduct effective research, both in college and beyond.

The Wadsworth Guide to Research is designed to be used in any class that has a research component, and it can also be a tool for research outside of academic contexts. The activities and principles in the book walk readers through a specific research project, or projects, regardless of the approach used in the class:

- **I assign one research paper throughout the entire semester. How can I keep students interested the whole way through?**

  - *The Wadsworth Guide to Research* walks students through three different projects that help them develop an effective, well-researched argument and a complex understanding of an issue. The first project carefully guides students through the process of choosing a topic that is relevant and interesting to them—one in which they're invested—that will help them maintain a semester-long interest in their research.

- **I assign two or more research papers a semester. How could I use this book?**

  - Students can work through the projects in *The Wadsworth Guide to Research* more than once during a semester. Consider spending more time on the assignments the first time through to give students a firm foundation in research. You could also emphasize different kinds of research each time through (i.e., research questions that arise from different disciplinary areas; gathering data and working with various technologies; or research questions that come from their personal, professional, and academic lives).

- **I assign a nontraditional research project that asks students to use new media to write in a multimodal format. How could my students benefit from this book?**

  - *The Wadsworth Guide to Research* could be an ideal fit for your class. No other book on the market helps students use as wide of a variety of technologies in their research process and assists them as thoroughly in documenting new media resources that they might use in their research.

SUPPLEMENTS

Cengage Learning offers many supplemental resources that will help you and your students as they develop their research projects.

Infotrac® College Edition with InfoMarks™ This online research and learning center offers over twenty million full-text articles from nearly six thousand scholarly and popular periodicals. The articles cover a broad spectrum of disciplines and topics—ideal for every type of researcher. Learn more at www.cengage.com/infotrac. (Access code/card required).

Wadsworth's Enhanced InSite for Writing and Research™ Easily create, assign, and grade writing assignments with Enhanced InSite™ for *The Wadsworth Guide to Research*. From a single, easy-to-navigate site, you and your students can manage the flow of papers online, check for originality, and conduct peer reviews. Students can access a multimedia ebook, private tutoring options, and resources for writers that include anti-plagiarism tutorials and downloadable grammar podcasts. Enhanced InSite™ provides the tools and resources you and your students need plus the training and support you want. Learn more at http://www.cengage.com/insite.

Turnitin® This proven, online plagiarism-prevention software promotes fairness in the classroom by helping students learn to correctly cite sources and allowing instructors to check for originality before reading and grading papers. (Access code/card required).

Merriam-Webster's Collegiate® Dictionary, Eleventh Edition America's best-selling dictionary delivers accurate, up-to-date information while students are working on writing assignments, composing email, and designing spreadsheets—you name it. This eleventh edition of *Merriam-Webster's Collegiate Dictionary and Thesaurus* contains nearly 60,000 alphabetical dictionary entries integrated with more than 13,000 thesaurus entries, including extensive synonym lists. This indispensable tool will give your students fast and easy access to the words they need to know today from all areas of human endeavor, including electronic technology, the sciences, and popular culture.

QUESTIA Six-Month Subscription Printed Access Card Questia is the online library that provides 24/7 access to the Web's premier collection of full-text books and academic journal and periodical articles in the humanities and social sciences. And it is more than a vast collection of online sources. Questia can help your students in the entire research process, from topic selection and research to organization of their notes and proper citations. Questia will help your students write better papers, providing a wider array of scholarly sources and enabling them to organize what they've learned into a better-thought-out paper.

English CourseMate with eBook for *The Wadsworth Guide to Research*, Second Edition Interested in a simple way to complement your text and course content with study and practice materials? Cengage Learning's English CourseMate brings course concepts to life with interactive learning, study, and exam preparation tools that support the printed textbook. Watch student comprehension soar as your class works with the printed textbook and the textbook-specific web site. English CourseMate goes beyond the book to deliver what you need! Learn more at http://www.cengage.com/coursemate.

ACKNOWLEDGMENTS

Writing a textbook requires a tremendous amount of support and a great deal of patience, and we have been fortunate to have much assistance along the way from folks who have encouraged us—and pushed us—when we needed it. First and foremost, we have not only been honored to work with Stephanie Carpenter, our top-notch development editor, but we've had a blast as well! Stephanie's thorough experience in the field has turned a solid first edition, written by first-time textbook authors, into a robust and mature second edition. We also greatly appreciate Leslie Taggart, our senior development editor, for her larger vision and wisdom for how the book will continue to grow within the field. We're also grateful to Kate Derrick, our acquisitions editor, and Monica Eckman, our publisher, who have been generously supportive of the second edition of this project. Stacey Purviance and Jason Sakos, our marketing sages, have never failed in their enthusiasm for this project and in their abilities to renew our excitement about it. Cara Douglass-Graff, media editor, has helped our online presence support the vision of the textbook. Rosemary Winfield and Aaron Downey painstakingly guided the text through the production process, and Josh Garvin, Jill Krupnik, and Alex Ricciardi carefully and enthusiastically tracked down the texts and images that we felt were essential for the textbook to convey meaning. To each of these people we owe a huge debt of gratitude—without them, our ideas would have no voice.

We are also extremely grateful to the students who were willing to share their writing in this book. Their examples are a critical component of the research guide, and their generosity in sharing their work truly appreciated.

We appreciate the outstanding comments and suggestions that we received from the following colleagues who took their time to review the manuscript while it was under construction:

Emory Reginald Abbott, Georgia Perimeter College
Devon Adams, Mesa Community College
Gillian Andersen, Eastern New Mexico University
Susan Ariew, University of South Florida
Ellen Barton, Wayne State University
Basak Tarkan-Blanco, Miami-Dade Community College—Kendall Campus
Richard Bogart, Essex County College
Arnold Bradford, Northern Virginia Community College
Eric Branscomb, Salem State College
Amy Braziller, Red Rocks Community College
Linda Brender, Macomb Community College
Carolyn Calhoon-Dillahunt, Yakima Valley Community College
Anita P. Chirco, Keuka College
Marisue Coy, Kentucky Wesleyan College
Barbara D'Angelo, Arizona State University
Kevin Eric DePew, Old Dominion University
Clark L. Draney, College of Southern Idaho
Don Erskine, Clark College
Elizabeth (Sharifa) Evans, Georgia Perimeter College
Douglas Eyman, George Mason University
Brian Fehler, Tarleton State University
Christina Fisanick, Xavier University
Cynthia Fischer, Harford Community College
Teddi Fishman, Clemson University
Letizia Guglielmo, Kennesaw State College
Christine Heilman, College of Mount Saint Joseph
Candy A. Henry, Westmoreland County Community College
Michael Hricik, Westmoreland County Community College
Greg Kemble, Yuba College
Cindy King, Berry College

Patricia Kohler, Syracuse University
Sharon L. Lagina, Wayne County Community College
Benjamin D. Lareau, Casper College
Gary Leising, Utica College
David C. Lowery, Jones County Junior College
Vickie Machen, Texas A&M University—Corpus Christi
Kate Mangelsdorf, University of Texas—El Paso
Janice Marshall, University of Wisconsin, Marathon County
Angela Megaw, Gainesville State College
Connie Mick, University of Notre Dame
Kathleen Mollick, Tarleton State University
Bryan Moore, Arkansas State University
Kris Muschal, Richland Community College
Fran O'Connor, Nassau Community College
Veronica Pantoja, Chandler-Gilbert Community College
Matt Porter, North Carolina State University
Colleen A. Reilly, University of North Carolina at Wilmington
Janet Ridgeway, Syracuse University
Jenny R. Sadre-Orafai, Kennesaw State College
Andrew Scott, Ball State University
Jeff Simmons, Syracuse University
Jennie Stearns, Georgia Perimeter College
Diane Svoboda, Mesa Community College
Jeremy Venema, Mesa Community College
Carol S. Warren, Georgia Perimeter College
Phillip Wedgeworth, Jones County Junior College
Anne Williams, Indiana University-Purdue University Indianapolis
David Wilson-Okamura, East Carolina University
Cheryl Windham, Jones County Junior College

We remain indebted to our former colleagues at Mesa Community College and current colleagues at North Carolina State University and Old Dominion University, especially the members of the First-Year Composition Committee at MCC and the faculty in the First-Year Writing Program at NCSU, who have provided inspiration and guidance that continually encourage us to refine our approaches to teaching research. Many of them used the first edition of the textbook and were willing to share their time and energy to help us imagine better ways to help students learn to be better researchers.

And most important, we would like to thank our families—Stacey, Sam, Harper, and Tom—who have been patient, encouraging, and endlessly giving of their time and energy as we worked on this project. We could not ask for more supportive partners.

The
Wadsworth Guide to Research

chapter 1

Research and the Rhetorical Situation

The word *research* strikes fear into the heart of many students. Why? Some students report that research is boring or that they're fearful of the grade that they'll receive when they turn in their assignments. Others are uncertain about their teachers' expectations, and they might be wary of the amount of time they'll have to put into a research assignment. These fears can be relieved if you understand how to do research, what the expectations are for your research, and how it will be assessed. In addition, choosing a topic in which you are interested and invested can make research helpful and enjoyable, even exciting, instead of boring. In Kendell's research scenario detailed on the next page, for example, she is interested in her topic, and she has experience with it. She will probably enjoy her research project because she sees an immediate purpose for the work she is doing.

we'll explore

▶ *the rhetorical situation's effects on writing and research*

▶ *similarities and differences between academic research and research for other purposes*

▶ *reasons for conducting research*

▶ *comparisons of writing and research in different academic disciplines*

Research in Action

Author: As part of the service learning component of a class she is taking, Kendell decides to volunteer at a local homeless shelter.

Topic: Kendell wants to understand how to help people in the homeless shelter who are also struggling with mental illness, so she starts to research schizophrenia and other serious psychological illnesses.

Brand X Pictures/Getty Images

Audience: Kendell's original audience is her professor, but when the managers of the homeless shelter realize that she is doing the research, they ask Kendell to share the results with the other volunteers.

Purpose: Kendell needs to find reliable information that she can condense into manageable pieces to pass on to the other homeless shelter volunteers.

Questions

1. How do the elements of Kendell's situation detailed above help develop her research topic?

2. How might Kendell present her research results to her intended audience? How do the elements of her situation suggest this presentation or publication plan?

3. What other things might Kendell want to find out about her situation before beginning her research?

4. Can you imagine other aspects of the situation that would affect researching, writing, and presenting or publishing in this case?

Recognizing Research Contexts

You might be surprised to realize that you've been conducting research for a long time. Whenever you have a problem to solve or a question to answer, you decide what kind of information you will need to solve the problem or find the answer; that is, you decide what kind of research you need to conduct to find an answer or solution. In school, you might be used to thinking of research in terms of going to the library, searching for information on the Internet, or writing a report. Research certainly takes place in academic contexts, but it also takes place in our everyday lives. For example, you might have conducted research about which college to attend, or you might research a particular company if you are applying for a job. Sometimes your research involves a large-scale investigation, but often it is pretty informal. The goal of this book is to help you develop strategies for conducting research in all sorts of scenarios: college classes, work settings, and various personal situations.

Although you'll be able to use the methods in this book to approach any kind of research, the key to remember is that research is highly situational. That is, research needs and processes change according to the circumstances. For example, imagine that someone close to you is experiencing heart problems, and you want him or her to go to the best doctor available. Answering the question, "Which heart doctor should my mother/father/friend/loved one go to?" requires some research. Not only do you need to do research on local doctors and their expertise, but you also have to consider the person's resources (especially medical insurance coverage) as an important element of the research situation. Although the final product of your research may simply be the name of a specific doctor, the reading, writing, and thinking you put into the process is considerable and depends on multiple variables within the situation.

People encounter problems that can be solved by carefully constructed research questions every day—questions about which car to buy, whether to lease or purchase that car, whether to adopt a pet, where (and how) to apply for a specific job, which utility company to choose, where to apply for scholarships and financial aid for school, which store to purchase textbooks from at the beginning of the semester, or which classes to take. While you are in school, you'll also conduct academic research to find answers to a variety of questions. Even school assignments are situational, though; they depend on the teacher's expectations, the course, the discipline, and a variety of other factors, such as:

▶ topic chosen or assigned

▶ length of the paper or project

▶ whether you conduct primary research

▶ whether you interpret something or critique someone else's interpretation

▶ whether you develop a theory about a phenomenon or test someone else's theory

▶ the expected product: a proposal? a developed argument? a report? an analysis? a description of a methodology? a review of previous research on the subject?

You will continue to encounter research situations outside of the academic setting. In the workplace, you might encounter research questions—either ones that are assigned to you (What do we need to include in our proposal in order to win the contract?) or issues that intrigue you (What salary would be competitive and fair for the work that I will be doing in my new job?). Working through the activities and projects described in this book will help you with the everyday research that you already do, the academic research you'll be expected to do, and the workplace research that you'll want to do in the future.

Regardless of the purpose of the research you are conducting, the general research principles remain the same, although your approach might vary depending on the situation and context of your research. This book will guide you through developing your own research process and developing arguments that consider the **rhetorical situation**. The rhetorical situation is the context surrounding a particular research or writing task. In other words, we will ask you to consider how several contextual factors influence your research:

- ▶ **topic**—what you are researching
- ▶ **purpose**—why you are researching it
- ▶ **audience**—to whom you are writing (reporting results)
- ▶ **author**—who you are and the experience you bring to the issue you are researching

When you consider the rhetorical situation of your writing, you are considering these elements. These factors influence not only the research that you do and how you conduct it but also your conclusions and your presentation of those conclusions to your readers. Additionally, becoming more thoughtful about your own research process will make you a more careful reader of the research and arguments of others.

How Have You Conducted Research Before?

reflect

Think of a situation recently in which you had to conduct research to solve a problem. Perhaps you had to solve some transportation problems in getting to school, or maybe you had to come up with a solution to a challenge at work. You might even consider the choice that you made about where to enroll in classes or which degree to pursue. Answer the following questions about that experience.

1. Describe the situation. Why did you need to conduct research? What did you need to find out? Try to state your challenge as a question that you needed to answer.

2. Who was involved in the situation—just you, or did the research and conclusion(s) affect others? Did you conduct the research alone or with others?

3. How did you explore possible answers to your question? Where did you look for information? Did you ask anyone for advice? Did you look for information that others had written, or did you gather information by talking to people?

4. What conclusion(s) did you come to? How did you decide on that conclusion?

5. Were you satisfied that you had considered all the options or did you make a quick decision? If time was a factor, was there something you would have done differently if you had had more time?

6. How did you share the results of your research? Who wanted or needed the information and how did you present it to them?

Identifying Research Purposes

You might conduct research for a number of reasons, but each time you're essentially doing the same thing—answering a question. In other words, there are a multitude of purposes you may fulfill by answering research questions. You might choose which college to apply to or what car to buy. You might decide where to live or which name to choose for your baby. You might point out an often-overlooked reason for the start of World War II or propose a more efficient process for your company. Each of these personal, academic, and work-related situations requires that you ask a question and then find an answer.

When most people think of traditional research purposes, they think of research to answer an academic question. For example, a history professor might ask the class to dig a little deeper into the history of World War II and to question the reasons that traditional textbooks give for the war. This research question requires the student not only to answer the question, "What are the traditionally cited reasons for the start of World War II?" but also to consider other possible causes of the war. After looking at numerous textbooks to understand which reasons are often cited, the student needs to access highly specialized references (history journals, discussion boards, even individual scholars) to search out other possibilities. Because this is an academic assignment, the student has access to traditional academic resources: library materials, databases, and professors. However, one student in the class may have a family member who fought on the European front in World War II. Another student's family may have emigrated from Japan after the war. These students may have access to personal and individualized resources that relate to the cultural situation at the beginning of and during World War II.

Such a research project is a fairly traditional example of the purpose and situation of a research assignment in a school setting. You will likely find that you will adapt your research process to the research question, the context in which you need to answer it, and the resources to which you have access. For any research question and context, it's important to be aware of the rhetorical situation.

reflect

How Do Research Processes Compare?

Think about two times you've conducted research in the past: one when you conducted research for a school project and one when you conducted research to answer a question for yourself. Think about the processes that you used in each situation and respond to the following questions.

	Academic Research	Personal Research
Why did you conduct this research? If you were given instructions, what were they?		
What questions did you ask?		
How did you start?		

>>>

>>>

	Academic Research	Personal Research
What went right and what went wrong?		
What were the outcomes of your research?		
How would you conduct your research differently if you were to do it again?		

Considering Elements of the Rhetorical Situation

Whenever we conduct research, and especially when we share the results of our research, we must consider each element of the rhetorical situation of our research and writing: the topic, purpose, audience, and author. In the history project example, the professor requested that students write an essay about possible causes of World War II. Such an essay would require that the students demonstrate their understanding of both the generally mentioned causes of World War II and possible alternative causes. On the other hand, the professor might request that rather than write an essay, the students use the results of their research in a letter to the author of the course's history textbook, proposing that a lesser-mentioned reason be given more attention in the textbook's next edition. In this letter, students would have to demonstrate their understanding of World War II (the topic) and how and why content decisions are made for textbooks (the purpose is to influence this decision), while addressing the needs of the textbook author (audience) and keeping in mind their own experience in studying with this textbook (author).

Each of the four elements of the rhetorical situation is shaped and influenced by the others. (See Figure 1.1.) The topic you choose to write about may be influenced by your

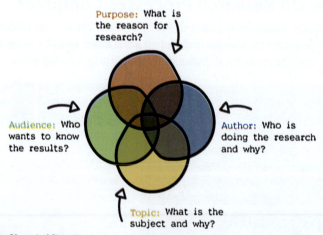

Purpose: What is the reason for research?

Audience: Who wants to know the results?

Author: Who is doing the research and why?

Topic: What is the subject and why?

Figure 1.1   The Rhetorical Situation

purpose for researching, especially if you are assigned a research paper in a class. Or your topic might be influenced by who you are and what you are interested in as the author. The way you approach and narrow your topic might also be influenced by the audience for your research and that audience's expectations. Being aware of the rhetorical situation for your writing and research will help you to answer your research question effectively.

Let's go back to Kendell's research situation outlined at the beginning of the chapter. If Kendell had been doing the research purely for her own interest, the author and audience for the research would completely overlap; in fact, they would be the same. (See Figure 1.2.)

Figure 1.2   Overlap of Author and Audience

As we know, though, Kendell's topic and purpose for researching originally arose out of the class she was taking. Therefore, Kendell's audience widens to include her professor; but her audience still overlaps somewhat with the author because Kendell is interested in the topic herself, too. (See Figure 1.3.)

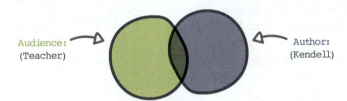

Figure 1.3   Kendell's Audience Widens

When Kendell shared her research goals with managers of the homeless shelter, she found that other people were interested in her research. Kendell's audience widened even more. She needs to be aware of this because different audiences have different expectations.

The rhetorical situation of Kendell's research and writing affects the way she conducts her research and the kinds of resources she chooses. What types of resources might Kendell have assumed were appropriate for just personal knowledge? How might she change her research processes and the types of resources she looks for if she is going to present her information in a formal research paper? And how might those shift even further if she presents her research more informally to other volunteers at the homeless shelter?

As another example, imagine that you are applying for scholarships so that you can continue your education. First, you must conduct research to determine

- which scholarships to apply for, and
- what to write in your applications.

Imagine that in the first stage of your research you locate two scholarships for which you would like to apply:

1. One is sponsored by the institution you attend and is given by the alumni association to a student who demonstrates financial need and has a promising academic record.
2. One is sponsored by a local charity organization and is given to a student who is actively involved in community service and also has a commitment to academic achievement.

For both scholarship applications, you must conduct research to determine what each organization values and which aspects of your experience you should include in the application. What would be relevant for both scholarship committees to hear? In your application to the alumni association, you might discuss your previous success in school and include specific praise for the institution you are attending. In your application to the charity organization, you might include information about your school record, but it will also be important to include information about your involvement in community service. The expectations and values of your two audiences will most likely result in your writing two different scholarship applications, even though the purpose is the same (asking for money for school), the author is the same (you), and the topic is the same (also you!). All elements of the rhetorical situation shape and affect your research and writing; any of the elements might carry more weight than the others in any given situation. (See Figures 1.4 and 1.5; for more information about cluster maps and how to use them in your writing, see Chapter 2.)

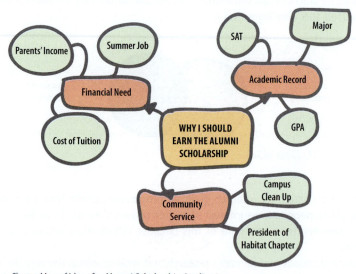

Figure 1.4   Cluster Map of Ideas for Alumni Scholarship Application

Considering the rhetorical situation of research and writing is central to the discussion of research in this book. You will be asked to reflect on your purpose for conducting research, your audience, your position and influences as the author, and the way your topic shapes (and is shaped by) your research. In addition, we will ask you to consider how each element of the rhetorical situation influences the others in the research you are conducting. Awareness of the rhetorical situation will help you conduct successful research and communicate the results of your research so that you can achieve your goals.

Figure 1.5   Cluster Map of Ideas for Charity Organization Scholarship Application

reflect

How Do Rhetorical Situations Compare?

Think of a situation in the recent past that required some research. Maybe you were planning a celebratory dinner at a restaurant and needed to look at menus, price ranges, locations, accommodations, and so on. Or you might focus on a research project that you completed for one of your courses. Think about the rhetorical situation of your research and fill in a Venn diagram like the following one with the four elements of your rhetorical situation. Try to pay attention to the size and placement of your circles based on the importance of and relationship between the different elements.

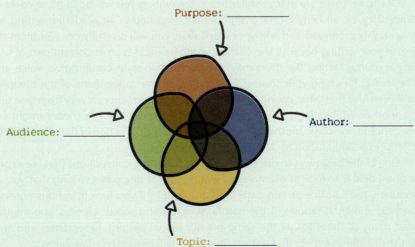

>>>

>>>

Compare and contrast your situation with other members of the class using the following questions:

1. What motivated you to conduct the research?

2. What was the topic, or subject, of your research? Was the topic tied to a specific time and location? Why or why not?

3. Who was the audience for your research? Who was affected by the results? Who might have been an unintended audience that was affected by your research? How did knowing your audience affect your research?

4. As the author, what was your experience with this topic before you began to research it? What was your experience with the audience? How did your experiences affect your research?

5. How do your rhetorical situations compare with those of other members of your class? How do your processes for adapting to the specific rhetorical situations compare?

Understanding Disciplinary Approaches

The rhetorical situations outlined so far in this chapter have included personal, workplace, and academic contexts. Academic contexts, as you may have already discovered, are just as varied as personal and workplace contexts. That is, from one class to the next you will come across different preferences, or what writing teachers often call **conventions**, for each discipline. As an extreme example, the writing that you do when completing an observational lab report in a biology class will be very different from the writing you do when completing a poetry assignment for a creative writing class. For example, in poetry it is generally okay to use the first-person pronoun *I*, whereas scientific writing generally uses passive voice, erasing the subject of the sentence altogether. Similarly, your writing in a literary analysis paper will probably have significant differences from your writing in an experimental psychology report. Other more subtle conventions may differ between disciplines as well, such as the width of your margins and the style you use for citing sources (in-text citations or footnotes).

Of course, there are many similarities in the writing you will do in these contexts, too. Since they are all fairly formal assignments completed in an academic setting, you will thoroughly proofread and edit your work. Also, you will carefully cite resources that you use in your writing because the citation of others' ideas is an important part of writing in any academic setting. But there may be differences in style, organization, voice, and even the format for citing your sources, depending on the conventions of the discipline. You will even find that what counts as evidence for an argument can vary from one discipline to another. While a logically constructed argument defending a theory might count as evidence in one class, another class might require the collection of data through observation or experimentation to defend a claim.

One of the best ways to discover the kinds of writing conventions that are expected in a given field is to look at examples of writing in that discipline, writing that you want to emulate. You'll notice certain patterns. For example, if you look at various observational and experimental reports in the natural sciences and social sciences, you might notice that many of them follow the same organizational pattern. Researchers and writers in these disciplines expect that reports, generally, will be organized as follows:

- introduction and review of relevant research
- description of the methodology used in the study
- presentation of the results of data collection
- analysis of the results
- discussion of the results and concluding comments

Exceptions to this pattern exist, too, and part of being an effective writer is determining when to follow the conventions and when to break them. In order to make that decision, you have to know the conventions in the first place. Learning about the discipline in which you are writing is an important part of your rhetorical situation if you are writing in an academic setting. Table 1.1 shows some of the distinct characteristics of academic disciplines in four main categories, the types of research in those areas, and the usual citation styles, but always keep in mind that such distinctions aren't absolute.

You have a variety of resources to help you learn about the conventions of different disciplines. Your primary resource is your instructor. Ask your instructor about expectations for

TABLE 1.1. Characteristics of Academic Disciplines

	Humanities	Social Sciences	Natural Sciences	Applied Fields
Example areas of study	Literature, art, philosophy, dance, film studies, religious studies	Anthropology, sociology, political science, psychology, justice studies, economics, linguistics	Biology, geology, physics, mathematics, chemistry	Engineering, computer science, nursing, education, business, pre-law
Primary areas of inquiry	Texts, artifacts, and other ways in which people create meaning and value	Society and social (especially human) interaction	The physical world	Application of scholarly knowledge to real-world situations
Primary role of the researcher	Interpreting and making meaning	Developing theories and looking for patterns	Systematically investigating and reporting results	Integrating and applying knowledge from one or more fields to practical context
Common citation styles	Modern Language Association (MLA), Chicago Manual of Style (CMS)	American Psychological Association (APA), Linguistics Society of America (LSA)	Council of Science Editors (CSE), American Psychological Association (APA)	Various, depending on field

writing and research in your discipline. Ask for a list of academic journals to skim through so that you can see those patterns. You might even ask your instructor for a sample of the writing he or she has done in that discipline. In addition, you could look at one or more of the many textbooks and references devoted to discussing writing in various disciplines.

write

Discover Disciplinary Patterns and Conventions

Begin by finding a teacher or professional that you could talk to in the discipline/major/career that you are interested in pursuing. You might talk to a professor that you know, or you might talk to someone who is currently in the kind of job you would like to have. Ask the following questions, and take careful notes on the responses you receive.

1. What kinds of writing are assigned in classes in this field? What kinds of writing do professionals in this field do on the job?

2. Are there specific patterns or conventions expected in the writing in this field? If so, what are they?

3. What are the most common problems that students or new writers in the field have? How could these problems be avoided?

4. What kinds of research are conducted most often in this field?

5. Are there specific research processes that people in this field/profession usually follow? How do they learn these processes? (For more about common research processes, see Chapter 2.)

6. What citation style is primarily used for research conducted in this field? Why is that citation style used? Are other styles sometimes used as well? If so, how should a new writer in the field choose an appropriate citation style?

7. Is there an example of writing in this field that you could share with me? (You might even ask to see something that the teacher or professional has written.)

If you do receive a piece of writing that you could analyze, look for the patterns and conventions that the teacher or professional identified for you. Then share your discoveries with your classmates. You might try filling out a table so that you can compare the similarities and differences among the disciplines you each investigated.

Entering a Conversation

As you can see, research does not happen in a vacuum. Research projects develop in a particular situation, from a problem that someone has or a question that someone asks. Sometimes it helps to think of your rhetorical situation as a conversation that you are entering—and you are entering that conversation by asking a question (or answering a question someone is asking you). So what does this mean, exactly?

Imagine that a friend has invited you to a party and you're a little apprehensive about going because you don't know many of the people who will be there. Perhaps you feel a little out of your element at first when you walk in the door. You don't see many people that you know, and there are already several groups around the room having lively conversations. Your friend immediately sees people that he knows and runs over to say hello. You're left on your own. What do you do? Perhaps you would circulate through the room, listening to what's going on, until you find a conversation that sounds interesting to you.

You might listen for a topic or person you know about already, or you might listen for something that is interesting for another reason. As you join the circle of people in discussion, you might listen for a little bit before saying anything—you wouldn't want to say something inappropriate, and it's best to find out what has been said already. It is wise to listen to the ongoing conversation before jumping in and adding to it. Perhaps an entry point into that conversation is a question—and you might think of your research in the same way.

As you choose a topic to research and a question on which to focus, you are entering a conversation in progress. People have most likely been talking about this topic for a while, and you can learn by "listening" to what's been said already. You might do this by reading things that others have written, paying attention to any disciplinary conventions you find, or you might interview people who are knowledgeable about the subject to learn what they know. The important thing is to remember that you're most likely jumping in mid-stream—the conversation has been going on already and you'll have some catch-up work to do before you can contribute to the discussion. Part of understanding the rhetorical situation of your research topic is learning what has already been said so that you can focus on how you want to enter the conversation.

Listening to conversations in progress

LINDEN/SIPA/News.com

techno tip

Listen to Conversations in Progress Online

With the prevalence of the Internet, many professional and academic conversations are occurring more quickly than ever, and sometimes a little less formally than in traditional print venues. A number of professionals have blogs, or online journals, in which they reflect and share their thoughts and processes on various topics. For example, Michael Wesch, a cultural anthropologist at Kansas State University, has published *Digital Ethnography*, both the blog as well as the YouTube channel (a video blog), for a number of years (http://mediatedcultures.net/ and http://www.youtube.com/user/mwesch).

In his blog and YouTube videos, Wesch reflects on various technologies and their incorporation into our society and various cultural processes. Both his students and his peers read his blog and follow his YouTube channel as a way to keep up on innovative ideas for researching and teaching with technologies.

One way to start listening to conversations in progress is to read dynamic Internet materials produced in blogs. You can find blogs on a variety of topics at the following sites:

- BlogCatalog: http://www.blogcatalog.com
- Technorati: http://www.technorati.com

>>>

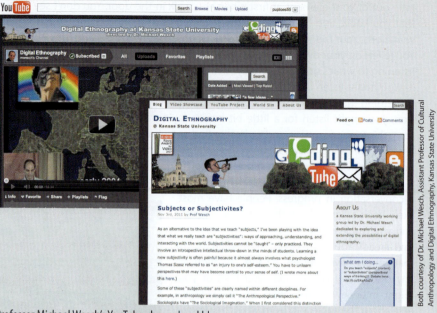

Professor Michael Wesch's YouTube channel and blog.

Both courtesy of Dr. Michael Wesch, Assistant Professor of Cultural Anthropology and Digital Ethnography, Kansas State University

▶ Google Reader: http://reader.google.com

▶ Google Blog Search: http://blogsearch.google.com

Find a blog dealing with a subject of interest to you, read through some of the posts and comments, and respond to the following questions:

1. What are people on this blog talking about?

2. How do the different blog postings relate to one another? How are they similar? How are they different?

3. What subtopics did you learn about while following the conversations? Do some of the subtopics cause you to reconsider your understanding of the subject?

If you'd like to read more about blogs, see the discussion of blogs in Chapter 4.

Many people come to college with some experience and skill in everyday research in their personal lives; some people also come with experience in academic research. Instead of claiming to teach research, this book helps the experienced researcher (you are experienced, after all, because you've been asking and answering questions for many years) become a more proficient and effective academic researcher, especially in contexts that may be unfamiliar, such as a college course.

chapter 2

Writing Processes

All writing and research has a context. Just as the different elements of the rhetorical situation (purpose, audience, author, and topic) affect a topic or research question, the rhetorical situation influences research processes and the writing of their results. For example, if your instructor says that you will need at least two academic journal articles to support the argument you present in your paper, then your research will probably focus (at least at first) on finding academic journal articles. Similarly, in the example on the next page, if Qi knows that he wants to attend a school in New York City, his research will be limited to schools within that area.

You will also likely be influenced by the subject matter that you are researching and writing about. Imagine that you are conducting a study in a physics class on the Doppler effect. Your research process will be influenced by the accepted research practices in the field of physics, and your final written product will probably need to follow a specified format for a laboratory report.

we'll explore

▶ *myths about writing and research processes*

▶ *classical writing processes*

▶ *contemporary writing processes*

▶ *basic research processes*

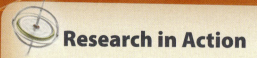

Author: Qi wants to come to the United States, New York City (NYC) specifically, to go to college. He has time to do research before coming to NYC, and he will be in NYC for six months before starting school.

Topic: Of the multitude of colleges in NYC that Qi could attend, which one should he choose and why?

Audience: Although Qi is the primary audience for his research and decision making, there are other stakeholders who are invested in his topic. Qi's family, especially if they are paying for a portion of his schooling, care tremendously about which school he attends. Also, many other international students who may want to come to the United States for college might be interested in his ultimate decision as well as his criteria and processes for selecting a college.

Purpose: Qi has to select the most appropriate college to attend with some of the following considerations: cost of tuition for an international student, language instruction and support because he is still learning English, commute time because he will not live in NYC proper, and curriculum—he wants to study to be an engineer.

Questions

1. What elements of Qi's rhetorical situation affect his research process?

2. What is going on in Qi's life that affects his research process? What resources does Qi have that will help him?

3. What obstacles might Qi have in his research process? What unexpected opportunities?

4. Can you imagine other aspects of the rhetorical situation that would affect researching, writing, and sharing the results of research in this case?

Myths about Writing and Research Processes

Writing and research processes are often described in simple, one-size-fits-all formulas, but no formula will fit every writing and research situation you might encounter. Although it can be helpful to start a project by following a formulaic research and writing process, you will often discover that you need to repeat some steps, skip others, and occasionally loop back to the beginning again. Not all research follows the scientific method, and even when it does, the scientific method is often a much messier process than the charts in elementary school led us to believe. Similarly, not all writing follows the step-by-step process of prewriting, drafting, revising, editing, and publishing. You might get to the editing stage, show the paper to a friend, and then realize that you need to start over from square one. Writing and research processes need to be flexible enough to meet the needs of each rhetorical situation. This research guide will introduce you to a variety of strategies and tools that you can use in research and writing. Our hope is that you will adapt these tools to help you address your specific research projects.

Before you get started, however, you should have realistic expectations of what your research and writing processes might look like. Many of us carry around common myths about writing and research in our minds, but those myths don't measure up to the reality of what we encounter as we start working. If you first recognize those myths as unrealistic, then you can avoid a lot of frustration later.

▶ **Myth 1: You must complete each step in the writing process.** The writing process is often described as linear, as shown in Figure 2.1. In this representation, writing is a simple process where you start at the top, with prewriting (or invention), systematically work your way down through each step, and finish with a perfectly written product. Writing often does not happen this way, though. We don't intend to say that people cannot, or do not, sometimes follow these steps in this order and finish with an effective piece of writing. In fact, this textbook presents a process of working through a major research project that appears to be linear, presenting one step at a time, chapter by chapter. Although we have a plan in mind, most of the time the actual process is much messier.

You already know that many casual writing situations do not require every step outlined in Figure 2.1. For example, a grocery list might require revising, especially to make sure everything is on the list. If someone else is going to do the shopping, you might also proofread the list before giving it to him or her, revising the list for clarity based on the new audience. But your prewriting and researching might be collapsed into one step as you flip through your stack of recipe cards and start to draft the list. One way you can make the writing process flexible enough to work for a specific rhetorical situation is by following the steps that are needed for a given writing task. Give yourself the freedom to skip steps if they are not necessary or to repeat steps if some require additional time (Figure 2.2).

▶ **Myth 2: Each step is equally important and time-consuming.** The linear image of the writing process also gives the faulty impression that each step involved in the process will take the same amount of time, energy, and work. Depending on the demands of the writing project and the rhetorical situation, you may spend lots of time in one area and very little in another (Figure 2.2). A student writing an essay in an exam for school may not spend as much time editing as drafting and revising. If you were conducting research on an upcoming election to determine which candidates to vote for, you might casually publish results in a posting on Facebook for your friends (if you choose to publish the results at all). For a sociologist studying demographic trends in elections, the majority of time might be spent conducting surveys and collecting empirical data, making the research portion of the process much larger and more time-consuming than other steps. Finally, not only can the steps of the process take varying amounts of time and energy, but your process could also change or shift in the middle of a project as a result of the process itself and what you have found in your research so far.

Figure 2.1
Mythical Writing and Research Process

▶ **Myth 3: The steps are linear.** Many people bounce back and forth among the steps, rather than proceed on a straight, one-way path (Figure 2.2). Your initial research might bring up some issues you had not considered, and so you need to move to a different step in the process. Likewise, many writers find that once they start drafting, or once someone else looks over their project, a large gap becomes evident and they need to go back to the invention or research stage. They might return to the peer review stage again after making revisions. The research of scientists publishing in the online journal *PloS One* (http://www.plosone.org), for instance, is subject to an initial peer review that determines whether the work is technically sound. Then the article is published online and opened up to peer review by the broader scientific community to determine the significance of the work. In this case, peer review happens at several stages, but the most public and significant portion of the peer review happens post-publication.

Although it is easier to teach and talk about writing and research as single, linear processes, in reality, writing and research processes are all variations on the theme of the mythical, linear process. Very rarely does research happen in a linear fashion and when it does, the researcher has usually missed something. Take this example from everyday life: While answering "What do I need from the grocery store?" you might refer to the household's weekly menu and refer to cookbooks for items on that menu. However, if you do not also check what is, or is not, in the refrigerator or cupboard, you could find multiple trips to the grocery store in your future. You might go several times from the list, to the refrigerator, to a couple of recipes, and to the coupons in the newspaper before finally answering your original question.

Good writers and researchers are aware of these recursive steps and even more aware of their rhetorical situations. Effective writers and

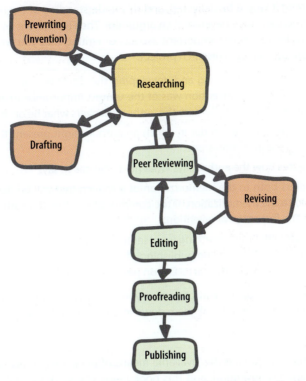

Figure 2.2   More Realistic Version of Writing and Research Process (Actual Experience May Vary)

researchers allow the individual rhetorical situation to influence their processes for every project and help them determine what step to take next. Writers have several processes to choose from when working on a writing project. The more you know about the options you have in tackling a research and writing project, the more successful you can be in completing it.

Elements of Writing Processes

You may have encountered descriptions of "the writing process" in classes you have taken. A listing of the steps of the writing process might include those shown in Figure 2.1: invention or prewriting, researching, drafting, peer reviewing, revising, editing, proofreading, and publishing. Some of these steps relate loosely to principles of classical rhetoric, and it is helpful to understand where some of these ideas came from. As you develop your own successful writing processes, you might find that a combination of some of these approaches will work best in certain situations.

Foundations in Classical Rhetoric

Aristotle defined rhetoric as "finding the available means of persuasion." He acknowledged that although you may not use all of the information and materials you have discovered and developed, it is important to identify a wide range of choices. Ancient Greek and Roman rhetoricians kept the purpose of writing (or speaking) in mind and the audience to whom it would be delivered, and this understanding of the rhetorical situation governed the ways they developed an argument. The Five Canons of Rhetoric these rhetoricians developed address important aspects of writing that you will need to consider as you work on your own research project.

▶ *Invention* refers to discovering and developing the possible arguments that might persuade an audience. Invention was of the utmost importance to ancient rhetoricians because it is the stage where the author discovers what he or she will say.

▶ *Arrangement* refers to the order in which an author might present the information found during the invention stage.

▶ *Style* addresses how the author says what he or she has to say.

▶ *Memory* refers both to the memorization of a speech that will be delivered or performed and to the memorization of the commonplaces that the author can recall to assist with the first stage of invention.

▶ *Delivery* deals with how something is presented, or delivered, to the audience. Today we might relate delivery to the publishing of a piece of writing. (Presenting a piece of writing is discussed in the Part 3 DIY on pages 215–240.)

Some of the canons may be more important to you than others, and in writing classes we often use specific strategies to break them down into manageable chunks.

Invention

Aristotle's emphasis on finding the "available means of persuasion" places a high importance on the canon of invention, and this book helps you work through the stages of invention in your own research and writing. Invention is similar to what you might have referred to as prewriting, a stage where the author (or *rhetor*) brainstorms, researches, and "invents" possible ideas and arguments. In this book, we prefer the term *invention* to *prewriting* because these kinds of activities can be useful at several stages of the writing process—not just before you start drafting. If we return to Qi from the beginning of the chapter, he might do some brainstorming about schools that he has heard of or read about at the beginning of his research process. But imagine that he has started drafting a letter to his parents about his top three schools after arriving in the United States, and then a friend mentions another school and program that he has not heard of. He might go back to the invention stage and do a little more brainstorming before he continues to draft his letter.

Careful and thorough invention leads to effective writing. You might have noticed that much of the research process contributes to invention—research itself is a means of discovering what you want to say. As you work through the activities in this text, you'll notice that many of the "Write" activities help with invention. We want to encourage you to think thoroughly about what you are going to say before you commit to a finished written product, and we believe that invention provides support for all stages of a writing process.

If you have ever been asked to write definition, comparison, or cause/effect papers, your instructor was relying on common topics, or *commonplaces*, derived from ancient rhetoric. (These topics are also called *topoi*.) The commonplaces help you generate ideas and argument by prompting you to think about how you might define your issue, what you might compare it to, and what the causes and effects are. Patterns of development based on commonplaces are discussed in more detail in Chapter 10.

During invention, writers try to explore and focus their topics. Even with the common use of computers and word-processing programs, many writers do a lot of their invention by hand with pen and paper. Exploring a topic or idea in a different modality from text can help the author "see" the topic in a different way, so many invention activities are visual. Common invention activities that you might be familiar with include brainstorming or listing, journaling, freewriting, looping, cluster mapping, asking journalistic questions, and outlining. You may be used to thinking about using these kinds of activities only at the beginning stages of working on a research or writing project, but the majority can be used at many points in your writing process. Because several of these activities can be particularly useful at specific stages of a writing process, we'll suggest certain invention activities as we discuss each stage. Keep in mind that invention activities can be mixed and matched as well.

Brainstorming or Listing   Brainstorming, or listing, is generating a list of ideas on a certain topic. Sometimes brainstorming takes place for a set period of time, and sometimes the goal is to come up with a certain number of possible ideas (or as many as possible). When we brainstorm, we know that some of the ideas might be discarded, but the purpose is to open up our minds to possibilities.

Many writers use brainstorming or listing activities to explore what they already know about a given topic. For example, when a student is first assigned a paper topic, she might brainstorm everything she knows about it. While brainstorming or listing, do not let your internal censor keep you from adding something to your list; in other words, keep your mind open to all ideas that might relate to your topic.

Brainstorming or listing can be helpful at the beginning of a project to choose a topic or to identify what you already know. It can also be useful during the middle of a research project so that you can list everything you have learned. It may even be useful to compare your pre-research brainstorming with your post-research listing; you will be able to identify what you've learned, what you may still want to research, and how your thinking has begun to shift.

Imagine that you are researching air pollution in the city that you live in. You could try brainstorming a list of possible causes that you know about, and it might look something like this:

- car exhaust
- poor mass transit in city
- lack of rain this year
- increased population
- industrial emissions

Once you have this initial list, you might also look at a few resources to see what you should add to your list.

Listing can also be useful when thinking about your writing project's purpose and audience, especially when identifying all of the purposes and audiences that your topic might address. Lists can then become checklists to verify that your writing project includes all of the information that your specific purpose and audience might require.

Brainstorming and listing can easily be done with traditional pen and paper or on the computer. Either way, it's a good idea to save your results in a notebook or computer file so that you can return to them later in your project.

The following are examples of brainstorming or listing activities that you might find helpful in your research process.

▶ Chapter 3: page 41, "Write: Analyze the Rhetorical Situation" is an example of using listing within a structured space; the activity asks you to fill in the blanks of a chart.

▶ Chapter 3: page 42, "Write: Find Out What's Important to You"

▶ Chapter 3: page 46, "Write: Focus Your Research Topic"

▶ Chapter 4: page 75, "Write: Develop a List of Search Terms"

Researching

Much like invention, research can be useful at any stage of your writing process. Research might include gathering information from resources found online or in the library, in the form of secondary research, or it might include gathering data firsthand through activities such as interviewing people, observing, or distributing and collecting questionnaires, as in primary research. As we discuss in more detail in Chapter 7, tracking your research is an important part of this step.

Journaling   Journaling can be very helpful in organizing a research project, and it can be an effective way to track your research. A journal is a collection of writing, composed of multiple entries, all generally related to the same topic. Therefore, it is a good idea to start a journal for any major research project that you undertake. In the journal (or you might try a blog if you would like to journal electronically), you can keep the following types of entries:

▶ any of the other writing activities suggested in this chapter

▶ an annotated bibliography or other notes about the resources you find

▶ timelines and checklists to help organize your research process

▶ reflections on research and/or writing sessions

▶ notes about discussions you've had with other people on the topic

▶ drafts of your writing

▶ any other ideas that you find relevant or interesting as you work through your research

By using a journal, you will keep everything related to your research project in one place. Whenever you are stuck on your project, look over the various entries in your journal to remind yourself of what you need to do and why this project is important to you.

To help keep your journal entries organized, it is generally a good idea to include the following information in every entry:

▶ the date of your entry

▶ a title that briefly describes your entry

▶ blank space to make more comments about the entry at a later date

Nearly all of the activities included in the "Reflect" and "Write" sections in this book could be considered journaling activities. Here are a few examples that could help you get started on journaling and see some of the ways that it can be used in your research.

Drafting

Depending on your rhetorical situation and writing preferences, you might find that you like to start with drafting and that sitting down to write actually helps you generate ideas. Drafting includes any part of your writing process that involves generating text that you could imagine ending up in a final version.

As you draft, you might prefer to start with a blank screen. Or, you might take all of the relevant invention activities that you've completed and try to weave them together (thus avoiding the blank screen). Invention and drafting are very closely related, and if you are doing invention from the beginning of your writing process, you probably are doing some drafting as well.

Freewriting   At one point or another, most writers have had writer's block. And almost all writers agree that the way to get over writer's block is just to write. Freewriting is a strategy to get yourself "just writing"—you simply sit down at your computer (or with a pen and paper) and write anything that comes to mind on your topic. During freewriting sessions, like brainstorming and listing, turn off your internal censor and just get words on the page or screen. To get going, many writers give themselves a brief topic or question and then set a time limit (usually five to fifteen minutes). Then they force themselves to write the entire time, no matter where their mind wanders. And if they get stuck, they can just write the same word or phrase over and over until they get new ideas or go back to the beginning idea or question and start over. The purpose of freewriting is just to get words down on paper or on screen.

Much of the writing produced during a freewriting session will never see final print or publication. Instead, this writing is meant to help the author think through elements of his or her project. At the beginning stage of a project, freewriting can be useful for exploring initial thoughts and feelings about a topic. During the research process, freewriting can help researchers make connections among multiple resources. And during the drafting stage, freewriting can help authors work through writer's block and get started with different sections of their projects.

Although you can easily freewrite with pen and paper, freewriting with a word processor on the computer definitely offers some advantages. For example, some writers turn off the monitor when they freewrite, or they might make the font color white so that they can't see what they are writing on the screen. When the text is not visible, writers are not distracted by what they've already typed, and they are not looking for misspellings or grammatical errors.

The following are examples of freewriting activities that you might find helpful in your research process.

Looping   Looping is an activity that writers usually use after freewriting, brainstorming, or listing. Once a writer has concluded one of these writing sessions, she could read the paragraph or list and look for one or two "hot spots" that resonate with her. They might spark her interest or surprise her. The point of looping is to discover a new perspective on your topic or to focus your thinking by taking that idea or phrase and making it the focal point for another round of freewriting, brainstorming, or listing. Looping is also another way to combat writer's block, and it's a good way to focus a topic if your initial subject matter is too broad. Looping might also help you work through connections in ideas and resources so that you can better arrange them in your writing.

Let's imagine that you were going to do a looping exercise with your list about air pollution from earlier in the chapter. The list of possible causes for air pollution looked like this:

- car exhaust
- poor mass transit in city
- lack of rain this year
- increased population
- industrial emissions

After completing this list, you might choose one of these to explore in more detail. You could copy and paste it and then freewrite or list for a while and see what you come up with. For example, if you chose to pursue increased population, you might write something like this:

Phoenix, Arizona, has one of the fastest growing populations in the country, especially in the suburbs surrounding the city. Several of the other items on the list come from the increase in population. For example, with more people driving, we have an increase in car exhaust that is contributing to the pollution problem. People are also resistant to carpooling here.

You can see that some of the ideas in this section overlap with ideas in the original list—that's okay. A looping activity might reveal ideas you hadn't considered, and it might help you come up with connections between ideas that you hadn't thought of before.

You can use any writing tool for looping: paper and pen, computer, blackboard, or whiteboard. Loop with whatever tools you used for your initial writing. If you use a word processor, you can use different colors, fonts, or highlighting options to identify hot spots, and then you can cut and paste before you start writing again.

The following are examples of looping activities that you might find helpful in your research process.

- Chapter 3: page 42, "Write: Generate Topic Ideas"
- Chapter 10: page 210, "Write: Draft an Effective Introduction"
- Chapter 10: page 211, "Write: Develop Closure"

Cluster Mapping   Clustering is a more visual activity than the methods already discussed; it helps writers see their work in a different manner. After producing a brainstorm or list, writers group like elements from their lists. After conducting research, writers

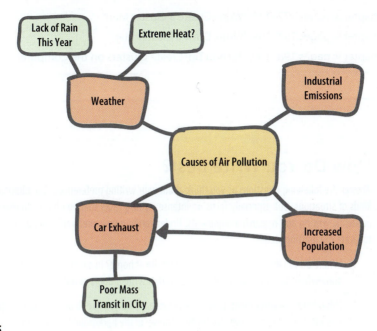

Figure 2.5

cluster resources that contain similar perspectives or ideas. If juggling multiple purposes and audiences, writers cluster the results of a detailed analysis of wants and needs.

Cluster-mapping exercises help writers and researchers not only to group like elements but also to understand connections among the groups. After grouping like elements, writers can draw lines connecting groups and describe the types of connections. Some cluster maps show hierarchies, like family trees. Others show working relationships, like flow charts. Some writers represent the size of each cluster in relation to other clusters so they know whether an area might not have enough ideas or examples to support it.

If we were to draw a cluster map of our air pollution example, it might look something like Figure 2.5. Cluster mapping can be done in a variety of modes. You can easily use paper and pen, maybe even many different colored pens, to group elements and map out connections. There are also a variety of computer and web-based programs that allow you to develop different types of cluster maps. Sometimes it helps to physically work with the elements, or groups of elements, by putting them on index cards or sticky notes that you can shuffle and rearrange as you explore different groups and connections.

The following are examples of cluster-mapping activities that you might find helpful in your research process.

▶ Chapter 1: page 11, "Reflect: How Do Rhetorical Situations Compare?" (Although this is not technically a cluster map, this activity shows another way you might use graphic representations throughout your research process.)

▶ Chapter 3: page 46, "Write: Focus Your Research Topic"

▶ Chapter 8: pages 170–171, "Write: Define the Rhetorical Situation"

reflect

How Do You Write Best?

Answer the following questions as you think about your writing preferences. You might consider all kinds of situations, but especially focus on intense writing tasks that you have completed such as academic writing and research assignments. Understanding your preferences might make it easier to tackle the drafting stage.

▶ Where do you like to write? Do you like to write at home? in a certain room? Do you like to go somewhere specific to write? Would you rather write indoors or outdoors?

▶ What kind of environment do you like to write in? Do you like to be around other people? Do you like to be alone? Do you like to have "noise" in the background (such as music, television, other people), or do you like to have a quiet environment?

▶ When do you like to write? At what time of day do you like to write?

▶ Do you prefer to write on the computer or on paper? Why?

▶ If you prefer to write on the computer, what software program do you use? Do you have other programs or applications open when you write? If so, which ones?

▶ If you prefer to write on paper, what kind of paper do you use? Do you write in a notebook? Do you use pen or pencil?

▶ Do you follow any special rituals when you write? Do you have a favorite place to sit? Do you like to have a cup of coffee next to you?

▶ Do you generally share your writing with others? If so, at what stage? If not, why not?

▶ If you share writing with others, what do you do with their comments? What kind of comments do you expect?

▶ Do you like to outline your ideas first? Do you draft first? In other words, what is the first step you take when you write?

▶ Where do you start writing? Do you start at the beginning? the end? somewhere in the middle? If there's a title, do you write it first or last?

▶ How do you know when you are finished writing?

Share your preferences with a classmate or friend, and see if you gather any new ideas about writing situations that might work well for you. Keep these preferences in mind as you draft because you'll do your best writing in *your* optimal circumstances.

techno tip

Dictate Your Writing

If you have difficulty getting started on your writing, or if you struggle with getting your thoughts onto the page or screen, you could try using a voice recognition software program to dictate your thoughts and have them translated onto the screen into text. Many writers with dyslexia and dysgraphia find it useful to use a voice recognition software program at the beginning of the writing process. Dragon NaturallySpeaking is a popular voice recognition software program that is often used for dictating writing. You can download a free trial to see if it works well for you.

Asking Journalistic Questions   Whereas brainstorming is an open form of idea generation, journalistic questions focus writers and researchers on specific aspects of their topics. Traditional journalistic questions use the following words to develop a list of information-seeking questions.

- who
- what
- when
- why
- where
- how

Dedicated writers and researchers might critically explore their topics with multiple questions from each category. The purpose of using journalistic questions is to try to see and understand the topic from a variety of perspectives. Journalistic questions can also be used by a peer reviewer to help focus response to a draft.

The invention tactic of asking questions can be generalized beyond the traditional journalistic approach, however. Exploring the topic in any structured manner will help a writer and researcher get to know a topic and the relevant resources much better. Other organized methods of exploring include the following perspectives:

- spatial: inside to outside, top to bottom, left to right
- oppositional: for and against, compare and contrast, denotation and connotation
- relational: cause and effect, parts to a whole

As you are writing and researching, be sure to keep and revisit any focused questioning activity. Many times thinking gets stuck in a rut; however, if you revisit your focused activity a few hours or days later, you might come up with different questions as well as different answers.

The following are examples of activities that use journalistic questions that you might find helpful in your research process.

- Chapter 3: page 47, "Write: Write a Research Question"
- Chapter 6: page 126, "Write: Track Bibliographic Information"

Peer Review

During the peer review stage you get to see your writing through the eyes of your audience, or an approximated audience, a luxury that you often don't have when you hand in writing for an assignment or send it out to be published. In a peer review workshop, you might be asked to read and comment on the work of another classmate while he or she reads and comments on yours. If you are in a work environment, you might share what you have written with a colleague who is knowledgeable about your project or who will be able to help you imagine how your audience would respond to what you have written. You might even share writing with friends or family members for feedback. Anytime you ask someone who is not formally evaluating your work to read it with the intention of commenting on it or helping you to see it from another person's perspective, you are participating in a kind of peer review.

Peer review is not the same thing as proofreading. Peer review includes reading and commenting on more global features of a piece of writing, like the development of ideas or the evidence used to support an argument; proofreading generally focuses on surface features such as correct use of grammar and consistent adherence to a particular citation style. The three types of changes you might make to your draft as you polish and refine it for publication are typically revising, editing, and proofreading. Peer review could include gathering comments and feedback on all three of these areas.

You might already have experience with peer review from a previous class. Unfortunately, many students report having unfavorable impressions of peer review, often because they didn't receive useful feedback from their peers. If you have ever had a classmate write something like "This looks good to me," during a peer review, or if you've had peers give you conflicting feedback, you might have an unfavorable impression as well.

The key to good peer review is asking the right questions of your peers and helping them understand what kind of feedback you need. Depending on your stage in the writing process, you might need different kinds of feedback. If you are at an early stage of writing, or if you don't have any specific criteria for the project you are working on, you might try variations of the following questions:

- What works well in this piece of writing?
- What did you want to know more about as you read?
- What was unclear in this piece of writing?
- What suggestions would you make for a revision?

These questions will prompt peer reviewers to give a balanced response, discussing things that you did well and things to consider in a revision. You might also draft some questions based on the specifics of your rhetorical situation. For example, have you done an adequate job of addressing the interests and expectations of your audience? If you were writing an annual report for your job, did you provide the information your superiors would be expecting? Are there other issues they might want to see addressed in the report?

Try following these guidelines the next time you participate in a peer review:

- Ask for both positive comments and constructive feedback. It's helpful to know what you're doing well—not just what you should revise.

▶ Ask your peer to ask questions if there are things he or she finds confusing in the text. Questions invite a response, and responding to questions written on your draft during a peer review will help you begin revising.

▶ If you have specific criteria for an assignment or project you are working on, ask your peer to address each of the criteria in his or her review. If there are numerous criteria to consider, perhaps have several peers read your work and have each one look at separate criteria.

▶ Finally, offer to review your peers' work as well. When you write a response for one of your peers, write the kind of review that would be helpful to you.

Outlining   Like cluster mapping, outlining is an activity that helps you to organize materials into meaningful patterns and relationships. Outlines can also be an effective method of peer review, helping a peer reviewer think about the arrangement of an argument. Outlines hierarchically group like topics, and detailed outlines begin to describe relationships between the groups. Writers might take the results of an initial brainstorming activity that explored what they already knew about a topic and try to outline the results so they can identify areas they need to learn more about. Many researchers use outlines as a predrafting technique to lay out what they are going to say and then plug in the various resources that they will include. A writer could then take that outline and start writing from easily manageable parts. For example, Chapter 7 of this book developed from this outline:

Formal Outline of Chapter 7

I. Copyright
    A. Fair Use
    B. Ideas vs. Words

II. Plagiarism
    A. Blatant Plagiarism
    B. Careless Plagiarism

III. Integrating Resources into Your Argument
    A. Introduction of the Resource
    B. Incorporation of the Data
        1. Quotations from Resources
        2. Summarizing and Paraphrasing Revisited
    C. Interpreting the Resource
    D. Documenting the Resource
        1. What to Cite
        2. How to Cite
        3. In-Text Citations
        4. Full Bibliographic Citations

By breaking the chapter into smaller parts, the authors were able to make the task manageable instead of being overwhelmed by it.

You might choose to write your outline in one of three ways: a formal outline, a sentence outline, or a scratch outline. The outline from Chapter 7 is a formal outline, with Roman numerals and carefully numbered headings and subpoints. You might choose instead to write a sentence outline, where each point is developed into a full sentence.

Such an outline will really help you get started on drafting. Written as a sentence outline, the first part of the Chapter 7 outline would look like this:

Sentence Outline of First Part of Chapter 7

I. **Copyright laws regulate the use of a particular expression of an idea.**
  A. Fair Use allows individuals to copy small portions of texts so that they may use them in other contexts, especially research and education.
  B. Copyright technically protects the expression of an idea, not the idea itself.
II. **Plagiarism is copying work from another resource without documenting it.**
  A. Blatant plagiarism is knowingly copying sections of other resources and submitting them as your own work.
  B. Careless plagiarism is using information from an outside resource without documentation because you think it is common knowledge or you do not adequately document the source.

At early stages of your writing and research, you might find a scratch outline to be sufficient. A scratch outline casually lists ideas in the order that you would discuss them without concern for headers and subpoints. A scratch outline for that same section of Chapter 7 might look something like this:

Scratch Outline of First Part of Chapter 7

Copyright laws
Fair use
What copyright protects
What copyright doesn't protect
Types of plagiarism
Blatant
Careless

You might experiment with a more formal outline and a less formal one to see what works best for you, and you might find that different kinds of outlines work at different stages of your research and writing process. As a peer reviewer, you might try drafting a scratch outline or more formal outline of the paper you are reviewing. An outline done during peer review can help you let the author know how you are reading his or her argument, whether you are making the connections he or she hopes you will, and whether each premise is supported by appropriate evidence.

As with cluster mapping, outlining helps you not only to organize your materials but also to evaluate the amount of ideas, resources, or support that you have for each category. If you only have one or two pieces of evidence for a particular category, and all the rest have more support, you may need to do more research or alter your inclusion of that category in your final project.

The following are examples of outlining activities that you might find helpful in your research process. Keep in mind that most word processors have numbering or listing tools that begin to label subcategories that you make in your outline when you indent the appropriate lines.

▶ Chapter 8: pages 185–187, "Write: Construct an Argument"
▶ Chapter 9: pages 197–198, "Write: Draw a Cluster Map"
▶ Chapter 10: page 208, "Write: Develop an Outline"

techno tip

Conduct Peer Reviews

Several technological tools can facilitate peer review, either in a classroom setting or in a work environment. If you have access to different kinds of technology, you might try one of the following variations on peer review:

▸ If you are using a software program such as Microsoft Word®, try using the "Insert Comment" feature to comment on specific parts of the text. If you have time, have several peers electronically comment on the same document. If you switch computers, be certain to update your user information in the word processor before entering your comments.

▸ If you have access to a closed discussion board for your class or workplace, you could post a draft of what you are working on with specific questions for peer review. Then your peers can post their responses.

▸ If you are comfortable using instant messaging software, you could schedule a chat with the peer(s) who read your writing. Chats work best one-on-one or, if you have access to a chat room, in very small groups. If you include more than four people, the feedback can be difficult to process in a chat environment.

 For an interactive tutorial about peer reviewing technologies, go to *Student Resources* in your English CourseMate accessed through cengagebrain.com.

Revising

Revising your writing generally refers to larger-scale changes you make to a document. As you revise, you will probably focus on the content of your writing. Revision can be challenging, especially when you have worked very hard on your original draft. You might be reluctant to delete things that you spent time writing, but revising is an act of refining. Sometimes revision will require the addition of ideas, sometimes movement, and sometimes deletion. The Nobel Prize–winning writer Elie Wiesel wrote that "Writing is not like painting where you add. . . . Writing is more like a sculpture where you remove, you eliminate in order to make the work visible." The important thing is to keep an open mind, and sometimes that requires having distance from what you have written. Having some time between drafting and revising will also help you to see your writing with new eyes (re-vision).

Editing

Similar to revision, editing is a way of refining and polishing your paper. When you edit, however, your focus is not on the larger-scale issues of content and organization but rather on issues of style and fluidity. Editing might include looking at your use of transitions, for example, to help the reader follow your train of thought in a piece of writing. You also might look at sentence variety in your writing or the overall tone of your piece. As you edit, you could pay attention to consistency in your writing. Try reading your essay out loud to "hear" how it sounds and how the language flows.

Read Your Writing Out Loud

It can be helpful to read your own essay aloud to hear how it sounds, and it can sometimes be even more beneficial to hear someone else read it; either reading will help you to hear things that you otherwise might not notice when editing silently. If you feel uncomfortable having someone read to you, however, or if you simply don't have someone you can ask to do it, you can have your computer read your essay to you. Granted, it's not quite the same thing, and the computer is not going to tell you when something doesn't "sound right." The computer also won't stumble over things that are awkward—it will just plow right on through. But hearing the computer read your writing is a very different experience from reading it yourself. If you have never tried it, you might find that you notice areas for revision, editing, and proofreading that you didn't notice before. You can download a free trial version of ReadPlease, a software package that will read your writing to you, at http://www.readplease.com.

Proofreading

Many instructors combine editing and proofreading under one label. They are separated here, however, because we want to highlight that there are several different steps to polishing your writing. In addition to looking at issues of style and fluidity when you edit, you will also need to proofread your work, focusing on surface features such as grammar, punctuation, and citations. Obviously, you can do a first round of proofreading by yourself, perhaps referring to the spelling and grammar checkers that are built into most word-processing programs. However, you need to be aware that they will not catch all of the errors in your paper. For example, many of them are "dumb" and do not know whether your sentence needs *there*, *their*, or *they're*. Automated grammar and spelling checkers might be a good place to start proofreading your writing, but you won't want to stop there for most rhetorical situations. If you are working on a piece of writing that needs to be polished in its final draft, you definitely will want to proofread carefully yourself and also have someone else proofread your paper.

What Are Your Writing Idiosyncrasies?

Over time, most people realize that they have a writing style that tends to rely on certain words and sentence structures, and they tend to make the same errors over and over again. For example, when one of the authors was in college she had an instructor who repeatedly marked her papers for passive voice. She spent an entire semester focusing on learning what passive voice was, how it functioned in a sentence, how to identify it in a sentence, and how to correct it. Now she is very aware of when she uses passive voice and only uses it to make a specific point in her writing. This was a trouble spot that she identified and keeps track of in her writing.

Answer the following questions to start a list of the idiosyncrasies of your writing style.

▶ What have friends, family members, and instructors identified as strengths in your writing? What have they said that you do well?

▶ What words, phrases, or sentence styles do you find yourself repeating in your writing?

> What things do you always find yourself correcting in your own writing? What things have friends and family members politely corrected for you?

> If you still have them, pull out graded writing assignments from past classes. Read through the comments. What common themes run through the comments?

> What parts of your own writing (paragraphs, complex sentences, semicolons, passive voice, etc.) do you already know you should spend some time focusing on and improving?

If you know you have problems in a specific area, ask someone to pay close attention to it when he or she is peer reviewing your writing. If you tend to overuse certain words or sentence styles, consider checking to make sure that you add variety to your writing. Also use this list to help you select one aspect of your writing that you would like to work on improving during a specific amount of time (perhaps during a semester). Consider sharing this list with your instructor to discuss methods that might help you address specific trouble areas.

Publishing

Once you have brainstormed, researched, drafted, revised, rethought, edited, drafted again, edited, and proofread (whew!), you will be ready to publish your writing. Publishing could include a variety of ways of presenting your writing to your readers. For example, you might print a paper and turn it in to your instructor. Or you might upload your research onto a web site. Or you might send an article to a newspaper. Or you might turn in a report to your supervisor at work. Your choice of publication method will be influenced, of course, by your rhetorical situation. The final "publication" of Qi's research and writing at the beginning of the chapter would likely be quite different from the final form of a paper that you might turn in for a class in school.

Introduction to Research Processes

Although *research* is listed as one of the possible steps in the list of contemporary writing processes, that step can be broken down into a series of smaller steps, or processes. And as we did with *writing processes*, we'll describe *research processes* throughout this book; however, realize that individual research processes are just as variable and dependent on rhetorical situations as writing processes. Although we present the steps as a list, and we put them in a specific order in this textbook, you should always adapt the approach you use for the specific writing/research project you are undertaking.

In Chapter 1 we mentioned that the simplest way to understand research is to remember that research answers a question. Many writing tasks qualify as research because they require the answering of a question—What do I need from the grocery store?—even though they do not feel like major research projects. When you take on a research project larger than a grocery list, however, there are five basic steps in research that you should follow:

1. Identify your topic/problem and develop a focused research question. (Chapter 3)
2. Assess what you know and what you need to know and develop a research plan. (Chapter 4)
3. Locate and document resources. (Chapters 4–7 and 11–15)
4. Analyze resources and develop the answer to your research question. (Chapters 8 and 9)
5. Present the answer to your research question while carefully citing your resources. (Chapters 9–11)

Many students make the mistake of simplifying their research process by focusing on step 3, locating resources. Without the careful preparation of steps 1 and 2, however, as well as the careful analysis and presentation of the results of your findings in steps 4 and 5, the work in step 3 can be completely overwhelming and not well represented in the results of the research project. Another way in which many students simplify the research process is by assuming that the only product of their research is the final report or presentation of the results. We hope you noticed that each step above includes an actual product (such as a research plan) that researchers should be developing as they work through the step.

This textbook will help you work through the five key steps of the research process for a variety of contexts, but you will need to adapt them to fit specific rhetorical situations. Chapter 3 will help you analyze your situation more closely and choose and focus a topic and research question.

chapter 3

Identifying a Topic

Any writing situation, academic as well as professional and personal, requires that you select and narrow your own topic. For example, a community organization might need to ask for money from a federal agency that is willing to fund projects to help low-income, single mothers. To receive the funding, the organization must write a successful grant proposal asking for the money. The proposal would need to specify what particular challenge the funding would help them resolve. In doing so, the organization would be narrowing its topic from a general request for money to a more targeted request for money to solve a particular problem. Similarly, in a film studies class you may be asked to research and write about a particular director's work. Although you have a general topic, you need to narrow it further. You might focus on a contemporary director whose movies you have always enjoyed watching, or you might focus on a director whose work has been mentioned in your class and that you would like to learn more about. Then, depending on the number of films the director has completed, you might need to determine if you want to focus on a particular time period or theme in the director's body of work. In both cases, the writer is given a general topic with which to start; however, it is his or her responsibility to narrow it further to a manageable, focused topic.

we'll explore

▶ *analyzing a writing situation*

▶ *choosing a topic*

▶ *focusing a topic by writing a research question*

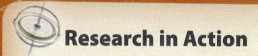

Author: Haley is taking a math course in college that is also designated as a writing-intensive course.

Topic: Haley's math professor assigns a writing project that asks her to report on an important person in mathematical history.

© Bonnie Kamin.com

Audience: Haley's audience for the math assignment is her professor.

Purpose: Haley needs to focus on a particular topic for her research paper that will be interesting to her and to her audience while fulfilling the requirements of the assignment.

Questions

1. What questions should Haley ask herself to get started on finding a topic?

2. What strategies might she use to create a list of possible topics?

3. Have you ever been assigned a paper in a class where you were given relatively free rein on the topic? Have you ever been overwhelmed with picking a topic or needing to narrow a topic to make it manageable? What did you do?

Analyzing the Writing Situation

Research and writing projects develop out of a specific situation, with a certain problem that needs to be solved or a goal that needs to be attained. An instructor might require you to research the chemical properties of a family of plants or your boss might ask you to research various shipping methods for a new product you are selling. In these cases, the context you are working and living in demands action; you have to write a paper to pass a class or you have to research shipping methods to keep your job. Whenever you are in a situation that presents the need to communicate, you experience **kairos**, a moment that inspires you or compels you to write.

Taking Advantage of Kairos

Elements of kairos, or of the "kairotic" moment, are usually present in both time and space. Let's focus on an everyday example. Imagine that you are eating at a restaurant and things keep going wrong. Your friend arrives twenty minutes late, your niece spills a drink all over you, your food is cold, and then you realize at the end of dinner that you need the check to be split among everyone and you forgot to ask the server. The server could get frustrated with all of these complications and convey that frustration by taking a long time to bring the food to the table, appearing irritated with the customers, or not refilling drinks. However, imagine that in this situation the server goes above and beyond to help resolve all the issues (he keeps everyone's drinks filled as you wait for your friend, he immediately helps clean up the mess from the spilled drink, he brings out a new plate of food for you, and he quickly splits the check four ways) and keeps on smiling. In that moment, you may think that it would be good to take the time to write the restaurant a letter to say how well this server interacted with your group. However, you know it is very unlikely that you will take the time to do so. But to your surprise, and luck, there is a feedback form included with the receipt. Without taking too much time out of your day, you now have the opportunity to respond to this situation and commend the server for his performance. All of these contextual forces combining to both motivate and set the conditions for your communication are an example of kairos. In other words, written communication needs to take advantage of a timely issue (the great job of the server) and have the material components necessary (the feedback form).

Successful communication, both written and oral, develops out of opportune times and places—out of kairos. To research and write about a topic that your readers will actually want to read about, you will need to be aware of and understand what is going on around you to find a topic that is both timely and appropriate.

Identify Kairos

Answer the following questions to explore what elements of kairos might shape your research.

1. What is your motivation for doing this research and writing? course assignment and grades? interest in topic? need to do/change something in your life?

2. What is going on around you that affects your understanding of this research project and topic? at school? at work? at home? in the community?

3. What has happened in the past and present, and what might happen in the future, that affects your understanding of this research project and topic?

write

Considering the Rhetorical Situation

To understand kairos better, think about how and why it is related to the concept of the rhetorical situation. Simply put, kairos presents the circumstance that then produces a rhetorical situation within which to research and write. You can test the timeliness, the kairotic fit, of an issue by analyzing whether the rhetorical situation emerging around your proposed topic "fits." The questions in Table 3.1 can help you do so.

TABLE 3.1. Kairos in the Rhetorical Situation

	Purpose	Audience	Author
Time	What has happened in the past, or is happening in the present, that motivates research and communication? What will happen in the future that will require research and communication?	What has happened in the past, or is happening in the present, that motivates this audience to care about this topic? What will the audience need to do in the future to motivate reading and learning about the topic?	What has happened in the author's past, is happening in the present, or might happen in the author's future that motivates him or her to research and write?
Space	What persons, places, or things will be affected by the outcomes of this research?	What "real-world" things can the audience do to impact this issue based on the research and writing?	What resources does the author have to facilitate research, writing, and publishing on this topic?

Table 3.2 analyzes the example of Haley from the beginning of this chapter.

TABLE 3.2. Kairos in a Specific Rhetorical Situation: History Report in a Math Class

	Purpose	Audience	Author
Time	Haley was never good at math in high school or college and dreaded taking this last math class. Haley was also taking a women's studies course and had been learning that the achievements of many women had been erased throughout history.	Haley knew that her math instructor wanted the students to recognize that math has a history and has developed and changed over time. She also knew that the math instructor was very interested in the history of math in different cultures. Finally, Haley knew her women's studies instructor would probably also like information about women in the history of math.	Haley wants to survive this last math class, so she wants to do well on this report. She knows she wants to focus on a topic that keeps her interested so she does well in the class.

Space	Haley's math professor was very excited by Haley's idea. The professor told Haley that there are significantly fewer women in math and science majors and professions.	Haley's math professor mentioned that a report on a woman in the history of math might motivate women to take more math classes and possibly become math majors.	Haley is excited about her access to resources because she has been learning about various women's studies resources in her women's studies class. Her math instructor has also provided starting places for historical research in math. Finally, her first Google hit listed four books to check out!

As you can see from Table 3.2, Haley's situation has many factors that help develop a kairotic moment for her math research project. One of the strongest elements is that she is also taking a women's studies class. And after she did a little exploratory research on the topic, including talking to her professors, she found that she has access to a variety of resources as well as a potential "real-world" purpose and audience. For Haley, this topic has moved beyond just a research report for a college class into something that can change people's lives. By taking the time to explore the timeliness of her topic, both for herself and for the community, Haley has now focused on a research topic that is exciting and will motivate her when the work gets tough.

write

Analyze the Rhetorical Situation

Start thinking about what is going on in your life and in your various academic, professional, and personal communities that might influence your understanding of possible research topics. Consider resources, both people and places, that you have access to while developing your research topic and/or during your research process. Focus on situations that would benefit from knowing more about your topic. How might your research impact the real world? Use Table 3.1 to help analyze your research project's rhetorical situation.

Generating Topics

A common element of the rhetorical situation for many students is being assigned a general topic to research. Like Haley's math professor, many instructors give students broad topics to research, usually based on the course's topics and/or themes. Your job in this situation, then, is to focus more carefully on a specific topic you are interested in researching within the guidelines of the assignment. However, if you are given free rein on your research topic, you may need to do a little searching for a general topic. Finding a general topic, and starting to narrow to a specific one, involves the same activities: finding out what is both important and motivating to you.

write

Find Out What's Important to You

Take some time to explore the various communities that you participate in:

▶ personal—home, family, leisure, and so on

▶ academic—school, past, present, and future

▶ professional—work and career, past, present, and future

▶ civic—community, political (local, national, global), and so on

Answer the following questions about these four communities you live in.

1. What discussions (in writing, on the Internet, verbally) engage you and other members of the community?

2. What events or experiences have happened that you still remember and that left you, or other members of the community, with questions or concerns?

3. What problems or concerns exist in this particular community?

Focus on one or two of your answers by digging deeper with the following questions.

4. Who, which individuals and groups, is involved in this discussion, event, or problem? Why are they involved?

5. When and where did/does the discussion, event, or problem take place?

6. What exactly is the topic of the discussion, event, or problem?

7. Why is the discussion, event, or problem significant to the community members?

8. How does the community usually start to resolve the discussion, event, or problem?

write

Generate Topic Ideas

As you think about topics to research, try writing down your responses to these steps.

1. Spend three to five minutes generating a list of topics that you find interesting and compelling (you might refer to your writing from the "Find Out What's Important to You" activity). List six to eight possibilities.

2. Go through your list and phrase each topic as a question. In other words, what would you like to find out? For example, if you listed, "Parking at my school," then you might write, "How could the

school provide more convenient parking options for students?" or "Why is the parking on campus so expensive?" You might even generate more than one question for a topic.

3. Now look at your list of questions and choose one that sounds particularly interesting to you. Freewrite for five minutes on why you think this topic is interesting and what you know about it.

4. Look at your freewriting and highlight or underline the most interesting idea you came up with. Copy (or copy and paste, if you're using a word-processing program) that idea below your freewriting and write about that idea for the next five minutes.

5. At this point, you might continue this exercise one or two more times until you find a focus that seems interesting to you. Or, if you find yourself stuck and think you might not want to research this topic, try one of your other questions and start the exercise at step 3 again. Remember that any of the invention strategies in Chapter 2 can also help you discover a topic.

Consider Audience and Purpose

write

As you make a final decision on your topic for research, freewrite for five minutes on each of the following two questions.

1. What might your audience be interested in? How could you relate your topic to your audience's experience?

2. Will this topic satisfy the purpose of your writing and research? What criteria must you keep in mind to make sure that you are meeting your writing goals?

Your answers to these questions might help you choose the best topic from several that you are considering.

Selecting and narrowing a topic can be one of the most important things you do before engaging in a research process. Consider talking about your answers with friends, family, coworkers, and classmates. Try putting down the questions and answers and returning to them a couple of hours, or days, later. Do you have new ideas? Can you add to some of your older ideas?

You, the author, are an important part of the rhetorical situation. If you are not engaged by the topic and motivated to learn about it, you will have difficulty being successful with your research project. Before committing to a specific topic, it is important that you explore various possibilities for your research. This is an opportunity for you to explore your own understanding of the topic. What issues and events is the topic related to?

Exploring and Narrowing a Potential Topic

Once you have a general idea of a topic you are interested in researching, you will want to spend time exploring it further to see what specific elements within it interest you. You should explore your topic prior to committing to it for two reasons. First, you need to verify that there are resources out there (people, places, and resources in the library and online) to actually use in conducting the research. If you don't have access to the proper tools, you can't do the work! Usually the best person to help you identify resources for starting your research is your instructor or any other person who "assigned" the research project (boss, community leader, or family member). Haley was able to find a wealth of information on her topic after talking to both her women's studies and math professors, for example.

techno tip

Use the Internet to Explore a Possible Topic

Depending on which of these descriptions best fits you, choose one of the following two activities to use the Internet to explore, or even find, a topic.

1. **I think I know what I want to research.** In this case, we recommend a variation on an activity that you might have done in the first chapter of this book. Try finding some running discussions about your topic. With the explosion of the blogosphere, there are lots of blogs on just about any topic. You could also consider looking at what has been written in Wikipedia on your topic.

   Keep in mind that this is the exploratory stage; blogs and Wikipedia won't likely be the most reliable resources you'll find. But they can be good starting points for understanding what people are saying about your topic. Try answering the following questions as you read what you find about your topic.

   ▶ What discussions are emerging around your topic?

   ▶ Who are some of the key players and groups interested in your topic?

   ▶ What subtopics emerged in discussions of your topic?

2. **I'm not sure what I want to research.** There are some resources that include lists of possible topics, and even include places to start reading about them.

   ▶ Web directories are a more linear way to search for resources on the Web. Instead of just dumping terms into a search engine, work your way through a Web directory. The directory starts with broad topic areas and allows you to continue narrowing down to subtopics. As you narrow, the directory will also provide resources to start reading. Try working through one of the following directories:

     ● The Open Directory Project (http://dmoz.org/)

     ● StumbleUpon is a useful resource for finding topics and resources that might interest you. You can try it out at http://www.stumbleupon.com.

- *CQ Researcher* is a publication for congressional leaders in their attempt to stay up-to-date on current events and issues. Forty-four weeks of the year a new report on a specific issue is published. The reports include lists of related issues, specific research questions with essays, and a list of resources to read more on the topic. *CQ Researcher* is published in both hard copy and in an electronic database. Most college libraries subscribe to one format or the other.

- Identify and read a few Web directory or *CQ Researcher* topics that you might be interested in. Then try answering the following questions:

  - What discussions are emerging around your topic?

  - Who are some of the key players and groups interested in your topic?

  - What subtopics emerged in discussions of your topic?

A second reason you should explore your topic further before committing is to broaden your understanding of the topic. By gaining a better understanding of some of the complexities of the topic, you can identify subtopics of interest to further narrow your research focus. Beginning researchers should learn more about their topic so they can then focus on a smaller piece of it. For example, when Haley searched online for "women in math history," she found a page that listed ten women with brief descriptions of their impact on math. As an English major, Haley was fascinated to find out that the poet Lord Byron's daughter might have been the first person to write computer code. By doing a little preliminary research, or exploration, of her topic, Haley may have found a specific subtopic she is very interested in; therefore, she is more motivated to do the research. Narrowing a larger topic, like the one Haley started with, to a more focused subtopic will make your research project, and your writing task, much more manageable.

reflect

How Can I Make a Topic Manageable?

When choosing a topic for writing, it is important to make sure that your topic is actually manageable and appropriate for the specific writing situation. Before continuing with your writing, take a moment to reflect on the topic you are working with by responding to the following questions.

1. How appropriate is this topic to the writing situation? In other words, will this topic fulfill the requirements of the assignment if you are writing for a class? If you are motivated by a situation at work or in your personal life, will exploring this topic satisfy the need that first prompted you to explore this topic?

2. How interested are you in your topic? Will you be able to sustain your interest long enough to complete the writing and research necessary? Is there a specific aspect of your topic that holds more interest for you that would be a good place for you to focus?

3. How doable is your writing task? Consider how broad your topic is right now. Will you have time to explore this topic thoroughly? Is there too much information available about the topic? If so, you might need to narrow it further. Is it difficult to find information about your topic? If so, you might need to refocus or broaden your topic.

Once Haley confirms that there are resources available on her topic and that other people are dialoguing about that topic, she needs to reassess whether her topic is appropriate for her rhetorical situation. Will her chosen topic be interesting to her audience? Is it appropriate for the assignment she was given? Will she be able to find enough information to meet the requirements of the assignment (or will she have too much information, which would mean she might need to narrow her topic further)?

Haley found many resources on Lord Byron's daughter, Ada Lovelace, but she had no idea how to narrow the topic further to help her decide what she needed to focus on while researching and reading. Although she was excited about all the material she was reading, Haley was overwhelmed with information. She decided to talk to both her math and women's studies instructors. Both asked her questions that helped her to decide what she was really interested in: Lovelace's impact on the field of software development.

Focus Your Research Topic

Take five minutes to brainstorm a list of the things that people debate regarding your topic. Think of conversations that people would have about your topic and points of disagreement. You might think of these as subtopics within the larger topic you're exploring. If you are in a classroom setting, pass your list on to your classmates and have them add to it. If you don't have access to other students, ask your friends and family to add to the list.

Once you have your list of related topics and subtopics, try visually depicting your topic by drawing a cluster map. Start by writing your topic in the center of a piece of paper. Write your various subtopics on branches. If you can break down any of the subtopics further, create additional branches that stem from the subtopics. You might see that some branches generate more ideas than others, and you may find that you are more interested in one or two branches than the others. These observations can help you pick a narrowed focus within your topic. You will probably want to focus your research and writing on one of the second- or third-generation branches away from your central, broad topic.

Developing a Research Question

Once you have discovered a topic that fits your rhetorical situation, and you've narrowed it down to a workable subtopic, it's time to really begin your research. Sometimes it is difficult to determine where to start, however. One of the most effective ways to get started on your research is to think of your topic in terms of a question that you would like to answer: your **research question**. Your natural inclination when you hear a question is to respond to it, and phrasing your chosen topic as a research question can motivate you to begin thinking of ways to answer. If you were having trouble narrowing your focus on your topic, writing it in the form of a research question is another way to work on focusing.

A research question should be clearly stated and provide the specific focus and scope of your research. For example, Haley might write a research question that looks something like this:

What influence did Ada Lovelace have on the development of computer code?

Try to avoid yes/no questions because they won't help you generate as much research and writing. For example, if Haley asked the following question,

> Was Ada Lovelace the first person to write computer code?

then it could be answered either "yes" or "no," but she might not have much more to say. An exception to this rule might be if there were a controversy surrounding the answer; in that case, Haley could write about the controversy. Even so, a more accurate research question would be:

> What is the controversy surrounding whether Ada Lovelace was the first person to write computer code?

Write a Research Question

write

1. To start developing possible research questions, begin with some basic question words. Try to write at least one question that someone might raise about your issue that starts with each of the following words: *who, what, when, where, how, why, should, would.*

2. Think about what your goal is in writing. Do you want to share information about your issue? Are you defining terms or aspects of your issue? Are you evaluating something or comparing/ contrasting it with something else? Are you identifying a solution? Take a look at your questions and circle any that specifically match your goal. Cross out questions that do not fulfill that goal.

3. Go back to the writing and thinking you have done about your audience and purpose in writing. Who are you writing to? What are their interests? What is your purpose in writing?

4. Use your responses to these questions to consider each of your preliminary questions from step 1. Cross out questions that would not meet the needs of your audience or fulfill your purpose in writing.

5. Finally, choose the one remaining research question that interests you most. Are there any terms you should define more clearly? Show your question to someone else and ask if it is clear. You might exchange your question with a classmate, a friend, or a family member.

Situating the Writer in the Research

Throughout our discussion of research, we have talked about the importance of choosing something to research and write about that interests you. Furthermore, the activities in this chapter have encouraged you to choose a topic in which you are *invested*. In other words, you have a stake in the outcome of your research.

For example, if you are researching whether you should purchase a standard automobile or one that uses alternative fuel, you have a stake in the outcome of your research. The answer you discover might determine what type of car you purchase. You are invested in your research because it will have an impact on you. You might be specifically invested in the topic because of various influences in your life—you might be living on a tight budget, so cost is a major factor to you. Or, you might be concerned about the environment and the emission of chemicals from standard automobiles. Any of these factors might influence the way that you conduct your research, the sources that you choose, the way you read and use those sources in your writing, and the criteria you develop for choosing the best answer to your research question. We call this **bias**, and it is the unique perspective that you bring to your research.

We are not using the term *bias* in a negative sense—everyone has bias. We all have unique experiences and backgrounds that influence the way that we see an issue. As you conduct your research, however, we want to encourage you to be *aware* of your bias and to consider how it might influence the way that you research and write about your topic. It's really not possible to be completely objective about an issue—we all see the world and the issues surrounding us through the lenses of our own perspectives, influences, and experiences. The audience that you envision for your research might not share your specific bias, though, so you will need to consider this if you are trying to persuade your audience to take action on your topic.

reflect

What Is the Writer's Place in the Rhetorical Situation?

Reflect on how and why you are interested in your narrowed issue and research question. Consider the following questions as you compose this reflection.

- ◗ What initially sparked your interest in this issue?

- ◗ What did you already know about the issue, and how well could you answer your research question right now?

- ◗ After conducting a preliminary exploration of the issue, have those interests been confirmed?

- ◗ What has surprised you as you've conducted the preliminary exploration?

- ◗ Why do you value this issue?

- ◗ What is your perspective on this issue?

- ◗ How might your values and perspective influence your research and writing on this issue?

- ◗ What specific experiences have you had with this issue (friends, family members, colleagues, community, news, movies, etc.)?

While answering these questions, you will want to be sure to explore past events that have molded your values and beliefs about this topic and issue. Do not simply discuss how you feel. Instead, focus on why you feel that way. What experiences have you had that make you believe what you believe? While discussing the experiences, use concrete details (sight, sound, smell, touch, taste, specific emotions, etc.) to make the reader feel like he or she has had the same experience.

Your Knowledge of Your Topic

If you have chosen a topic in which you are interested and invested, chances are that you already know something about it. You might not be an expert, but you will still find it helpful to reflect on what you already know about your topic before you begin to think about what other resources you will need to find.

If you choose something you are invested in, however, then you have a specific bias about that topic. Therefore, you must not only identify what you already know, but also look for different perspectives in order to understand the complexity and controversy surrounding the issue. If you are researching the debate about marriage equality, for example, you will want to look at arguments for the extension of marriage rights to all people as well as arguments defending the preservation of marriage between a man and a woman. If you already have a specific opinion on the issue that you are researching, be very careful to find resources that both agree and disagree with your opinion. If you start with what you know and believe, however, you will be able to piece together a plan for what you still need to find out. The first step, though, is determining what you already know.

Take an Inventory of What You Know

reflect

As you make your final decision about the topic you will research and write about, take a personal inventory of what you know.

▶ What is the central issue that people debate when they talk about your topic or discuss your research question? In other words, what is the main controversy (or, what are the main controversies)? What do people disagree about?

▶ What do you believe about this topic? What evidence makes you believe this? Where did you find or learn about this evidence?

▶ What different people, or groups of people, are interested in your research question? What do you believe others think about this topic? What evidence do you believe they base their opinions on? Where do you think they found that evidence?

▶ Where do these people discuss their positions on your issue? In other words, where would you go to find out what people are saying?

▶ Based on what you already know, what perspectives do you need to learn more about?

Try conducting this activity more than once, returning to it numerous times as you research. And don't do this activity alone—get friends and family members to participate in a dialogue with you. Keep in mind that there is a difference between what we *know* as fact and what we *think* we know. This activity should not only help you figure out what you know as fact, but it should also give you a sense of what you *think* you know but need to verify.

Writing a Research Proposal

At the beginning of any major research project, a researcher needs to identify the focus and purpose of the research, something you have been working toward in Chapters 1–3. A researcher may write a research proposal to establish the focus and purpose of research, especially if seeking permission, funding, or approval of some sort: proposals ask the reader to make a decision about the proposed project. Depending on the nature of the research project and the rhetorical situation, a formal written proposal might or might not be necessary. Whether or not the researcher writes a proposal, though, the questions outlined in this section are valuable for defining a focus.

In this section, we offer guidelines and examples of research proposals along with a sample assignment for a research proposal, but keep in mind that proposals can take many forms. We'll introduce you to three kinds of research proposals:

- **Topic Proposals**
- **Conference and Article Proposals**
- **Funded Project Proposals**

Common Features of Research Proposals

The goal of a research proposal is to help the audience understand the focus of the proposed research. Because the audience will base an approval or funding decision on the proposal, it is also an important persuasive document in its own right. To achieve their persuasive goal, nearly all research proposals share some common key features, the wording of which also can serve as subject headings for longer proposals:

▶ **Introduction to the subject of the proposal:** The introduction should provide enough information about the subject of the proposed research to inform the audience adequately but should avoid providing too much information that the audience would already know. Readers need to have an understanding of the subject of the research project and/or the issue at stake in order to make a decision about the project (to approve a topic, to provide funding or resources, etc.), and the author of the proposal should have an understanding of the readers' familiarity with the subject.

▶ **Explanation of the significance of the project:** In addition to explaining the subject of the proposed research, the author must give a rationale for why the project is important and relevant. You might think about this section in terms of kairos, as discussed in Chapter 3: why is this research, at this time, in this context, to this audience, important to pursue? This section could include a description of the researcher's interest in and experience with the subject, where the idea for the project came from, and/or what kind of contribution the project will make. If appropriate to the guidelines for the proposal you are writing, evidence or data to support the need for the proposed project can appear here as well.

▶ **Clear research question:** Research proposals should always contain a clear research question (or set of questions) that highlight the specific focus of the project. The research question(s) might appear before or after the "significance" section in a research proposal, depending on the requirements of the proposal and the author's preference. Some authors like to use the significance section to lead up to a research question, while others prefer to state the question after the introduction of the subject and then use the significance section to justify the importance of the question. In Chapter 3, we discuss principles for writing a research question in more detail.

▶ **Statement of objectives:** At some point in the research proposal, the author must clearly state the objectives (goals) and expected outcomes for the research. What do you hope to achieve through this research? What is your purpose in researching this subject? The objectives might be stated in a separate section, or they might be incorporated into the description of the significance of the project. In either case, the author should indicate a clear connection between the research question(s), the intended audience, and the expected outcomes, or purpose, of the research.

▶ **Statement about the researcher's ability to complete the project:** Again, depending on the requirements for the research proposal, this section might include a description of the author's credentials, past research, or experience with and knowledge about the subject matter. Additionally, this section could include a list of resources available to the researcher to complete the project, if relevant. For example, if you are planning to conduct a survey, how will you do so? Do you have access to the participants who would complete the survey? Will you conduct the survey online or in print, and do you have access to the resources to do so? Finally, this section should include an indication of the researcher's commitment to the project.

▶ **Timeline for the research project:** Most research proposals include a timeline for completion of the project, breaking the project down into manageable steps with clear deadlines. Even if a timeline is not required, it can be helpful to draft a timeline for yourself to make sure that the scope of the project you are proposing is manageable given the amount of time that you have.

Additional Features Found in Some Research Proposals

Some other features are not as universal, but you may find them in certain kinds of research proposals:

▶ **Review of prior research:** Depending on the nature of your research, you may include a brief review of research already conducted on the topic. The purpose of the review of research is to show your knowledge of the work that has already been done on the subject and to demonstrate that your research fills a gap in the existing knowledge or thinking about the subject. For more information about writing a review of prior research, see the Part 2 DIY on pages 149–164.

▶ **Description of methodology:** Detailed proposals often include a description of the methodology that will be used to complete the project. Depending on the nature of the research project, the description of methodology might take various forms. For a research project that proposes conducting secondary research, the author might describe where and how he or she intends to find relevant resources for the project. (See Chapter 4 for help with conducting secondary research.) For a research project that involves primary research, the author should include a specific description of how he or she will conduct that research (conducting observations or interviews, distributing surveys, analyzing data). (See Chapter 5 for help with conducting primary research.) Additionally, the proposal might include a copy of any interview questions, surveys, or observation methods used in the project. If the research proposal you are writing requires a description of methodology, we recommend reading Chapters 4 and 5 before proceeding.

▶ **Budget:** If you are requesting funding, your proposal must include a detailed budget that justifies the amount of the request. In a research proposal budget, you should include specific expenses with justifications for those expenses. In some cases, you might also attach evidence in support of the amount you request (for example, if you ask for funding for a subscription to SurveyMonkey.com to conduct an extensive online survey, you should include a link to or printed copy of the fees for use of the software).

Types of Proposals

Research proposals can take many forms, mainly depending on purpose. In this section, we describe the specific features of topic proposals, conference or article proposals, and funded project proposals. We also include examples of two types you are most likely to write as an undergraduate: the topic proposal and conference proposal.

A Topic Proposal

Features of a Topic Proposal

Topic proposals are often written in an academic context, usually for an instructor who requires a research project for the course. In such a context, depending on the formality of the proposal and the requirements of the instructor, a topic proposal would include all of the features listed on pages 52–53 ("Common Features of Research Proposals").

Some of the elements might be unnecessary if the assignment already dictates specific parameters for the research project. For example, the instructor might give you a specific timeline to follow, rather than require you to specify one. Additionally, the instructor might not expect you to discuss your ability to complete the project, but he or she might expect you to talk about your prior knowledge of the subject and any perspectives that might influence the way you approach the subject.

In addition to these features, topic proposals might include the following:

▶ brief description of methodology

▶ statement of the intended audience

▶ review of prior research

Again, the specific requirements of the topic proposal should be drawn from the assignment given by the instructor.

Example of a Topic Proposal

The following example of a topic proposal was written by Alexandra McMullin, a student in a first-year writing class. She wrote this proposal in response to an assignment that asked her to propose a topic for research that is potentially controversial. The assignment also asked that she do a little reading and thinking about the topic prior to writing her proposal. Alexandra chose to write about the option of attending a community college instead of a four-year college or university. She discusses her reasons for pursuing this topic and what she believes her focus will be in her research. As you read, keep in mind that there are both strengths and opportunities for revision within the final proposal. We have included the instructor's comments on Alexandra's final proposal so that you can see the feedback that she received on this paper.

Alexandra McMullin
Professor Miller-Cochran
English 102
19 February 2011

Is Starting a Degree at Community College Best?

In the past two years the economic state of the country has gone from bad to worse. The housing market is filled with foreclosed and bank-owned homes. Jobs are being lost. Now, education is taking a hit. University tuition prices are being raised all while students are not able to keep up with payments. While the economy is taking a turn for the worse, it seems one aspect of education seems to be thriving: community colleges. As stated by the Center for American Progress, "America's future economic success may well depend on how we invest in two-year institutions" (Fitzpatrick 1). In comparison, many universities are having to cut funding, or turn away thousands of applicants ("To Save UC, Cut Enrollment").

The question I'm trying to answer is whether or not community colleges are a reliable option for earning or starting a degree while saving money. I am a current community college student, and I started my degree at a community college less than a year ago, even though right out of high school I had the option to start classes at a university. What I didn't have was money to pay high tuition costs. I chose Mesa Community College because I knew I would save money, and I didn't even know what degree I wanted to get. A community college, I felt, was a great way for me to explore what I wanted to do, while not paying as high of a price tag.

Although I personally feel very excited about my education, many people weren't too thrilled that I opted for a community college. When I told my high school teachers that I chose MCC they seemed less enthused and almost disappointed that I'd chosen that route. The same has been true for many other people. Once I tell them I'm a community college student, they seem to think less of me and it's almost as if they think I'm less qualified. I think there is a certain stigma attached to community colleges. People presume two-year colleges are less prestigious than four-year colleges, and that the people who attend couldn't make it at a university.

> Interesting—you're doing a good job of establishing ethos here and explaining your experience with the issue. Can you discuss actual dollar amounts? What was the difference between what you would have paid at the university you would have attended and what you pay at the CC?

> I'm glad you included this part of your experience—this is an important part of the decision-making process.

This stigma is what I will really be delving into. I'm interested in whether or not prospective employers will accept degrees from community colleges as credible. Also, since the economy has affected how much time students can spend in college, I want to research how universities and community colleges have started collaborating to accept transfer credits.

My purpose in writing about this issue is to help inform people looking into getting a higher education in a tough economy. I would like to lay out opinions from professionals about the positive aspects of going to a community college. I would also like to show how completing two years at a community college, before transferring, could be as beneficial as completing all four years at a university. The audience I will target in my research is high school graduates looking into alternative educational options. I would also like to present my research to anyone who is interested in furthering their education, while gaining credibility in a failing economy.

It's clear that you have already determined your perspective that you want to argue.

The topic is controversial because many negative stigmas are attributed to community colleges. Even though community colleges are financially much more reasonable than universities, there are presumptions that two-year colleges are less prestigious and less rigorous than four-year colleges. Another controversial debate is whether or not saving money at a community college for the first two years will be a financial pay-off in the long run. The argument is whether or not community college transfer students get equally well-paying jobs after graduation. This topic is relevant to everyone, especially my designated audience, because the recession has affected every aspect of life. The economic downturn is causing people to be resourceful and flexible about change. By looking into all the different ways to gain an education, not just the traditional safe route, students are preparing themselves to be adaptable to whatever hardships may come out of a bad economy.

My research plan includes finding the best current sources for my information. I want to find statistics that are effective and reliable. Resources could include magazine and newspaper articles which will display how this topic is relevant to the general public. Along with the articles, I would like to find opinions from professionals about what correlation there may be between the job market and community colleges in the next few years. The timeline I will follow is first to research what the differences are between universities and community colleges and how they may change in the next few years. My biggest challenge in this research is to check my bias because of my own personal experiences with community colleges. I plan to give a clear informative presentation unhindered by my own encounters.

Good—I'm glad you're acknowledging this.

Overall, I look forward to presenting my research about such a controversial and relevant issue to anyone looking into educational alternatives. I hope that I can inform readers about the positive aspects of community college, using my personal experience, along with the opinions of experts in education and the job market.

Works Cited

Fitzpatrick, Laura. "Can Community Colleges Save the U.S. Economy?" *Time*. Time, 20 July 2009. Web. 12 Feb. 2011.

"To Save UC, Cut Enrollment: The Options Are All Grim, But the Priority Must Be to Maintain the System." Editorial. *Los Angeles Times*. 21 Jan. 2011. *ProQuest*. Web. 4 Feb. 2011.

Discussion Questions

▸ Can you clearly tell what Alexandra McMullin's research question is? If you think it needs clarification, what suggestions would you make to the author?

▸ What is the author's purpose in researching this topic? Where does the author discuss the purpose, and what recommendations would you make for clarifying the purpose?

▸ Whom does the author intend to address with the final research project? What suggestions would you make to clarify the intended audience?

▸ If you were going to make suggestions to Alexandra about issues she could clarify or expand upon in her proposal, what would you say?

A Conference or Article Proposal

Features of a Conference or Article Proposal

Conference or article proposals are similar to topic proposals in that they propose a research topic that is of interest to the author. Two major differences exist, however. First, the proposal is often written in response to a specific Call for Proposals (especially in the case of the conference), and it has to follow the guidelines given for proposals to that conference or journal. Second, conference or article proposals tend to be far more concise than topic proposals written for a class. For some conferences, proposals might not be allowed to exceed two hundred words, which is generally less than a page, double-spaced. When they are required to be concise, conference and article proposals rarely use subject headings. Other conferences and journals might expect proposals to be longer and more detailed. The author must make sure that the subject matter is appropriate for the conference or journal and carefully read the requirements for writing the proposal for that context.

Conference or article proposals generally share most of the features of topic proposals, except that they are written more concisely. In addition, they nearly always include:

- review of prior research
- description of methodology, especially if the author proposes to conduct primary research

Because these proposals are generally written for academic audiences, readers are specifically interested in the researcher's sound knowledge of the subject matter and the suitability of the methodology to the research project.

Example of a Conference Proposal

The following example of a conference proposal was written by an undergraduate student. She was interested in presenting her work at a conference on science fiction and fantasy literature. This proposal is for an individual presentation, but some conference proposals discuss a theme and include multiple speakers who will address different topics. Most conference proposals have a word count limit; therefore, it can be tricky to include references to outside sources and full bibliographic citations. Check with whomever is collecting the proposals for guidelines about whether to include a Works Cited page. Also note that, although we have included the author's name below, conference proposals are generally submitted with no identifying information on them so that the proposal can be reviewed without bias related to the author's identity.

Alexis Catanzarite
November 30, 2011

Analyzing Female Role Models in
Romantic Vampire Literature for Young Adults

Many critical reviews of supernatural romance novels, especially ones that are geared towards the teenage female demographic, are so focused on the vampires (or whatever supernatural creature is featured) themselves that the female protagonists featured in them are often left by the wayside when the analysis is being conducted. Charlaine Harris's *Dead Until Dark*, Stephenie Meyer's *Twilight*, and PC and Kristin Cast's *Marked* represent three such novels that are

> You mention there are "many" reviews; you should include in-text citations for 2–3 of them as evidence of your claim. Including citations will demonstrate you have been paying attention to the conversation in progress.

told from the female's point of view; readers are meant to identify with the female protagonists of these books, creating a new and questionable kind of role model for the reader. While it should be noted that *Dead Until Dark* is not classified as a YA novel due to sexual content, it is widely acknowledged that many teens that read the *Twilight* series also read the *Sookie Stackhouse* series. With as much as these novels are consumed by young readers, the characters in them have the ability to make a much larger impact on their impressionable audience than anyone seems to acknowledge.

> Acknowledged by whom?

Whether the authors are aware of it or not, they have created a role model in each of the lead female characters for readers to look to for guidance. As such, their characters should receive more scrutiny from reviewers and the topic should be given appropriate credence. In each of these novels, the female protagonists are confronted with their sexual awakening with (or in *Marked*'s case, *as*) a vampire. Their reaction to this experience, how they handle such an overwhelming feeling, is critical to their role model status. While it's true that most critics seem to concur that *Twilight*'s Bella presents young female readers with an almost disturbing example of how to conduct one's self in a relationship, the articles I examined did not compare her to similar characters in literature so as to create a standard. In most cases, scholars simply point out Bella's deficiencies as an independent female character, but offer up no alternative model as to how she should have acted. This paper will bridge the gap between Bella, Sookie, and Zoey, showing how they all experience similar feelings, but handle them very differently, thus presenting readers with three alternative role models.

> Great job pointing out a gap in the current scholarship and demonstrating how your project will fill the gap.

Discussion Questions

- What is the overarching purpose of the research proposed for this conference presentation?

- What kinds of external sources does the author refer to? What might be the advantage of including both primary sources (the literature she is analyzing) and secondary sources (scholars who have already written about themes in these books)?

- Who does the author intend to address in the conference proposal? What suggestions would you make to clarify the intended audience?

- If you were going to make suggestions to the author to revise this proposal, what suggestions would you make?

A Funded Project Proposal

Features of a Funded Project Proposal

Sometimes researchers write proposals to ask for resources or funding to conduct a specific project. The request might be modest or it might be quite large, depending on the scope of the research project. Some funded project proposals are written in response to a specific call for grant proposals. In other words, a funding organization advertises that they are willing to fund research about a specific topic, and the researcher must fit her or his request into the parameters of the Call for Proposals. At other times, researchers might write unsolicited requests for funding or support, directed to an audience who might have interest in the project and the resources to fund it, but who hasn't advertised a specific grant to fund such work.

Research proposals which ask for funding generally share features that are unique to this type of request. In addition to the features mentioned in the two types of proposals above, funded research projects include:

- connection between the research and intended audience
- budget

The connection with the intended audience should address the specific interests of the funding agency. The budget should carefully justify each item requested.

Steps to Developing a Researched Topic Proposal

If you are writing a topic proposal, your goal is to introduce the issue that you are interested in exploring in your major research project. This might be a topic that you will develop throughout a course (perhaps for the entire semester), or one of several you might eventually research and write about. Either way, you will want to narrow your focus to one issue that you could explore through this assignment. Your topic proposal should include the following features:

- introduction to the subject or issue you wish to research
- explanation of why that subject or issue is significant
- one clearly stated research question
- identification of a rhetorical situation for the project that includes
  - discussing your own interests and prior experience with the issue
  - articulating your purpose in researching the specific issue (your statement of objectives)
  - focusing on a specific audience to whom you will communicate the results of your research
  - discussing how all of these elements construct a rhetorical situation in which you will be researching and writing
- brief timeline that presents the plan you will follow to complete the project

You will likely follow four major steps in completing this research proposal: first, choosing a focused topic; second, exploring what you already know about the topic; third, writing a research question; and fourth, determining your audience.

Choosing a Focused Topic

The proposal is an opportunity to narrow down your research to a specific, guiding research question and focus. Depending on the specific assignment prompt, you may not need to use many, if any, outside resources for a proposal assignment; your primary resource is your own experience and knowledge of the issue. You are exploring what you know, what you need to find out, what your focus is, and who your audience is. For more information about developing your credibility, or ethos, as an author, see Chapter 8, "Developing an Argument."

To keep yourself interested and inspired in your research topic, be sure to select something that interests and engages you. In addition, you need to choose a topic that will interest and engage your readers. To complicate things further, if you are writing in the context of a class for which you have to complete an assignment, then you must choose a topic that will meet the criteria for the assignment.

No wonder it can be so difficult to choose a topic—writers have to balance the needs and interests of several different groups! Sometimes those needs and interests can compete with one another, too. Perhaps you can think of a time when you heard someone go on and on about a topic to the point of completely boring the people who were listening. It's very possible that the speaker was interested in the topic, but the audience wasn't. Or imagine taking a course on Ethics in Science and the instructor assigns a term paper having to do with one of the ethical issues discussed in class that semester. If you write a paper about the development of the designated hitter rule in baseball, then you probably won't meet the criteria for the assignment—even though you may be very interested in the topic.

What we suggest is that you start with your own interests and then think about what the purpose for your writing is and who your audience will be. Weighing each of these factors into your topic choice will help you find something to write about that you will be interested in, that your audience will enjoy reading, and that will fulfill your purpose in writing.

▶ "Write: Find Out What's Important to You," on page 42 of Chapter 3

When students are confronted with a research assignment where they need to choose a topic, the most difficult part often is finding something to research and write about. Sometimes we are able to start with an idea of what we're interested in, and then we can go to the Internet or other research sources to find more information and focus our topics. Other times, we don't really know where to start and we need some help thinking of possible topics to focus on.

▶ "Techno Tip: Use the Internet to Explore a Possible Topic," on pages 44–45 of Chapter 3

Once you have chosen a broad topic for your writing, it is important to focus your attention on a particular issue that you will research and write about. Topics are broad, general subject areas, and issues are specific conversations, and sometimes points of disagreement, within a topic. If you've had difficulty in the past with researching and writing about something for which you found too much information, then you might have been researching a topic instead of focusing on a specific issue within that topic. For example, let's say we're back in that Ethics in Science class. One of the students decides to write about the use of animals in laboratory testing. This topic is rather broad, and it doesn't tell us what the student is interested in within that topic. The student would need to think about what kinds of conversations people have about animal testing, and he or she might specifically brainstorm a list of the points on which people disagree. Each of these points is an issue, and the student could then choose one of them for extended research and writing.

▸ "Reflect: How Can I Make a Topic Manageable?" on page 45 of Chapter 3

▸ "Write: Focus Your Research Topic," on page 46 of Chapter 3

Exploring What You Already Know about the Topic

One way to focus a research topic is to think about what you already know about a subject and why you are invested in researching it. This step can help you determine what aspect of a subject will be most likely to sustain your interest long term and be most satisfying to you. Additionally, exploring what you already know about a subject can help you think about your own personal biases and how that might influence your research. Part of our responsibility as researchers is to understand that we all work from specific frames of reference, and an awareness of our own biases can help us adopt the most neutral stance possible when conducting our research. Your experience and interest in the issue are part of your rhetorical context. Nobody looks at an issue entirely objectively, so by describing the perspective you already bring to the table you will begin to define your unique position on the issue. For example, a single mother who chooses to write about the controversy over spanking a child might describe her struggle to determine the best way to discipline her own children and whether or not she chooses to spank them. She might describe her experience with discipline as a child, or she might choose to describe the influence of others on her decision. Finally, she would describe how these experiences influence her opinion on the issue of whether or not parents should spank their children.

▸ "Techno Tip: Use the Internet to Explore a Possible Topic," on pages 44–45 of Chapter 3

▸ "Reflect: What Is the Writer's Place in the Rhetorical Situation?" on page 48 of Chapter 3

Writing a Research Question

An important component of your research proposal will be a clear statement of your research question. Writing a clear research question can be one of the most difficult parts of the research process, however, and it is an essential link between your purpose in writing and the methodology you use to conduct your research. Be certain to give yourself plenty of time to draft and revise your research question.

▸ "Write: Write a Research Question," on page 47 of Chapter 3

Determining Your Audience

Your final researched argument will be addressed to a specific audience whose thinking you want to influence. Your credibility as a reliable researcher will be very important in persuading this audience to adopt your evaluation of the issue or position. To establish this credibility, you should present yourself as someone who is well-informed about the issue you are discussing. You might choose an audience that is open-minded about your evaluation, or, if you want to attempt something a bit more difficult, choose an audience that is skeptical or even hostile to you or your evaluation. If you are evaluating the merits of gun control, for example, you could imagine yourself writing to members of the National Rifle Association. A primary goal of this particular assignment is to focus on the specific audience you will address in your final research paper and to determine the purpose of addressing your argument to that audience.

You have multiple audiences for this assignment. If you are completing this proposal in the context of a class, one of your audiences is your instructor and potentially your fellow classmates. If you were assigned a research project for work, you may want to share your research proposal with your supervisor to be sure you both understand the requirements of the research project. In addition, your audience is yourself—this is a chance to explore your own perspective on your issue and become more aware of the ways in which your perspective influences how you research. You should also, however, identify an audience whose thinking you want to influence on your issue. Be specific about that audience, and think about what you need to include or consider in order to persuade that audience.

As you consider potential audiences for your research, take a moment to think about who you would want to persuade to see the issue you are researching differently or to take action on the issue. Who might be able to make a difference? As you brainstorm potential audiences, you might think about the rhetorical situation of your research as a whole to determine the audience you think would be most appropriate. Once you have narrowed your choices down to a specific audience, you need to think about the expectations, needs, prior knowledge, and motivations of that audience. What should you consider in order to make your work most persuasive? What does this audience already know about your subject, and what do they think about it? How much do you know about your audience, and is there anything you should strive to find out?

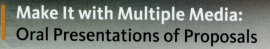

Make It with Multiple Media: Oral Presentations of Proposals

In professional settings, many research project proposals are delivered as oral presentations. Organizational officers and managers usually have to approve research projects because of the time and money the organization will dedicate to the project. Oral presentations of proposals generally include the same information listed above in the various features lists; however, most of the information is conveyed orally. Oral presentations generally include three major components:

- **Oral script:** This is the information you will convey orally. You can do this in real-time (speaking) or through software such as VoiceThread.

- **Visuals:** This is the information you will convey visually (many people use presentation software like Microsoft PowerPoint, Prezi, or Keynote to visually supplement their oral presentations).

- **Informational handout:** This is the written information you will provide to every member in your audience to supplement your presentation and to remind your audience later of important aspects of your presentation.

Good presenters do not duplicate the information in each component. The majority of your information should be conveyed orally. In other words, if someone only gets copies of your visuals and your informational handout, he or she will not have all of the details of your proposal, only a general overview. The informational handout should only include bibliographic information (name, title, date, etc.), summative information, and any critical details the audience might need to refer to later. The visuals should only visually enhance what is being said; therefore, they should primarily be pictures, tables, or key words. It is a good rule of thumb to never use smaller than 30-point font in presentation slides; 30-point font is big enough for the audience to see and keeps you from putting too much text on the slides.

 For an example of a student's proposal delivered in multimedia through VoiceThread, access your English CourseMate through cengagebrain.com.

part 2

Conducting Research

chapter 4

Finding Resources through Secondary Research

Many students are often paralyzed by the overwhelming number of options for answering a research question. Where should you start looking for information? What search terms should you use to locate resources? Should you gather information from other people and conduct field research? If so, who should you ask? Or, should you rely solely on published resources? The options can seem limitless.

The good news about conducting large research projects is that you can break the process down into manageable steps. If you completed a thorough rhetorical analysis of your writing situation and a critical self-evaluation of your perspectives, experiences, biases, and knowledge, you are already off to a good start. You have an idea of why you are interested in your topic and what information you need to balance the perspective you are developing on your issue. Chances are that you have already read a few things to begin thinking about the topic. And if you focused your research project on a few key research questions, you already have the beginnings of your search terms.

we'll explore

▶ *determining what you know about your topic*

▶ *identifying what you need to learn*

▶ *developing a plan for finding secondary resources that will support your research*

Research in Action

Author: Ricardo needs to complete a project on a Renaissance painter for an art history class. He is required to use outside resources, write at least a ten-page research paper, and then make a five- to ten-minute presentation to the class about his research.

Topic: Ricardo knows that he really likes Donatello's sculptures, especially his *St. George*. He visited a Renaissance exhibit at a local art museum two weeks ago, and he was inspired by Donatello's work.

Audience: Ricardo's audience includes his art history instructor as well as his classmates.

Purpose: Ricardo needs to develop, conduct, and produce a research project in the five remaining weeks of the semester.

George Tatge for Alinari/Alinari Archives, Florence—Reproduced with the permission of Ministero per i Beni e le Attività Culturali/Alinari Archives/Alinari via Getty Images

Questions

1. How will Ricardo get started with this project? How might he incorporate the Donatello exhibit into his research plan?

2. How will Ricardo know what types of information he will need?

3. How will Ricardo know where to look for information?

4. Have you ever had a project where you were responsible for locating large amounts of information? How did you know what you needed to find? How did you know where to look?

Conducting Research

You have an abundance of information about nearly any topic available at your fingertips, so it is critical to carefully plan how you will conduct your research. An Internet search engine like Google or bing is probably not the best place to begin. Searching for the key terms from your research question in Google will probably give you thousands (if not millions) of potential sources and web sites that you will need to comb through, and that can be quite overwhelming (not to mention inefficient).

When Ricardo searched for "Donatello St. George," he had approximately 87,000 hits.

A better plan is to

▶ reflect on what you already know about your topic,

▶ decide what kind of information you need about your topic,

▶ narrow your research results by developing specific search terms, and

▶ plan where to look for that information.

As you respond to the writing activities in this chapter, think about the rhetorical situation for your writing. Who is your audience, and what is your purpose for writing? Keep this in mind as you respond, and you will have the tools you need to develop a research plan that will give you useful results.

Identifying the Information You Need to Find

What kind of information do you need to find for your topic? The first step is to "take inventory" of your knowledge about your topic. Once you have determined what you already know, you can start developing specific lists of what you need to learn and what resources you need to find. By taking the time to develop a detailed list of the types of resources you hope to find, you will be able to check categories on your list as you find resources that fit into them.

Primary and Secondary Research   One big decision you will need to make is whether to conduct primary research or to rely solely on secondary resources. **Primary research** entails going straight to the resource to answer your research question. There are two criteria for defining primary resources. First, the resource itself must be the primary object of study. Primary resources include the data collected from field research as well as from works of art or other texts when they are the primary object of the study. Therefore, if Ricardo's research question is about the meaning of masculinity in Donatello's sculpture *St. George*, the sculpture itself would be a primary resource. If the Renaissance exhibit at his local art museum happens to include a reproduction of *St. George*, Ricardo could observe the sculpture himself and draw his own conclusions. Likewise, if a student in an education class had a research question about how elementary school students learn multiplication tables, her primary resources would be the students themselves, their work, and probably the teacher and his or her lesson plans. All of those materials would be part of the object, or the primary focus, of the research question.

The second criterion defining a primary' resource is that you, the researcher, are the one collecting the data. The data from the resources are not filtered through any other person. For example, if Ricardo's research question was "How have art scholars in the past one hundred years discussed the meaning of masculinity in Donatello's sculpture *St. George*?" the sculpture itself would no longer be his primary resource. Instead, scholarly articles about masculinity and the sculpture would be his group of primary resources. He would be collecting his own data about how a variety of scholars discussed masculinity in *St. George*. Independent of the type of resource—book, painting, or person—the label "primary" is based on the focus of the research question and the person collecting the data.

Secondary research, on the other hand, deals with resources produced by someone else. In other words, your knowledge and experience of the primary resource to answer your research question is mediated through another author or authors. Therefore, journal articles about elementary education and elementary levels of math would probably make up the list of secondary resources for the research question about children learning multiplication tables. And again, if Ricardo's research question is "How do historical ideas of masculinity contribute meaning to Donatello's sculpture *St. George*?" articles about Donatello, his sculpture, and historical definitions of masculinity are secondary resources that mediate Ricardo's understanding of the primary object of study, the painting itself. However, if Ricardo's research question is "How have art scholars in the past one hundred years discussed the meaning of masculinity in Donatello's sculpture *St. George*?" those articles that were secondary resources for the first research question become primary resources for this second question.

To decide whether you will be conducting primary or secondary research, return to your rhetorical situation. The type of information you need will be partially determined by your research question, your perception of your audience, and your purpose for writing. Although it is critical that Ricardo conduct primary research for either research question about masculinity in the *St. George* project, it is advisable that he also see what scholars say because he is not an expert in art interpretation. However, if the initial project was just a journal prompt for his art history class, his instructor may not expect secondary research. In this case, it's important to consider the expectations of your audience (your instructor) and the requirements for the assignment.

Should You Conduct Primary or Secondary Research?

To help you determine what type of research will best answer your research question, fulfill your project's purpose, and appeal to your intended audience, you will want to make sure that you are gathering the right types of resources. Use the following chart to help you decide what types of resources you will need and what types of research you will conduct based on your rhetorical situation. You might not be able to think of both primary and secondary resources for every category—that's okay. If you are having trouble thinking of examples for one column or the other, try asking a classmate, a teacher, or a friend. If you are still having trouble thinking of possibilities, that might be a clue as to which type of research you should conduct.

	Primary	Secondary
Purpose: What types of resources will help you achieve your purpose and motivate your audience to action? (Consider what you want readers to do after reading your paper.)		
Audience: What types of resources/data does your audience value—numbers and statistics? anecdotes and stories? case studies and ethnographies? expert testimonies? What will be most convincing?		
Topic/question: What type of information can help you answer your question thoroughly?		
Author: What types of resources do you have access to? Who can help you locate and gather information? What and who do you have access to for gathering information? (Be sure to consider the project's time frame as you ask yourself these questions.)		

If you are still having difficulty determining where to start, you might want to begin with secondary research because it will give you a foundation in what others have said and written in response to your issue. Secondary research helps you understand the rhetorical situation surrounding your issue, and it can give you a solid foundation before embarking on primary research. The remainder of this chapter focuses on strategies for conducting secondary research (see Chapter 5 for detailed information on conducting primary research).

Locating Resources

If you have spent time and energy preparing to research, the process of locating resources will be much simpler than if you start with a blind Internet search. Use the following list to help you get started.

1. Find the resources you already know about.
2. Find the resources that emerged during your planning.
3. Ask a librarian to help with your search.
4. Systematically search new resources.

Once you have tapped the resources that you, your friends, your family, your classmates, and your instructor(s) have suggested, go to the librarian. Librarians are experts at finding information; however, they cannot serve you well if you haven't prepared for meeting with them. Instead of thinking of the librarian as the starting point, think of him or her as a place to go for additional help once you have begun to determine the direction of your research. A good thing to prepare before you talk to the librarian is a list of potential search terms.

Specific Search Terms

When you begin to search for secondary resources, you need a list of specific terms that will help you locate those resources. Obviously, you will need to use specific terms to locate secondary resources in the library or on the Internet. However, have you considered that terms that seem like synonyms might return a different group of hits? For example, try searching with the terms "distance learning" and "distance education." Although there will probably be some overlap, the search will also yield a lot of different sources. Sources dealing with "distance learning" focus more on the actual teaching and learning activities in a "distance" class and sources discussing "distance education" focus more on institutional and programmatic concerns like how many courses to offer, how to retain students in classes, and how to train teachers. Therefore, you may want to use closely related terms to help you locate more resources during your research. Be aware, though, that subtle differences in meaning might impact your search results.

In the quest to identify search terms, you already have a key resource, your research question. Obviously, the key words in your research question will be your principal search terms. The key words are the descriptive nouns, verbs, and adjectives in your research question. If you can't easily identify key words in your research question, you may need to go back and continue narrowing and focusing your question. And if the key words seem a little vague or you find that you are collecting an abundance of data, again, you may need to continue narrowing and focusing your research question. Once you have that initial list of key words from your research question, developing a larger list of search terms is a relatively easy process.

Ricardo decided he was most interested in examining how art scholars have discussed the concept of masculinity in Donatello's sculpture *St. George*. Ricardo circled the following key words in his research question:

How have art scholars

in the past 100 years

discussed the concept and image of masculinity

in Donatello's sculpture *St. George*?

Although adding these extra key words to Ricardo's search did help diminish the number of hits, Google still returned approximately 8,080 hits.

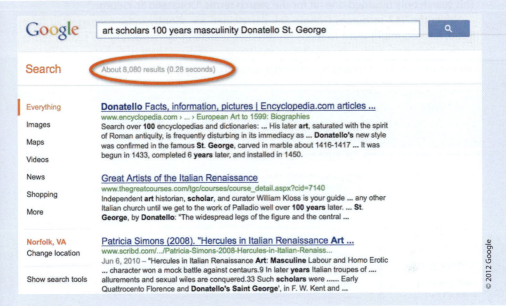

With a deadline in five weeks, Ricardo did not have enough time to search these 8,080 resources, as well as all the leads that his art history instructor gave him. Ricardo had a couple of options: he could try a search engine that would give him more-focused results or he could focus his search terms further.

One strategy Ricardo should try is to get away from the standard Google search. General search engines such as Google can return many different resources, but because they do not limit the kinds of resources returned they are not a helpful starting point for Ricardo. Because he is focusing his research on scholarly interpretations of masculinity in Donatello's sculpture, he should start by using a search engine or a database that looks for academic articles and re-sources. By simply changing his search engine from Google to Google Scholar, but still using the same search terms, Ricardo would limit the number of resources returned from 8,080 to 117.

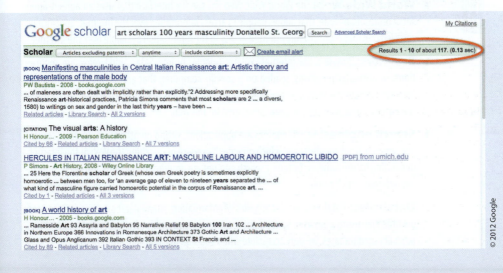

He could also try searching in an academic journal database, such as Gale's Academic OneFile. This type of academic database would be available through his school's library. This search only returned one hit for the search terms "Donatello St. George."

While the 117 resources Google Scholar yielded are slightly more manageable than 8,080, Ricardo might want to focus his Internet searching by narrowing his search terms further. However, with only one hit in the library database, he'll definitely need to use alternative search terms and speak with a librarian.

© Cengage Learning

Internets, Browsers, Databases, Oh My!

techno tip

Many people struggle with understanding the differences between resources found on publicly available web sites and resources found in library databases. Having a general understanding of how the Internet works helps make the distinction clearer.

▶ **Internet:** The Internet is a network of computers that holds information that other computers can access through the same network.

▶ **World Wide Web:** The World Wide Web is a specific interface that uses an agreed-upon set of protocols, or code, that allows people to access information over the Internet. Specifically, the Web provides more visually oriented access to the information available over the Internet.

▶ **Browsers:** Browsers, like Internet Explorer, Google Chrome, Safari, and Firefox, are applications, or computer programs, loaded on a specific computer, that access information on the Internet through the Web. In other words, browsers are tools that access the Internet by using the agreed-upon protocols, or code, developed for the Web.

▶ **Search engines:** Search engines are applications, sitting on other computers or servers and separate from your browser, which provide the service of searching the Web or the Internet, depending on the browser. Different search engines are programmed in different ways, providing different search results.

▶ **Databases:** Databases are repositories of information. Many databases can be accessed over the Web using a browser. Some databases are only accessible after paying a fee; therefore, most library databases are only accessible when you sign in using your student ID.

Expanding and Focusing Search Terms

There are three primary methods to help identify, evaluate, and further focus key words.

1. Be sure to carefully acknowledge the literal differences between the words in your research question. Using a dictionary, look up the definitions for each key word from your research question as well as two or three alternative words. Notice the subtle distinctions between the definitions. Are any of those distinctions completely inappropriate to answer your research question? Will your intended audience heartily approve or disapprove of specific definitions? For example, Ricardo knows that his instructor will accept the ideas and perspectives of art "scholars" but not art "critics."

2. Try adding modifying phrases to the key words in your research question. For example, if you are researching the differences between Chevy automobile models in the 1950s, you may find a lot of information. You might first focus on a specific model, like the Bel Air. You may decide you want to focus only on specific years, like the major differences between '55, '56, and '57. The further you focus, the more modifying words you add to your key search terms.

3. As you conduct your research, identify the alternative phrases people use when talking about your subject. Once you've identified some of those alternative phrases, carefully distinguish why one person refers to your topic using one phrase and another person uses a different phrase. As you did with the literal, or dictionary, definitions, search for subtle differences to help you further focus your research as well as to start processing your data.

write

Develop a List of Search Terms

After you circle the key words in your research question, write them in the accompanying chart. Brainstorm alternative terms for each key word. After you've run out of ideas, ask your friends, family, classmates, and instructors to help you.

	Key Word 1	Key Word 2	Key Word 3
Alternative terms from your brainstorming			

Once you have your list of key words and alternatives, be sure to talk to a librarian. The librarian will help add and cull terms from your list based on his or her experience as a researcher. The librarian should also be able to help you identify related Library of Congress classification terms that will help you find information in the library more readily. Keep your chart of search terms with you as you collect your data. While reading articles or listening to interview responses, other useful terms might emerge during your research process.

	Search Term 1	Search Term 2	Search Term 3
Librarians and the Library of Congress classification terms			
Terms you find during your research process			

After spending so much time narrowing and focusing your research question, developing a list of search terms broadens the possible field of resources. To keep yourself sane, try to keep your search terms narrowed and focused as well. You may even find that you need to remove some search terms entirely.

Search Engines and Web Directories

Ricardo's searches in Google and Google Scholar provide one example of how a researcher's choice of search engine can make a difference in the resources he or she finds. Different search engines yield varied results because they are programmed to search differently. Depending on how the search engine has been programmed, it might rank returns differently as well. If you have not tried more than one search engine, you might try your search terms on a couple of different search engines to see what results you receive. A few of the most popular search engines are:

- Ask.com (http://ask.com)
- Google (http://www.google.com)
- bing (http://www.bing.com/)
- Yahoo! (http://www.yahoo.com)

You might also try a couple of metasearch engines that compile the results of multiple search engines for you. Several popular metasearch engines are:

- Dogpile (http://www.dogpile.com)
- Excite (http://www.excite.com)
- WebCrawler (http://www.webcrawler.com)

If you are having difficulty finding helpful sources on your topic, then a metasearch engine might be a useful tool.

In addition to search engines, web directories such as the Open Directory Project (http://www.dmoz.org) can be useful starting points for locating online resources dealing with your research topic. Web directories are different from search engines because they do not list links, or hits, based on key words. Instead, they list links by categories and subcategories. Whereas search engines are programmed web "crawlers" that search available web sites automatically, web directories are edited by people who submit sites for inclusion in different categories and review the appropriateness of sites included in the directory. Many university and college libraries also include directories of school resources on popular research topics; check with your local librarian to see if your school has library-specific directories.

techno tip

Refine Your Search Results

Many search engines, as well as database search tools, now include an option to use various advanced search and results filtering options to help narrow the results of your search. For example, once you have your results in Bing or Google, there are easy filtering options. Bing has these options, as well as a link to an Advanced Search page, along the top of the search results.

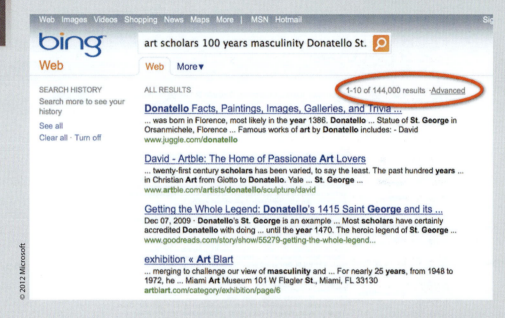

© 2012 Microsoft

Google has a longer list of filtering options in a menu along the left-hand side of the search results (click the "More" buttons to see even more options).

Many search engines also allow you to limit your search results by typing commands into the search box. As shown on page 78, typing "filetype" into the search box limits the results to particular kinds of files, such as PDFs or PowerPoint slides ("filetype:pdf" or "filetype:ppt").

Other filtering options you might include:

▶ Donatello **"St. George"** (The quotation marks treat the title as a specific phrase instead of searching for the words separately).

▶ Donatello St. George **–review** (The minus sign excludes the word "review," filtering out many art reviews.)

▶ Donatello St. George **language: en** (Adding "language: en" would filter the results so that you only had results in the English language.)

▶ Donatello St. George **site: worldcat.org** (Adding "site: worldcat.org" would only search for results within the "worldcat.org" web site.)

>>>

>>>

> ▶ Donatello St. George **AND (masculinity NOT gender)** (Incorporating a layered search with parentheses and different Boolean terms further clarifies your search. In this case we add the term "masculinity" but not the term "gender." The parentheses act as in algebra, keeping different functions together.)

> ▶ **Define: renaissance** (Using "define" would search for a definition.)

Not all search engines use the same filtering options; be sure to check the individual search engine's "help" page.

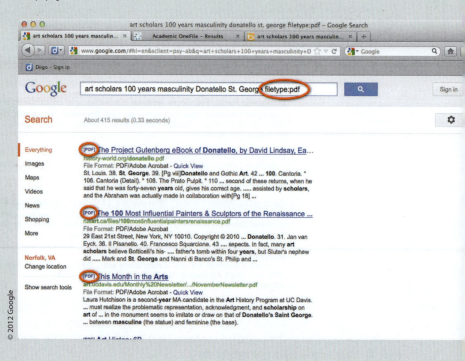

© 2012 Google

Types of Resources

In this text we categorize resources according to two characteristics: how they change over time and how they are reviewed. When you begin to evaluate your resources and consider how you will interpret them and incorporate them into your writing, you first need to understand the nature of the resources that you find. Understanding the nature of the resource is important so that you can begin to evaluate it and so that you can determine how to cite it in your research. (For more information on citing sources, see Chapters 11–15.)

How Texts Change over Time

One of the defining characteristics of a resource is how it changes (or does not change) over time. Resources can be categorized in these three ways:

> ▶ **Static.** Static resources change the least of all three types. They are only "published" once, even though they may be redeveloped as other editions. Examples include books, paintings, films, and basic html coded web sites.

▶ **Syndicated.** Syndicated resources are released over time under the same general title. Examples include periodicals (magazines and journals), television shows, blogs, and podcasts.

▶ **Dynamic.** Dynamic resources are never permanently published in a final form. If there are repeat performances or publications, they are different every time. Examples include plays and other live performances, wiki publications, and field research (observations, interviews, and surveys).

How Texts Are Reviewed

Another important characteristic of the resources you find is the process by which they are reviewed. Review generally takes place before publication, but with the technological capabilities that individuals now have for publishing material, review sometimes happens after the fact.

▶ **Edited.** Before the resource is published, someone with some type of authority or certification (besides the author) reviews the resources and provides suggestions for revision.

▶ **Peer reviewed.** Before the resource is published, it must not only pass the editor's criteria but must also be approved by peers in the same profession as the author.

▶ **Self-published.** The author publishes the resource. There is no authoritative editor or other gatekeeper. Whoever provides the author with resources to help publish, however, may function as some form of gatekeeper.

Understanding the review process of your resources will also be helpful as you evaluate the usefulness and credibility of the resources that you find.

Library Resources versus Internet Resources

In the past, you might have thought about resources as being either "in the library" or "on the Internet." This is an easy distinction, but it is not always accurate or applicable. Consider an article that you might find in the *New York Times*, a newspaper that can be read in print or online. You might find the same article in the print version of the paper and on the World Wide Web. If it's the same article, does it matter where you found it? For the purposes of evaluating the credibility or usefulness of the resource, probably not. It's still a newspaper article, published in a syndicated publication that was reviewed by an editor. If you are determining how to cite the resource, however, the location of the resource does matter.

When you are reviewing and analyzing your resources, keep in mind that the library/Internet distinction is not quite as simple as it might seem at first. The Internet is where students often turn when they are having difficulty getting started. Many instructors warn students against using Internet resources because they are easily alterable and because anyone can construct and publish a web site. These are important points to remember, but it is essential to use clear evaluative criteria when you are looking at *any* resource. Print resources can be self-published as well. Analyzing how easily a resource is changed, how often it is changed, who changed it, who reviews it, and who is responsible for the content will help you choose resources that are reliable and credible, wherever you might find them.

Some Internet resources, because of the nature of their publication and review processes and the ease with which they can be accessed, need to be scrutinized especially carefully, however. Many instructors warn students about using information from *Wikipedia* (http://www.wikipedia.org). *Wikipedia* is an online encyclopedia whose entries any user can revise. *Wikipedia* has an elaborate review system under which various users take responsibility for reviewing and monitoring content, but it is not foolproof. If you have never tried making a revision to an article in *Wikipedia*, you should—if for no other reason than to see how easy it is for any user to change the content of the reference. You might also notice whether or not someone else makes a change to the page you edited. How often is the information shifting? Is someone reverting the information you changed back to what it said originally? Who is responsible for maintaining accuracy on the page?

An equally important point to remember is that *Wikipedia* is not just an online resource—it is the online equivalent of a reference book. Reference books can be good places to learn general information about a subject, but they are not the most authoritative resources to use as evidence in an argument. Because they are compilations of the research done by others, reference books are not primary resources or even necessarily secondary resources. (You could think of them as *tertiary* resources.) They can be helpful at the beginning stage of a project, though, because they often include useful bibliographies that point you to other helpful resources. They might also help you identify potential search terms.

Review the History of a Wikipedia Page

Not only can pages in *Wikipedia* be edited easily, readers also have ready access to a list of the edits by clicking the "view history" tab at the top of a *Wikipedia* page. Looking at the history of a page will also give you a good idea of how often the information in *Wikipedia* changes. Of course, some topics are edited more often than other topics. The accompanying web screen gives an example of the "history" page for the entry on "secondary research"; readers can click on any of the links to see previous versions of the page.

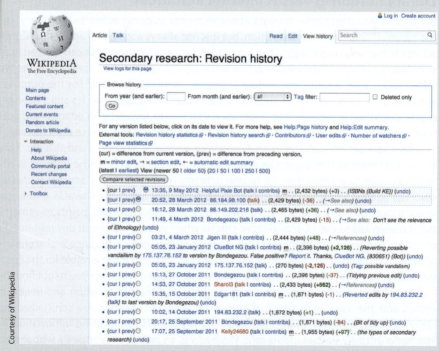

Pages for topics that are in the news frequently, however, are not open to public editing. On these pages you can view the "history" of the page, but there is no option to "edit" the page. You'll also find that pages for major celebrities and political candidates are closed to public editing. The "talk" tab is always open for public comment, though, and that can provide access to insightful exchanges about the topic.

One of the best methods for finding the most reliable perspectives on a specific topic is to search through and compare a variety of types of resources. As we mentioned earlier, you should not limit your research to an online search of a few terms. Yes, you can find some valid and useful resources on the Internet; however, you should also search more traditional resources found in your school or public library. Consider looking through and/or using the various media and digital resources described in the next sections to help you find resources on your topic. The resources listed are divided according to how they change over time: static, syndicated, and dynamic. They are also discussed in terms of the review processes that they might use, when appropriate.

Static Resources

Static resources are often the ones that students think of first when they start to conduct secondary research. Static resources are usually published once and rarely revised. If they are revised, as in the case of books, web sites, or software applications, they are usually released as a separate edition.

Books

Many students think of books as the most authoritative and desirable resource for a research project. After all, if someone took the time to write an entire book, then they must have a lot of useful information to share, right? And if someone expended the effort and money to publish the book, then it must be authoritative. Right? Well, sometimes . . . but not always. Books can be useful because they compile a great deal of information into one publication. However, books can also take a long time to publish, so they are not always the best place to start looking for cutting-edge research on a current issue. On the other hand, books are generally more extensive, in-depth treatments of a topic, so they often have excellent bibliographies and can give a researcher a good sense of the background and context of an issue. Depending on what your topic is and how important it is for you to find timely information about it, books might or might not be the best place to start.

If you look for books on your topic, you will want to scan several things that will help you quickly evaluate the usefulness of a book in answering your research question.

1. **Copyright.** The date of publication will give you a sense of how current the information in the book is.
2. **Publisher.** If the publisher is a reputable one (e.g., an academic press or a press that publishes a great deal in a particular area or field), then it could help you determine how reliable the information in the book is. An academic press also probably has a peer review process, which means that other professionals in the field reviewed the information and suggested revisions and corrections prior to publication. See what information you can find about the publisher's review process. You might also search for any reviews of the book. Be aware that the

Internet has made it quite easy to self-publish books; in such cases, it will be of the utmost importance that you verify the author's credibility.

3. **Table of contents.** If you have been looking for information on this topic already, a quick scan of the table of contents will give you a sense of whether the book presents a balanced and thorough treatment of the subject.

4. **Bibliography.** The bibliography should provide evidence that the author(s) consulted a multitude of other resources in writing the book. Scanning the bibliography will give you a sense of how balanced and thorough the author's research was.

One of the best places to start looking for books is at a university or college library. Searching the online catalog will give you a sense of whether or not the school has any books that might be useful for answering your research questions.

write

Search the Library Catalog

You might start your search for resources by browsing your library's online catalog. As you search, answer the following questions.

1. Enter your search terms into the keyword search in the library catalog. How many resources does the catalog return? Which ones look potentially useful to you? Make sure you note the call number of particularly promising resources so that you can find them on the library shelves.

2. Use variations on your search terms. What kinds of results did you find when you altered your search terms or used them in different combinations? Which key terms were most useful?

3. Your campus might have multiple libraries, or you might have access to libraries on other campuses through interlibrary loan. What resources could you request from other locations? (If you do request resources from other libraries or campuses, make sure that you leave enough time to receive the resources and look through them before an assignment or project is due.)

4. Your library might also have access to electronic books, or ebooks. If you are doing your search remotely, ebooks can be an especially useful resource. Does the library catalog list any ebooks on your topic?

5. Go to the shelves and look for the resources that sound most promising to you. Once you find the section in the library shelves that has books on your topic, browse the shelf. You might be surprised at the useful resources you find by reading the spines of books surrounding yours on the library shelves. What titles do you see that look promising?

Web Sites

Well-chosen web sites can provide some of the most up-to-date information on a subject. If your research question requires that you find the most current information available, you might want to search the Internet for appropriate and useful web sites. As we mentioned earlier, though, the amount of information available (and the number of web sites on some popular subjects) can be completely overwhelming. If you decide to surf the Web for information on your topic, you should carefully narrow your search to find resources that will be applicable and useful. To determine how reliable the information is on the web site you have found, look for the following key pieces of information.

1. **Author.** Who wrote the information on the web site? What are the author's credentials? If you cannot find an author, that is not always cause for alarm. In such a case, look for a sponsoring organization and see if that alleviates your concerns.
2. **Sponsoring organization.** Is there an organization sponsoring the information on the web site? For example, is the web site published by a government entity? Is it a corporate web site? Sometimes you'll have to dig for information, but you should be able to find an author, sponsoring organization, or both. Sometimes the extension on the URL can give you a hint as to where the information came from. For example, .gov indicates a government-sponsored web site, .edu is generally an educational institution, .org is a nonprofit organization, and .com is a commercial web site, most often a corporate or personal web site. If you cannot find either an author or a sponsoring organization, then you should be skeptical about the information you have found.
3. **Date of publication and/or last update.** When was the information on the site published? This might be important for your topic, depending on your rhetorical situation. You might also look at how recently the information was updated.

One of the biggest concerns about Internet resources is that there is not always a clearly stated review process. If a resource you have found is located in an online publication, you might be able to find specific details about its review and publication process. And if the web site is published by a sponsoring organization, you could probably conclude that the organization approves of the content (unless a disclaimer is attached to the article/site).

Audio and Video Files

If audio and video clips would provide useful data for answering your research question, you might try looking for audio or video files in your school's library and on the Internet. Your library might even provide remote access to some audio and video files, if you have a password-protected connection to the library's collection. On the Internet, you can search iTunes for audio files, and some search engines (such as AltaVista) provide audio- and video-specific searches. If you are interested in video clips, try searching YouTube, TED, and Explania. You may also find useful podcasts, which we discuss in greater depth under "Syndicated Resources" below.

The considerations that apply to web sites also apply to other resources that you find online, such as audio and video files. You'll want to ask similar kinds of questions as you consider the reliability of those resources, especially about who uploaded the information. Also, be certain to check that the person who uploaded the material did not violate copyright if you are going to use it in your research.

Syndicated Resources

Syndicated resources are published in installments over time, usually under the same general title. For example, magazines and newspapers are syndicated resources because they publish issues periodically that include new articles and information. Likewise, blogs are syndicated resources because the authors publish new entries over time.

Periodicals

Periodicals include newspapers, magazines, academic and trade journals, and other publications that are released "periodically" under the same title. They can be found in print and online, and sometimes the same publication can be found in both places. Many newspapers, for example, have both print and online versions. If you choose to cite periodicals as references, it is important that you understand what kind of periodical you are reading. **Newspapers and magazines** tend to report on research others have done rather than present original research. They often include ads and are affiliated with commercial publishers. They tend to fall into two categories: consumer periodicals and trade/business periodicals. Each type is targeted to a different audience. **Journals** have various degrees of review and are often affiliated with particular organizations or universities. They have different standards for research appropriate for different audiences. Journals can be divided into at least two categories: trade journals and academic journals.

Academic journals are often considered most authoritative because of their rigorous review process, but your topic might not be discussed in academic journals. As you choose resources for your project, think about who your audience is and what your purpose is in writing. What kind of publication will be most authoritative and convincing to your readers?

The most efficient and effective way of searching for periodicals is through the online databases available through your library. Most libraries have two kinds of online databases—general databases and subject-specific databases. General databases for academic journals include Gale's Academic OneFile and Academic Search Premier. Google Scholar is a search engine that is specifically focused on academic resources, and it is available to the public. Your school library probably also has databases for newspapers and magazines as well as subject-specific databases for academic journals.

write

Search for Resources in Periodicals

Try the following steps to find resources in periodicals that will help you answer your research question. As you complete each step, take careful notes on what you find so that you can locate the resources again later.

▶ Use an academic database through your school library. Enter the search terms that you have decided on. Then try a different set of terms in the same database to see if you get a different set of results.

▶ Choose a subject-specific database, appropriate to your topic, and search for your terms again.

▶ Search for your terms in Google Scholar, an academic search engine. What resources do you find that are different from the journal databases?

▶ Enter your search terms into a newspaper database to see if you can find any news stories about your subject.

techno tip

Databases, Microfilm, and Microfiche

Libraries used to house paper copies of all of the periodicals they subscribed to. As the library space began to fill, many libraries provided access to older periodical information and rare pieces in their collection through microfilm and microfiche (also called microforms on some campuses). If you are researching a historical topic, microforms can be invaluable. If you have never used a microform reader before, don't hesitate to give it a try. You just might find a treasure trove of useful information that you didn't realize was available to you.

Instead of subscribing to individual journals, libraries increasingly find it easier and more economical to subscribe to periodical databases that include a number of journal titles. Databases are repositories of resources that were, usually, published elsewhere first. Companies that own databases such as Academic OneFile or Academic Search Premier collect multiple resources, in this case scholarly journals, and then sell libraries digital access to the entire collection of journals. That is why you have to log into your school library to access the databases: your school has to prove they have paid for your right to access the materials. Websites like iTunes and Hulu are also databases to which individuals subscribe. You purchase songs or albums through iTunes and might access a few episodes of your favorite show through Hulu; however, they want you to subscribe for access to more materials.

Podcasts

Podcasts are audio files that are published in installments. They operate almost like an audio version of a magazine or blog. The difference between an individual audio file and a podcast is simply that podcasts have more than one episode, or installment. Podcasts and individual audio files can be evaluated similarly, but they are cited slightly differently.

Blogs and RSS Feeds

A blog (which is a shortened version of the phrase "Web log") is a web site where entries are published over time and usually organized chronologically. Many people keep blogs as a sort of public, online journal, while other blog sites are collectively written by a group of people. Some blogs focus on a particular subject while others deal with a wide range of topics. For example, Twitter is a microblog that usually focuses on an individual person's day-to-day activities.

Because blogs can be hosted on free public sites and started by anyone willing to take the time to set up an account, you need to be particularly careful when choosing blog entries as resources in your research. Be aware of who the author is. The blog should have an "About" tab that gives information about the author(s), and if you have difficulty finding such information, you might question the credibility of the site. Try to determine what makes the author a reputable source of information on the subject. If you choose to cite a blog entry in your research, give the resource an appropriate context. Explain where the information came from, and consider whether you need to defend the relevance of the blog entry in your argument.

If you are interested in looking for blogs that deal with your topic, try searching an online blog directory. Several such directories exist, and you can find personal and professional blogs on a variety of topics. Try looking for blogs at:

- Blogarama (http://www.blogarama.com/)
- BlogCatalog (http://www.blogcatalog.com)
- BlogHub (http://www.bloghub.com)
- Technorati (http://www.technorati.com/)

If you find a potentially interesting blog, you could follow it for a while and watch for new posts. An easy way to do this, without having to visit the blog on a regular basis, is by subscribing to an RSS (Really Simple Syndication) feed. An RSS feed will alert you when new blog entries or updates have been posted on web sites that you are "watching," and all of the new information can be gathered in one place for you by using an RSS aggregator.

Set Up RSS Feeds

Several RSS aggregators are available online:

▶ Google Reader (http://www.google.com/reader)

▶ Bloglines (http://www.bloglines.com)

▶ Gritwire (http://www.gritwire.com)

An easy, and free, RSS feed aggregator to start with is Google Reader. If you start at the Google homepage (http://www.google.com) and click the "More" link, you'll find "Reader" on the list of other options. Set up an account by clicking the link on the Google Reader homepage.

Once you have created your account and logged in, you can easily add blogs or web sites that you would like to subscribe to by clicking the "Add Subscription" link. Google Reader will compile the blogs you are watching, and you can read new entries in the center of the screen.

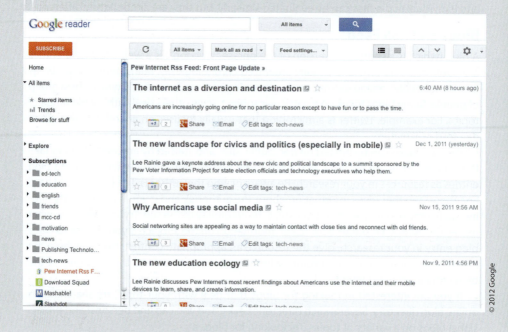

Dynamic Resources

Dynamic resources are meant to change. They are continuously changeable over time through repeated revisions or performances. Dynamic resources are often not edited or peer reviewed before publication, but they are usually reviewed (or perhaps just revised by a reviewer) after they are published. The reviews might be in the form of comments or suggestions. They might also take the form of discussion such as that found under the "talk" tab in *Wikipedia*. In such cases, it is important to remember that the credibility and authority of the resource should be measured by looking at the entire context of the source—not just the original text but also its revisions and reviewers.

Email Lists and Newsgroups

Email lists and newsgroups are probably the least "changeable" of the dynamic resources. Individual email messages and postings to newsgroups often cannot be changed or altered, but other participants in the list or group can respond to the message by affirming, disagreeing, or revising. Depending on the topic of your research, you might find an email list or newsgroup dedicated to your issue or area of interest, and you might find it helpful to join the list or group and "listen" to the conversations in progress. Some lists will have an archive of past messages that can be searched as well. If you are interested in looking for email lists or newsgroups, check out Google Groups (http://groups.google.com) and Yahoo! Groups (http://groups.yahoo.com).

Social Networking Sites

Social networking sites, such as Facebook and LinkedIn, provide opportunities to connect with and communicate with other people in a Web-based environment. Many social networking sites have groups within them that are interested in specific subjects, and you might find a group that is discussing the issue that you are researching. You can also create your own social network through applications such as Spruz (http://www.spruz.com/) if you'd like to invite people to talk who are interested in your research question.

Online Communities

While email lists, newsgroups, and social networking sites are all different types of online communities, they are all primarily *asynchronous* environments; that is, participants do not generally interact at the same time. In *synchronous* online communities, participants communicate at the same time and can instantly respond to one another. Instant messaging (IM), or chat, discussions are an example. Chats are usually between just two individuals; some IM technologies, however, like Google Talk and Skype, allow multiuser chat sessions. IM and chat technologies generally allow you to record a transcript of the live discussion, making it easier to use the chat as a resource later. MUDs (Multi-User Dungeon or Domain) and MOOs (MUD Object-Oriented) are text-based multiuser virtual environments. MUDs and MOOs have slowly been replaced by graphics-based virtual environments like SecondLife (http://secondlife.com/) and World of Warcraft (http://www.worldofwarcraft.com/). Depending on the software that runs the virtual environment, you may be able to record a live session.

Synchronous online communities can often be useful for conducting primary research, either by observing the environment or by meeting individuals in the environment to talk about your research topic. In either case, the strength of conducting research in an online synchronous community is the ability to get instant feedback. If you have a question, you can ask it; if you need clarification, you can get it immediately.

If you are using an online synchronous environment as a primary resource, you need to carefully consider the ethical concerns of working with human participants. (Chapter 5 offers guidelines for such ethical considerations.)

Wikis

Wikis are software applications that allow users to create and edit pages easily, often in a collaborative environment. Wikis exist for all sorts of purposes, but they are often used for collaborative writing and development. *Wikipedia* is arguably the most famous wiki, but wikis exist for other purposes as well. Not all wikis are public, and not all wikis that can be viewed online are open to editing by the general public. If you are interested in searching for a wiki that focuses on your subject, try searching at WikiIndex (http://wikiindex.org).

Several resources are available if you would like to try setting up your own wiki, which can be especially useful if you are working on your research project with one or more collaborators. Try one of the following applications to set up your own wiki space:

▸ Google Sites (http://sites.google.com).

▸ PBworks (http://pbworks.com/)

Performances and Broadcasts

Although a manuscript of *Romeo and Juliet* might be considered a static resource, an actual live performance of *Romeo and Juliet* is considered a dynamic resource. Too many variables exist in a live performance for it to be considered exactly the same, day after day. Actors may misspeak a line, the wardrobe or setting may be slightly altered, the understudy may be playing the lead. Similarly, a lecture or speech, even if repeated in a different location on a different day, should be considered slightly different and therefore accounted for accordingly. Although the manuscript of the speech might be the same, the audience is different, and the audience's interaction with the text and the speaker could even alter the performance. In other words, when you track information from a live performance, you should keep track of the day and time you were in the audience.

Like live performances, television and radio broadcasts might initially work as static resources (a television episode or a song); however, the actual live distribution will be slightly different each time. For example, TV stations vary in their editing methods, commercials placement decisions, and approach to choosing commercials. Now that many stations include banner ads or logo bugs at the bottom of the screen that actually cover the television content on the show, what you are able to see on the screen varies based on the size or location of the banner ad. Again, like live performances, it is important to track the day and time you watched or listened to the broadcasted material.

write

Search for a Variety of Resources

Once you have read about all of the different kinds of resources, take a few minutes to brainstorm some ideas about how you might use various resources to answer your research question. Write down your responses to the following questions.

1. What kinds of resources could you use in the invention stage of your research process? Could you look at blogs to help refine your research question? Could you browse news-related web sites to search for ways to focus your research? Would browsing through recent periodicals help you think through your topic? Look through the different kinds of resources listed in this chapter and write down a few that might be useful as you plan your research and writing.

2. Where might you find the most authoritative, persuasive resources that will help you answer your research question? What kinds of static, syndicated, and dynamic resources might you search for?

3. How will you evaluate the credibility of the resources that you find? What criteria will you use to determine if they are persuasive, reliable resources? Consider your rhetorical situation and compare it with what you know about your resource: who wrote it and when; how and when it was updated or revised; how it was reviewed and by whom.

Developing a Research Plan

Finding useful resources is the heart of research—collecting information and data about your topic in general and your research question specifically. To be successful in this step, it is important to have a clearly defined research plan. Many students become easily overwhelmed at this step because of all of the possible resources they might access for information. For example, imagine a student in an English department who is doing a study on contemporary adaptations and representations of Charles Dickens's *Oliver Twist*. During the first step of her research, she would develop a focused research question: "How do historical representations of Charles Dickens's *Oliver Twist* impact interpretations and representations in the first part of the twenty-first century?"

TABLE 4.1. Types of Resources on Oliver Twist

	STATIC Published once and does not generally change	**SYNDICATED** Released over time under the same general title (e.g., magazines, newspapers, journals)	**DYNAMIC** Continuously changeable through repeat performances or revisions
EDITED Reviewed before publication by someone with authority or certification	Novel form of *Oliver Twist*; contemporary films and filmic adaptations of *Oliver Twist*	Original syndicated version of *Oliver Twist* published in *Bentley's Miscellany*	Videotape of a live theater production of *Oliver Twist*
PEER REVIEWED Reviewed by others in the same profession	Scholarly books about Dickens, *Oliver Twist*, the history of the novel, and contemporary references to *Oliver Twist* in popular culture artifacts like advertisements and television shows	Articles from the following types of scholarly journals: *Dickens Quarterly*, *Dickens Studies Annual*, *Victorian Literature and Culture*, and *Sight and Sound* (for articles about film adaptations of *Oliver Twist*)	*Wikipedia* entries about Dickens and *Oliver Twist* that include comments and citations from noted Dickens scholars
SELF-PUBLISHED Published and revised by the author	A Dickens scholar's personal web site	Blog publication of "*Oliver Twist* in 10 minutes" (http://asgt .livejournal.com/ 36313.html)	Observation of restaurant in Seattle called *Oliver's Twist*; video footage of a group of students reading *Oliver Twist* aloud

During the next step this student would develop a research plan that includes a detailed list of the types of information she needs to find. She might also keep a checklist or chart, like Table 4.1, of the various types of resources she should search to find information; she wouldn't want to miss something in her research process. In Table 4.1, notice the variety in changeable resources (static, syndicated, and dynamic) as well as the variety in who reviews the information, usually before it is published (edited, peer reviewed, and self-published).

Now that you know what you need and have an idea of how and where to look for it, you need to develop a research plan. "But wait," you might ask, "I know what I want and how to get it, so why don't I just get started?" You can, but how will you know what you still need to find during the process if you don't first outline a research plan? Good research is a systematic study of a specific topic. Medical professionals don't just ask random patients about the results of a new surgical procedure; instead, the researchers carefully plan which patients will be asked to participate in the research, in what manner and how often they will be assessed, and what criteria will be used to evaluate the patient's progress under the new method.

The components, structure, and steps of your research plan will depend on your rhetorical situation. However, all research plans are based around the following key questions.

- What data do you need to collect?
- In what way will you collect that data?
- On what timeline will you collect that data?

In other words, what, how, and when will you conduct your research project? If Ricardo decides to conduct both primary and secondary research for his project, his research plan might look like Table 4.2.

TABLE 4.2. Ricardo's Research Plan		
What types of resources does Ricardo need to find?	**Where will Ricardo locate these resources?**	**When will Ricardo locate these resources?**
Primary documents articles by art scholars that discuss masculinity in Donatello's *St. George* • Gender and art scholars	Ask his art instructor Ask other art instructors Ask librarian Search "Google Scholar"	Week 2: Monday Week 2: Tuesday Week 2: Wednesday Week 3: Monday Week 3: Tuesday
Secondary documents articles that discuss how art scholars have talked about masculinity in Donatello's *St. George* • Art scholars • Gender and art scholars	Ask his art instructor Ask other art instructors Ask librarian Search "Google Scholar"	Week 2: Monday Week 2: Tuesday Week 2: Wednesday Week 3: Monday Week 3: Tuesday

For now, consider the secondary resources that you will need to find for your project. If you are interested in conducting primary research, take a look at Chapter 5.

What's Your Plan?

If you have already completed, and possibly reflected upon and revised, the various activities in this chapter, you have a working draft of your research plan, without the timeline component. You can fully develop a research plan in three steps.

1. List the different types of data and resources you need to collect. If possible, break the types of data and resources into smaller pieces. For example, if you are searching for statistics about whether or not the Earth has a population problem, you can break it into smaller groups of statistics about rising birth rates, rising life expectancies, and rising population numbers based on continents or countries. Ask classmates and family members to help you break down your data and resource needs into the smallest possible groups.

2. For each piece of information, describe where and how you will locate and collect that data. Be specific about where you will be looking—list not only that you'll be using the school's library databases, for example, but which specific databases. If for some reason you have to stop searching in the middle of a session, you'll be able to refer back to which databases you wanted to search (and if you tracked your data collection well, which ones you already searched). Ask your instructors and librarians for help with ideas on where you might locate different types of resources.

3. Provide a timeline, preferably with deadlines, for each task that you have to complete. Just think, the smaller each task is (the smaller each group of data to collect, the smaller each step of collecting it), the easier it will be to "fit" your research into your already busy schedule. If you leave your research plan in big pieces of work, you will only be able to work in big pieces of time. If you take the time to break your research up into smaller, more manageable pieces, you'll be able to fit it into smaller portions of your day; therefore, you'll work more consistently and chip away at your research project.

Types of Resources	Location of Resources	Deadlines

chapter 5

Conducting Primary Research

As you search for an answer to your research question, you need to determine what kind of research will best fit your rhetorical situation. Will you need to collect data on your own (primary research), will you need to read the research results of others (secondary research), or will you need to do both? Secondary research is likely more familiar to you, but you shouldn't avoid primary research just because you have never conducted an interview or designed a survey. Sometimes primary research is essential for answering a research question. If your question deals with a specific local situation, for instance, primary research might be the best way to answer it. For example, Kira's situation detailed on the next page requires primary research to answer her research question adequately.

This chapter provides a basic introduction to conducting three common types of primary research: observations, interviews, and surveys. Each method provides distinct possibilities for the kinds of information you can gather and the ways in which you might answer a research question.

we'll explore

▶ *when and how to conduct interviews, observations, and surveys*

▶ *important ethical considerations to keep in mind*

▶ *how to interpret and present the results of primary research*

▶ *how to develop a research plan*

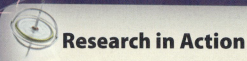
Author: Kira, a student at a community college, is taking a biology class and her professor has asked the class to consider community practices that affect the environment. Her assignment includes writing an investigative report on one issue and its implications on the environment.

© Kharidehal Abhirama Ashwin/Shutterstock.com

Topic: Kira has noticed that the students on her campus fail to use recycling bins for aluminum cans and plastic bottles, and she decides to investigate the reasons students don't recycle on campus.

Audience: Kira's primary audience is her biology professor, and her secondary audience is the staff on her campus who might be interested in recycling efforts.

Purpose: Kira's immediate purpose is to write a report to fulfill the requirement for her biology class. An additional purpose, though, is to raise awareness among students, faculty, and staff about the importance of recycling.

Questions

1. How would Kira gather information about the frequency of recycling on her campus?

2. How might Kira use the research that others have published to support her investigation?

3. If you were Kira, what would be your first step in working on this project?

Types of Primary Research

As you read the descriptions of the three methods of primary research shown in Table 5.1, keep in mind that researchers often use more than one method of gathering data in order to avoid inaccuracies in the research and to confirm findings. Validating the research results is the researcher's responsibility, and you could confirm your research conclusions by finding two or three reliable sources or methods that provide similar results. For example, as she prepares to investigate the question about recycling on campus, Kira realizes that she can't answer her question solely by reading the research that others have published. She might be able to gather some general information through secondary resources about why people don't recycle, but she won't be able to determine reasons for lack of recycling on *her* campus. Instead, she plans to form a hypothesis about whether or not people recycle on her campus (based on the general information she gleans from her secondary resources), and then she will test that hypothesis by conducting a series of observations to determine the extent of the problem. She could also develop a hypothesis about why people don't recycle on campus and test it by conducting interviews with students on campus and designing and distributing a survey. Her secondary research will help her determine the extent of the problem (and might help her fine-tune her research question), but the results of her primary research will form the basis of her response to her research question. Such a combination of methods will help her interpret the data more accurately, especially if that analysis is paired with background investigation from secondary resources that help her understand the results of her primary research.

TABLE 5.1. Types of Primary Research	
Type of Primary Research	**Method of Data Collection**
Observations	Gathering data through your own senses
Interviews	Asking questions of one or more people in person
Surveys	Asking questions of larger groups of people

Observations

When researchers conduct observations, they use all of their senses to note everything they can about a subject and its environment. Observations can be a useful way to gather firsthand information about a subject by relying on senses and note-taking skills. Observing a subject directly is sometimes a useful way to narrow your research question during the invention stage, to determine the extent of a problem or issue that your research question addresses, or to answer the question itself. Observations are often a central part of a research project, as the following research questions show.

▶ **How do bilingual speakers switch back and forth between English and Spanish in casual conversation?** In this case, a researcher would observe the conversation of bilingual speakers and note when they switch back and forth between languages.

▶ **At what times of day are voting locations most busy on election days?** To answer this question, a researcher might observe voting locations at various times of the day.

▶ **To what degree does "light pollution" obscure the view of the night sky in a particular metropolitan area?** Part of the response to this research question should include an observation of the night sky on various occasions.

Including Observation in Your Research Plan

Your rhetorical situation may or may not call for observation. Consider the following questions as you determine whether observation would be a useful data-gathering technique for your project.

▶ **Is there a person, place, activity, or ritual that you might watch, hear, or experience in order to answer your research question?** If so, you might want to directly observe your subject.

▶ **Would observing your subject over time provide data that would help you answer your research question?** In this case, you might schedule observations at certain intervals that would help you collect the appropriate data.

▶ **Would your presence as an observer influence the subject that you are observing?** This influence is often called the **observer's paradox**—the presence of the observer sometimes affects the environment being observed and, therefore, the data collected. Sometimes it cannot be avoided, but it is important for the researcher to be aware of his or her potential influence on the subject being observed. (The activity on page 48 can help you determine how your perspective can influence your research.)

▶ **Could you participate in an event, ritual, or environment that would give you unique insight into the subject you are studying?** If so, you might consider being a **participant observer**, an ethnographic term for a person who is collecting data and researching a subject while participating in it. In such a case, you need to be clear about your relationship to the subject when you describe your data-collection method, and consider your perspective as a participant in your analysis of the data.

Conducting an Observation

Once you have decided to conduct an observation, what should you do? First, determine where and when you will observe and have a plan for taking clear notes about your subject as you observe. Some researchers keep notes in a journal, and many organize their journals as **double-entry journals** to keep their observation and analysis/response separate. In a double-entry journal, one side is generally reserved for the observations themselves (which might even be organized by senses or themes) and the other side is

Observation

Eleven customers present
All are white, apparently middle-class
Four appear to be under the age of 30
Only two are sitting together talking;
   everyone else is either reading or
   working on a computer
Tables are small; could only accom-
   modate two people comfortably
Free wi-fi provided to customers
Extension cord with additional outlets
   is extended into the middle of the
   floor
Microwave in the corner
Conference room is being used by
   three people working individually on
   computers
Background music is classic jazz
Temperature is slightly cool; around 65
   degrees

Response

Specific clientele, could be influenced
   by the neighborhood
Shop is organized to cater to people
   who come here to work or get away,
   more than for socializing

Could almost function as an "office
   away from work"

Even the space that is designed for
   group gathering is being used by
   individuals who are working

Figure 5.1   Example of a Double–Entry Journal

used for interpretation, response, or comment on the observations. For example, if some-one were observing the coffee shop where one of the authors of this textbook likes to sit and write and were keeping notes in a double-entry journal, it might look something like Figure 5.1. The observations are listed on the left-hand side, and the observer writes com-ments and interpretations about what he or she observes on the right-hand side. Such notes could be taken in either a journal notebook or on a laptop.

Careful note-taking is essential to completing a useful observation, especially if you are the sole person responsible for data collection. Ideally, you will conduct your obser-vation and then have time to return to your notes later, when you will have a different perspective. You might write down some of your interpretations as you conduct the observation (or immediately after), but then you might add interpretations in the right-hand column when you read your notes later. As you read the notes, especially when you have some distance from the subject, patterns will emerge that might lead to interesting conclusions about your subject.

In addition to having a clear plan for taking notes during your observation, you should keep in mind that it is not possible to be entirely objective when you observe. Your goal, rather, should be to remain as neutral as possible in your observations. Your experi-ences, beliefs, and perspective will influence you, drawing your attention to certain sights, sounds, and smells (among other things). You should strive to experience as much as pos-sible, though, and to be aware of—and try to limit—the influences that could bias your observation. One way to do so is to have a method for conducting the observation. If you have never done an observation, try the following exercise to practice observation skills, and then consider using the strategy for collecting data to answer your research question as well.

Practice Observing Your Subject

Choose a space to observe for ten minutes. It might be a location on your campus, at your place of work, or in your home. Make sure that you won't be interrupted for the ten minutes that you are observing, and bring a double-entry journal with you to record your observations. Note: You might practice this method by observing a space with which you are familiar before beginning your observation for your research project.

▶ Start by observing the space immediately surrounding you, only going out one or two feet from where you are sitting. First, observe what you see, then what you hear, then what you smell, touch, and taste.

▶ Extend your observation by a few feet. Again, record what you observe with each of your five senses.

▶ Again, extend your observation, this time by about ten feet. Record what you observe through each of your five senses.

▶ Finally, focus on each sense and write down everything you observe—as far as you can see, hear, smell, touch, or taste.

Once you have finished noting your observations, take a moment to write comments on your observations in the other column of your double-entry journal. What patterns do you see? What surprised you?

Record Your Observation

Taking notes in a double-entry journal can be a great way to collect data during an observation, but other kinds of technology can help facilitate your observation as well. Depending on the nature of your observation, you might choose to record your subject either through a video or audio recording. For example, if you want a transcript of language use or of sound, an audio recording might be an ideal method of data collection. Be sure to keep in mind the guidelines from the "Ethical Considerations" section of this chapter: any recording should only be made with the permission of the subjects being recorded.

Interviews

For some research projects, the researcher needs to ask questions of someone directly involved with an issue. Like observations, interviews might be used when you are trying to determine how to focus your research question, and they might also be used once you have defined your research question and want to answer it. Interviews are often integral to answering a research question, as in the following examples.

▶ **What are the writing practices of individuals in the software engineering field?** In this case, the researcher might interview one or more professionals in the field to find out what kinds of writing they do.

▶ **How do international students use social networking applications to connect with friends and family?** A research question such as this might include an interview to hear the student's perspective, as well as an observation to learn how the student uses social networks for this purpose.

▶ **How might climate change impact the flora of the eastern coast of North Carolina, and how soon would that change be evident?** For this project, the researcher might want to interview one or more experts on the subject. An observation wouldn't be feasible for a short-term research project since the research question is projecting into the future. If the researcher could conduct an extended project, though, observations might also help answer this question.

Including Interviews in Your Research Plan

You might notice from the preceding research questions that interviews can be used in a variety of ways. You might interview an expert in a specific field in order to gather data that will help you answer your research question. You might also interview people who are participants in or members of a community (such as a profession) that you would like to study. Depending on your research question, you will also need to determine how many people to interview. As you consider whether interviewing might be a good method for your research, consider the following questions.

▶ Would talking to experts in a particular field help you to answer your research question?

▶ Would speaking with participants in an activity or members of a specific community help you to answer your research question?

▶ What could you learn from speaking with someone that you can't learn from reading published information or from conducting an observation?

▶ Could you conduct an interview on the phone or online if it is not possible to conduct the interview in person?

Conducting an Interview

If, after answering the previous questions, you have determined that you should conduct an interview for your research project, then you will need to start planning your interview. First, you need to do three things:

▶ **Set the interview time and location with the person (or people) you will be interviewing.** Try to select a location that will make the interviewee feel comfortable but not distracted, and keep the length of the interview reasonable. Thirty minutes to an hour is a reasonable length of time. Keep in mind that your interviewee is doing you a favor by setting time aside for you, so be careful to schedule around the interviewee's commitments. If you realize you need more time, ask to schedule a follow-up interview. Sending a confirmation before the interview and a thank-you note afterward is a nice, courteous touch.

▶ **Write your interview questions.** If you are conducting an interview, you should come prepared with specific questions so that the interview is efficient and you get the information you need to answer your research question. Remember that the interviewee is giving you his or her time, so be prepared and professional. As you write your questions, avoid closed questions that elicit short yes/no responses (i.e., "Are professionals in your field expected to write much?"). Instead, write open-ended questions that will invite the interviewee to talk about a particular subject. Open-ended questions generally start with *who, what, when, where, why,* or *how,* such as "What kinds of writing are professionals in your field expected to write?" or "How much writing is expected of professionals in your field?" In addition, make sure that you keep the number of questions reasonable for the time allotted. You might have a few questions in reserve in case you have additional time, and you might want to order your questions based on importance in case you run out of time.

▶ **Decide how to record the interview.** You might want to digitally record the interview or you might take notes. When you choose your method, consider how important it will be to have the interviewee's exact words. Note-taking, as done in an observation, could work if you can just paraphrase and summarize the responses of your interviewee. An audio recording will work if you need the exact words of your subject, and a video recording might be best if it is important for you to notice expressions or gestures. Keep in mind that each method of recording (note-taking, audio recording, and video recording) could be increasingly distracting to your interviewee, and that will likely affect his or her responses. If you don't need a video recording, for example, then opt for a less distracting method. And if you do need a video or audio recording, make sure that your recording device has enough memory and a power supply to record the entire interview. Of course, in order to do a video recording, you would need to interview the subject in person (or have the subject use a webcam if your subject is agreeable). And for any recording, be sure to obtain permission from your subject before proceeding.

write

Draft Interview Questions

Before you begin to write questions for your interview, write your response to the following prompts.

▶ What do you need to know from your interviewee? Why do you want to interview this particular person? Freewrite for five to ten minutes.

▶ Once you have finished your freewrite, read your response. Look for patterns. Are there specific things that you need to know? Generate a list.

▶ Now go through your list and prioritize the things you would like to know.

▶ Finally, write a question for each item on your list; keep them open-ended. If you find you have several closed questions (questions that will elicit only a yes/no response), try inserting "Why?" at the end of such questions.

Once you have finished a preliminary list of questions, consider how many questions you will have time to ask. Are there some questions you should combine? Are there some that should be separated? Then try your interview questions out on a friend. Revise as you ask them, looking for questions that are awkward or confusing.

TABLE 5.2. A Triple-Entry Journal for an Interview

Interview Questions	Responses	Comments/Analysis

Regardless of whether you make an audio or video recording of your interview, you might want to use a double-entry journal during the interview, too. The double-entry journal will look much like the double-entry journal created for an observation. You can record your questions on one side and your interviewee's responses on the other. You could include a third column for notes and analysis that you might add later, as shown in Table 5.2.

If you are doing an audio or video recording, a double-entry journal could be used to take notes that will help you refer to specific parts of the interview when you review your recording. Even though you would not write comments as you are conducting the interview, you'll have the space to go back and insert your analysis later.

Conducting a successful interview takes a tremendous amount of practice. If you haven't had much experience in conducting an interview, preparing well is the best thing you can do. Consider "trying out" your interview questions and technique on a trusted friend before going to your official interview.

techno tip

Conduct Interviews Online

Interviews can be conducted in person or on the phone, but they can also be conducted online. The most common ways to conduct interviews online are through email and instant messaging (IM). If you choose to conduct an interview in email, ask fewer questions than you would during an oral interview. It takes more time (and often more effort) for most people to respond to questions in writing than it does to talk about them. If you conduct an interview via IM, make sure that you save a transcript of the interview before you log out. If you conduct the interview using Google's IM client (among others), a transcript of the interview will be saved automatically for you.

Another possibility is to have a synchronous voice interview using an application such as Skype (http://www.skype.com), an online phone/video conferencing service that is free. Both you and your interviewee would need to create Skype accounts, and you would both need microphones (and webcams, if you want a video recording) in order to use such an application.

Surveys

Some research projects require asking questions of a large group of people and would not be manageable by doing individual interviews. In such cases, surveys are often the best option. Because a survey can take a considerable amount of time to design, distribute, and assess, it works best when the researcher has a well-defined research question that clearly calls for the kind of data a survey would produce—that is, data from a large group of people that could help to identify a widespread trend or phenomenon. Surveys can provide essential data for answering some research questions, as in the following examples.

▶ How do American college students rate speakers of different dialects of American English on multiple characteristics such as intelligence, likeability, and friendliness?

▶ How many citizens in my town generally vote on election days, and what reasons do they give?

▶ How well do graduating seniors from my college feel the required first-year writing class(es) prepared them for the writing they did in other college classes?

Including a Survey in Your Research Plan

To decide if a survey would fit the criteria for your rhetorical situation, consider not only the kind of data you would need to answer your research question but also how feasible it would be to conduct a survey. Surveys can take a tremendous amount of time to do well, and you would need access to the appropriate people who would be willing to complete your survey. As you determine whether or not you will conduct a survey, consider the following questions.

▶ **What can I learn from a survey that I can't learn from an interview or observation?** Surveys enable a researcher to ask questions of a large group of people and also have the advantage of providing the researcher with the exact responses of the participants in text form. (Of course, an email interview would do the latter, too.)

▶ **How many people would I like to poll in order to answer my research question?** If the number is larger than you could reasonably interview, a survey might be the way to go. The number for your research project must be small enough to be manageable but large enough so that you will have the interpretive power necessary to answer your research question. Many students who are designing surveys for the first time make the mistake of surveying an unrepresentative group. For example, in the recycling scenario at the beginning of the chapter, if Kira surveys twenty of her friends, she is not likely to get a representative sample (because they're all her friends, and twenty is a fairly small number if she's generalizing her results to the whole campus). If she surveys the students in a few different classes, however, she might come closer to getting a better representation of the student population on her campus (especially if the classes are in different departments).

▶ **Do I have the time to design a successful survey, distribute it, collect responses, and analyze the data?** Surveys can be quite time-consuming, and you will want to consider how much time you have to devote to your project as you design your survey.

Conducting a Survey

If you have determined that you should conduct a survey for your research project, in addition to choosing a representative group of participants, you need to pay close attention

TABLE 5.3. Types of Survey Question

Type of Question	Issues to Consider	Sample Questions

Closed Question
• Multiple choice
• True/false
• Yes/no
• Rating on a Likert scale
	Gives a certain set of possible responses, so they are easily comparable with the responses from other participants.	• Which item are you most likely to recycle?
		  a. Cans
		  b. Bottles
		  c. Paper
		  d. I don't recycle
		• I regularly place used soda cans in the recycling bin on campus. ___ True ___ False
		• Do you have access to the Internet at home? ___ Yes ___ No
		• How confident do you feel in anticipating the needs of different types of readers when you write?
		  1—Not confident
		  2—Somewhat confident
		  3—Confident
		  4—Highly confident

Open-Ended Question	Allows participants to give more information, but responses are not as easily compared as answers to closed questions.	• What technological support do you receive as a student? • What differences do you perceive between taking a course online and taking a course in person?

to two issues involved in design: (1) writing successful survey questions and (2) distributing and collecting your survey.

First, as you write the questions for your survey, think about how many responses you will be analyzing. In other words, keep your project manageable. It is also critical to consider the kinds of questions and responses that will help you answer your research question. Two kinds of questions are most common on surveys: closed, or fixed-response, questions and open-ended questions. Take a look at the different kinds of questions in Table 5.3.

Many surveys incorporate both closed and open-ended questions so that the researcher has statistics that can be compared but participants can also explain their answers, giving the researcher interesting information that helps to interpret the results of the survey.

write

Draft Survey Questions

Before you begin to write specific questions for your survey, write your responses to the following prompts.

▶ Who will you survey? How and why did you choose this group of people?

▶ What do you need to know from your survey participants? Why do you want to survey them?

Read your responses to these questions. Look for patterns. Are there specific things that you need to know? Generate a list. Now go through your list and prioritize the things you would like to know. Next, consider the kind of data that would be most useful in responding to your research question. Should some questions be closed questions in order to collect quantitative data? Which ones should be open-ended? Finally, write a question for each item on your list.

reflect

Is the Survey Valid and Reliable?

Before using your survey with a large group of people, test it on a few friends. Look for points of confusion in the survey. Which questions should be revised for clarity?

As you test your survey, you'll also be determining whether the survey is valid and reliable. Ask the following questions as you revise the draft of your survey.

▶ Is it **valid?** Does the survey actually assess what it's supposed to assess? For example, in the recycling scenario, asking "Do you think recycling is important?" doesn't tell the researcher whether the person recycles. Also, if the questions are confusing, you might not be "testing" the same thing for everyone.

▶ Is it **reliable?** Is the survey conducted in a similar way and scored identically for all participants? Your survey must be administered and scored consistently in order to be reliable. For example, participants should have a similar amount of time to respond, and if you are looking for patterns in open-ended responses, you should consider **inter-rater reliability.** (See page 107 for more on reliability.)

Distributing Surveys and Collecting Responses

Once you have designed your survey, you will need to plan how to distribute and collect responses. One of the biggest challenges in conducting a survey is getting people to respond, so you might consider some strategies that would help increase your response rate. Some researchers offer incentives to survey participants (but the incentives shouldn't influence the data). For example, incentives could be food, a gift certificate, or something else that would be of value to the participants. Another strategy is to conduct the survey in a closed space, like a classroom (with the teacher's permission, of course). One of the disadvantages of this strategy is that it limits the group of participants, but it might increase the number of responses. All strategies should be disclosed when you report the results of your research.

Consider Online Survey Services

One way to increase response rates on a survey is to make the survey easy and convenient to complete by putting it online. You might look at an online survey service such as Survey Monkey (http://www.surveymonkey.com) to see if it would be a useful strategy for your research project. Many online survey services will help you analyze the data by displaying graphic representations of the results.

Ethical Considerations

If you are conducting research that will include other people (especially if you are asking questions of them), then you'll probably need approval from a group on campus that oversees research that involves **human subjects**. Such a group is usually called an **institutional review board (IRB)**, and it exists to make sure that research on humans is conducted ethically and doesn't violate anyone's rights (especially privacy) or have adverse effects on health or well-being. Many institutions of higher education have IRBs, although schools that are less focused on research might not. Ask your instructor if your project would need to be reviewed by an IRB and if your school provides a process for gaining IRB approval for a project.

Even if you do not need IRB approval, you will need consent, or permission, from the people that you are interviewing or surveying. You might also ask for consent for an observation, if you are observing in a closed space. An observation in a public space, like a restaurant, would not generally require consent. To ask for consent, you would disclose as much as you can about your project (without altering the data you are hoping to collect) and then ask for the participant's consent and signature. If you are collecting data electronically, you cannot collect a physical signature from the participant, so you might use an electronic signature or include an "I grant permission" button in the survey form. In either case, you'll want to phrase the letter differently. Figure 5.2 shows a letter of consent written for a research project that included completing online surveys. The goal of the study was to compare how well students believed they had achieved the objectives of a course in two learning environments, but notice that the letter of consent does not go into much detail (so as not to influence the students' responses). If you are submitting your project for approval by an IRB, your institution might have a template consent form that you could adapt for your project. Ask your instructor for guidance on this as well.

If you are working under an instructor's supervision, you could include the instructor's name in the letter of consent as your project advisor. Make sure that you show any research plans and your letter of consent to your instructor before starting your research project.

ENG 101/102 STUDY

Dear Student:

I am a graduate student under the direction of Professor Jane Smith in the Department of English at XX University. I am conducting a research study to compare instructional environments for teaching ENG 101/102.

　　I am requesting your participation, which will involve completing two surveys that will ask about your perceptions of your experience in ENG 101/102, one at the beginning of the term and one at the end of the term. Your participation in this study is voluntary. If you choose not to participate or to withdraw from the study at any time, it will not affect your grade and you will not be penalized in any way. Although the survey will ask for your name, your name will only be used to identify your survey if you should choose to withdraw from the study. The results of the study may be published but your name will not be known.

　　If you have any questions concerning the research study, please call me at 480-555-4653 or Professor Jane Smith at 480-555-9427.

Sincerely,
Susana Rodriguez

Figure 5.2　A Letter of Consent

techno tip

Gather Data Online

If you gather data in an online environment, you still need to get consent from your participants. The lines are somewhat blurry, though, in spaces such as online gaming environments, chat rooms, and virtual worlds such as Second Life. The best rule of thumb to follow is to obtain consent from anyone you are observing, interviewing, or surveying. A simple consent letter can be provided to participants that either collects their electronic consent through a signature or permission button, or that indicates that if they participate in the activity you are observing while you are observing it or complete the interview/survey you are conducting, their participation indicates their consent. It is also a good idea to check the documentation for any gaming environments, chat rooms, or virtual worlds in which you would like to conduct research to see if procedures for conducting research or limitations on research are stated.

Interpretation of Data

You might remember from the beginning of the chapter that it is best to collect data from a variety of sources and in a variety of manners to compare responses and interpret the results. Researchers call this **triangulation** of the data. Consider this scenario: imagine that you conduct a survey and receive several similar responses to one question. But one of your participants gives a response that is completely opposite to all the other responses. If the survey was not anonymous and you have the opportunity to do a follow-up interview with that participant, you could ask about his or her response to understand it better—instead of jumping to conclusions about that response or dismissing it without knowing the purpose or reasoning behind it.

As another example, think about the ways that you have seen your teachers evaluated. Most likely, you've had to fill out an evaluation survey for a teacher at the end of a course. You likely have also been in a classroom when a teacher was being observed by someone, perhaps another teacher or an administrator. When the teacher is evaluated, all of the data can be considered. For example, if the students' written evaluations note that the instructor is particularly good at leading class discussion, the observer might be able to elaborate on that evaluation by describing several specific things the teacher did in class that facilitated discussion. Likewise, two separate types of data can pick up different trends. For example, if the students note in their evaluations that the teacher is particularly helpful in office hours outside of class, the observer would not have seen that by sitting in a class session. In this case, it would be important to have both survey data and observation data in order to fairly assess the teacher's performance as a whole.

Once you collect your data, search for patterns that will help you draw conclusions. There are two major categories of data—quantitative and qualitative—and your analysis and interpretation will vary depending on which type of data you have collected.

Analyzing Quantitative Data

Quantitative data can be analyzed numerically. You can tally results and compare averages, look for statistical patterns, and determine whether a majority of respondents said the same thing. Of the types of research discussed in this chapter, only surveys can generally be used to collect quantitative data. Quantitative data are often valued because they are more generalizable; that is, they are collected from a large population.

Analyzing Qualitative Data

Qualitative data are not intended to be analyzed statistically in the same way quantitative data are, but they can provide insight into a subject. Interviews and observations provide qualitative data, as do the open-ended responses on surveys. When you analyze qualitative data, you look for patterns and trends. In some cases, you might be searching for the number of times you observed a certain phenomenon or the number of times a participant used a certain word or phrase, but because of the small number of participants you would not draw statistical conclusions about the significance of a phenomenon or generalize the results to a larger population. In this case, you would want to carefully aggregate the data and have a second person also aggregate the data, identifying the occurrences of a phenomenon. This process is called **coding.** The second coder would help to provide inter-rater reliability. In other words, the results are more powerful because the researcher is not the only one verifying the patterns in the data. You can check your interpretation of the data with another person.

Regardless of whether you collect quantitative or qualitative data, strive to phrase your conclusion in a way that is appropriate to what is called the **interpretive power** of your study. You'll want to provide your readers with a clear understanding of the limits of extending your results, based on the scope of your study and the way you define your rhetorical situation. You could also use hedging terms to provide for the possibility that another researcher would find a different result since you will be unable to observe all situations or interview/survey all possible participants. Hedging terms include words like *generally*, *usually*, *often*, *might*, and *could*. For example, let's imagine that Kira, when conducting the recycling project, surveyed seventy-five students and found that eighty percent of the survey respondents mentioned that the recycling bins on campus were not conveniently located. She could write in her conclusion that "The location of the recycling bins is a *likely* reason that students do not recycle regularly." Using the term *likely* allows for the fact that she did not survey all students, and not everyone responded the same way on her survey. Yet, eighty percent is a strong response rate for such a large number of students.

Presenting the Results of Primary Research

IMRAD Format   When you present the results of primary research in a written format in many disciplines, especially those in the sciences and social sciences, your audience might expect you to follow what is often called **IMRAD** format. IMRAD is an acronym that stands for the following steps:

▸ **Introduction**—generally an introduction to the subject, an overview of the secondary research on the topic, and a clearly stated research question. This section should answer "What's the subject and why is it important?"

▸ **Methodology**—a clear description of the methods used to conduct the research, including a description of the participants, how they were selected, what was observed, what questions were asked, how data were collected, and how they were analyzed (i.e., if you had a second coder look at the data, this is where you would explain your process). This section should answer "What did you do?"

▸ **Results**—a presentation of the data collected. This is generally separate from any analysis of those data, which comes in the next section. This section should answer "What did you find?"

▸ **Analysis**—conclusions you have drawn from the data you collected. This section should answer "What do the results mean?"

▸ **Discussion**—implications of the results of your research or suggestions you are making based on the results and analysis of your data. This section should answer "What are the implications of the results?" or, more informally, "So what?"

If you're not sure what format to use to present the results of your research, IMRAD provides a useful outline to follow.

Presenting Data Visually   While IMRAD format provides an arrangement pattern for the written presentation of your primary research, you might also be interested in presenting the results of your data visually. A graphic depiction of data can often communicate the impact and importance of results more effectively and efficiently than a textual description can. Many researchers incorporate visual representations of data into written reports or oral presentations. Three of the most popular ways of presenting data are tables, charts/graphs, and maps. Depending on the nature of the data you have collected and the results you would like to highlight, you might find one of these methods more appealing and persuasive than the others:

▶ *Tables* provide, in essence, a graphic organizer of data collected through primary research. They are especially useful for presenting the results of qualitative data, since tables are not restricted to representation of numerical data. If you wanted to display common responses to survey questions, for example, a table would be a good way to do so.

▶ *Charts/Graphs* (bar chart, line chart, pie chart) are used to represent numerical data and to show the relationships between data. Three of the most common types of charts are bar charts, line charts, and pie charts. A bar chart can be used to compare results between groups. Line charts are generally used to show a progression of a trend, perhaps over time. Pie charts often show distributions of responses to a particular question. (The Techno Tip that follows suggests ways to create these charts and graphs.)

▶ *Maps* are useful ways to present results if you have collected data that have geographical significance. In one of the examples earlier in the chapter, we suggested that a researcher might be interested in determining how American college students rate speakers of different dialects of American English for various personality characteristics. For such a study, it might make sense to use a map of the United States to show where different dialects are most common and to present some of the interpretations that students have of the dialects common to those regions.

techno tip

Making Charts and Graphs

Spreadsheet applications like Microsoft Excel and Google Docs include functions that convert data into charts and graphs. In many cases, it can be difficult to format the data so the applications can easily make the charts and graphs. Refer to the help documentation and/or look for help resources on the Internet if you run into difficulty (YouTube is always a good place to begin). Once you've identified the correct span of data, Google Docs allows you to easily test what your results will look like as different charts and graphs (see Figure 5.3, for example).

Figure 5.3   Google Docs' Chart Editor

reflect

What Does Your Research Plan Look Like Now?

At this point, take some time to plan the kinds of research you need to conduct. At the end of Chapter 4, you might have started a research plan that sorted through the different kinds of secondary resources for your project. If you are interested in conducting primary research, you can take that information and put it into a more comprehensive research plan, using the chart below.

You also need to decide when you are going to complete your research. Keep in mind that it will be of the utmost importance to manage your time well if you are conducting primary research; be sure to plan enough time to collect and analyze data.

Types of Resources	Location of Resources	Deadlines
Primary Resources		
Secondary Resources		

chapter 6

Rhetorically Reading, Tracking, and Evaluating Resources

This chapter's research situation involves someone who will be filtering through a huge amount of resources on buying cars. She will have to filter through not only what individual people (for example, friends, family, and maybe even some bloggers) say about different types of cars but also through the large amount of material published by the car manufacturers and materials distributed by more "objective" resources, such as independent research firms. The strategies presented in this chapter will give you, as well as Yoshi, methods to read resources effectively and pick out elements related to your specific rhetorical situation.

we'll explore

▶ *identifying the context of a resource*

▶ *annotating while you read*

▶ *summarizing, paraphrasing, and quoting from resources*

▶ *finding, tracking, and responding to the resources that you find*

▶ *filling any gaps in your research to build a strong argument*

Research in Action

Author: Yoshi has recently been promoted in her social services job, and her new position will require that she travel across the state at least three days per week. While Yoshi has really enjoyed the Honda Fit that she purchased right out of college, she's not sure that it's the best choice for increased highway driving. Yoshi would like to find a car that will be reliable but will also be environmentally friendly and help her maintain low gas costs. She'll receive a small bonus for her promotion, and she's willing to put that toward a down payment on a new car.

Topic: Yoshi needs to research her options for purchasing a new car.

Audience: Yoshi's research is primarily for herself.

Purpose: Yoshi would like to find a reliable, environmentally friendly car that would be appropriate for frequent highway driving related to her job.

Questions

1. What are the various elements of the rhetorical situation in this research scenario? How do they affect one another?

2. What types of resources might Yoshi seek out for her research?

3. When was the last time you had to make a large purchase? What did you buy? What criteria did you consider for your purchase? What elements of your rhetorical situation affected your selection of criteria? Your purchase choice?

4. Do you have a big purchase to make in the near future? What do you need to buy? What criteria will you need to consider? What elements in the rhetorical situation will affect your choice of criteria and ultimate purchase?

Rhetorical Reading

You've been reading for a long time. And not only have you been reading, but you've been reading to learn and to gather information. You may have also been doing what we call **focused reading.** Simply defined, focused reading is reading with a specific goal in mind. It is paying attention when you read. For example, before voting in an election, you might closely read the candidates' statements to decide if your ideals and goals align with theirs. You read their statements with the focused goal of deciding which candidate will receive your vote, and as you read you are choosing which statements most closely align with your values and beliefs.

To get the best results from resources you consult for any research question, it is wise to go one step further and **read rhetorically.** To read a resource rhetorically, you not only read for a purpose but also pay attention to the context of the document you are reading, closely analyzing its rhetorical situation. Let's say you are watching a movie. If you just watch the movie and zone out, you will probably laugh when everyone else at the theater is laughing and not remember much of it the next morning. In this case, you are just passively "reading" the movie. If you go to the movie to be entertained, you will be engaging in focused reading of the film as you watch it. The next morning you would be able to explain to someone whether you liked the movie, whether you found it entertaining, and why. However, if you were to read the movie rhetorically, you would be paying attention to how certain people are depicted (e.g., women and characters of color), considering the historical context in which it was made, or comparing it to other films by the same director, screenwriter, or editor.

Let's consider an example from a different research situation. Imagine you're conducting research on gun control laws and you come across a web site titled, simply, "Gun Control." The web site begins with a quote from Thomas Jefferson and includes sections on "The Second Amendment" and "Gun Control: A Statistical Perspective." The web site asks and responds to many of the questions you have been considering in revising your research question:

▶ How often are guns used in self-defense?

▶ Does gun ownership deter burglars?

▶ What does the Second Amendment mean and how should it be interpreted?

On the surface, this web site might seem like a perfect match for your research. If you were doing a focused reading of the site, looking for information on your research topic, the site provides a wealth of responses to relevant questions. A careful *rhetorical reading* of the web site, however, reveals that the site has a clear bias toward an interpretation of the Second Amendment that protects gun owners and limits gun control. The web site gives very limited attention to other perspectives on the issue. Additionally, you would have difficulty establishing the credibility of the source because the authors are not clearly identified. The site refers to "GunCite" as the sponsoring organization but offers no specific information about that organization or the authors of the site. Reading your resources rhetorically will help you to evaluate them for usefulness in your research project.

reflect

Is Your Reading Focused or Rhetorical?

To help distinguish between a *focused* and a *rhetorical* reading, list the various texts that you have read during the past couple of days. Then label each reading experience as either focused or rhetorical. Ask yourself the following questions to help categorize your reading experiences.

▶ What was the goal in reading the material?

▶ Did I consciously have this goal in mind before reading the material?

▶ Did I pay attention to the rhetorical elements of the material (the text's author, purpose, audience, and topic)?

▶ Did understanding the rhetorical elements of the material affect my goal for reading the material?

In your list, circle the reading experience that you are most confident was focused, circle another experience that you are most confident was rhetorical, and circle a third that you had the most difficult time labeling as either focused or rhetorical. Discuss these three experiences with a friend or classmate. Does your friend or classmate agree with your labeling? Why or why not?

Like all the activities related to writing that are described in this book, reading rhetorically requires paying attention to the rhetorical situation. To be successful in reading something rhetorically you must first be aware of your purpose for reading the material. You will use your purpose as the criterion for deciding what material is important and worth remembering and what material is worth only skimming. In many cases, when you read rhetorically you end up reading a document more than once. Suppose you buy a new car. You might not read the owner's manual at all when you first get the car (you already know how to drive, right?). However, once you've decided you are tired of the stereo's clock flickering the wrong time at you, you would read the manual to find out how to change the time on the clock. Your reading would be focused. If you had lost the manual, you might go online to find the instructions for setting the time or search YouTube for a video that shows how to change the time. You would read rhetorically, considering who was writing and publishing the Internet resource before following the instructions. You wouldn't want to damage the clock in your new car! In this case, you would read rhetorically to determine which source is credible, and then a focused reading would be necessary to find the information that you need and to follow instructions.

When you rhetorically read documents in an academic setting, you generally have to read them more than once to obtain all the information you need. While reading resources for a research project, you probably want to read through them at least three times:

1. Read (or perhaps even skim) for the main point or claim of the resource so that you can decide whether it is worth your time and energy to read the material closely.

2. Read to identify the rhetorical situation of the resource so that you can understand the context as well as figure out how it will fit into your research project's specific rhetorical situation.

3. Read closely for details. In this reading you will probably annotate the resource and take notes paraphrasing the claim, reasons, and evidence presented in the resource.

Sometimes you will want to rhetorically read materials from another person's perspective. To argue a particular claim effectively and to influence people who believe differently from you, you must demonstrate that you understand their point of view. To help understand those who might think or feel differently about your topic, and to make better connections with that same group later, it is important that you rhetorically read materials from their perspective. This means (1) seeking a variety of materials and perspectives while doing research on your topic, especially secondary research, and (2) taking care to read rhetorically and take notes on those resources. Much of the rest of this chapter is devoted to helping you develop these reading strategies for your own research.

write

Choose Resources to Read

As you conduct your secondary research, you will find a large number of possible resources. Knowing that you can't possibly read them all, you need to quickly assess whether a resource is worth your time to read more closely. Practice choosing relevant resources to read by using an Internet search engine to do a search with one of the key terms of your research question. After reading only the introduction, conclusion, and subject headings, answer the following questions about the first four hits.

▸ Are you able to quickly identify who wrote the resource, on what subject the resource is focused, when it was published, where it was published, and what the purpose of the resource is?

▸ How does the material in the resource directly respond to your specific research question, not just your research topic?

If the resource is organized enough to answer the first question and is specifically addressing your research question, it is probably worth your time to read it more closely. Reading rhetorically is the first step in choosing and evaluating resources, but to determine whether you'll use a resource in your project requires even more intense reading and evaluation.

Considering Context

As a piece of communication in its own right, every resource you read has its own rhetorical situation, or context. Just like everything that you write, each resource you read has a purpose, an audience, a topic, and an author that help to define the context in which it was produced and distributed. Rhetorically reading a resource means carefully understanding not only what it says but also its purpose in saying so. You need to know the rhetorical situation of a piece of writing in order to truly understand what it says.

write

Situate a Resource Rhetorically

Select one of the resources you have found that could help you answer your initial research question. Respond to the following questions about that resource.

▶ Who is the author of the resource, and what are his/her/their credentials?

▶ With whom is the author affiliated (employer, organization, or other group)?

▶ For what purpose(s) did the author write the resource? In other words, is the author trying to provide information? persuade readers? entertain? What clues help you to identify the piece's purpose?

▶ Who is the audience? How do you know? How might the audience have affected the way that the resource is written?

Once you have responded to all of these questions, consider the resource as a whole. How might the answers to these questions have influenced the writing of this resource?

Annotating Resources

Simply put, annotating is writing on or about something you read. You can annotate a resource in a variety of ways. Usually, the method in which you annotate your resource is based on your purpose for reading the resource. For example, if you are enrolled in a literature class that is currently discussing tone and rhythm and you are reading the *Odyssey*, you will probably mark sections and take notes about language choice. However, if you were reading the same work in an ancient world history class, you might mark sections and take notes about passages that refer to specific historical events. In both cases you are reading the same text; however, the method in which you annotate is based on the information you need from that text.

The annotation method you use is directed not only by your reading purpose but also by the materiality of the text itself. The least complicated way to annotate resources is to physically write on them. However, if you borrowed the book from someone or from a library, it is better to use sticky notes or notebook paper for annotations instead of writing on the pages. If you are reading a web site, you might use software, such as Diigo, that allows you to take notes onscreen, but many people take notes from the Internet on paper.

Claim

While reading resources for larger, more complex research projects, spend some time identifying and annotating the resource's claim, reasons, and evidence. The **claim** is the overall point that the resource is making, or its thesis. Whereas identifying the claim in a scholarly, academic resource is fairly easy (it is usually located somewhere within the first few paragraphs), identifying the claim of a more informal resource—a blog, a newspaper editorial, a song, a movie—may be more difficult. For example, all commercials claim that some specific product is good and, furthermore, that you should spend money purchasing it. A primary claim might be explicit, but it is often implicit, and you might need to read the resource multiple times to identify a claim.

Reasons

After identifying the claim that the resource is making, you will want to identify the **reasons** that the author is using to support his or her claim. The overall claim of car commercials is that a specific car is better than all others and that you want or need that car. However, different commercials provide different reasons for claiming that a car is good. Engine size and speed are often the primary reasons given in commercials for sports cars, but secondary reasons might include that the car would make you more popular, attractive, or envied by your neighbors. On the other hand, fuel efficiency and safety are often the primary reasons in commercials for more family-oriented vehicles. These reasons support the argument, or claim, in an advertisement that a specific car is good enough to spend thousands of dollars on it.

Evidence

Finally, resources need to provide **evidence** to support their reasons and claims. Evidence is material provided about the object being discussed as support for the reasons and claims. Car companies might cite how quickly a car can go from zero to sixty miles per hour as evidence of a specific sports car's speed. They might also cite how many cylinders the engine has, or how much horsepower it puts out, as evidence of its engine size. Commercials for family cars might cite the number of air bags in the vehicle as evidence of the car's safety, or they might cite independent researchers who agree that the car gets more than forty miles to the gallon as evidence of fuel efficiency.

As you annotate a resource, make notes about how you think it might help you to answer your research question. When you read rhetorically, consider not only the rhetorical context of the resource but also your research context. How might this resource fit into your research plan? Does it provide a perspective that is lacking in the resources you have found so far? See the final activity in Chapter 5 for an example of a research plan.

In the following advertisement for the Toyota Prius, Toyota is clearly addressing an audience concerned with the environment. First, most of the advertising space is taken up with the image of blue sky and blue water, with the car appearing to have emerged from a green forest. The sky and forest are reflected in the water, providing a mirror effect that creates the image of an arrow pointing to the car as it emerges from the forest. By placing the forest on the right-hand side of the page, taking the space of a trail of emissions, the company emphasizes the environmentally friendly nature of the car and conveys the car's lack of impact on the environment. The white text resonates with concepts of clean clouds and clean emissions. Even the choice of font size and type are meaningful; the font is thin and barely visible, emphasizing that the car isn't marring the beauty of the environment. The text at the top, "Today—thinking green. Tomorrow—planning for blue," reflects the image the company wishes to foster of thinking toward the future and making little negative impact on the environment.

Both the unadorned style and white color of the text evoke images of clean emission

Car appears to emerge from green forest.

Predominance of blue sky reflected in blue water emphasizes harmony with environment.

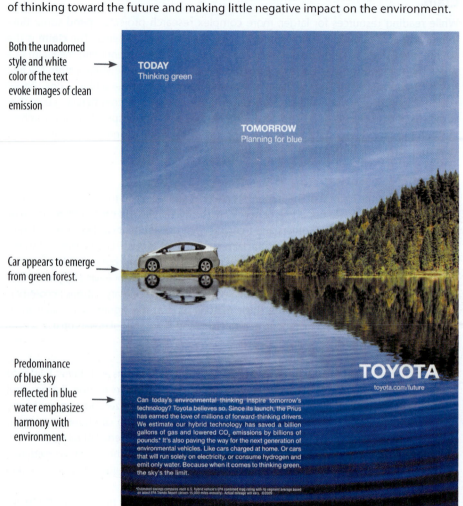

Image Courtesy of The Advertising Archives

Annotate a Resource

write

Once you have chosen at least one resource to help you answer your research question, use the following strategies to practice annotating it.

▶ Print source: Write on the pages directly if you printed it yourself or "mark" it with sticky notes if it's a borrowed book.

▶ Electronic source: Take notes on screen or paper, or print sections so that you can mark them and keep track of your thoughts.

Annotate your source by responding to the following questions.

1. Who is the author of the text and what are his/her/their credentials?

2. What is the purpose of the text and who is its intended audience?

3. What is the major claim made in the resource?

4. What are the reasons given for supporting that claim?

5. What evidence is provided to support those reasons?

6. How useful will this resource be in your own research? How does it fit with the other resources that you have found?

techno tip

Search Electronic Documents

Have you ever been confident that a book has the information that you need but you can't find the information in it? Perhaps the title seemed promising but the chapter titles and index didn't help you navigate the book. Or perhaps you had read something interesting when you first skimmed the item, but then couldn't find that information on a second reading.

With electronic documents—whether a word-processed text, a web page, or a PDF file, you can easily and quickly search the document, word by word. To try this feature, select an electronic resource that you aren't positive you will want to use in your research. Then locate your extended list of search terms that you developed in Chapter 4. Electronically search your document for each of your terms. For every "hit," be sure to read the surrounding sentences, and consider skimming the entire paragraph. After you have searched for your terms, you'll know better whether the document is worth reading more carefully.

You can also use the search function to help you identify the claim and reasons of a text. First reread the introduction to the text, identifying any words that you think are key to the argument's reasoning. Then search for those words or phrases to see if they lead you to the reasons developed in the argument. This process doesn't always work perfectly, but it can be a good way to trace an argument's overall structure.

Summarizing

A summary gives the main points of a resource, but is briefer than the original. After you read one of your resources, you should be able to summarize it briefly. It is important to summarize the resource for two reasons. First, you need to be sure that you understand the main point of the resource. What is it trying to say? What does the author want the reader to do or think after reading the resource? Although you will want to read it again more closely to accumulate details about the information and arguments presented in the resource, it is important that you initially understand what the resource is doing.

At minimum, summarizing the resource will help you to understand whether it applies to your specific research project.

Summarizing a resource also helps you keep your research organized. A short summary of the resource will be a reminder of what is in the document when you start organizing, and reorganizing, your resources. With summaries of various documents, you will be able to quickly assess whether you have enough information in one area of your project and if you need more in another.

The easiest way to summarize a document is to briefly answer the standard journalists' questions. In other words, you will want to know the *who, what, when, where, why*, and *how* of the resource. A helpful guideline is to remember that your summary should be no more than ten percent as long as the original resource. In many cases, you can summarize a source in one or two sentences. Your summary will also probably reflect what you found most interesting in the resource and hint at your purpose for using the resource.

write

Summarize One of Your Resources

Now, choose one of your own resources that you plan to use in your research project. Do a first reading of the resource (which you may have already done when you chose the resource in the first place) and summarize the main point of the resource. Keep the journalists' questions in mind as you summarize, and also try to maintain a balance between keeping your summary concise and making sure it is thorough enough to be helpful as you work on your research later.

Swap your summary with someone in your class, or a friend or family member. Ask him or her to read the summary. Did you provide enough information? If you have time, ask the person to skim the resource and recheck your summary. What information might he or she include in the summary? What information should be cut out? Why?

Paraphrasing

Another way to take notes on your resources is to paraphrase them. When you paraphrase a resource, or a part of a resource, you put the author's argument or ideas into your own words. Such a strategy might be helpful if you don't want to quote the resource or idea in its entirety but you also don't want to condense the ideas that were interesting and useful to you. For example, if you found a long passage in a print resource that had some great information in it but the resource was written for a very scientific audience (and your research is not), you might paraphrase the ideas to use in your writing later. In this case, you don't want to condense, and possibly lose, some of the ideas in the resource, but you'll need to use different language when you share the information with your audience. Of course, when you paraphrase, you need to provide a citation to tell where the ideas came from.

One other guideline to keep in mind when paraphrasing is that you need to put the ideas in *your own* words—not just change a word or two here and there. If you find yourself keeping the same basic sentence structure as the resource but changing just a few words, it might be best to just quote the resource. For more information on **when** to cite resources to avoid plagiarism, see Chapter 7, "Understanding Plagiarism and Integrating Resources." For more information on **how** to cite resources, see Chapters 11–15.

Blog postings can be a good source for independent reviews of products. On his blog, *The Prius Diary*, Sean Paterson provides updates on the "everyday experience of owning and driving a Toyota Prius." The following posting offers insight into the conditions that have been helping him maintain 50 mpg.

Top Safety Rating - The Prius makes me feel safe in its solid cabin, surrounded by copious air baggery. In the UK, I find the Parkers website a very useful source of car data and information. You can see for yourself that the Prius scores well and has a top Euro NCAP 5 star rating. With more safety-feature related acronyms than you can shake an oily stick at, the Prius gives me the reassurance that my family's safety is being well catered for.

*****

What I don't like so much about the Prius:

Driving

Sat Nav Destination Setup – the Sat Nav doesn't take full UK post code as a way of setting the destination. Now, this is the most common and convenient way most people I know set destinations on their Sat Navs. Why this is not the case on the Prius beats the tripe out of me. I'm not sure if USA models can accept full ZIP codes, or what the equivalent is in other parts of the world. I'd love to know.

Dim Instruments – when it is poor visibility during daytime driving (like when it gets gey dreich as we say here in Scotland) then I'll put on my side or main headlights in order to be more visible to other vehicles on the road. However, the digital instrumentation dims because it presumes I am driving at night time and therefore needs to reduce instrument intensity. Maybe there is a setting to address this, I'm not sure. In the meantime, it means I am hesitant to put on my headlights in the daytime, which can impinge on road safety.

Inappropriate paraphrase of the first sentence: The Prius makes a driver feel safe because its cabin is solid, and the passengers are surrounded by many air bags (Paterson).

This paraphrase uses much of the original phrasing of the first sentence. Even though a citation is included at the end of the paraphrase, it is inappropriate because too many of the original words and phrases are used without quotation marks and the sentence structure is too similar to the original.

Appropriate paraphrase: According to Paterson (2012) on his blog *The Prius Diary*, the carefully designed safety features of the Prius, such as the solid cabin and the placement of the air bags, help the driver feel assured.

Notice that there still is an in-text citation at the beginning of the paraphrase to indicate the source of the information being paraphrased.

write

Paraphrase One of Your Resources

Now, choose one of the resources that you plan to use in your research project. Skim through the resource to find a passage that is particularly interesting or that you think you might use in your research project. Try paraphrasing the passage, putting it into your own words. Once you have paraphrased the passage, reread the original passage and decide whether it would be better to use your paraphrase (with reference to the source) or to quote the resource.

Selecting Potential Quotations

Sometimes you might decide that it is best to quote directly from a resource. You might choose to quote, instead of summarizing or paraphrasing, for several reasons:

▶ You are doing direct analysis of a written text and need to provide the specific examples you are analyzing.

▶ The section of text that you would like to use is short and could easily be incorporated into your larger text.

▶ The author(s) of the resource used language that you believe to be particularly powerful and/or persuasive for your intended audience, and you would lose meaning or emphasis if you paraphrased it.

▶ The text is well known and your audience might be familiar with the quotation you have chosen.

▶ You know you will want to comment directly on the author's ideas and/or language.

As you are reading your resources, take note of quotations that you think might be particularly powerful to use in your research project. As your research project develops, you might find that some of those quotations are more useful than others.

write

Take Detailed Notes on a Resource

As you choose resources for your research, you might subconsciously be thinking that some of the resources are particularly useful. Often in the first stages of a research project we mentally categorize the resources we are finding into *resources I'll definitely use* and *resources I might use*. If you did this as you were doing your preliminary research, pick one of the resources that you think you would *definitely use* for this activity.

Now try using several of the strategies discussed in this chapter to rhetorically read your resource. Note: If you are completing one of the writing assignments in the Part 2 DIY on page 159, you will want to complete this activity for each resource you include in your review.

As you read your resource, take the following steps.

▶ Physically annotate your resource. Use a method that you are comfortable with—write on the document itself (if it is yours, you have printed it, or it is a copy), use sticky notes to keep track of ideas as you read, or keep notes on a separate piece of paper or on your computer as you read.

▶ Summarize the claim or main point of the resource.

▶ Paraphrase the reasons given in the resource for its claim or main point.

▶ Make note of the evidence used to support the claim and reasons for the claim in the resource.

▶ Contextualize the resource by noting its purpose, intended audience, author, and topic.

▶ Project how and why this resource might help you answer your research question.

▶ Finally, note sections that include evidence or reasons that you would want to quote directly. Carefully note specific phrases and sentences you might want to quote.

Tracking and Evaluating Data

The rhetorical reading strategies described in this chapter will help you read through, understand, take notes on, and comprehend the resources you have chosen during your preliminary research. By completing these tasks, you are beginning to evaluate the usefulness of the resources you have collected. But you also need to keep track of the information that you collect during your research process, and we encourage you to do more than just pile it up in a shoebox or computer file. It is much more efficient, and will better prepare you for the final presentation of your research, if you systematically track the data you collect.

Keeping track of a few resources is not a difficult task; however, chances are that a lack of resources will not be your problem. Instead, with the proliferation of information on the Internet, you are more likely to have too much information. Imagine a first-year writing student who has chosen to research water conservation efforts and legislation in her city. She might collect general information about water conservation, documentation about water conservation in her community, minutes from city council meetings, interviews with city council members, and perhaps observations or interviews with people in her community. To keep her resources organized in a meaningful way, she will probably want to track her data in four ways:

▶ **Verify.** She should verify that she has collected everything that she needs.

▶ **Copy.** She should keep copies of the actual data collected.

▶ **Respond.** She should reflect on and respond to her data, considering how the data answer her research question, compare to other resources, and might affect her intended audience.

▶ **Fill gaps.** She should use the results from her consistent verifying and responding to identify gaps in her research that she still needs to fill.

Each of these methods includes an evaluation phase that would help her to determine whether she has collected useful, credible, and valid data. These strategies will help you to track and organize your resources as well.

Verify—and Evaluate Usefulness

The downfall of many novice researchers is that they get stuck in the "data collection" mode. By not developing a well-thought-out research plan, they just continue to collect data because they do not know when they have enough. To help keep you organized and consistently moving forward in your research project, you need to compare what you have found with what you actually need according to your research plan. In other words, use your research plan as an initial data-tracking checklist.

As you start collecting resources, both primary and secondary, be sure to quickly check them against your research plan. A quick evaluation of resources at this stage will help you determine if they actually focus on your research question. Another important criterion to keep in mind as you verify the importance of resources is their potential usefulness to your project.

▶ How well will each resource help you respond to your research question?

▶ What does each resource bring to your research project?

As you find and verify the importance of your resources, you may have to make changes to your original plan based on what you have found. If you do have to make changes (and who doesn't?), be sure to take note of them. Instead of writing the changes in a separate document, handwrite them or type them as bold or italic notes in your original research plan.

Copy—and Evaluate Credibility

Once you've verified that a resource is worth keeping, it is critical that you copy it carefully or take detailed notes from it. If you are doing secondary research, we suggest that you obtain a complete copy of the secondary text. At some point, you might need to refer to the larger context of the piece, and documenting your resources will also be much easier if you have complete copies of them. Therefore, if you find a journal article in the library or in the library databases, photocopy or print it. If you find a blog posting on the Internet, print or bookmark it.

techno tip

Register with a Social Bookmarking Application

Many researchers have begun using various free social bookmarking services like Diigo (http://www .diigo.com) to keep track of electronic resources they find on the Internet. Like your Internet browser, a social bookmarking service saves the URL of web pages you want to visit again. If you've used "My Favorites" in Internet Explorer, or bookmarks in Firefox, you already know the usefulness of bookmarks; however, bookmarks saved on your computer cannot travel to other computers or be shared with anyone. Since the social bookmarking services are web-based, you can access your list of resources from any computer connected to the Internet. The services also track the date you located your resource, which is one of the many pieces of information required for bibliographic citations. Finally, most social bookmarking services allow you to tag, categorize, rate, and comment on resources you find.

One of the authors of this book tracks her research in Diigo, and you can see her bookmarks with the tag "Blooms" in the accompanying screen shot.

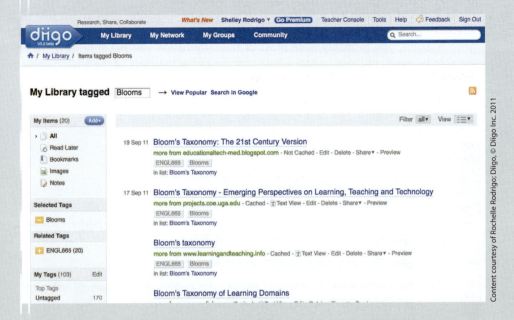

These bookmarks are web sites that the author found that relate to her research and teaching. Notice the different categories and bundles of tags listed on the right side of the screen. These are categories that the author has created to find resources that might be helpful for a variety of projects. You might also notice that the resources listed on the screen usually have more than one tag associated with them, indicating that there are multiple ways to find the resource. Social bookmarking accounts can be infinitely customized to your interests and research.

If you are conducting primary research, you will want to carefully store your original texts (questionnaire results, interview tapes or files, highlighted literary work, etc.). You may even want to make copies of your primary data to work with and put your originals someplace safe. Whether your primary data are in hard copy or electronic format, it is always advisable to make a backup copy. For example, imagine that a student conducts observations of her coworkers while they are working on a collaborative project to understand how they are collaborating. She videotapes them as well as asks that they install screen capture software on their computers so she can record what they are doing on the computer. Having the information in several formats (observation notes, video files, and screen capture files) gives the student backup information if any of her data are lost.

If for some reason you cannot obtain a complete copy of your secondary, or even primary, resource, be sure to take careful, thorough, well-organized notes that focus on the content of the text (exactly what is in it), not your reaction to it. For example, if your library holds a book in its special collections that includes information you need and photocopying the pages isn't allowed because it will damage the book, consider directly hand copying the parts of the text that are important to you. Be sure to write careful summaries and paraphrases before returning the primary document.

As a part of copying, be sure to capture as much bibliographic data as possible to prepare for writing your bibliographic citations. If you are able to photocopy or print your resource, you probably have most of the information you need; however, it is good to be overly cautious and take note of more, rather than less, of the bibliographic information.

write

Track Bibliographic Information

The easiest way to take note of the various types of bibliographic information you will need for a resource is to use the journalists' questions. Select one resource that you know you will use in your research project and answer all of the following questions.

▶ Who is the author? editor? publisher? owner/webmaster?

▶ What is the name of the article? journal (page number, volume number)? web page? web site? chapter? book? blog entry? blog title?

▶ When was it published? posted to the Web? When did you find it? (Be as detailed as possible—day/month/year.)

▶ Where did you find it? What is the name of the library? name of database? name of search engine? URL/web address? (If a book, what city was it published in?)

techno tip

Track Bibliographic Information Online

Several web-based software applications will help you track bibliographic information online. Your school might give you access to a program, such as RefWorks, that will help you track bibliographic information and generate a references or works cited list when you are ready to do so. If your school does not give you access to such a program, you could use Zotero for free (http://www.zotero.org). Zotero is an online research project management package that will capture bibliographic information from the sources that you are looking at online. It will recognize and capture bibliographic information from web sites and also from articles you find in library databases. You can take notes on the source in a Zotero page.

This screenshot shows an article in the database ScienceDirect in the top half of the screen and a Zotero note card on the bottom half of the screen. There is space to take notes and organize information within the Zotero program. It works as an extension in Firefox.

Another part of the copying step in your tracking process is to write a brief summary for every secondary source you collect. These summaries will help you to keep your secondary sources organized as the pile of resources grows. The summaries will also allow you to group like sources together as you start working with your data.

As part of your note-taking during the copying phase, remember you should also carefully note the purpose and audience of the resource. To help prepare for your analysis of the resource, you need to know who produced it as well as their purpose in producing it. For example, if you were doing research on breast cancer, you might find legitimate information from accounts of survivors as well as articles reporting the research of doctors working with patients. However, to adequately assess how and why you might use each resource in the answer to your research question, you need to understand the credibility and authority of its author.

Respond—and Evaluate Validity

A common mistake many students make is simply to combine several quotations and summaries from different resources and call it a paper. They miss the opportunity to make the project their own. In the first project described in this book (Part 1 DIY), you made the research question your own by reflecting on how and why you are invested in the topic. While conducting the research, you need to make research your own by making personal connections to your resources. In other words, you need to spend time with your data—to know the information that you have collected—and respond to it.

Responding to your data goes beyond just "taking notes" on it. Notes are reminders of the original information documented—the *who, what, when, where, why,* and *how* of the original resource. Responding to your data goes beyond reminding yourself of the content of the resource; it includes analyzing the resource in relation to your research question. When responding to your resources, consider the following questions.

▶ How does the resource answer your research question?

   ▸ Does it provide an answer? What evidence does it provide for support?

   ▸ Does it introduce more questions? If so, what questions? How do these new questions affect your understanding of your original research question?

▶ How does the resource compare with other resources?

   ▸ Does it say the same thing as some of your other resources? If so, which ones? How are they related?

   ▸ Does it say something different from some of your resources? If so, which ones?

   ▸ Does it use similar language and ideas?

   ▸ Does it refer to similar people, places, and other resources?

When discussing primary experimental research, "validity" means something very specific. It refers to the logical appropriateness of the methods for a specific study. Evaluating the validity of a resource in your own research is somewhat similar; you are assessing the content of the resource itself. This step differs from evaluating credibility, when you are looking at who conducted the research and wrote or sponsored the document you might use as a resource. When evaluating validity, you will need to look at two areas:

▶ **Internal structure.** Look at whether the argument or presentation of information follows coherent lines of reasoning with easily identified claims and reasons and logically connected evidence.

▶ **External comparison.** Look at how the types of information or conclusions being presented compare with other resources that present or use similar types of information and draw similar conclusions.

Therefore, when you are evaluating the validity of your primary research, pay close attention to your methods for inspecting and collecting data from your primary resources. If you are interviewing people, you should document how you chose your interviewees, what questions you asked and why, and the rate of reply. You can then compare your methods and your results to similar studies that you found in your secondary research. (See Chapter 5 for other factors to consider in primary research.)

When evaluating the validity of secondary resources, you are critically assessing the information in the text. You might assess how current the information is that is cited in the source (if currency is important to your topic), how authoritative the sources are that your resource relies upon, and how well developed the claims, reasons, and evidence presented in the source are. Although we are suggesting that you compare your resources as a test for validity, do not automatically throw out a resource that radically stands out from the rest. Sometimes when new ideas emerge, they are shockingly different from everything that has come before them. Some of the most groundbreaking work throughout history was questioned in terms of its validity in the beginning—for example, consider the work of Galileo and Albert Einstein. If you have a resource that fits into the "radically different" category, then it will be of the utmost importance to evaluate its validity by critically examining its internal structure to make sure that it contains a logical and well-supported argument. Also, be aware that if you are using such work as support for your argument, your audience (depending on who they are and what they value) might question such a resource, so you might need to defend its validity in order to use it effectively as a reference.

write

Evaluate Validity

Select one of the scholarly secondary resources that you will be using in your research project. Ask yourself the following questions about the resource.

▶ Can you easily identify the claim, reasons, and evidence provided in the resource?

▶ Do the evidence and reasons logically support the claim? Why or why not?

▶ Do you have a similar resource that either argues the same perspective or conducts a similar study?

▶ If so, did the two resources use similar methods for gathering and presenting data for their argument? How are they similar and different?

Fill the Gaps—and Evaluate the Balance of Your Resources

Do not wait until you've collected all of your data to start verifying, copying, and responding to it. First, you'll want to carefully copy everything as soon as possible so you do not lose information. Second, you will need to know what you've collected so that you do not waste time collecting too much of the same information. Third, the trends and themes you begin to identify as you respond to and reflect upon the resources and data might identify gaps in your original research plan. You may find that you need to collect other types of resources and data to answer your research question effectively.

Imagine Rajiv, who works for a transglobal company. He has been asked to research collaborative writing/document-sharing software that allows people from around the world to work synchronously. Once he started researching different technologies, he noticed that the various software applications had sections in their advertising that discussed security measures. He quickly realized he had overlooked an important area in his research and his bosses would be very concerned about security. Security was a "gap" in his research he needed to fill.

write

Make Cover Sheets

Consider using the following cover sheet for each resource you collect (especially secondary resources).

Bibliographic Information

▶ Date you found the resource: _____

▶ Name of the resource/article/book chapter/web page/blog entry: _____

▶ Journal (page no., volume no., issue no.): _____

▶ Book: _____

▶ Web site/blog title: _____

▶ Author: _____

▶ Editor: _____

▶ Publisher and place of publication (city): _____

▶ Owner/webmaster of the web site: _____

▶ Date of publication/copyright/posting to the Web (day/month/year): _____

▶ Medium of publication: _____

▶ Name of library : _____

▶ Name of database/search engine: _____

▶ URL (web address), if needed: _____

Summary

_____

_____

_____

Verification

_____ Checked off on your research plan

Usefulness

How does the material in the resource directly respond to your specific research question, not just your research topic? _____

_____

_____

Copies

_____ Photocopy or printed copy attached to this worksheet

_____ Detailed notes attached to this worksheet

Credibility

Who is the author of the resource, and what are his/her/their credentials? With whom is the author affiliated? _____

_____

For what purpose(s) did the author write the resource you have chosen? In other words, is the author trying to provide information? persuade readers? entertain? What clues help you to identify the piece's purpose? _____

_____

_____

Who is the audience for the resource? How do you know? How might the audience have affected the way that the resource is constructed? _____

_____

_____

Response

How does the resource answer your research question? _____

_____

How does the resource compare with other resources? _____

_____

_____

Validity

Is the resource internally consistent and logical? If not, what problems do you see? _____

_____

_____

Are the resource's content and methods similar to other resources you have collected? If not, is that a concern? _____

_____

_____

>>>

>>>

Balance

Is this a _____static, _____syndicated, or _____dynamic resource?

Is this a(n) _____edited, _____peer-reviewed, or _____ personally published resource?

Does this resource include any of the following types of data?

_____ statistical evidence

_____ experimental results

_____ expert opinions

_____ personal experience and/or testimony

_____ observations?

chapter 7

Understanding Plagiarism and Integrating Resources

Following the conventions of documentation and avoiding plagiarism are key responsibilities of researchers. As a researcher, you must document how and where you locate your resources for three primary reasons:

▶ to give credit to the original author/artist/speaker,

▶ to help your audience find the same resource, and

▶ to build your credibility as a researcher.

Documentation is your ethical responsibility to the individuals who produced the resources from which you are drawing your information, and you demonstrate good will to your audience by providing them with the information they need to find the original source in a manner that they can easily understand. By understanding and abiding by the principles of copyright and by documenting how and where you locate information or ideas that are not your own, you are following legal guidelines and demonstrating your high ethical standards.

we'll explore

▶ *principles of copyright and fair use*

▶ *how to avoid plagiarism by accurately documenting resources*

▶ *ways to effectively integrate resources into research-based writing*

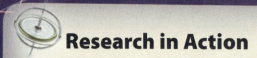

Research in Action

Author: Jeff is a graduate student in clinical psychology, and he would like to work as a school counselor when he is finished with his graduate degree. He is particularly interested in working at a two-year college.

© Steve Dunwell

Topic: Jeff is conducting research on first-year, first-generation college students. He wants to be prepared to work with students dealing with depression, and he realizes that the pressures and demands of college are often overwhelming to first-year students, especially those who have no college graduates in their immediate families to act as mentors and role models.

Audience: Because of Jeff's career goals and the topic of his research, he could publish the results of his research in several places. Other scholars in the field of psychology might be interested in his research, so he could publish his work in an academic journal. He might also look at a less research-oriented magazine geared toward teachers and school administrators. In addition, Jeff might think about sharing his work with parents of first-year students in a newsletter or other publication marketed to parents of college students.

Purpose: Jeff wants to share the results of his research with others who can help first-year students deal with the pressures of academic life, and he also wants to contribute to the ongoing research in this field.

Questions

1. Where might Jeff look for research that has already been done on this topic?

2. Can you find appropriate publications that Jeff could consider as venues for sharing the results of his research?

3. Looking more carefully at one of those publications, what documentation conventions do you see? Are sources cited carefully in the text? Are reference lists provided at the end of articles? Why do you think the authors follow the conventions they do in this publication?

4. What citation style is being used in the publication? Why do you think that style is used?

Copyright

One of the reasons we document resources is to uphold the copyright laws that protect the information that we use. Copyright laws regulate the use of a particular expression of an idea. Ideas that are considered "common knowledge" are not protected by copyright, but many people disagree about what constitutes common knowledge. Therefore, if an idea you include in your writing is not your own, you must cite it as someone else's work and give that person the credit.

Copyright laws protect the author, or producer, of any given text (written, audio, visual, performance, etc.) from people who might reproduce that text without permission. The entertainment industry, both in music and movies, fights to keep very strict copyright regulations on their texts so that they will continue to earn money for the work and resources that went into the production of those texts. Similarly, scholars, and the publishing houses that publish their work, also want to retain control over their materials. You should be aware that even though you might not see a copyright symbol, ©, or the statement "all rights reserved" on a text, copyright is automatically granted to the author or producer of a work once it is published in a tangible form. For example, you own the copyright to all of the papers you write for various purposes.

Copyright does not last forever, however. The length of any text's coverage under copyright law depends on when and how the text was published, among other things. Copyright coverage can expire after a certain length of time. But remember, the ethics of documentation are not only about following copyright law but also about giving credit where credit is due and being responsible to your audience by providing pertinent information about the resource so they can find it themselves.

Fair Use

What should you do if you want to refer to something in a resource that is still protected by copyright? Fair use allows individuals to copy small portions of texts to use them in other contexts, especially research and education. If you are doing a critical analysis of a book that has been written in the past fifty years, you may quote a few small excerpts from it under the fair-use doctrine. Always keep in mind that even though fair use gives you this right, you still need to document how and where you found the information. This gives credit to the copyright holder while providing your audience with the information needed to find the original sources.

Ideas versus Words

Copyright technically protects the expression of an idea, not the idea itself. However, in academic research it is expected that you will also document where and how you found specific ideas. For example, imagine that a doctor who specializes in hip replacements has conducted research into a new method for connecting the replacement hip to the patient's thighbone. When writing his article about the new method, he needs to briefly discuss the methods currently in use to demonstrate why his new method is better. When referring to the other methods, he is not reprinting the exact details of them; however, he still must cite the resources that originally presented the other methods. If the audience wants, or needs, to read more specific or detailed material about the other hip replacement methods, his documentation will provide the way.

Plagiarism

Remember, documentation and plagiarism are ultimately about ethics. Therefore, if you plagiarize by copying the work of others without documenting, you are being unethical in two ways:

1. you are most likely breaking copyright law, and
2. you are not acknowledging the work of others.

When we are talking about plagiarism in an academic setting, most instructors are highly concerned about the second issue. The production of original ideas is valued in academic settings, and it is important to give credit to the original author(s). Writing assignments are one of many methods that instructors use to evaluate how much you have learned in the course. If you copy someone's work without documenting it, you have committed plagiarism: you have stolen someone's ideas and you are not demonstrating your own learning.

Part of the difficulty in talking about plagiarism, however, is that it can be difficult to define. Plagiarism, as it is generally defined by academic institutions, includes many kinds of academic violations, including the following:

▶ turning in an entire work composed by someone else and claiming it as your own

▶ using someone else's exact words in your writing without acknowledging the source

▶ paraphrasing someone else's work or using someone else's ideas in your writing without acknowledging the source

In addition, some professors classify turning in work that you have completed for another class as a form of academic dishonesty. To complicate matters, plagiarism (as it is defined in academic settings) happens in other settings as normal practice. In some contexts, copying parts of a text into a new document is considered normal, accepted practice (in the writing of contracts, for example). Furthermore, in different cultures and settings, the "rules" of documentation and plagiarism shift. Simply put, plagiarism is a complex issue, and the rules of plagiarism are shaped by rhetorical context, just like everything else that we have discussed in this text.

Two kinds of plagiarism are commonly viewed as academic violations in American higher education. In academic contexts, students who plagiarize often fall into one of two categories:

1. **Blatant plagiarism.** Someone knowingly copied sections of other resources and submitted them as his or her own work.
2. **Careless plagiarism.** Someone knowingly used information from an outside resource but thought that it was considered common knowledge or did not adequately provide in-text and full bibliographic documentation within the paper.

Both kinds of plagiarism have serious academic consequences, and it is important to understand the conventions of citing sources in order to avoid them.

Blatant Plagiarism

Is there a difference between copying a whole paper and copying and pasting text from several sources into a paper? For the purposes of following an academic code of conduct, not really. In either case, the writer is knowingly copying another resource and presenting that work as his or her own. Obviously, if you submit an entire paper that was written by another individual, you are plagiarizing. However, if you copy and paste small sections from another resource, shouldn't that count as fair use? Yes, if you document where and how you found that resource both within the paper (through the use of quotation marks or block quotations and in-text citations, explained later in this chapter) and in the bibliographic citations at the end of the paper. If you do not properly cite those copied and pasted sections, however, you are plagiarizing.

Why would a student plagiarize on purpose? There are a few common reasons, and at least two of them are completely avoidable with proper planning:

1. The student didn't understand the assignment or the material and relied on someone else's work instead.
2. The student ran out of time to work on the assignment and copied someone else's work out of desperation.

In the first instance, the student who doesn't understand the assignment or material could seek help from the instructor, or perhaps from someone else in the class or in an academic support center, to understand the requirements of the assignment. Planning ahead and seeking help early can prevent this situation. Planning ahead will also help you avoid the second circumstance, running out of time and plagiarizing from desperation. The assignments laid out in this text will also help you avoid that circumstance; a carefully written research plan, for example, will help you plan the time to find all of the information you need to complete your own work.

Careless Plagiarism

Many cases of plagiarism are what we call "careless plagiarism"—plagiarism that could have been avoided by an understanding of the rules of citation and careful documentation of outside sources. The first step in avoiding this type of plagiarism is learning to identify appropriate and inappropriate uses of secondary sources and understanding when to use in-text citations. Take the time to learn how to correctly paraphrase and summarize so that you avoid plagiarism.

Most of the time, careless plagiarism could have been easily avoided if the student had left enough time to double- and triple-check the documentation. Understanding the conventions of documentation will go a long way toward helping you avoid plagiarism due to carelessness. Make sure to give yourself enough time to carefully document and double-check your research before turning it in for a grade or sharing it with someone else. As much as possible, avoid making last-minute revisions to a text that involve changing, adding, or removing resources. Even with the best of intentions, mistakes can happen at the last minute if you don't give yourself time to review and revise. (For standard conventions of documentation, see Chapters 11–15.)

Integration of Resources into Your Argument

Once you have developed your argument and know what resources, data, and evidence you will incorporate into the final published product, you should start thinking about how to incorporate those resources into your writing. For every outside piece of information that you present in your writing, whether it is from primary research or from a secondary resource, make sure to do the following four things.

▶ Introduce the resource.

▶ Incorporate the resource as a summary, paraphrase, or quotation into your writing.

▶ Interpret the resource, connecting it to your argument.

▶ Document the location of the resource.

If you follow these four steps when incorporating resources into your writing, you will be sure to avoid plagiarism as well as provide your readers with the information they need.

Introduction of the Resource

One of the common challenges students face in research-based writing is figuring out how to elegantly incorporate resources into their own argument. What often happens is that a student ends up "dumping" a quotation into a paragraph, or stringing several quotations together, or just putting a quotation in a paragraph by itself. The problem with that approach is that the audience (1) has no context for the quotation and (2) is disoriented because your text shifts from your own words to those of your source with no warning. If you take the time to introduce your resource, you will avoid this common problem. First, you'll have a transition from what you were previously discussing in your argument. Second, and more importantly, you'll provide a context for the resource itself—what it is and, if needed, where it comes from. In the following example, in, American Psychological Association (APA) format, the authors (Marini et al., 2007) introduce the summaries of multiple articles with a brief introduction about why they are important—they are recent studies.

> The cardioprotective effects of exercise training are well known and out of any dispute. Recent studies have clearly shown that training at >60% VO2max increases myocardial tolerance to ischemia-reperfusion (I-R) (Strøm et al., 2005), improves cardiac performance and ameliorates the cell defence capacity against stress (Powers et al., 2002; Freimann et al., 2005).

The emphasis on this example is the date of the studies and what the studies demonstrate. The authors of the studies are not the main point here; the resource is supporting the statement that the studies are recent; therefore, the authors' names do not need to be introduced into the actual text of the manuscript—the names appear only in the in-text citation. However, in the next example, the author's name is incorporated into the sentence. Yan Le Espiritu is a well-known Asian American scholar; therefore, by building Espiritu's name into the sentence, the writer (Han, 2006) is not only making the point about Asian American identity formation but is also backing the point by showing that it came from a well-known scholar.

> However, as Espiritu (1992) points out, identity formation for Asian Americans in the United States is more a reflection of common experiences they found within Western borders than the discrepant histories and cultures of their homelands. (p. 9)

To put this in a completely different context, think about how you might use a movie review in a conversation. If you quote a reviewer about a particular movie, you might just emphasize what the reviewer said. However, if you were trying to convince a friend that this movie is worth going to you might say, "Ebert gave it a thumbs up." Not only would you be quoting the source on the quality of the movie, you would also be working the well-known reviewer's name into your reference to give it more weight and authority in your argument.

If you are doing primary research, like Jeff at the beginning of the chapter, you will also need to introduce the primary data. In Jeff's example, he might give pieces of background information about specific students to help his audience understand how to interpret the information he is giving them. For example, he might describe how old they are and if they have children before he incorporates a quote about the stress of balancing a personal and home life with attending college.

write

Introduce Secondary Resources

Find a specific section of a resource that you are fairly certain that you will use in your final research paper. Answer the following questions about this specific information or piece of evidence.

▶ Why might this resource be helpful in the development of your argument?

▶ What might be important to point out to your audience about the information so that they pay attention to this resource in your argument?

▶ Who is the author? Is the author well known in the field? Will the audience know the author's name? Does the author have very strong credentials related to this topic? (If so, you might consider incorporating the author's name, and maybe even his or her credentials, when introducing the resource.)

Now try writing an introduction to the information from that resource that you could include in your final paper. Include the relevant information that will help your audience interpret the resource you are presenting to them. Here are two examples.

> Leading researchers in child psychology agree that spanking can be damaging to a small child . . .

> According to Glenn, a respected researcher in child psychology . . .

Incorporation of the Data

Once you've introduced the information from your resource, you then need to incorporate the actual data you are using into the sentence. You can directly quote the resource or more casually refer to it by summarizing or paraphrasing the information provided in the resource.

Quotations from Resources   Many beginning researchers make the two common mistakes of incorporating lots of direct quotes and incorporating very long quotes into their papers. To avoid committing these common errors, make sure that you are directly quoting for the right reasons. Generally, you only need to quote a resource directly for one of the following reasons.

▶ You are doing direct analysis of a written text and need to provide the specific examples you are analyzing.

▶ The section of text that you would like to use is short and could easily be incorporated into your larger text.

▸ The author(s) of the resource used language that you believe to be particularly powerful and/or persuasive for your intended audience, and you would lose meaning or emphasis if you paraphrased it.

▸ The text is well known, and your audience might already be familiar with the quotation.

▸ You want to comment directly on the author's ideas and/or language.

If you can articulate why you chose to quote directly instead of paraphrase a resource, you generally are doing it for the right reasons. If you are only directly quoting a resource because you have the resource and want to include it in your argument, you probably should summarize or paraphrase instead. Summarizing and paraphrasing give you the opportunity to present the resource in a way that gives the most support for your position.

Many scholars examine texts and language and are interested in the specific phrasing that someone might use in an expression. While analyzing any text, they must refer to the specific words on the page as well as the specific utterances of individuals. In this case, the scholars are focusing on the choice, order, and style of words, among other things. They must include detailed quotations from the texts that they then continue to analyze in their papers. Obviously, this type of scholarship requires writers to include direct quotations from resources into their papers.

Although other scholars may not be specifically studying language and texts, they are sensitive to highly expressive moments where someone wrote or said just the right thing. For example, in 1964 when the U.S. Supreme Court ruled in the case *Jacobellis v. Ohio* on whether a specific film was pornographic, a portion of Justice Potter Stewart's concurring opinion attempted to define pornography and included these words: "I know it when I see it." Since then, many arts and humanities scholars who have written about the difficulty of defining pornography quote Stewart when referring to his attempt at a definition. The exact language is striking ("I know it when I see it") and the sense of ambiguity would be lost if someone paraphrased it.

Many arguments that revolve around definitions use direct quotes to distinguish specific ideas, concepts, and perspectives from one another. As Jeff, from the beginning of the chapter, starts to write about his research about depression in first-generation college students, he will need to define both "depression" and "first-generation college student." Especially in the case of depression, Jeff will have to explain clearly how and why he defines depression in a certain way. To articulate his definition, he will need to refer to different psychologists' definitions. He will probably quote some he agrees with, focusing on expressive and "perfectly stated" language. Jeff might also quote psychologists' definitions that he disagrees with, and he could use direct quotes to emphasize the difference between his definition and theirs.

Ultimately, it is important to remember that you do not always need to directly quote individuals who support your opinion, perspective, or argument. Unless the specific language is essential to your argument, you should try to summarize or paraphrase your resources.

Summarizing and Paraphrasing Revisited   Unless you need to quote directly for one of the reasons listed, you should either summarize or paraphrase the resources you are incorporating into your argument. Summarizing might be useful if you want to condense some of the ideas of a particular resource to support your argument. If you don't want to condense the ideas but you don't have a reason to directly quote the original author, you might paraphrase the source. This could be a useful strategy if the original language of the source might be inaccessible to your audience, for example.

Interpreting the Resource

Another important step when incorporating resources into your writing successfully is to interpret the resource for your audience. Earlier in this chapter, we gave the example of novice researchers who tend to "dump" quotations or statistics into their writing. When a writer doesn't make explicit connections between the source and his or her argument, the writer leaves the audience to make the connections themselves. A better approach is to provide the connection for your reader, which prevents him or her from making the wrong connection or interpreting the resource in a manner that does not support the argument. By interpreting your resources for your audience, you are also ensuring that your voice, not someone else's, remains the dominant one in your research.

This final connection can take place either in the sentence that includes the information from the resource (as well as the introduction and in-text citation) or in a separate sentence. Sometimes getting everything (introduction, resource, interpretation, and in-text citation) into one sentence is overwhelming and it is easier on both the writer and the reader if you interpret your resource in the following sentence. If you choose to do the latter, always interpret the resource immediately following the sentence in which you included the resource to avoid confusion.

Some resources might not need interpretation, however. If you have found a particularly effective quotation, for example, you might want to have it stand alone without interpreting for your reader. Such cases should be conscious choices, though. In other words, if you choose not to interpret a resource you have included, you should have a clearly understood reason for not doing so, knowing that the quotation will draw attention to itself because there is no interpretation.

Good interpretations can be challenging to write. Try to avoid the trap of writing, "This quotation means that. . . ." Instead, think about how to use your interpretation to point the reader back to the argument that you are developing. Consider the earlier example about Justice Stewart's language for defining pornography. A student writing about the difficulty of regulating pornography on the Internet might write the following passage:

This phrase incorporates the quotation into the sentence.

This phrase introduces the quotation.

In *Jacobellis v. Ohio* (1964), Justice Stewart defined pornographic material by claiming "I know it when I see it." If even a Supreme Court justice has difficulty coming up with a less ambiguous definition than this, it is no wonder that the judicial and legislative systems in the United States have had difficulty identifying and regulating pornography on the Internet.

This sentence interprets the quotation and relates it to the author's argument.

Documenting the Resource

After introducing and incorporating information from the resource, documentation is the next step. You must document the resource in the same sentence as you refer to it in your argument. Most guidelines require a two-step documentation process for previously published resources:

1. **In-text citation.** In-text citations give the reader just enough information to locate the correct, full bibliographic citation elsewhere in the document. In-text citations are brief so that readers are not distracted by them and can continue to read with the flow of the text.

2. **Full bibliographic citation.** Full bibliographic citations provide detailed information on how and where to locate the resource. Since full bibliographic citations are bulky and do not fit well within the flow of the text, most are found in either footnotes (at the bottom of the page) or endnotes (at the end of the paper).

What to Cite   You should cite any information that you locate from an outside resource. The only exception is if the information is considered common knowledge within the context in which you are writing the document. (In other words, is this common knowledge to your specific audience?) Your citations should be included in *every sentence* that incorporates information from an outside resource.

How to Cite   Before figuring out how to construct your in-text and full bibliographic citations, you need to determine which citation style you will follow. This book contains guidelines for four of the most popular citation styles, which have been developed by professional organizations for academic writing.

▶ **Modern Language Association (MLA).** Scholars who study literature, languages, and other humanities generally follow MLA documentation style.

▶ **American Psychological Association (APA).** Scholars who study psychology, sociology, and other social sciences usually follow APA documentation style.

▶ ***The Chicago Manual of Style* (CMS).** CMS includes two types of citation styles, one designed for the humanities and one designed for the social sciences. History scholars tend to follow CMS documentation style.

▶ **Council of Science Editors (CSE).** CSE is a good example of a citation style in the sciences; however, engineers, chemists, and doctors often have discipline-specific citation style guidelines as well.

As with any other decision you make during your research process, your selection of citation style should be based on your rhetorical situation. See Chapter 11 for information about choosing the most appropriate citation style for your research.

In-Text Citations   One of the challenges in citing resources accurately is figuring out what the in-text citations should look like. A second challenge is figuring out where and when to include citations in the text. The rules for when and where to include in-text citations are fairly consistent across citation styles. In-text citations should be included for every idea, quotation, and piece of information that you take from another resource. When in doubt, cite.

Take a look at the following paragraph, noting where in-text citations have been included—and where they have not. The annotations explain why citations were or were not included. This example is in MLA format.

A citation is included for the quoted resource. No page number is listed because it is from an Internet-based article in the *Chronicle of Higher Education*.

No citation is listed after the first sentence because this could be considered common knowledge.

Many students have difficulty figuring out how to define plagiarism and don't understand when to include citations in their work. According to a study of Internet-based plagiarism in student writing, students may have "an attitude that anything on the Internet is public domain, and they're not seeing copying it as cheating" (Kellogg). But students need to understand that in academic writing, attribution is expected—not just of exact words but also of ideas. Many students also don't realize that borrowing the word choice or phrasing of the original author is also considered plagiarism if it's not put in quotation marks (Howard 799); changing a word or two does not create an appropriate paraphrase.

The in-text citation is included in the middle of the sentence, just after the information that came from the resource. The reader can assume that the rest of the information in the sentence is the author's own ideas or interpretation.

Practice In-Text Citations

write

Open a research-based document you wrote before—perhaps a paper you finished for a different class. Save it as a new file and delete all of the in-text citations (if it is a long paper, you might just copy and paste a small portion of it for this activity). If you are in a class, switch documents with a partner and mark all of the places in your partner's document where you think an in-text citation should go. Then switch back and see if you agree with what your partner marked in your document. Compare the marked sections with your original paper—did you include all of the in-text citations that you should have included? Where do you and your partner disagree?

Full Bibliographic Citations   Compiling a full list of references at the end of your research is an important part of the research process. Your bibliography, list of references, or works cited list will provide further information and resources for your readers in case they would like to follow up and discover more information about your topic for themselves. For example, a works cited list (MLA format) for the paragraph excerpt included in the preceding section would look like this:

Works Cited

Howard, Rebecca Moore. "Plagiarisms, Authorships, and the Academic Death Penalty."
   College English 57.3 (1995): 788–806. Print.

Kellogg, Alex P. "Students Plagiarize Less Than Many Think, a New Study Finds."
   Chronicle of Higher Education. Chronicle of Higher Education, 1 Feb. 2002.
   Web. 25 Nov. 2011.

As you compile your list, keep in mind that you are providing a trail for your audience to find the same resources that you used in conducting your research. So, even though you might be able to find the same article in several places (online and in a print-based newspaper, for example), you should provide the correct information for your audience to find the version of the article you read.

As you think about the different places that you might be able to find the same resource, consider this example from a student's research for a social work class. Tasia is a college student in New York City. Her social work class has gotten her to think a lot about the economy and its impact on senior citizens. On December 6, 2011, while sitting at a local coffee shop, she picked up the *New York Times* and read an article about how many public employees are retiring at a younger age. If she were to write a full bibliographic citation in MLA format for that article, based on the one she read in the physical newspaper, it would look like this:

Davey, Monica. "Many Workers in Public Sector Retiring Sooner." *New York Times*
   6 Dec. 2011: A1. Print.

Once Tasia started the spring semester, she emailed a couple of her friends about the article. She just gave them the name of the article, the name of the author, and that it was in a December issue of the *New York Times*.

Sarah, one of Tasia's friends, looked for it on the *New York Times* web site and decided she might use it in a paper as well. Sarah's full bibliographic citation in MLA format would look like this:

Davey, Monica. "Many Workers in Public Sector Retiring Sooner." *New York Times*.
   New York Times, 6 Dec. 2011. Web. 3 Feb. 2012.

Notice that Sarah does not have the section and page number; this is because that information is not provided on the web site, and she only accessed the article online. However, if the section and page number had been provided, she should include it in the citation (see Chapter 12 for an example of how to do this in MLA format).

Teresa, another one of Tasia's friends, looked in one of her library's databases for the article. Her citation in MLA format would look like this:

Davey, Monica. "Many Workers in Public Sector Retiring Sooner." *New York Times*
   6 Dec. 2011: A1. *Newspaper Source Plus*. Web. 13 Feb. 2012.

Notice that Teresa did include the original print page numbers because that information was included with the electronic copy in *Newspaper Source Plus*.

Each of the citations has distinct features that would help a reader find that exact version of the article. While this might seem inconsequential at first (they're all the same article after all, right?), consider this: in an online version of a periodical, many publishers provide a space where readers can comment on an article, similar to a blog. Such additional commentary might have been helpful to you in interpreting the content of the article, and you might want to point your readers to that discussion. In addition, some periodicals only include portions of the full article in the online version, and readers might not be able to find the section you are quoting if you read the print version and then reference the online version. See Chapter 11 for another example of how these differences can prove to be important in citations.

Avoiding Common Documentation Pitfalls

As you put together your full list of resources at the end of your research, follow the guidelines for the citation style you have chosen. Each style has its own unique details, but you'll see commonalities among them. We've found that students encounter some common problems, regardless of the style they are following. Try to avoid these common pitfalls.

1. **Incorrect formatting of authors' names.** Check the formatting guidelines for the citation style you are using to make sure you are listing the authors' names correctly. For example, in MLA format you include the author's full first name, but in APA format you include only the initial of the author's first name.

2. **No author listed.** If you cannot find an author for your resource, consider the following steps:
   ▶ Really search for the author. On web sites, the author's name may be listed on a different page. Take some time and really search.
   ▶ Government agencies, organizations, and corporations can be authors.
   ▶ If you really can't find an author, do not start your citation with the date. Use the title of the work in the place of the author.

3. **Incorrect use of italics.** Titles of major works (books, films, television shows) and periodicals (magazines, newspapers, and journals) are italicized. Specific articles, chapters, and television episode titles are not italicized. In some citation styles, they are put in quotation marks—see the specific guidelines for your citation style for more guidance. Also note that some citation styles specify when and how to capitalize the title of the work.

4. **Incorrect punctuation.** Follow the exact punctuation guidelines for your citation style for every period, comma, semicolon, and quotation mark. Each style has its specific rules, and they are important to follow. For example, in APA you should not include periods at the end of a full bibliographic citation with a URL.

5. **Inaccurate listing of URLs for digital resources.** Styles differ in the specifics for listing URLs and databases. See the detailed examples included with your citation style's guidelines. You should always keep a copy of the exact URL or database name in your notes in case you change citation styles.

Writing a Review of Research

At some point during the process of gathering information for a project, a researcher needs to compile the notes on various resources in one location. By doing so, you are able to get a broader perspective about the information you have, what you still need, and what themes, trends, and connections you are starting to see. Most researchers are good about seeking information that supports their initial position on or impression about a research topic. However, effective researchers know that in order to get a broader under-standing of a rhetorical situation, they need to search not only for resources that agree with their initial perspectives, but also the opinions and perspectives of other groups in-vested in the issue.

Compiling a review of research can be a helpful step in the research process to organize and present the information you have gathered on a topic. In this section, we introduce you to two types of reviews of research:

> **annotated bibliographies**
> **literature reviews**

Common Features of Reviews of Research

The format of your final written review of research will depend on whether you are writing an annotated bibliography or a literature review. The basic process of writing both types is similar, however. Reviews of research should contain a list of resources with a description and a summary of each one. At a minimum, your annotated bibliography or literature review should include the following elements:

▶ **Overview.** Provide a picture of the conversation that is in progress on this issue by giving an overview of what people are saying and what research has been conducted.

▶ **Summaries.** Write brief summaries of what each resource concluded about your topic, including differing perspectives.

▶ **Citations.** Include accurate citations in a standard documentation style so that readers can find the original sources (included in the citations in the text of an annotated bibliography or in the references/works cited list at the end of the literature review).

Additional Features Found in Some Reviews of Research

▶ **Context.** Some reviews of research will also include information about the rhetorical situation surrounding each resource's different perspectives.

▶ **Evaluation.** You might be expected to include evaluative information about the resources based on how credible they are, how useful they will be in your research, how current they are, or how they measure up to other evaluative criteria relevant to the project.

▶ **Purpose for inclusion in your review.** Some reviews of research include a sense of how the resources will help the writer respond to the research question.

Types of Reviews of Research

Annotated Bibliography

Features of an Annotated Bibliography

An annotated bibliography is a list of citations of sources on a topic with a paragraph of description following each citation. The citations are generally listed in alphabetical order unless they are organized by theme. The description of each source usually summarizes its main points and expands the understanding of how its author perceives the issue. In addition, annotations might evaluate the various positions taken by people who are concerned with the issue. As you write an annotation, you may wish to list key themes that appear in the source, and you might want to speculate as to why the author holds the position he or she does. Consider including contextual information for the source to help understand the author's claim and position. A useful annotated bibliography illustrates the complexity of an issue by mapping out the positions on an issue and reflecting on the various parties' investments in them.

Traditionally, scholars construct annotated bibliographies on a specific topic. Normally primary research, especially qualitative and quantitative data, is not included in an annotated bibliography. However, you, or your instructor, may want to include descriptions of primary data (if you are collecting any) so that your annotated bibliography provides a complete picture of your research process. Most citation styles do not provide guidelines for citing full bibliographic entries of primary research (the data are usually just presented in the research report). If your instructor wants you to include annotations on your primary research, you will need to determine how to construct a bibliographic entry based on the citation guidelines provided in Chapters 11 through 15.

Example of an Annotated Bibliography

Amelia Cooper is a first-year writing student who wrote an annotated bibliography on why students procrastinate. Her instructor had specifically asked her to focus on academic sources, describing research conducted on procrastination, so you will notice that all of her sources come from academic, peer-reviewed journals. Depending on the assignment your instructor has given you, it might be appropriate to include sources written for a more general audience (see Chapter 4 for more information about the types of resources you might include). Amelia wrote an annotated bibliography of her resources, and she included her initial research question as her title. As with all examples of writing in this book, keep in mind that there are strengths and opportunities for revision of this annotated bibliography. Amelia's annotated bibliography is written in MLA format.

Amelia Cooper

Prof. Cochran

English 101

10 Nov. 2011

Why Do Students Procrastinate?

Ferrari, Joseph R. "Self-handicapping by Procrastinators: Protecting Self-
esteem, Social-esteem, or Both?" *Journal of Research in Personality*
25 (1991): 245–61. Web. 4 Nov. 2011.

Ferrari is a Professor in the Department of Psychology. He claims
procrastinators have both low self-esteem and high social anxiety.
He studies how individuals try to protect their social- and self-esteems.
Specifically, he looked at whether procrastinators or nonprocrastina-
tors actively seek ways to block their ability to complete a task as a
way to save face. Not surprisingly, procrastinators were more likely to
find ways to handicap themselves. However, if the activity was public
and would somehow explicitly demonstrate the lack of ability by the
procrastinator, they would not self-handicap. Logically, if the activity
did explicitly demonstrate lack of ability but was private, the procrastinator was more likely to self-handicap.

Schraw, Gregory, Theresa Wadkins, and Lori Olafson. "Doing the
Things We Do: A Grounded Theory of Academic Procrastina-
tion." *Journal of Educational Psychology* 99.1 (2007): 12–25.
PsycARTICLES. Web. 18 Oct. 2011.

Schraw and Olafson are both professors at the University
of Nevada and in the Departments of Educational Psychology.
Wadkins is professor at the University of Nebraska and in the
Department of Psychology. First, the authors conduct a review
of literature of the definitions and characteristics of procrastination. Specifically they "define the construct of academic
procrastination as intentionally deferring or delaying work that
must be completed" (12). They then completed a study asking
students about their own procrastination. Their research resulted
in a paradigm model of academic procrastination that included:
contexts and conditions (unclear directions, deadlines, lack
of incentives), antecedents (self, teacher, task), phenomenon
(adaptive, maladaptive), copying strategies (cognitive, affective),
and consequences (quality of life, quality of work). Based on

---

Margin notes:

I noticed you had the name of the databases in some of your resources and not in others. MLA does want the name of the databases in all resources found in databases.

I like how you quickly provide ethos (see page 116) for the author as a way to evaluate the credibility of your source.

Do you and/or your readers really need to know which institutions the authors are from; is it enough just to know they are professors in psychology? If so, consider combining these sentences.

These look like very specific details, or at least very precise terminology. Again, you probably need to provide an in-text citation to identify what page/s you found these concepts on.

this paradigm, the researchers developed a list of six principles of academic procrastination: minimum time, optimum efficiency, peak affective experience, early assessment or work requirements, open escape routes, and close proximity to reward. Their concluding discussion focuses on some of the possible benefits of procrastination and how instructors and students may want to cultivate positive versions of it.

Sommer, William G. "Procrastination and Cramming: How Adept Students Ace the System." *Journal of American College Health* 39 (1990): 5–10. Web. 4 Nov. 2011.

According to Sommer, university students adapt to time constraints by cramming. And, he argues, they actually do well and succeed academically! In his study he finds "Many students [who] outwardly adapt to this system, however, engage in an intense and private ritual that comprises five aspects: calculated procrastination, preparatory anxiety, climactic cramming, nick-of-time deadline-making, and a secret, if often uncelebrated, victory. These adept students often find it difficult to admit others into their efficient program of academic survival." Based on the success of the students, Sommer argues that these school rhythms actually shape the workplace. In the article Sommer also presents methods for helping students trapped in these cycles. This is a credible source from a peer reviewed journal.

Tice, Dianne M., and Roy F. Baumeister, "Longitudinal Study of Procrastination, Performance, Stress, and Health: The Costs and Benefits of Dawdling." *Psychological Science* 8 (1997) 454–58. Web. 27 Oct. 2011.

Tice and Baumeister are both professors at Florida State University in the Department of Psychology. The authors conducted two longitudinal studies that ultimately concluded that procrastination is a self-defeating behavior. Specifically, procrastinators did much worse in terms of their grades. Interestingly, although the studies found that procrastinators might be healthier in the short term, they were more likely to be more stressed and ill over the long term. The authors did confess their study allowed participants to self-select into "procrastinator" or "nonprocrastinator" groups which could weaken the results of the study.

> This is a long quote for an annotated bibliography entry, but it does include very detailed information you would want in your notes. Although you have the citation above, you should include an in-text citation of the page number from where you took this quote.

> I like that you include criticisms of their research methods so that you are aware of the authority and credibility of the resource.

Tuckman, Bruce W. "The Development and Concurrent Validation of the Procrastination Scale." *Educational and Psychological Measurement 51* (1991): 473–80. Web. 20 Oct. 2011.

Tuckman is a professor at Ohio State University. The purpose of the study was to develop a new survey method for students to self-assess their procrastination tendencies. The article reports out on a first study that developed and piloted the new research instrument. The article then reports a study where the authors compared the results of the newly developed self-assessment procrastination with an "actual self-regulated performance." In short, the study concludes that students are very aware of their own procrastination tendencies and that students who self-identify as procrastinators doubt their own abilities and spend less time on work that would help them achieve academically.

Van Etten, Shawn, Geoffrey Freebern, and Michael Pressley. "College Students' Beliefs about Exam Preparation." *Contemporary Educational Psychology* 22 (1997): 192–212. *SciVerse*. Web. 4 Nov. 2011.

Etten, Freebern, and Pressley are all in the Department of Educational Psychology and Statistics, at the University of Albany, and the State University of New York. The authors studied college students as they prepared for exams. Their methods included collecting and interpreting data before collecting and interpreting more data. The study looked at four major categories of student beliefs: motivations for studying, strategies for coping with test demands, affect about test preparation, and external factors affecting test preparation. Motivations for studying were tied to desire for specific grades and beliefs about ability to achieve the grade. Strategies include reading, attending class, as well as managing time, materials, study spaces and study partners. Not surprisingly, external factors included instructors, prior experiences, as well as social and physical environments. In the discussion, authors mentioned that many of the results align with results in earlier published studies.

Most of your resources are coming from psychology journals; you might consider switching from MLA to APA (American Psychological Association) style.

This is interesting information about the research methods; however, it is too vague to really understand what you mean. If their research methods were important enough to comment upon; you should probably include more details about what they did and why they did it that way.

Discussion Questions

▶ The author chose MLA format for this paper, and the instructor suggested she consider APA format. What choice would you make for this annotated bibliography? Why?

▶ How well do you think the author develops the annotations in the piece? What suggestions would you make for revising the annotations themselves?

▶ Based on the sources included in the annotated bibliography, what kind of conclusion would you draw about student procrastination?

▶ Do the sources in the annotated bibliography represent a variety of opinions on the issue? Do you think any perspectives are missing? If so, which ones, and why?

Literature Review

Features of a Literature Review

A literature review includes much of the same information as an annotated bibliography, but it is written in the form of an essay. Instead of breaking the writing into annotations, the literature review provides a snapshot of the ongoing conversation by drawing relationships among the sources found on the issue. In essence, the literature review weaves the different resources together to show how the authors represent a part of the discussion taking place about the issue.

The point of a literature review is to make that discussion clear for the reader; literature reviews are not meant to argue positions on an issue. Rather, they provide background information about what has already been said, and sometimes that is done prior to starting to develop a position on an issue. A literature review should make a point about the conversation that has taken place on the issue (Perhaps the researchers haven't considered a particular perspective? Perhaps the arguments are centering around the definition of a particular term?), but that point should not be to develop a unique position on the issue. In other words, literature reviews highlight the information that will eventually help you answer your research question, but they don't answer the research question themselves.

Many researchers find it helpful to write the basic summaries of the sources first and then look for connections among them before drafting the literature review. You must include a list of sources at the end of your literature review since the full citations will not be included in the text of the review.

Example of a Literature Review

In this next example Meridian Salazar revised her annotated bibliography of ten resources into a review of literature using nine resources. While the annotated bibliography generally just lists the resources, Meridian's review of literature has to look carefully at the connections between the sources. Pay close attention to how she puts the sources in conversation with each other and the similarities and differences she notes between them. Be sure to look for rhetorical strategies Meridian uses to move between discussions of specific topics and sources, as well as methods she uses to demonstrate her awareness of the authority and credibility of the authors she is citing.

ECOTOURISM AND THE WHALE COMMUNITY   1

Note: Since this is a classroom paper, the instructor asked for an adapted APA title page that included the date.

Meridian Salazar

April 1, 2013

Review of Literature

The Relationship Between Ecotourism

and the Whale Community

In recent years, ecotourism has been growing extensively. People are becoming more and more interested in the world around them and interacting with nature. The downfall of this newfound interest is the impact it is having on the environment and its inhabitants. One of the most popular ecotourism activities is whale watching. At every marina and beach resort you can find advertising for whale watching expeditions. Many families are more than willing to pay money for this close encounter opportunity. It's not everyday that you can see a whale in its natural habitat. These ecotourism trips provide entertainment, education, and awareness for the community and a large amount of revenue for the sponsoring companies. While these benefits are clear, a look at the changes occurring to the whale populations frequently visited by these ecotourism vessels raises concern.

You've done a great job of setting up the focus of the review of literature by highlighting the controversy in the topic.

As humans, when something unexpected happens in our lives or an unknown person invades our home, we experience stress. Animals also experience stress when these situations occur in their lives. If there is a constant stress in our lives then our immune system is compromised, and we are therefore more likely to become ill. This applies to whales as well. Constantly stressing over the presence of a tour boat in their habitat has an effect on their overall health or lifespan. We need to consider a limit on these boating excursions to alleviate some of the stress caused to these innocent marine animals. Although we have overexploited and pushed thousands of species to extinction with our activities, we never learn our lesson and still continue to participate in harmful practices toward the environment. Too often, few are concerned with a species' well being until only a handful of that species remains. We need to consider serious changes and regulations to protect our marine community from the negative effects of ecotourism.

Did any of your sources back up this assertion?

Great use of a topic sentence to transition from your description of the issue to your overview of published research.

Several studies have investigated the effects of whale watching on surrounding whale populations. Erbe (2002) observed and researched the impact that ecotourism boats were having on the killer whale

ECOTOURISM AND THE WHALE COMMUNITY   2

population in southern British Columbia and northwestern Washington State. He used an impact assessment model and a software sound propagation to determine how intense the interference of boating noise was on whale communication and to what degree it caused behavioral avoidance and hearing loss (Erbe, 2002). He found that fast-moving boats had worse effects on whales and their behaviors compared to slow-moving boats. He also found that an excessive amount of boats circling whales caused them to have long-term hearing loss with extensive exposure (Erbe, 2002). Hearing loss for whales is a serious problem because it diminishes their communication with other whales and, therefore, affects their mating and hunting skills (Erbe, 2002).

> You've done a nice job of consistently using in-text citations to let readers know where information originated. Make sure you include a citation in every sentence that includes information from an outside source.

Sousa-Lima and Clark (2009) conducted a study concerning boating noise as well; they investigated its effects on the humpback whales in a Brazilian marine park. Their main focus was the effect of ecotourism boating noise on the vocalization of whales in that area. To collect their data they sent four pop-ups into the water that could record all noise for the duration of their study. The researchers began the study out of concern for the whales' reproductive success because male humpback whales use vocalization for reproductive display. Since boating noise can mask some of the important sounds or qualities in a whale's communication, this is a big concern. Their study lasted three months and the results showed that all of the whales left the area or moved great distances away when the boats came near them. Some of the whales, 44.5%, also ceased vocal activity when the boats were present and usually didn't resume for another 20 minutes (Sousa-Lima & Clark, 2009). A total of 55.5% of the whales continued their vocal activity while moving away (Sousa-Lima & Clark, 2009).

> This sentence makes a helpful connection to the previous paragraph and the previously mentioned study.

Clark, Simmonds, and Williams-Grey (2007) investigated other short-term behavioral differences such as changes in dive times/depth, direction, swim speed, and changes in acoustic behavior. The changes in dive times, depth, and swim speed are all avoidance strategies created by the whales in an attempt to escape commercial boating. Changes in acoustic behavior, however, were the result of boating noises being so loud that they masked the whales' communication and feeding signals. Richter, Dawson, and Slooten (2006) also conducted a study prior to Clark, Simmonds, and Williams-Grey (2007) that investigated behavioral changes such as blow intervals

> This is another helpful connection for readers to the previously mentioned research that shows how this study contrasts from them.

ECOTOURISM AND THE WHALE COMMUNITY   3

and time at the surface, but their data showed the effects to be less detrimental. Their study lasted three years and the results yielded that while sperm whales off Kaikoura do respond to ecotourism activities, the changes brought on by the activity are small. They also noticed that resident whales were less responsive to whale watching activities than transient whales; they speculated that this could be the result of habituation (Ricter, et al., 2006).

While habituation minimizes distress effects, habituation itself is not the answer. A more significant decrease in distress effects can be achieved with stricter regulations. Chion, Cantin, Dionne, Dubeau, Lamontagne, Landry, Marceau, Martins, Menard, Michaud, Parrott, and Turgeon (2013) recently studied the regulatory aspect of ecotourism. In their research they used a newly developed Agent-Based Model (ABM) called the Marine Mammal and Maritime Traffic Simulator. This ABM evaluates the benefits of new rules compared to the current standing ones. To effectively use the ABM, three areas of sustainable development needed to be examined. These included the impact on whales, the whale-watching companies, and the tourist experience. It was found that there would only be a minimal impact on ecotourism due to new rules studied by Chion, et al (2013), but they would improve the tourist experience and whale conservation. Sustainability of whale populations and the companies supporting ecotourism activities involving the species is also a concern of Valentine, Birtles, Curnock, Arnold, and Dunstane (2004). Their 2004 study focused on the growing popularity of the new ecotourism "swim with the whales" operation. They discussed the nature and development of this practice thoroughly because this new activity raises a lot of concern for long-term management. After observing and investigating the new activity they found that new regulations would need to be put in place to sustain the whale population and the companies supporting it.

To effectively sustain the marine environment and its inhabitants, maritime regulations must be strictly followed. Unfortunately, this is not always the case. Wiley, Moller, Pace, and Carlson (2008) had suspicions that companies weren't abiding by the restrictions set for whale watching tours so they decided to inspect companies that were in the northeast region of the United States. This area has a voluntary conservation

You've shifted your focus here, and these two sentences set up a transition to talking about the potential solutions to the problem instead of the effects. Great job!

Would it be helpful to readers to summarize what those new rules were?

ECOTOURISM AND THE WHALE COMMUNITY   4

program for ecotourism and although companies had joined this program, it was questionable whether or not they followed the rules. The program has in place 3 speed zones within specified distances to whales. The goal of Wiley, et al. (2008) was to determine if companies were complying with this program or if more programs or rules need to be set in place to ensure efficacy. They gathered volunteers to travel on the whale watching tours of these companies and collect data on their speed and distances from whales. They found that all companies approached their maximum speed in speed zones and that many companies were noncompliant with the restrictions (Wiley, et al., 2008).

There are some ecotourism companies however, who are concerned with protecting the whales and have put in place their own conservation regulations. This is currently happening in Baja. PBS aired a documentary about their conservation efforts in the lagoon (2009). Gray whales travel to this lagoon during the winter to breed. In this area, several groups have come together in collaboration to protect the whales and other marine life in the lagoon. They have created an observation area for the whales and dolphins in which they only allow 16 boats in at a time and for only 90 minutes each. If the whales and other marine life are outside of the observation area then they cannot be followed or disturbed by tourists or boats. There are no exceptions to these rules. All of the organizations here regulate each other to ensure that everyone abides by these regulations.

Whale-watching tours are a huge source of revenue for many companies. Limiting the number of boats allowed to view the whales at one time, putting a restriction on the speed that the vessels can travel in the viewing areas, or putting a cap on the number of excursions allowed in one day could significantly lower their profits. Some non-governmental organizations also support the whale watching industry, mainly for four reasons. These reasons are that observation encourages conservation, ecotourism boats serve as locations for research, viewing animals in the wild is better than viewing animals in captivity, and it is an alternative to whaling that is economical (Corkeron, 2004). Whale conservation organizations however, argue that economic profit should not be put before the wellness and protection of marine species. The damaging effects to the whale community could lead to declines in their population and with prolonged intense exposure, their extinction.

Your concluding paragraph pulls together the research in the review of literature and draws conclusions about what it tells readers about the issue. Nicely done!

ECOTOURISM AND THE WHALE COMMUNITY   5

References

Chion, C., Cantin, G., Dionne, S., Dubeau, B., Lamontagne, P., Landry, J., . . . Turgeon, S. (2013). Spatiotemporal modelling for policy analysis: Application to sustainable management of whale-watching activities. *Marine Policy*, *38*, 151–162. doi:10.1016/j.marpol.2012.05.031

Clark, J., Simmonds, M., & Williams-Grey, V. (2007). Close encounters: whale watching in the UK. *Biologist*, *54*(3), 134–141.

Corkeron, P. J. (2004). Whale watching, iconography, and marine conservation. *Conservation Biology*, *18*(3), 847–849. doi:10.1111/j.1523-1739.2004.00255.x

Erbe, C. (2002). Underwater noise of whale-watching boats and potential effects on Killer whales (Orcinus orca), based on an acoustic impact model. *Marine Mammal Science*, *18*(2), 394.

PBS. (2009). *Saving the ocean: Destination Baja* [Video file]. Retrieved from http://video.pbs.org/video/2286020756/

Richter, C., Dawson, S., & Slooten, E. (2006). Impacts of commercial whale watching on male sperm whales at Kaikoura, New Zealand. *Marine Mammal Science*, *22*(1), 46–63.

Sousa-Lima, R. S., & Clark, C. W. (2009). Whale sound recording technology as a tool for assessing the effects of boat noise in a Brazilian marine park. *Park Science*, *26*(1), 1–7.

Valentine, P. S., Birtles, A., Curnock, M., Arnold, P., & Dunstane, A. (2004). Getting close to whales--passenger expectations and experiences, and the management of swim with dwarf minke whale interactions in the Great Barrier Reef. *Tourism Management*, *25*(6), 647–655. doi:10.1016/j.tourman.2003.09.001

Wiley, D. N., Moller, J. C., Pace, R. M., & Carlson, C. (2008). Effectiveness of voluntary conservation agreements: Case study of endangered whales and commercial whale watching. *Conservation Biology*, *22*(2), 450–457. doi:10.1111/j.1523-1739.2008.00897.x

> Unless you accessed articles in print publications, you need to include the digital publication information. If your article is from a database, you should either include a DOI, or if you can't find a DOI, look up the URL (web address) of the journal. Do not include the URL from the database.

Discussion Questions

▶ How do the forms of a literature review and an annotated bibliography differ? What are some of the key similarities?

▶ Do you think an annotated bibliography or a literature review would be the best choice for your project? Why?

- How well does the author of this essay explain the conversation taking place about environmental concerns related to whale watching?
- What suggestions would you make to the author in terms of the resources included in the literature review? Would you recommend she look at any other perspectives?
- Based on the instructor's comments made in the example, what seems to be a common difficulty authors struggle with while writing a review of literature?

Steps to Developing a Review of Research

For this assignment, your task is to develop a list of resources that provide a picture of the developing conversation on the issue that you are researching. You might do that in the form of an annotated bibliography and/or a literature review. Regardless of the form that your review of research takes, all reviews of research should include the following features:

- a clearly focused issue, ideally articulated in a research question
- a variety of sources that show a multitude of perspectives and a snapshot of the developing conversation (pay attention to any requirements from your instructor about the number or types of resources you should include)
- summaries of resources and perhaps some evaluation of them
- citations for all resources, listed in a consistent and appropriate documentation style

You will likely follow four major steps in completing your review of research: first, searching for resources; second, summarizing and annotating your resources; third, organizing your review of research; and fourth, checking documentation.

Searching for Resources

Your first task is to find a group of resources that will give a sense of how people are discussing your issue. Depending on the nature of the assignment you have been given by your instructor, your list might be a representative sample of resources or a comprehensive list. Your instructor might also give you specific instructions about what types of resources to include (academic peer-reviewed journal articles, for example), or a minimum number of resources to include in your review of research. If you do not have such guidelines, we recommend including at least seven resources so that you will get a balanced perspective on your issue. Additionally, you should strive to find resources from a variety of publications and types of venues.

As you search, we recommend tracking your resources very carefully. You can follow the guidelines for tracking resources in Chapter 6, or you might start by at least keeping a table or spreadsheet that includes a column with each of the following types of information:

- basic bibliographic information
- summary notes
- themes in the resource
- keywords
- methods used (especially if the resource describes a research study)
- the kinds of evidence referred to in the resource
- other research referred to (so you can easily tie resources together if you are writing a literature review).

Here are some additional activities to try as you search for resources:

- ❿ "Write: Develop a List of Search Terms," on page 75 of Chapter 4
- ❿ "Write: Search the Library Catalog," on page 82 of Chapter 4
- ❿ "Write: Search for Resources in Periodicals," on page 84 of Chapter 4
- ❿ "Write: Search for a Variety of Resources," on page 88 of Chapter 4
- ❿ "Reflect: What's Your Plan?" on page 91 of Chapter 4
- ❿ "Reflect: What Does Your Research Plan Look Like Now?" on page 110 of Chapter 5

Summarizing and Annotating Your Resources

Your annotated bibliography or literature review will list the resources you have found, providing information about each one in the form of short summaries and perhaps descriptions of the rhetorical situation of the resource. Once you have found a list of resources that you think you would like to include, you will need to read them and write summaries.

In an annotated bibliography, a paragraph of summary is usually expected, and that summary should include information about the findings of the resource. Your instructor might also ask you to include other information in your annotations and/or your literature review. Some common things to include are evaluations of resources, information about the rhetorical situations represented, comments about how the resources might be used in your own research, or notes about how the resources link together.

In a literature review, summaries are sometimes a paragraph long, but they are generally discussed in the context of other sources (see Organizing, below). As you write summaries for a literature review, it might help to write a one-sentence summary and a one-paragraph summary for each of your sources. You can then choose how much to include about each source in your final literature review based on the importance of the resource to your research.

Activities to do as you summarize and annotate:

- ❿ "Write: Choose Resources to Read," on page 115 of Chapter 6
- ❿ "Write: Situate a Resource Rhetorically," on page 116 of Chapter 6
- ❿ "Write: Annotate a Resource," on page 118 of Chapter 6
- ❿ "Write: Summarize One of Your Resources," on page 120 of Chapter 6

Organizing Your Review of Research

The organization of your review of research will depend largely on whether you are writing an annotated bibliography or a literature review. If you are writing an annotated bibliography, resources should be listed in alphabetical order unless you explicitly choose another organization (by topic, for example). Before you choose an alternate organizing structure for your annotated bibliography, you should discuss it with your instructor. Some lengthy annotated bibliographies also include subheadings that organize resources according to topics or themes within the larger structure.

If you are writing a literature review, then you should determine whether you want to organize your resources chronologically or thematically, depending on the main point you want to make about the research conducted on your issue. What story do you want to tell about the research? A literature review should make a point about the resources included, so organize your resources around that idea or theme.

Organizing your resources will help you map out the perspectives you have researched so that you can determine what patterns are starting to emerge. You will also be able to determine if you might be missing important perspectives or have an imbalance of resources reflecting a particular perspective.

Activities to do as you organize your review of research:

▶ **Timeline.** Consider developing a timeline to map the progression of research on your issue. Looking at your resources chronologically can help you track the development of research on your issue over time as you consider how to put the resources in dialogue in a literature review. Developing your timeline through an interactive online application such as Timeglider (http://www.timeglider.com) can help you track your resources as you write about them. You can embed links, videos, and other media into your timeline as you write.

▶ **Cluster Map.** Another tool for sorting and organizing your sources is a cluster map. You might try drawing a simple cluster map, as discussed in Chapter 2, or you might try creating your map on the computer, as discussed in Chapter 9.

Checking Documentation

You should follow a consistent documentation style throughout your review of research. In Chapter 11, we discuss how to choose the documentation style that fits your rhetorical situation. You should also speak with your instructor about his or her expectations for which documentation style you will use. See Chapters 11–15 for specific guidelines on different citation styles.

Activities to do as you check your documentation:

▶ "Techno Tip: Format a Document," on page 246 of Chapter 11
▶ "Write: Practice Citations," on page 251 of Chapter 11

Make It with Multiple Media:
Hyperlinked Review of Literature

Many of the resources you use for your research might be available online, either through a library database or a public web site. One way to digitally track your resources and develop your annotated bibliography at the same time is through a social bookmarking tool such as Diigo. Diigo allows you to bookmark resources online, annotate them, and put them together in a list for future reference. The bookmarks will provide readers with hyperlinks to the digital resources.

You might also post your annotated bibliography as a hypertext document that provides links to the digital resources. You can do the same thing with a digital review of literature as well. Meridian Salazar could have made a research project portfolio website that included digital versions of her review of literature and annotated bibliography. In this instance, the links in the review of literature link to the specific resources in the annotated bibliography. The links in the annotated bibliography link out to the digital versions of the text, as shown on page 164.

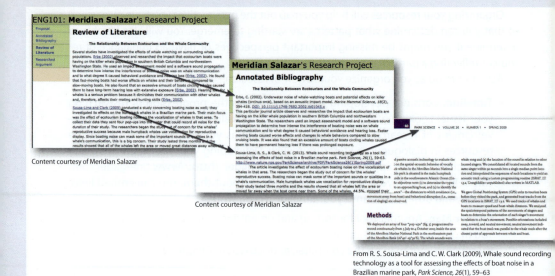

Content courtesy of Meridian Salazar

Content courtesy of Meridian Salazar

From R. S. Sousa-Lima and C. W. Clark (2009), Whale sound recording technology as a tool for assessing the effects of boat noise in a Brazilian marine park, *Park Science*, *26*(1), 59–63

You could also post your annotated bibliography in a timeline. This would also allow you to include images and, depending on the timeline application, videos as well. Sometimes it is nice to see a chronological display of your resources; you might see a gap that needs filling. We made a timeline version of Amelia Cooper's annotated bibliography.

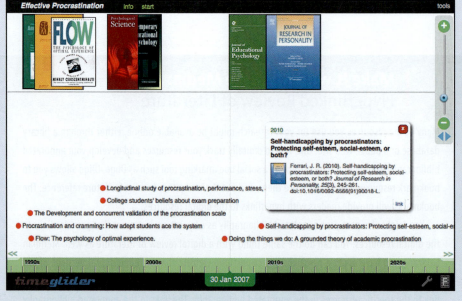

chapter 8

Developing an Argument

The research scenario described on the next page might be similar to assignments you have had or will have in college. Sam knows that there are a number of issues related to political science that he could write about for his college class. Likewise, there are a variety of ways he could approach an argument on the subject he chooses, a Supreme Court case. Sam will have to consider the rhetorical situation of his project while researching and writing, and he will also have to consider elements of how to construct a convincing argument based on the data he finds. As you read the research scenario, consider how Sam's rhetorical situation might shape his research and writing. How would you go about developing a researched argument in response to this assignment?

we'll explore

▶ *responding to the research question*

▶ *developing a thesis*

▶ *constructing an argument through ethos, pathos, and logos*

▶ *considering counterarguments*

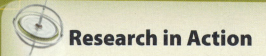

Research in Action

Author: Sam is a college student, taking his first class for his political science major. Sam wants to go to law school when he finishes his undergraduate degree.

© Photofusion Picture Library/Al—

Topic: Sam's professor for the course has assigned an end-of-semester paper that must present an argument about a legal issue that has been discussed in class and has been heard by the courts. The only guideline is that the topic should deal with something controversial and current, an issue that has been in the news within the last ten years. Students must take a position on the court's decision and argue for their position using their knowledge of legal precedence.

Audience: Sam's audience is his professor.

Purpose: Sam decides to write a report on a court case that is of particular interest to him, but he's in the awkward position of reporting on a topic to someone who already knows quite a bit about it. In his textbook, he read about a Supreme Court case from 2006 that dealt with whether or not college campuses could ban military recruiters. He thought he might be interested in learning more about it because he had two connections to the case: he is of legal draft age and the controversy took place on a law school campus.

Questions

1. What are the various elements of the rhetorical situation in this research scenario? How do they impact one another?

2. Where could Sam look for specific information about the case he is researching, and where might he look for information on related court cases?

3. In what ways could Sam develop his argument, and where should he start?

4. What kinds of strategies might help Sam organize the ideas and information he has gathered?

5. Have you ever been assigned a paper and you felt you had lots of information but didn't quite know how to organize it all and where to start writing a draft? What did you do?

Reporting versus Arguing

Sam faces another challenge—when he first sits down to write a draft, he finds himself primarily summarizing the background information for the case and the things that different people have said about the case and the decision. He writes about three pages when he decides to visit the campus writing center to see if he is on the right track. At the writing center, a tutor reads what he wrote, and she points out that he isn't really "arguing" for a position on the case yet but is "reporting" what others have said. Sam needs to figure out one legal issue to focus on, his position on it, and how to defend it. He is spending too much time summarizing his research instead of using it to defend his position. The tutor suggests he reconsider his goal in writing the paper to make sure that he is actually accomplishing it.

Table 8.1 gives some examples of activities that generally fall into either the reporting or the arguing category.

TABLE 8.1. Reporting versus Arguing

Reporting	Arguing
Summarizing	Interpreting
Paraphrasing	Analyzing
Quoting	Concluding
Describing	Claiming
Telling	Persuading

Sam realizes that he is probably writing a lot of summary because he is learning about the case himself, but he probably doesn't need to include all of the summary in his final draft because his audience (his professor) is already familiar with the specifics of the case. He needs to refocus his writing on the purpose of the assignment, but the writing he has already finished is helping him understand some of the controversial issues surrounding the case. The tutor suggests that Sam consider some of this writing to be part of his invention; he should keep all of it for later reference, but he might not include it all in his final draft.

Many of us need to revisit the rhetorical situation of our writing when we begin interpreting our research and drafting. Sam's preliminary writing and summarizing is useful because it helps him to identify and understand the controversy surrounding his issue. At this point in his writing, though, he needs to refocus and pick one aspect of the controversy to defend in an argument. Sam also realizes, though (as you might realize when you complete the "Reflect: Is It Reporting or Arguing?" activity), that when summarizing and reporting on a topic, he is presenting a version (or an interpretation) of what he has read and learned; therefore, he is starting to present a kind of argument. In other words, he is implicitly arguing what he thinks is important about the topic (what he includes) and what does not matter (what he excludes). Sam is pretty certain that this type of argument isn't what his professor is looking for in this paper, though; he needs to refocus his draft on a more explicit claim about the Supreme Court case. After conducting in-depth research on an issue and looking at so many people's perspectives, it can be easy to lose the original focus of the writing task. One of the best things to do as you sit down to write is to remind yourself of the rhetorical situation.

reflect

Is It Reporting or Arguing?

To help distinguish between texts that report and texts that argue, list the various pieces of writing you have completed in the past six months or so. Then label each of them as either something you reported (such as an email with show times for a movie at the local theater) or something you argued (for example, an email claiming that you should watch one film instead of another on the upcoming Friday night). In other words, was the primary goal to provide information to your audience (reporting) or to persuade your audience (argument)? Ask yourself the following questions to help create your list and identify your writing as either reporting or arguing.

▶ What pieces of writing have you done for school? your job? in your personal and home life? in your civic or community life?

▶ What was the purpose for the piece of writing? What was its goal?

▶ Who was your audience for the piece of writing? What did you want your audience to do after reading your text?

In your list, circle the writing experience that you are most confident was reporting, circle another experience that you are most confident was arguing, and circle a third that you had the most difficult time labeling as either reporting or arguing. Discuss these three experiences with a friend or classmate. Does your friend or classmate agree with your labeling? Why or why not?

write

Define the Rhetorical Situation

Before you start to dig into drafting, take a moment to remind yourself of your rhetorical situation. This activity will help to focus your thoughts as you begin to write. It will also give you the chance to rethink some elements of the rhetorical situation that might have shifted as you conducted your research. For example, you might have come across some resources that suggested a specific, different audience than you had originally imagined. Use this as an opportunity to fine-tune your focus before developing a direction for your argument and a complete draft. Write down your answers to the following questions.

▶ What is the research question you are trying to answer? If you need to rephrase or refocus the research question, this is a good time to do so.

▶ What is your purpose for researching and writing about this issue? Consider multiple purposes that you might have, and try to list them in order of priority.

- Who is the audience you are addressing? Be specific and describe as much as you can. Also consider the possibility that you might be addressing direct and implicit audiences in your research and writing.

- How do you fit into the context? In other words, how might your beliefs and understanding affect what you write and how you interpret your resources?

- Where do your answers to these four questions overlap? How might those overlapping answers further focus your research topic?

Once you have written responses to these questions and/or completed the Venn diagram below, consider sharing them with a classmate, friend, parent, or coworker. Encourage the person to ask you questions that will help to refine your focus.

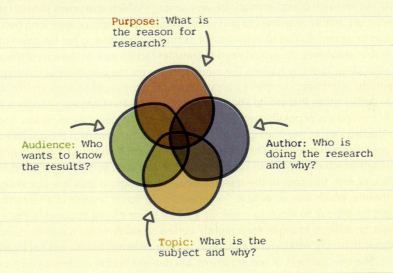

Purpose: What is the reason for research?

Audience: Who wants to know the results?

Author: Who is doing the research and why?

Topic: What is the subject and why?

Responding to the Research Question

Arguments are often, at their cores, responses to questions. Sometimes the questions are asked directly and sometimes they are implied. In the case of the research that Sam is doing, and in the research that you are completing, the argument is developed in response to the original research question. As you plan how you will respond to your research question, consider what the answers might be, what responses might work best for your purpose and audience, and what you can support with the evidence and resources you have found. This is the point in the research process where all of your work starts to come together.

A clear focus on your research question and rhetorical situation, along with an understanding of the resources you have gathered on your topic, will help you generate a list of possible responses to your research question. Sam wants to focus his research question on the Supreme Court decision in *Rumsfeld v. Forum for Academic and Institutional Rights, Inc.* As he began his research, however, he quickly discovered that the Court had been unanimous in its opinion, so perhaps it wouldn't make sense for him to develop an argument for or against the Court's decision. The Court had ruled that institutions of higher education who receive federal funding must allow military recruiting on campus. Sam began to wonder if there were any circumstances in which military recruiting could be banned, so he drafted the following research question:

> Under what circumstances could an institution of higher education ban military recruiting on campus?

By looking through resources dealing with earlier courts' decisions on the case, as well as reading the Court's final decision, Sam was able to begin drafting a list of possible responses to his research question.

Generating possible responses to a research question is important in other kinds of research as well. For example, imagine someone who is looking for her first apartment to rent. Her research question might be very simple ("Which apartment should I rent?"), but her list of possible responses to that research question might be very long because there would be several factors to consider. For example, in narrowing her list down to the "supportable" responses, she would need to consider factors such as the cost of the apartment in view of her monthly budget, the safety of the area, the possibility of sharing the apartment, the apartment complex's policy on pets, her commute to work and/or school, and many other issues that would affect her final decision. Her first step, though, is to find out all of the options, or possible responses to the question. Then she can narrow down her list.

The first step in developing your argument is to consider all of the possible responses to your research question. Then you must decide which answers fit your rhetorical situation and which ones you can support with the evidence you have gathered. Part of the difficulty with this step in the research process, though, is that it is not always easy to determine which answer is best. Sometimes a particular answer to a research question might be difficult to argue to a specific audience, but it's not impossible. For example, it might be difficult to argue for a nightly curfew to students on a college campus (more difficult than, say, making the argument to their parents), but it's not necessarily impossible. The effectiveness of the argument will depend on the evidence you provide, how appropriate and convincing it is to your audience, and how you develop your argument. Once you have generated a list of possible responses that is narrowed down to those that are *reasonable*, *supportable*, and *feasible* for your rhetorical situation, the next step is to choose one response and develop it into an effective thesis.

write

Create a Cluster Map

To focus on thinking of the possible ways to respond to your research question and then generate a position that you could support, we suggest putting your responses in a cluster map, like the one in Figure 8.1. In order to complete this activity, you will need access to your gathered resources, along with your previous writing and brainstorming about your rhetorical situation. Write your answers to the following prompts, working through them in order.

1. What is your research question? Write it down. Make this the central bubble in your cluster map.

2. Think of all of the possible answers to your research question. Start by responding with what you know and have learned from researching the issue. Take a look at some of your resources to see how others have responded to this issue and if there are possible answers you should add to the cluster map. There's no need to put specific details about how you would support the answers at this point; just generate all of the responses you can. You might also share your research question with someone else—a classmate, friend, or other person interested in this issue. Ask them to help you generate responses that are not already on your map. Make these responses the branches that generate from the central bubble on your cluster map.

3. Now start to narrow down the list. Start by considering the purpose of your research—why are you completing this research? Take a look at your possible answers (the branches) and cross off all that do not accomplish this purpose.

4. Consider the resources you have gathered on your topic. At this point, consider which responses you could actually defend and support with meaningful, reliable evidence. Try listing resources as branches of responses to the research question on the cluster map. Cross off all responses that you think you would have difficulty supporting.

5. Consider the audience for your research. Which responses to your research question would be most feasible to that audience? Who will read or hear your research? What do they already know and think about the topic? Which responses to your research question could you support and defend to your audience? Consider the research you have gathered on your issue, and think about what evidence your audience might find convincing. Cross off all responses that you do not think you could effectively argue to your audience.

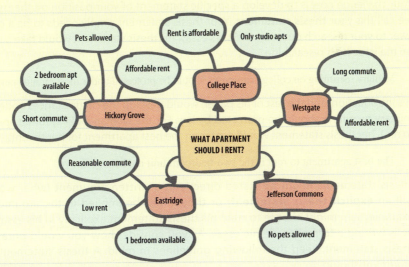

Figure 8.1   Cluster Map of Apartment Options

Your cluster map probably resembles the one in Figure 8.2 at this point, showing fewer possible answers, and maybe even the one answer you want to pursue. For more help with cluster maps, see Chapter 2.

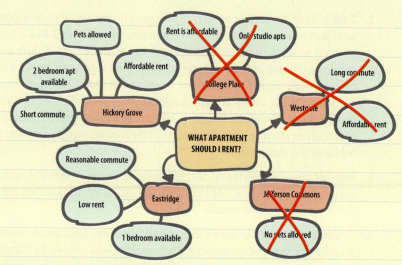

Figure 8.2   Narrowing Down the Possibilities

Developing a Thesis

At this point in your research, you have considered different possible responses to your research question and narrowed your list down to those that you think you could defend. Your challenge now is to develop a specific statement of your position on the issue, and we call this your **thesis statement.** Your thesis statement simply needs to be a clear answer to your research question. In Sam's essay, his thesis statement would take a position on the issue he is researching.

> Military recruiting on college campuses should be protected under most circumstances.

His introduction, and the rest of his paper, would develop the circumstances under which military recruiting should be protected by law. For the woman looking for an apartment to rent, her thesis statement would center on the best apartment for her to rent.

> The best apartment to rent is the two-bedroom unit at Hickory Grove.

Thesis statements might be stated directly in a written argument (what we would call an **explicit thesis statement**) or they might be implied in the argument. For example, Sam might choose to state his thesis statement explicitly in his essay, since he is writing a formal academic essay. As you consider how you would phrase your thesis statement, keep the following guidelines in mind. A thesis statement for an argument should

- be a statement and not a question.
- make a precise claim and not be merely a statement of fact or observation.
- be clear, avoiding unspecific language.

Depending on your rhetorical situation, your thesis statement most likely should also

- be a complex statement, not simply a "yes" or "no" answer to your research question.
- give your audience an idea of what to expect in your argument.

Sam's thesis statement is somewhat vague, so he should either clarify the circumstances he is talking about in the introduction or revise his thesis statement to be clearer. As you draft your thesis statement, you might think of it as containing two parts: the precise claim itself and the reasons for your claim. You might not include the reasons in an explicit thesis statement in your argument, but for now it will be helpful in thinking about how to defend your claim to consider and write down your reasons for that claim.

Example Thesis Statement 1

Precise Claim: The best apartment to rent is the two-bedroom unit at Hickory Grove.

- **Reason:** It has the shortest commute to my office.
- **Reason:** The apartment complex welcomes pets.
- **Reason:** The rent is reasonable for my monthly budget.

Example Thesis Statement 2

Precise Claim: ABC University should enforce a nightly curfew for students.

- **Reason:** Violent crime on campus has escalated after 1 A.M. in recent years.
- **Reason:** Students would study more for classes.
- **Reason:** Students would sleep more.

A thesis statement can also do more than simply answer the original research question.

- It could identify areas that will be developed in the argument, providing a basic outline for the argument itself. This might be the case for Example 1 if the three reasons are listed as a "because" statement after the claim:

    The best apartment to rent is the two-bedroom unit at Hickory Grove because it has the shortest commute to my office, the apartment complex welcomes pets, and the rent is reasonable for my monthly budget.

- It could invite the audience to take action on the thesis statement or to be part of a solution to a problem. This might be the case for Example 2 if the argument is directed toward administrators at the university.

The way you choose to write your thesis statement, of course, depends on your specific rhetorical situation.

write

Draft a Thesis Statement

As you work on this activity, keep your original research question in front of you along with your list (or cluster map) of possible responses. Use these steps to draft the two parts of your thesis statement (your claim and your reasons). Keep in mind that your claim is the answer to your research question, and the reasons could be thought of as "because" statements that support the claim. Read the example, and use it as a guide to write your own thesis statement.

>>>

>>>

Sample research question: Should a law be passed to make English the official language of the United States?

Precise claim: Congress should pass a law making English the official language of the United States.

Reasons/blueprint:

▶ A common language would encourage unity among citizens.

▶ Learning English is empowering to people because of its status in global communication.

Complete thesis statement: Congress should pass a law making English the official language of the United States because it would encourage unity among citizens and empower people to participate in global communication.

Now it's your turn. Write your responses to the following prompts for your research project.

▶ **Research question:**
_____

_____

▶ **Precise claim:**
_____

_____

▶ **Reasons/blueprint:**
_____

_____

▶ **Complete thesis statement:**
_____

_____

Note: Even if you choose not to use both the claim and the reasons in your thesis statement, you have begun supporting your argument by developing the complete thesis statement.

Using Qualifiers

As you develop your argument, you will realize that there are often exceptions to any claim and line of reasoning. One way to address a potential exception is to offer a **qualifier**, a word or phrase that "hedges" or limits the claim. Consider Sam's thesis statement again: Military recruiting on college campuses should be protected under most circumstances. Sam used the qualifier "most" to allow for circumstances where military recruiting is not, or should not, be protected. In the case of Example 2 in the previous section, the thesis might be written in any of the following ways:

▶ ABC University should suggest a nightly curfew for students.

▶ ABC University should enforce a nightly curfew for freshmen and sophomores.

▶ ABC University might consider a nightly curfew for students.

Each of these thesis statements has a slightly different meaning based on the qualifiers. Sometimes qualifiers are simply words that are included in a claim or reason in order to allow for an exception. Such qualifiers include words like *often*, *generally*, *usually*, *most*, and *many* (instead of definitive words such as *always* and *all*). For example, in the first sentence of this section, we used the word *often* to qualify our claim that there are exceptions to any claim and line of reasoning. It would probably (another qualifier) be too strong a statement to say that there is *always* an exception to a claim or line of reasoning. On other occasions, it might be more appropriate to include a phrase or sentence as a qualifier for a claim or even an entire section of the paper as a qualifier for the argument. For example, someone arguing that parents should spank their children might offer a qualifier that spanking should only be used under certain circumstances or done in a certain way.

Using qualifiers in the development of an argument can be tricky, however. You don't want to discredit the argument that you have developed by qualifying it too much or in a way that makes it less persuasive. You might even consider trying different versions of your claim and reasons—with qualifiers, without qualifiers, and with different kinds of qualifiers—on a willing listener to see how he or she responds.

reflect

Can You Recognize Qualifiers?

Most scholars leave a little wiggle room in their arguments because they've seen too many exceptions to the rule. Writers also know that if they are discussing a heated subject, they must provide qualifiers as a form of ethos, acknowledging there are almost always exceptions.

Practice identifying qualifiers by looking at the beginning of this article about women's body types from *Psychology Today*. How do they qualify their claims? What terms do they use to allow for exceptions and dissent? What qualifiers function to leave "logical" space for exceptions? Which qualifiers function to develop an ethos that the author knows there are always exceptions?

Eternal Curves[1]

Men "know" something significant about women's bodies that women don't. And it all has to do with nature's mandate to produce children with the greatest array of survival skills. Sculptors immortalize them. Poets regularly regale them. Even ordinary men pay tribute. American males, it has been calculated, spend some $3 billion a year to gaze at women with hourglass figures, those whose small waists blossom into sinuously curvy hips.

Men rate women as most attractive when they have a waist size that is 60 to 70 percent of their hip size, the late psychologist Devendra Singh found in a series of pioneering studies begun 20 years ago. And in more than a hundred other studies, men all over the world—including isolated groups unexposed to modern media—prefer a similar shape. Singh and cognitive neuroscientist Steven Platek found that viewing women with curvy figures stimulates a powerful internal reward system, lighting up the same pleasure centers in men's brains that are targeted by cocaine and heroin.

That this kind of hourglass figure is not only typical of the women men pay to look at, such as *Playboy* Playmates and adult film stars, but is also a preference found in many different social groups and cultural settings, suggests it has been shaped over millennia by evolutionary forces, like our tastes for sugar and fat. The preferred women are remarkably alike, and the similarity of their measurements and men's reactions to them further suggests that there is a specific template buried deep in men's minds.

It is likely that men who preferred curvy hourglass figures in women had more children who carried their fathers' preferences down to the present. Still, how could an hourglass figure relate to a woman's success as a mother? The answer is not at all obvious. But over the past several years, we have been demonstrating that it has a lot to do with intelligence. And just as much to do with what people eat and where it comes from. The evidence also suggests why American women increasingly dislike their bodies and misjudge what men like in women. It may even explain why American children fare increasingly poorly academically compared with kids in the rest of the world.

What it comes down to, in a word, is fat. But not just any fat.

---

1   Lassek, Will, Steve Gaulin, and Estroff Marano. "Eternal Curves" *Psychology Today*, last modified July 3, 2012, http://www.psychologytoday.com/articles/201206/eternal-curves

Supporting an Argument

Once you have defined the claim that you are going to make in your argument, you need to support it with reasons and evidence. As with the other research-based writing discussed in this book, supporting an argument is rhetorically situated. You could choose from numerous methods for developing, supporting, and organizing your argument, and you could reason with your audience in many ways, based on your purpose and goal. In this chapter we will present a variety of reasoning methods you might use to support your argument.

Ethos, Pathos, and Logos

One way to support an argument is to develop specific appeals to your audience. As mentioned in Chapter 2, Aristotle defined rhetoric as searching for "the available means of persuasion." He divided what he saw as the various kinds of persuasive appeals that a speaker could make to an audience into three categories:

- **ethos**—appeals to credibility and authority
- **pathos**—appeals to emotions
- **logos**—appeals to reason and logic

You can find examples of each of these appeals all around you. If you observe a classroom immediately after a teacher has handed back a graded test, you might find several varieties of appeals (with varying degrees of persuasive success) if students are unhappy about their grades on the exam. For example, one student might appeal to ethos by pointing out a passage in the textbook that supports an answer marked as incorrect on the exam. Relying on the passage in the textbook would be an appeal to a credible authority. Another student might appeal to logos by reasoning through the different answers to a question and showing how the answer marked as correct doesn't make logical sense if interpreted in a certain way. And yet another student might appeal to pathos (probably unsuccessfully) by explaining to the teacher that he or she must get a high grade in the class to keep a scholarship. While these are somewhat flippant examples of rhetorical appeals, they illustrate different approaches that one might take in constructing an argument. Depending on the rhetorical situation, of course, some kinds of appeals may be more effective than others.

Let's consider another example. Imagine a boxing enthusiast who wants to develop an argument that Muhammad Ali was the greatest boxer of all time. She first might appeal to ethos by quoting an authority on boxing who says that Ali was the greatest boxer of all time. If she wanted to appeal to logos, she might use statistics from Ali's career record or cite and analyze an example of a specific boxing match, such as his legendary fight against George Foreman in 1974. And finally, she might appeal to pathos by describing the way that Ali overcame adversity to reestablish his career after being out of boxing for several years. Depending on the person's audience and purpose for writing, one of these appeals might be more persuasive than the others, or it might be best to include a combination of different kinds of appeals.

Ethos   Arguments based on ethos refer to the credibility and authority of an individual or a group of individuals. When providing evidence from expert or personal testimony, you are making an argument based on ethos. You, as the author of a researched argument, also need to develop your own ethos as a credible and authoritative researcher and writer. If you do not provide evidence that you have done your research carefully and systematically, your audience will not trust your results.

Much of the time *expert* credibility and authority are demonstrated through education and training. Experts usually have degrees and high positions in the field of their expertise. Sometimes, however, experts are also certified by their vast amount of experience. Degrees and highly ranked positions usually imply experience; however, some fields do not necessarily have degree programs. For example, although a water purification expert may only have an associate's degree, there are not yet many educational programs for that field. Most of the experts in water purification gain their ethos from years of experience.

Individuals who provide evidence based on *personal testimony* also have to demonstrate the ethos of the personal experience. For example, if a pre-med student were doing research on diabetes, she might find personal testimony of people diagnosed with diabetes as well as people who live with diabetics. Both groups have a certain amount of credibility and authority to discuss the topic with personal anecdotes. Obviously, a doctor who specializes in diabetes would have the ethos of an expert. Personal testimony, though, often needs to be qualified when it is used to support an argument to avoid overgeneralization.

When using arguments based on ethos, it is critically important to provide evidence of the individual's credibility and authority. The easiest way to do that is to introduce the source (e.g., an expert or an established agency), as well as its qualifications, before quoting or paraphrasing it in an argument. For example, the pre-med student writing about diabetes might include the following statement in her argument about developing an elementary school support program for diabetes:

> Both the U.S. Department of Health and Human Services (2003) and the Centers for Disease Control (2001) emphasize that schools need to take responsibility in teaching students, especially those with diabetes, about healthy eating habits.

The pre-med student would also need to develop her own ethos in researching and writing about diabetes. Her student status would give her some credibility because the audience would assume she has taken some classes that would give her more information on the topic. By providing a well thought-out, researched, developed, and organized argument about diabetes, she would provide evidence of being a careful and systematic researcher and writer.

write

Develop Your Authorial Ethos

As you begin to develop and support your argument, consider how you could construct your own ethos in the argument.

▶ What is your experience with this topic? Do you have firsthand or detailed knowledge about the topic that gives you authority to research and discuss it?

▶ What is your experience with your audience members? Do you have firsthand or detailed knowledge about them that will allow you to make explicit connections to their wants and needs?

▶ What resources have you located that demonstrate authority and credibility? Do you have resources by experts on the topic? Do you have research studies or experiments conducted by qualified researchers?

And finally, what would be most persuasive to your audience? Which members of your audience would be most persuaded by an appeal based on credibility?

Pathos   Arguments based on pathos appeal to an audience's emotions, attempting to persuade through the power of emotional response. Personal testimony can also be a way to develop pathos. If you have ever watched the president of the United States give the State of the Union address, you have most likely seen a compelling use of personal testimony as pathos because the president always has at least one special guest in attendance whose story he can tell to underscore one of his initiatives that year. A personal testimony might be an effective way to open an argument (or even to frame an argument). If the story is used to encourage an emotional response from the audience, it is an example of pathos. If it is used to develop the credibility of a source or of the argument's author, it is an example of ethos. Sometimes, of course, personal testimony can be used to do both at the same time. For example, when the president refers to the experience of a special guest in the audience at the State of the Union address, he appeals to pathos because he is drawing on the audience's emotions, and he also appeals to ethos because the guest has had personal experience with the issue at hand.

Many authors use pathos to motivate their audiences to action. For example, many of us admit that although the reward would be nice, we would not do something with extreme physical risk just to "win" a lot of money. However, many parents will put themselves into extremely risky situations to save their children from harm. Whereas the "logical" argument of earning more money does not motivate an individual, saving a family member might.

In Western culture, pathos is generally not the sole foundation of a persuasive argument. Audiences often want to be convinced based on reason (logos). However, we do see pathos used frequently in introductions and conclusions as a way to motivate audiences to read or listen to the argument and then act on it.

write

Develop Emotional Arguments

Now consider how you could incorporate appeals based on pathos into your argument. Write down your answers to the following questions.

▶ How and why are you invested in this topic? What motivates you to continue researching and writing about this topic when you are tired and worn out?

▶ How and why are your audience members invested in this topic? How does this topic affect

- ▸ your audience members' finances?
- ▸ your audience members' living situations?
- ▸ your audience's families or close circles of friends?
- ▸ your audience members' employment or employment processes?

Logos   Most academic arguments are primarily based on reasoning and logic, categorized by Aristotle as logos. Many include four major elements: claims, reasons, evidence, and warrants.

▶ **The claim** is a precise statement about your topic, usually an answer to your research question.

▶ **Reasons** are statements that demonstrate *why* your claim is valid.

▶ **Evidence** is provided to demonstrate that each reason you provide is valid. The evidence supports your claim.

▶ **Warrants** are the assumptions that the audience must accept in order to believe your reasons and evidence. Warrants are ideas, concepts, and beliefs that connect the reasons to the claim, as well as the evidence to the reasons.

Many presentations of arguments do not explicitly include all four elements; however, these elements are usually present implicitly. Because we discussed claims and reasons earlier in the section on developing your thesis, we'll jump right into talking about evidence and warrants.

Offering Evidence

Evidence can take many forms, but one thing remains consistent—evidence is an essential part of developing and supporting an argument. Evidence is the key component that persuades your audience to accept your claim. While reasons answer the audience's implied question "Why?" evidence responds to an audience that challenges you to "Prove it!" Evidence might include any of the following kinds of information (and you might be able to think of others to add to this list, based on your research topic).

▶ **Statistical data.** Although statistical data provide concrete numbers that people like to rely on in an argument, it is critical that researchers carefully check the method used to collect, interpret, and report the statistics. If the collection method is not valid, the numbers are meaningless, and the use of them to support an argument is questionably ethical.

▶ **Experimental results.** Like statistical data, many people place high credibility on the results of an experiment. And, again, like statistical data, it is important for the researcher to carefully examine the methods of conducting the experiment, as well as collecting and reporting the results.

▶ **Expert opinions.** Relying on expert testimony is useful as long as you clearly outline how and why the individual is considered an expert in that field. Be sure that your audience values those criteria of expertise. In other words, if the audience doesn't think the person is an expert, then the testimony doesn't matter.

▶ **Personal experience and/or testimony.** Sometimes research questions require feedback from people who have some experience with the topic; however, they might not necessarily be considered experts. As you would with expert opinions, carefully identify how and why a person's experience is relevant to your topic.

▶ **Observations.** Although personal observation of a person, place, or thing can be a powerful form of evidence, you have to carefully describe what you observed (who and what), the circumstances in which you observed (when and where), and your method of observation (why and how).

Just like every other choice you will make in writing and research, the selection of effective, persuasive evidence depends on the rhetorical situation. Especially consider your audience as you select which evidence to include in your argument: What would this audience find persuasive? What resources would your audience find authoritative? For example, an advertisement for a specific product might rely on one person's endorsement about how well that product works to convince potential customers to buy the product. If the product is a new type of testing kit for diabetics, then the advertisement might have someone sharing his or her personal experience that the testing kit is more reliable and hurts less than other testing kits (diabetic testing kits must have a sample of blood to read the person's blood sugar level). It will most likely be persuasive to the target audience (diabetics) if the person in the commercial is also a diabetic (ethos). However, what if the advertisement were targeting diabetics who are children? The advertisement appeals to both logos (reliability) that the parent might find attractive and pathos (less pain!) that the child having her fingers pricked would appreciate. In this case, both types of appeal arise from one type of evidence, testimony.

Researchers should select a good balance of different kinds of evidence to make an argument more persuasive to their audiences. For example, we mentioned personal testimonies as an example of ethos and pathos. Personal testimony could be used to convince your audience, but it generally won't be effective as the only piece of evidence in an argument. Even multiple personal testimonies might be insufficient. Instead, an effective argument will generally incorporate a variety of kinds of evidence from a variety of sources. For example, Sam's paper on the court case might include the following types of evidence:

▶ precise language from the ruling

▶ interpretations of the ruling by experts in the field

▶ comparisons to similar court cases

As another example, a person researching health care providers for her company might include different types of evidence in her report, such as:

▶ survey results from employees about their health care wants and needs

▶ statistics on how many other companies use a particular health care provider

▶ comparisons to similar companies who use a particular health care provider

▶ referrals from human resource specialists and other employees from companies who use a particular health care provider

Finally, the most persuasive arguments generally include a similar amount of evidence for the different reasons given in the argument. Of course, every argument has weaker and stronger points, and the stronger points can be emphasized based on the pattern of organization you choose. (See Chapter 10, "Sharing the Results," for further discussion on patterns of organization.)

A researcher should seek some balance in the argument, though. If you have three or four good pieces of evidence for one reason and only one piece of evidence for another reason (and not a very convincing piece of evidence at that), consider looking for more evidence to support that point or think about taking it out of your argument. As you seek this kind of balance in your argument, also look for a balance among elements of ethos, logos, and pathos—the most convincing arguments do not solely rely on one type of persuasion. (Chapter 9 goes into more detail about selecting and incorporating evidence into your argument, and also includes a discussion of the various kinds of evidence.)

Determining Warrants

Warrants are the connections between the claim and the reason in your argument and between a specific reason and its evidence. They are the assumptions that the audience must accept in order for a claim to seem plausible and, therefore, persuasive. Sometimes the warrant, or assumption, is one that you can assume your audience will readily accept because it is not controversial (see Example 1). If this is the case, then you could develop your argument based on that warrant without explicitly stating it or defending it. However, if the warrant itself is controversial (see Example 3), then you will need to defend the warrant before you can assume that the audience will accept and agree with your reason and/or evidence.

In the examples below, we have identified the specific claim, a reason for that claim, and the warrant, or assumption, that the audience must accept in order for the reason to support the claim.

Example 1

Claim: You should not drive while intoxicated.

Reason: Intoxicated drivers can cause serious, and often fatal, accidents.

Warrant: Situations that cause serious accidents should be avoided.

Most people would agree that serious accidents should be avoided; therefore, this warrant does not need further support in the argument.

Example 2

Claim: Cell phones should not be allowed in restaurants.

Reason: I think it's annoying to listen to people's conversations in restaurants.

Warrant: What I don't like should be eliminated.

Although many people might find use of cell phones in public somewhat annoying, most realize that one individual not liking them is not a valid reason to disallow them entirely. However, if the reason were that a large number of people do not think cell phones in restaurants are appropriate, the warrant might have more sustainability (what a lot of people do not like should be abolished).

Example 3

Claim: My father should be elected town mayor.

Reason: Our family has lived in this town for five generations.

Warrant: A candidate with a long family history in the town will make a better mayor.

In this third example, the audience may or may not agree with the warrant about family history and suitability to lead the town. This writer may need to provide some evidence to support the warrant. For example, perhaps members in this person's family have historically participated in key elements of the town's development. As a member of this family, this person has grown up knowing detailed history of the town as well as being surrounded by family members with a civic commitment to the town's well-being. Such an explanation would help to connect the reason to the claim.

While deciding whether a warrant needs further support, be sure to think about your audience. You might think the warrant is solid, but your audience might have different ideas.

Example 4

Claim: I should purchase the new iPad with more memory.

Reason: A newer technology with larger capacity is better than an older technology with less capacity.

Warrant: Bigger and newer are worth purchasing.

Are bigger and newer always better? Do people always have to have the newest thing to get the job done? If the person already has a fairly new iPad with a medium-range memory capacity, does she really need a new one? What if the audience is the parents paying for the new iPad? Would they agree with this warrant? Always double-check your warrants with your audience's specific beliefs.

Remember that these descriptions of claims, reasons, evidence, and warrants are guidelines and not a formula to follow. Each argument is different and might not follow this pattern exactly. Just use the principles to get started and develop your argument as it fits your rhetorical situation.

Understand Your Warrants

write

Revisit the complete thesis statement you have developed, the one that includes your claim and reasons. Focus on one of the reasons. As you might notice from the preceding examples, all warrants have two parts, one explicitly connected to the claim and one explicitly connected to the reason. State the warrant connecting your claim to your reason and decide whether you need to further support your warrant. Use the following questions to help articulate your warrant.

1. Does your warrant include one section for your claim and one for your reason?

2. Does your warrant sufficiently connect your reason to your claim?

3. Will your intended audience undeniably agree with your warrant? Why or why not?

If your answer is "yes" to the third question, you probably do not need to support your warrant any further. However, if your answer is "no," be sure to develop reasons and evidence to support your warrant.

After you have explicitly stated your warrant and decided whether it needs to be supported further, talk to a classmate, friend, or colleague about your claim, reason, and warrant. Do they agree that you have identified the correct warrant? Do they agree that you do or do not need to further support your warrant?

Providing Counterarguments

Sound reasoning to support your claim is key to developing your argument. However, it is often necessary to acknowledge alternative perspectives and provide counterarguments. For example, if Sam claims that military recruiting should be banned on college campuses in some circumstances, he realizes that there are many who would disagree with his opinion. If he does not acknowledge that he has accounted for these differing perspectives, readers who understand the issue might think he has not done his research well. To bolster his own ethos, it is important that Sam acknowledge alternative perspectives and then provide counterarguments that demonstrate why his perspective is better.

Sam can provide counterarguments using two methods: rebuttals and qualifiers. He could openly acknowledge an alternative perspective and offer his rebuttal. Or he could qualify his claim about military recruiting on college campuses by clarifying the circumstances under which it might be banned.

Including Rebuttals

Once you acknowledge your research topic is part of a larger conversation, you usually recognize that there are multiple perspectives on the issue. If there are very popular and well-supported perspectives that differ from your own, address them. You might also have to provide rebuttals if any of your warrants is debatable. Finally, be sure to have a classmate, friend, or family member carefully read a draft of your argument. If they come up with serious questions or concerns, you need to refute those issues as well.

write

Develop Counterarguments

Start identifying possible counterarguments. Look back over your research and identify perspectives that are different from your claim. Rank the differing perspectives from strongest (has the most validity, legitimacy, and credibility) to the weakest (is incomprehensible, unbelievable, and dismissible). Construct a rebuttal against the two strongest alternative perspectives on your list.

Once you've constructed your rebuttals, have a classmate, friend, or colleague look them over. You may also want to ask that person if they think any of the other alternative perspectives on your list require refutation.

write

Construct an Argument

This guide can help you construct your argument, and you can add and subtract elements as needed. Many writers find templates or guidelines like this helpful to start planning their written project; however, they will break away from it as the project's rhetorical situation demands.

▶ Research question: _____

▶ Answer/thesis/claim: _____

▶ Ethos: Would your audience find appeals based on ethos to be persuasive? Where and how will you demonstrate your credibility and authority as an author? _____

_____

▶ Pathos: Would your audience find appeals based on pathos to be persuasive? Where and how will you include appeals to the audience's emotions? _____

_____

>>>

>>>

▶ Logos: Would your audience find appeals based on logos to be persuasive? Where and how will you appeal to your audience through logic and reasoning? _____

_____

▶ Reason 1 _____

    Warrant connecting reason 1 to claim _____

    Evidence 1 _____

        Warrant connecting evidence 1 to reason 1 _____

    Evidence 2 _____

        Warrant connecting evidence 2 to reason 1 _____

    Evidence 3 _____

        Warrant connecting evidence 3 to reason 1 _____

▶ Reason 2 _____

    Warrant connecting reason 2 to claim _____

    Evidence 4 _____

        Warrant connecting evidence 4 to reason 2 _____

    Evidence 5 _____

        Warrant connecting evidence 5 to reason 2 _____

    Evidence 6 _____

        Warrant connecting evidence 6 to reason 2 _____

▶ Reason 3 _____

    Warrant connecting reason 3 to claim _____

    Evidence 7 _____

        Warrant connecting evidence 7 to reason 3 _____

    Evidence 8 _____

        Warrant connecting evidence 8 to reason 3 _____

    Evidence 9 _____

        Warrant connecting evidence 9 to reason 3 _____

▶ Reason 4 _____

    Warrant connecting reason 4 to claim _____

    Evidence 10 _____

        Warrant connecting evidence 10 to reason 4 _____

    Evidence 11 _____

        Warrant connecting evidence 11 to reason 4 _____

Evidence 12 _____

    Warrant connecting evidence 12 to reason 4 _____
- Objections your audience might have: .

  Objection 1 _____

    Refutation 1 _____

  Objection 2 _____

    Refutation 2 _____

  Objection 3 _____

    Refutation 3 _____

Qualifiers: Which claims, reasons, or refutations might you need to qualify? _____

_____

techno tip

Use Technology to Gather and Organize Your Evidence

You can use project management software designed for research such as Zotero (http://www.zotero.org/) or RefWorks (your institution might have a license for this application) to gather your evidence and to begin organizing it. In Chapter 6, you read about how to use project management software to track your data (see page 124, "Techno Tip: Register with a Social Bookmarking Application"). Most project management software applications that are designed for research will also help your organize your data so that you can begin structuring the evidence that you will use in your argument.

chapter 9

Selecting and Integrating Evidence

In order to develop an effective and persuasive argument, a writer must select evidence that will be convincing to the audience and relevant to the context. Each writing situation is unique, and there may be specific circumstances that a writer must consider in choosing evidence and developing reasons for his or her argument. As you constructed your argument in the previous chapter, you developed specific reasons for your position that establish your claim. For each reason, you need to provide evidence to convince your audience that the reason is valid, and the evidence will be most convincing if it comes from sources the audience values and respects.

we'll explore

▶ *evaluating your resources as possible evidence*

▶ *integrating resources into your argument*

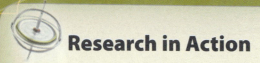
Author: Raj specializes in developing mass transit systems, and he has been working at a civil engineering firm for one year.

©Ken Hurst/Shutterstock

Topic: His firm would like to bid on a project to develop a light rail system for commuters, and he has been charged with the task of leading the team that will develop and submit the proposal.

Audience: Raj has at least two primary audiences: the city government, who would award the project, and his supervisors at the engineering firm, who will be interested in his performance in leading a project team and his success in the proposal process.

Purpose: Raj must write a successful bid that will carefully balance the needs of commuters, the desires of city planners, and the requirements of a structurally sound and efficient light rail system.

Questions

1. What types of resources and evidence does Raj need to find for each audience?

2. How will Raj decide what evidence is appropriate for each audience?

3. Have you ever needed to meet the needs of different audiences within one writing project?

4. If so, how did you identify the resources and evidence you needed for the different audiences?

5. Were there types of evidence that members of your audience absolutely had to have? Were there types of evidence that members of your audience absolutely would not accept?

Developing Project-Specific Evaluation Criteria

To choose the evidence you will incorporate into your argument, you need to evaluate the resources you have found and select the ones that are most appropriate to your rhetorical situation. Because each writing and research situation is distinct, you need to develop evaluation criteria that are specific to your project. You must consider what evidence your audience will find most convincing and what is most appropriate to the topic and argument you are making. You must also consider issues such as audience and purpose, but you might also consider timeliness and relevance, as well as other criteria applicable to your project.

Audience and Purpose

Raj is addressing multiple audiences in his proposal. The primary audience, of course, is the city government and the authorities who will be selecting the firm to build a light rail system. Raj also has at least two other audiences: the citizens of the city (who might be paying for the light rail system through their taxes) and his supervisors at work (who might consider him for a promotion and/or raise if his bid is well-written and successful). He realizes that he might need to include a variety of evidence and different kinds of resources to address these multiple audiences.

Consider the audience for your argument. Do you have one explicit audience? Is there also an implied audience (or audiences) that you need to consider? What kinds of evidence will be most convincing to your audience(s)? In order to answer this last question, you might think about what your audience values. Understanding the audience's values will help you choose evidence that will be persuasive to them, and it will also help you determine the best way to construct and phrase your argument and reasons. In addition, consider what your audience already knows about your topic. What do you know that they already believe about your topic?

As you consider the way your audience shapes the kind of evidence you choose, also consider your purpose. What do you want your argument to accomplish? What are you hoping your audience will do in response to your argument? Will the evidence you have found persuade your audience to accomplish your purpose? In Raj's case, he needs to choose evidence that will be persuasive to all three of his audiences, and he needs to consider his purpose in addressing each of these audiences. He needs evidence that will persuade the city authorities to adopt his proposal over others, and he also needs evidence that will persuade the citizens that funding his light rail system is a good use of public resources. Finally, he needs to choose evidence that will be respected by his supervisors at work. He knows, however, that if he wins the bid, then that will be the most convincing evidence of all to his supervisors.

reflect

Are You Addressing Your Audience's Wants and Needs?

As you begin to think about which evidence to include in your argument, start by reflecting on your audience. Try responding to the following questions to help you determine which evidence might be most useful and persuasive to include in your argument.

1. Who is/are your audience(s)? Think about who your primary audience is, and then consider whether there are other audiences that you are also addressing. You might have an explicit audience that is more defined and also an implicit audience. For example, if you are writing a paper

>>>

for a class, you might address an explicit audience that would be appropriate for your topic, but then you always have the implied audience of your instructor to consider as well.

Now answer each of the following questions for each audience that you identified in item 1.

2. What does your audience value? What is important to them?

3. What will your audience be expecting in terms of evidence? What types of evidence are you required to include (if any)? Have you found evidence that would be undoubtedly convincing to your audience?

4. What does your audience think about your issue? Do they already have well-formed opinions in response to your research question? Do you know whether they already agree or disagree with you? Your response to this question will help you determine not only which evidence to include but also how much. If your audience disagrees with you, then you may need to include more evidence. If your audience is open to different ideas or already agrees with parts of your argument, then you might use less evidence in certain parts of your argument.

Timeliness, Relevance, and Other Criteria

Several additional criteria might help you determine which evidence to choose. First of all, consider the timeliness of the evidence that you are considering. Does this matter for persuasive effect in your argument? For example, doctors doing cutting-edge research on how to replace worn-out hip joints need to know what other doctors are doing. How will a research doctor's paper on a "new" method for hip replacement be received if the readers (other orthopedic doctors) realize she does not know about a successful method that was published in the past two years? What will lack of knowledge, or lack of acknowledgement, do to the research doctor's credibility? To sustain her credibility, the research doctor must know the most up-to-date information. Similarly, eco-friendly arguments about recycling and global warming often depend on the most current research both to set the stage for the crisis and to provide evidence that the proposed solution will help.

Research projects about literature or a historical topic, however, may not require the most "timely" research. Instead, such research usually requires that the writer demonstrate an extensive knowledge about what has already been written on the topic. For example, if an undergraduate English major is writing about Shakespeare's play *Romeo and Juliet,* his professor will probably not expect him to focus on the most recent research, nor will he expect him to read everything ever written about the play. Instead, his professor will expect that the student read enough scholarship on *Romeo and Juliet,* and incorporate it into the course paper, to demonstrate a broad understanding of the play and how other scholarship fits into the paper's argument.

While some research may require the most current information and other research may not rely as much on timeliness, certain research projects may require research from a specific time. Instead of defining "timeliness" simply as "current," "timeliness" may refer to specific historical information. If a movie reviewer wanted to comment on the reception of the *TRON* sequel, *TRON: Legacy* (2010), she may have to do research comparing the reception of the first *TRON* film (1982). Since the two films cover a three-decade span, the reviewer may need to know not only how the different films were received but also what was going on historically when each film was released.

Relevance is just as important as timeliness. How relevant is the evidence you have found to the purpose and scope of your argument? For example, Raj may have found great resources and evidence from an ongoing light rail project in another city; however, many of his primary audience members recognize that the other city might be in a radically different setting. If Raj is to incorporate this evidence into his argument, he will need to carefully acknowledge the differences in the situations of the two cities. Similarly, the student doing research on Shakespeare's *Romeo and Juliet* may have found a recent article about dialogue between the female characters in the play, but if he is writing about symbolism in the play, the article is probably outside of the purpose and scope of the project.

What other criteria should you consider for your topic/project? Look to elements of your rhetorical situation to develop more criteria. For example, Raj might have to consider how his plan will affect the environment because the city council might also be considering various types of environmental legislation. Similarly, a child care agency that is researching methods to help parents get involved in reading to their young children might have to consider evidence that takes into account the radically different socioeconomic backgrounds of the children and their families.

write

Develop Evaluative Criteria

To help develop criteria to use while constructing arguments and selecting evidence, write your answers to the following questions.

1. Who is the audience(s) for this research project? What do they want to know? What do they need to know?

2. What is the purpose of this research project? What must be conveyed for that purpose to be achieved?

3. How timely is this research project? What types of contemporary information must you address? What types of historical information must you address? How recent must information be to be relevant and persuasive?

4. How did you continue to narrow and focus your research question? What type of information must you find to fit within that scope? What information may be only tangentially relevant?

5. What other elements or issues about your topic must be covered?

6. What elements or issues about your topic might be interesting but not useful since they do not fit the purpose or scope of your project?

Use these criteria to start reevaluating your research. Based on these criteria, divide the results of your research into three piles.

>>>

▶ information you must include in your project

▶ information you might include because it is tangentially relevant

▶ information that you will not include because it is not useful or relevant

Put the information that is not relevant in an envelope, shoe box, or separate computer file. Tuck it safely away somewhere. Although you will probably not use it and do not want to be distracted by it any longer, do not throw it away yet. Depending on the direction your project takes, the information might be useful later.

Resources as Evidence

Evidence can emerge from any type of resource; however, different types of resources often need to be evaluated in different manners. For example, you may find expert testimony in a variety of resources: individually published blogs, edited trade publications, or peer reviewed journals. However, since these three types of publications have different processes of editorial review, a researcher needs to evaluate appropriately. We're not claiming that a researcher shouldn't evaluate a peer reviewed journal article, but he or she knows that other scholars in the same field evaluated the article before it was published. Similarly, an article in a trade publication was reviewed by an editor who likely knows a lot about the particular industry the publication represents. However, the researcher may need to do a little bit of extra research to check the validity of the blog posting. Unless it is noted on the blog, it is highly unlikely that anyone edits an individually published blog; therefore, the researcher must verify the blog author's identity and credentials for publishing on the subject. This means that it is important to evaluate some of your evidence based on where you locate it.

With the invention of the Internet and the resulting relative ease with which individuals could publish their ideas, opinions, histories, and other information on the Web, many scholars started to distinguish between paper or hard-copy resources and electronic or soft-copy resources. In other words, secondary resources could suddenly be found outside the library; however, many times these resources were less authoritative and trustworthy. To be more specific, scholars were worried that much of the information found on the Internet did not have an editorial review process. For example, although popular books, magazines, and newspapers do not necessarily have resident experts on all subjects, they do have knowledgeable editors that help to filter the information that goes into print. What made scholars wary of electronic resources is that so many people could publish to the Internet without any form of editorial evaluation or review. As we mentioned in Chapter 4, many writing textbooks distinguish between library and Internet resources, often stating that the Internet resources are not to be trusted without a critical and thorough evaluation.

However, with the turn of the century and the proliferation of Internet-based electronic resources of originally printed materials, we can no longer easily dismiss electronic, soft-copy, or Internet-based resources. For example, many school libraries no longer subscribe to the paper copies of many scholarly journals; instead, they subscribe to various

TABLE 9.1. A Resource Evaluation Matrix

	Static	Syndicated	Dynamic
Edited	State and local legislation and other government documents about public transit issues for the city and comparable metropolitan areas	State and local newspaper articles from the city and comparable metropolitan areas	
Peer Reviewed	Books by engineers about metropolitan public transit	Scholarly journal articles about metropolitan public transit and ecocriticism of public transit systems	Wikis of similar projects by other groups of engineers
Self-published	A web site published by a special interest group about the light rail system's role in reducing air pollution in a major city	Blogs about local public transit and "green" issues in the city and comparable metropolitan areas	Observations of public legislation sessions in the city

databases that provide electronic copies of those journals. And students access these databases through web browsers on the Internet. Likewise, new types of solely electronic resources, such as blogs, wikis, and listservs, can be scholarly, authoritative, edited, and even peer reviewed. Similarly, the technologies that have helped proliferate numerous self-published electronic resources have also contributed to a larger number of authors self-publishing in hard-copy media as well, especially books.

In Chapter 4 we classified resources by how easily and how frequently they change (static, syndicated, and dynamic) and by who filters the information before it is published (edited, peer reviewed, and self-published) on pages 78–81. Table 9.1 provides definitions and examples of each type of resource in the context of Raj's project.

Your audience will want to know that you critically evaluated your evidence in an appropriate manner, regardless of where you found it. It is important to carefully evaluate Internet-based resources because of the fluidity of the Internet and because of the ease with which information can be changed, especially when that information is self-published. To evaluate a self-published resource, it is helpful to answer the following types of questions.

▶ What is the purpose of the self-published resource? How can you tell? How might its purpose bias the information being presented? Who is the primary audience? How can you tell?

▶ How detailed and thorough is the information being presented? Is there documentation of the information? What other methods can you use to evaluate the credibility of the information presented? How does the information in the self-published resource cross-reference with information in edited or peer reviewed resources?

▶ Who has the authority to publish or update the self-published resource? Who is paying for or hosting the publication? If it is an Internet-based resource, what is the suffix on the end of the URL (universal resource locator, which is the web address)? Where does the site link from? Where does the site link to? Are there advertisements on the site? If it is a hard-copy resource, who is the publisher? What other types of resources does that publisher produce?

▶ When was the self-published resource last printed or updated? How can you tell? Can you contact the author or the webmaster?

The criteria and scrutiny we apply to self-published resources isn't so different from what we apply to edited and peer reviewed resources:

▶ Critically evaluate the resource based on its rhetorical situation.

▶ Know when the resource was published and if it has ever been updated.

▶ Evaluate the credibility of the information it contains by checking its documentation and cross-referencing it with other resources.

On some level, evaluating the credibility of the information in a self-published resource and an edited or peer reviewed published resource is identical, but we often trust the editorial and peer review processes to weed out "bad" information for us.

Generally, it is much easier to locate the information needed to evaluate your resources in static and syndicated resources than in dynamic resources. Most static and syndicated resources imply some desire for longevity; static resources remain permanent and syndicated resources continue syndicating material. Therefore, the authors of a static resource (e.g., a new book, film, or song) generally want credit for their publication so that they gain notoriety and can make, publish, and sell more static resources. And the producers of syndicated materials (e.g., periodicals, television shows, and podcasts) generally want audience members to know where the information comes from so that the audience will come back and possibly pay for more. Dynamic resources, on the other hand, may be a little more difficult to evaluate.

Obviously, you cannot evaluate the results from your own experiment or originally collected field research in the same way; however, you can explicitly describe how you designed the experiment and collected the data. For example, scientists always give explicit details about how they construct their experiments and collect their data so that other scientists can duplicate their experiments. A social scientist would be sure to include copies of interview questions or survey instruments as a part of the publication process. Duplicating original research is one way that researchers evaluate one another's work. Other dynamic resources, like live play performances, would similarly require detailed descriptions of the methods by which the researcher documented the resource as well as careful documentation of the specific time and date of the performance. And although it is possible to quote a dynamic resource, such as lines from an audience participatory play or an entry in a wiki, the line from the play or the wiki entry may change the next day. It is critical that you, the researcher gathering and evaluating this dynamic resource, carefully document the date and location of the resource you quoted. That way the readers of the paper based on your research can verify your dynamic resources by checking with others who saw the play that same day or use a program like Wayback Machine (http://www.archive.org/) or the wiki's version tracker to evaluate an Internet-based wiki page.

Evaluate Types of Resources

Select one of the resources you categorized as something you *must* include based on the previous activity. Categorize it as static, syndicated, or dynamic. Also categorize it as self-published, edited, or peer reviewed. Answer the following questions based on your categorization of the resource.

▶ How would your audience react to this type of resource? Would they find this to be a reliable source? Why or why not? If not, what information do you need to provide to persuade them? For example, could you emphasize the credentials of the author or perhaps the timeliness of the information?

▶ What types of information would your audience need to know about this resource? Is that information already included in the full bibliographic citation? What information do you need to provide for them to locate the exact resource you looked at or worked with?

▶ How critical is this resource to your research? Does your rhetorical situation demand that you incorporate this resource into your project?

Matching Reasons with Evidence

At this point in your research process, you have been thinking about your research topic, your resources, and your position for a while. You know what your motivation is for researching, and you've identified a potential audience that would be interested in what you have discovered. Now is the time to pull everything together and match specific resources and pieces of evidence with your reasons. Because you have gathered so much information about your topic, and you have begun to construct the reasoning for your argument, it is time to think about what resources and pieces of evidence will best support your claim, purpose, and audience and how you will structure your argument and include that evidence.

Draw a Cluster Map

Depending on how focused your argument is at this point in time, complete one of the following clustering activities. After you develop the cluster, try sharing it with someone who knows something about your topic and someone who knows nothing about your topic. Both people can give you insightful ideas about the connections you have made.

▶ **Option 1: You have collected a lot of information and are still trying to process and organize it to develop a thesis and reasons for your argument.** Start with your research

>>>

>>>

question written in the middle of the page. What are the major issues explicitly connected to your research question? What are the major "answers" to your research question? Either the major issues or the major answers, and possibly both, will be your first round of satellite clusters. Write those in a circle spaced around the research question and connect them to the middle with lines. Now, start filtering through your research notes. Add subtopics and/or notes from specific resources as satellites to their relevant research-related issue or answer. If you have research notes or resources that do not fit in your initial cluster, think about whether you need to add a satellite point from the research question. And if you have large groups of information or notes around one of the satellites, try grouping them into further levels of satellites.

▶ **Option 2: You have already developed a tentative thesis and reasons for your argument, but you are still figuring out how your research fits together and how it should all be arranged.** Start with your thesis statement or argumentative claim in the center of the page. Put your reasons as the first round of satellites in the cluster map and connect them back to the center. Now filter through your research and connect specific resources, notes, and evidence to each reason. If you have a large number of resources or evidence linked to a specific reason, see if you can group them into like categories. If you only have one or two resources or pieces of evidence associated with a reason, you may need to rethink your line of reasoning or conduct a little more research.

Once you have completed your cluster map, try transferring it to the form of an outline. What information would you put first? second? third? Begin to consider how you would prioritize information in your argument. See Chapter 2 for more information on outlining.

Instead of just starting to write, or drafting blindly, we suggest that you spend some time thinking about the natural grouping or clustering of the materials you collected and the lines of reasoning you have developed.

You may consider doing clustering activities at a variety of points during your research process; however, we definitely suggest you do them at one, or both, of the following points:

▶ after you've collected all of your data and are trying to make meaning of it.

▶ after you've drafted a thesis statement with reasons and are trying to make connections to your research to organize everything.

techno tip

Create Clusters on the Computer

If you would like to construct your cluster on the computer instead of on paper, there are a variety of clustering, or mind/idea mapping, types of applications. Microsoft Word® has a simple diagram or organizational chart tool embedded in the program. Go to "Insert" and then "Diagram" to insert one of the visuals into your document. MS Word allows you to switch the type of diagram being used without changing the text you have entered. Switching the diagrams with your information might give you different ideas about how to cluster, or organize, your ideas and materials.

Four other tools are also worth checking out:

1. Mindmeister (http://www.mindmeister.com/)

2. Mindomo (http://www.mindomo.com/)

3. Popplet (http://popplet.com/)

4. Cmap Tools is a more robust mapping program that you can download for free (http://cmap.ihmc.us/download/). However, it is both more difficult to use and more difficult to export your cluster/concept map into a usable format.

Find Additional Resources

write

Based on the claim, reasons, and evidence you have brought together so far, what holes still exist in your argument? Where is your audience most likely to disagree with your argument? Identify two areas in your argument cluster that you are concerned about. For each area of concern, take the following steps.

1. List specific types of information, resources, and pieces of evidence that you would like to find to support your areas of concern. Talk to an instructor, mentor, or librarian to help you identify where you might find the items on your list.

2. Share your cluster map or an outline of your argument with a classmate, family member, or friend. Ask them to identify your two weakest spots.

3. Share your cluster map or an outline of your argument with a different classmate, family member, or friend. Specifically identify your areas of concern; ask them if they agree with your concerns. Ask for suggestions on strengthening your argument.

Based on this feedback, produce a new cluster map, outline, or draft of your argument.

chapter 10

Sharing the Results

Now is the time to pull everything together, to share the results of your research with your audience in a way that will interest them and accomplish your initial goals. Because you have gathered so much information about your topic, and you have begun to construct the reasoning for your argument, it is time to think about how to arrange your argument and how to present it to your audience. You'll want to consider your rhetorical situation once again, choosing an organizational structure and medium of presentation that will communicate your research results in a way that will suit your purpose and persuade your audience. In the research scenario on the following page, Kristi has several possibilities for how she could present the results of her research. As you read, consider what presentation format you would choose for such an assignment.

we'll explore:

▶ *arranging your final project*

▶ *writing introductions and conclusions*

▶ *designing your final project to share the results of your research*

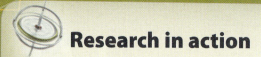

Research in action

Author: Kristi, a senior in college, is taking a history course.

Topic: Kristi's history professor has assigned a family history project and asked students to think of a unique approach that they might take to writing their families' histories. Kristi is also engaged to be married, and she has asked her professor if she could write a combined history of her two families (her birth family and her in-laws), looking at the intersections between them.

Gazimal/The Image Bank/Getty Images

Audience: The audience consists of Kristi's professor, but she also plans to share her project with both families.

Purpose: Kristi needs to investigate the histories of both families to find points of intersection. She would like to develop a visual representation of the history to accompany her written research report; she thinks that looking at family photographs would be a good starting point for identifying patterns of intersection between the two families. She needs to talk to members of both families and also find photographs that will demonstrate connections.

Questions

1. How could Kristi present the "results" of her research visually?

2. How might she organize the photographs, and what form do you think the presentation might take?

3. How might she connect the visual representation with her essay?

4. Can you imagine another way Kristi might approach this research project, given the purpose and audience for the research?

Arrangement of Your Argument

As you consider possible patterns of organization for your research project, you will want to choose the organizational strategy that will best support your claim, purpose, and audience. The pattern of arrangement you choose depends upon a balance between the reasoning of your argument and your rhetorical situation (your purpose, audience, and topic). Since you have already been constructing the reasoning for your argument in terms of your rhetorical situation, you now need to do two things:

1. Decide on a pattern of argument (evaluation, definition, proposal, cause and effect).
2. Determine how to organize the argument that you are constructing (most important to least important, least important to most important, or chronological).

In Kristi's case, she decides to start her research by asking that members of both families pull out old photo albums and other memorabilia. After going through and picking out the photos and other documents that are sturdy enough to withstand being scanned, she starts trying to group them into like piles. She looks for connections between them and tries a number of arrangements. First she tries making piles based on the family members in the photos (Figure 10.1). Then she tries organizing the photos based on theme (Figure 10.2). Then she considers a chronological organization. Just by spending time with the photos, the "evidence" of her family history, she gets to know the "data" better and she starts to construct an arrangement pattern for her project.

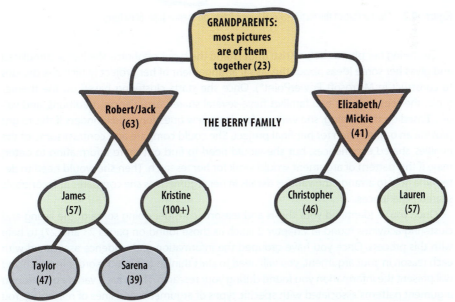

Figure 10.1   Cluster Map of the Pictures Kristi Found Based on Family Member (includes number of photos per person)

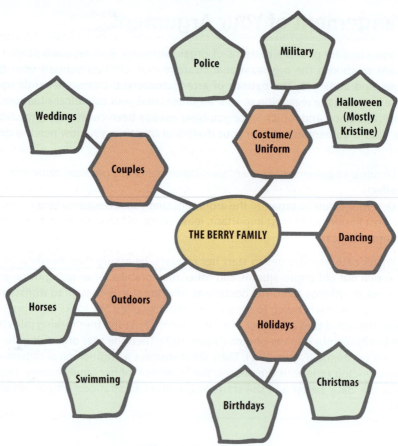

Figure 10.2   Cluster Map of the Pictures Kristi Found Based on Theme/Topic of Pictures

Clustering her photos helps Kristi understand the types of photos she has accumulated and gives her some ideas about the visual arrangement of her project (which she decides to construct in Microsoft PowerPoint®). Once she starts clustering based on the theme/topic, she sees that the two families have several shared experiences, traditions, and values. Based on this finding, she writes a few interview questions and wonders if this might provide an organization for her final project. She could compare and contrast some of the families' shared experiences, but she would need to find out more information to determine if this pattern of argument would work for her research. Then she would need to determine how to arrange the various details in her argument as she compares and contrasts shared experiences.

Once you've identified your thesis and reasons, consider doing some of the listing and clustering activities found in Chapter 2 (such as those found on pages 23 and 27) to help with this process. Once you have grouped the information and evidence associated with each reason in your argument, you will need to start thinking about the order in which you will present the information you found during your research. There are a variety of common argument patterns associated with specific types of arguments and lines of reasoning. You might choose one of these common argument patterns for your researched argument, or you could just start with one and then adapt it to fit your argument and rhetorical situation.

Common Argument Patterns

Although there are a variety of types of arguments, the vast majority of them fall into the following four categories: evaluations, definitions, proposals, and cause-and-effect arguments. More sophisticated or complex arguments, usually associated with more complex research questions and issues, often include more than one of these types of argument. As you read through the following descriptions, first think about your thesis or argumentative claim. Does it appear to clearly fit into one of these categories? If yes, you might want to follow the argument pattern outlined. If not, focus on each line of reasoning: does it fit into one of these categories? If yes, you might want that section of your argument to follow the argument pattern outlined.

Evaluation   In evaluations people judge an object against a specific set of criteria. For example, movie reviews evaluate a movie based on the criteria provided by the reviewer. However, if you don't agree with the reviewer's criteria of "what makes a good movie," you might not agree with the evaluation. Therefore, evaluation arguments become two-layered arguments: the first layer argues for a specific set of criteria, and the second layer argues for how a specific object meets that set of criteria. Here's an outline of what an evaluative argument might look like.

Claim: A specific object is a good/bad example of a specific group.
Section 1: Describe the first evaluative criterion (justify the criterion if needed) and apply the criterion to the specific object.
Section 2: Describe the second evaluative criterion (justify the criterion if needed) and apply the criterion to the specific object.
Section 3: Describe the third evaluative criterion (justify the criterion if needed) and apply the criterion to the specific object.

Repeat this pattern as often as needed, depending on the number of evaluative criteria in your argument.

Comparison and Contrast   Sometimes arguments pit one specific object against another, or group of others, by comparing and contrasting them. For example, a film reviewer might compare *Pirates of the Caribbean: On Stranger Tides* (2011) to the first *Pirates* movie *Pirates of the Caribbean: The Curse of the Black Pearl* (2003). Or, instead, the reviewer might compare *On Stranger Tides* with a variety of pirate movies that came before it. In either case, the comparison and contrast requires a set of criteria, or categories, on which to base the comparison, so it is also a type of evaluation. A comparison and contrast argument can be structured in two ways, the first arranged based on the criteria and the second arranged according to the objects being compared or contrasted.

Claim: A claim compares or contrasts one specific object in relation to another (or others).
Section 1: Describe the first evaluative criterion (justify the criterion if needed) and apply the criterion to all the objects being compared/contrasted.
Section 2: Describe the second evaluative criterion (justify the criterion if needed) and apply the criterion to all the objects being compared/contrasted.
Section 3: Describe the third evaluative criterion (justify the criterion if needed) and apply the criterion to all the objects being compared/contrasted.

OR

Claim: A claim compares or contrasts one specific object in relation to another (or others).
Section 1: Establish and argue for the set of criteria.
Section 2: Describe one of the objects in terms of all the evaluative criteria.

Section 3: Describe another object in terms of all the evaluative criteria.

Section 4 (if needed): Describe another object in terms of all the evaluative criteria.

Depending on the goal of your argument, one of these patterns might fit better than the others. You can decide which pattern might work best by considering which section of your argument will need the most development.

Definition   In an argument of definition, the author makes a claim about how a specific object fits in a category (an evaluation of what a specific object is) or how a group of specific objects fit together to make a specific category (comparison of multiple objects to develop common criteria). Therefore, the argument might be arranged in two different structures. For example, in the first instance, an author might claim that a specific object, an electronic book, still remains a "book" based on the definition of "book." The argument is then arranged around the specific elements of the definition—in other words, the criteria for "book."

Claim: A specific object is (or is not) a part of a group based on the definition of the group.
Section 1: State the first criterion for definition of the group and specific evidence for the object demonstrating that criterion.
Section 2: State the second criterion for a definition of the group and specific evidence for the object demonstrating that criterion.
Section 3: State the third criterion for a definition of the group and specific evidence for the object demonstrating that criterion.

In the second type of definitional argument, the author has a group of objects that he or she then compares, and possibly contrasts, to identify a common group of elements the objects share that make a definition for the group. For example, an author might make a claim to define the concept of a "book" by looking at the common elements of different types of texts that could be considered "books," to include ebooks and printed books.

Claim: The common elements of a group of objects form the definition of the category of objects.
Section 1: Describe the first common element and provide evidence from all the objects in the group.
Section 2: Describe the second common element and provide evidence from all the objects in the group.
Section 3: Describe the third common element and provide evidence from all the objects in the group.

For either of these patterns, you would include as many sections as you needed, based on the number of criteria or common elements you need to include in your argument.

Proposal   In some arguments, it is appropriate to propose a plan for action that will solve a problem identified in the argument. Such arguments generally contain two primary parts: a section identifying the problem and a section describing the solution. If we use the terms often used in formal debate, the argument proposes a "case" (the establishment of the problem) and a "plan" (the solution). If you would like to offer a proposal as part of your argument, you will likely rely on one of the other organizational patterns to develop the case section, establishing the problem that you are identifying.

Proposals usually follow an organizational plan such as the following.

Claim: A specific problem needs to be solved and your solution is the best option.
Section 1: Establish the problem or dilemma that needs to be solved (the case).
Section 2: Describe your proposed solution to the problem, and show how this solution is the best for addressing the problem (the plan).

Depending on the emphasis of your argument and the nature of the issue you are re-searching, you might spend more time on either of the two main sections. Think about what you need to convince your audience of the most, and spend more time develop-ing that section. You will also need to consider how much space you should devote to convincing your audience that your solution actually solves the identified problem.

Cause and Effect   If the purpose of an argument is to demonstrate why something has happened, then a cause-and-effect argument might provide the best pattern to follow. In an argument of cause and effect, the author describes the causes of a situation and connects those causes with the result, showing how certain circumstances, actions, or other instigators contributed to creating the existing situation. Cause-and-effect arguments can be particu-larly useful in conjunction with proposals to structure the first part of the proposal argument (establishing the problem). If the author can demonstrate what caused a particular circum-stance or situation, then the author can show how a specific solution would solve the problem.

Cause-and-effect arguments are often structured in one of two ways: establishing the causes and then their effect(s), or describing the effect and then showing what caused it. The organizational structures might look something like this.

Claim: A specific set of circumstances caused a situation.
Section 1: Describe the circumstances.
Section 2: Demonstrate the relationship between those circumstances and the situation, showing that they caused the situation to occur.

OR

Claim: A specific set of circumstances caused a situation.
Section 1: Establish the nature of the situation.
Section 2: Describe the circumstances that caused it.

As with the previous argument structures, the option you choose might depend on what you would like to emphasize in your argument.

Common Presentational Patterns

No matter which argument pattern (or set of patterns) you might select, you also need to think about the order in which you present reasons and evidence. Generally, you base this organizational decision on the relative strengths and weaknesses of your reasons and pieces of evidence. Depending on the subject, the pieces of evidence might be presented chronologically as well.

Least Important to Most Important   Sometimes an author chooses to start with the least important reason and build toward the most important. Such an organiza-tional structure leaves the audience with the most important, or most convincing, reason and pieces of evidence in mind as he or she finishes reading the argument. This strategy is especially effective for a long argument because audience members tend to "tune out" during the middle of the argument. This strategy might not be as effective if an audience is resistant to the argument from the beginning. In other words, if already resistant readers think it is a weak argument from the start, then they'll stop reading.

Most Important to Least Important   If the author really needs to keep the audi-ence engaged and convinced from the beginning of the argument, he or she might begin with the most important reason and then present the remaining reasons that further support the one main, most important reason. If an author goes with this organizational strategy, he or she will reemphasize that first, and most important, reason during the conclusion section to motivate and persuade the audience to agree with the argument.

In both of these organizational structures, an author might use a variation in order to place strong reasons both at the beginning and at the end. For example, an author addressing a somewhat resistant audience might put the strongest argument at the end, but he or she might put the second most compelling argument at the beginning to convince the audience to continue reading.

Chronological Organization   Depending on your topic, it might make sense to present your evidence and reasons chronologically. If Kristi is making an argument that her two families share certain values and experiences, for example, she might want to present the evidence of her argument by chronologically describing events in the families' histories. Kristi could use an argument pattern of comparison and contrast (comparing the two families) but then present the evidence for the argument chronologically.

write

Develop an Outline

Using the various structures presented here, develop an outline for your argument. Start with your claim and list your reasons and evidence. After you have produced the outline, describe what structural patterns you used and why you used them.

You can develop your outline as a formal outline, sentence outline, or scratch outline. (Chapter 2 can provide additional help with these types of outlines.) If you're not certain in your choice of argument pattern or organization, try using another set of structures and develop a second outline for your argument. Describe what structural patterns you used for this second outline and discuss why you used them.

Share your outline(s) with a classmate or a friend. If you developed more than one, ask which argument or organizational pattern he or she preferred and why.

Introductions and Conclusions

Although introductions and conclusions are sometimes considered the most important parts of your argument (i.e., you can't persuade people to change their minds if you can't even persuade them to read the argument), many authors write, or at least revise, these sections of the argument last. Generally, both introductions and conclusions carry a large amount of responsibility for the effectiveness of arguments. People tend to use ethos (arguments developed from personal authority) and pathos (emotion-based arguments) more blatantly in introductions and conclusions. The introduction needs to motivate the audience to continue to read, or listen to, the argument. Similarly, the conclusion needs to motivate the audience to go out and do something with the information. Both introductions and conclusions have other work to do as well, however, and it's important to keep these multiple responsibilities in mind as you write.

Are You Grabbing Your Audience's Attention and Motivating Them to Action?

Good writers know they need to motivate their audience, both to read the document and to take action on the argument. By this point in the process, you have narrowed your audience enough that you have a very good idea about who they are and what they care about. To help construct introductions and conclusions that motivate your readers, answer the following questions about your primary audience.

▶ Why is your audience invested in this topic in general? Why are they invested in the answer to your specific research question?

▶ What interests your audience about this topic? What could change from the status quo that would greatly satisfy your audience?

▶ What scares your audience about this topic? What could change from the status quo that would concern your audience even more?

Ancient rhetors claimed there were three possible sections for an introduction and, based on the rhetorical situation, you could include any one, or all, of the three parts. First, authors need to prepare the audience for receiving the message. In other words, the author needs to make sure the audience is sincerely engaged in hearing the argument. The second section includes a brief introduction to or history of the topic, and the third section outlines the argument. Depending on your rhetorical situation, you might include one or more of these sections in your introduction. Regardless of which sections are included, you need to carefully understand the purpose and audience of the argument to develop a powerful introduction.

Many contemporary scholarly writers start with showing how their research identifies a gap in what is known about an issue. In other words, they demonstrate that no one else has asked a specific research question (or answered it sufficiently). By identifying the research gap, the author implies that his or her answer to the question will fill the gap. Introducing the gap, or problem, that your research is going to fill is one way to get your readers' attention and motivate them to continue reading. For example, Kristi could explain that looking at the histories of the two families together provides insight that isn't possible if their histories are written in isolation. Indeed, she might be able to make connections with her families' shared histories and larger historical events or trends. She can introduce her family history, and her method of looking at both histories together, as filling a gap in the knowledge of either family's individual history. Her research will enrich the families' understanding of their individual and shared histories.

write

Draft an Effective Introduction

As you draft your introduction, keep your rhetorical situation in mind—especially the purpose of your argument and the audience you are addressing. Freewrite in response to the following questions to help draft your introduction.

▶ Why is this topic important? How does it affect the audience? the community? the world?

▶ What is the audience's stand on the issue? How does it differ from yours? If their perspective is different from yours, how might you show respect for their perspective so that they might read yours?

▶ What is your authority on this topic? Who are other major "players" that write or talk about this topic? What are their strengths and points of authority? their weaknesses?

▶ Does your audience know the topic, or its history, well? What do they already know? What do they need to know to understand your perspective?

▶ How long will your paper be? How complex will your argument be? Do you need to give the audience a road map to prepare them for your argument?

Once you have drafted your responses to these questions, look for the most compelling point in what you wrote. Copy and paste that below what you wrote (or even highlight it or circle it if you're writing in a notebook), and then freewrite about that idea for another five minutes. Is this something you could develop into an introduction for your argument? You could try this looping activity a couple of times until you find something that you think you could develop into your introduction.

An important thing to remember is that you do not have to start writing your draft with the introduction. Although it might help you to start with the introduction, most likely you will revise it radically before completing the final version. Similarly, you do not have to wait to write your conclusion until after you've written the entire paper. Sometimes it helps to write a draft of your conclusion earlier to continue reminding yourself of the main point or purpose of your research project. In other words, the main goal of the conclusion is to motivate your readers to action. However, also like the introduction, conclusions can do much more.

A common mistake many student writers make is to simply summarize their argument in the conclusion. While argument summary is one possible function of the conclusion, a summary, like everything else, needs to be rhetorically situated. If your argument is a twenty-page proposal for making your college campus sustainable and "green," the reader might need a summary to remind him or her of the most important information in the last twenty pages. However, if the argument is much shorter, the reader might be able to remember the argument without requiring a summary in the conclusion.

Instead of ending the paper with a summary, try returning to the purpose of your writing. Why is it important that the audience read the results of your research? What do you want them to do with the information you give them? Keep in mind that suggesting change and motivating someone to change are two different things. Both logical arguments and emotional arguments can be effective motivators for change. Ancient rhetors had a list of what might be included in conclusions as well as introductions. If the argument is long and complex, you may need to summarize it at the end of the paper. However, ancient rhetors also realized that people are more likely to leave an argument energized if the author appeals to their emotions, whether through excitement, anger, or fear. Is there a consequence to your argument that you should highlight in your conclusion? Or is there a memorable point that you want to remind your audience of as they finish reading your argument?

Develop Closure

write

Continue to keep your rhetorical situation in mind as you work on a conclusion for your argument. Remember that you are trying to bring a sense of closure to your argument, and consider what you want your audience to be thinking or feeling when they are finished. Freewrite in response to the following questions to begin drafting your conclusion.

▶ What issues raised in your argument need to be repeated for your audience? Is there any support offered in your argument that bears repeating?

▶ What will happen if the current situation continues as it is? What effects might impact your audience, and what effects might impact others that your audience will be concerned about? How could you demonstrate the importance of these effects?

▶ How could you demonstrate that the current problem violates the shared values of a community?

▶ Is this present issue parallel in any way to a previous situation? Are there circumstances or effects from a previous parallel situation that might spur your audience to action (perhaps because they want to avoid those effects or because a previous situation was resolved well and you'd like to see a similar resolution)?

▶ To which person, or group of people, should your readers address their concerns? How might you encourage them to share those concerns?

▶ Will this situation continue if nothing is done? If so, how will the audience be impacted?

Once you have drafted your responses to these questions, look for the most compelling point in what you wrote. Copy and paste it below what you wrote (or even highlight it or circle it if you're writing in a notebook), and then freewrite about that idea for another five minutes. Is this something you could develop into a conclusion for your argument? You could try this looping activity a couple of times until you find something that you think you could develop for your conclusion.

Once you have drafted an introduction and conclusion, you might even try switching them in your paper. Sometimes authors find that what they originally wrote as a conclusion actually works well as an introduction, or vice versa. In either case, you'll get a better sense of the impact on your audience, and the effectiveness of what you have written, if you try changing the order of your introduction and conclusion when you read through your draft one time.

Another strategy you might consider as you draft is to provide a similar image, quotation, or reference in both the introduction and conclusion. This technique is called **framing**, and it can be an effective way to bring closure to a piece if you feel that an image or reference you have used in the introduction is particularly compelling. Writers often engage ethos or pathos in both their introductions and conclusions, and repeating a meaningful image, or reminding your audience of what interested them in reading your argument in the first place, can be an effective way to bring closure to your argument. Often the same things that grab the attention of readers are the things that motivate them to action. If the frame is too heavy-handed, however, it might not be effective.

Identify Possible Frames

write

Reread the draft of your introduction and highlight the most effective, or persuasive, image, quotation, or reference. If you are reading a digital version of your paper, copy that section of your introduction. Then read (or scroll down to) your conclusion. Reread what you have written, looking for a location where you could effectively insert the reference from your introduction. Then copy (or paste) the image into your conclusion, and write effective sentences to contextualize that reference in your conclusion. You might look toward the beginning or the end of your conclusion for an opening point, and keep in mind that repeating that reference will signal to your audience that you are wrapping things up in your argument.

Putting Everything Together

At this point in the process you have spent a lot of time thinking about what you are going to say, why you are going to say it, and even in what order you will say it. You may have written small portions of your argument, or you may have large sections drafted. Regardless of where you are in the process, this is the time to write. Start with compiling all of the pieces that you have started drafting for your final argument, and begin putting everything together.

Draft Your Final Argument

write

Open a new document in your word processor and either type in or cut and paste your outline. Select one of the sections that you think you can write about without needing to check your resources. Even if that section is in the middle of the outline, it's okay to start writing there. Once you have completed all that you can, without help from your resources, stop. Now go and find the resources that will help you develop that section. Once you have completed the section you worked on first, move on to the next one. Before you know it, you'll have a complete draft.

As you write, or once you have completed several successive sections, look at how you can make effective connections between those sections. Even though you may draft in chunks, moving back and forth to different sections in the paper, you need to make connections between the sections and even out the prose so that the final version reads as one fluid argument.

techno tip

Use Document-Sharing Technologies

As you draft, you may want to have others read and comment on your work. Depending on your writing preferences, you might share your work along the way or wait until you have a complete draft. If you are sharing your work electronically, consider using a document-sharing application to have readers look at, comment on, and even make changes in your document. Document-sharing applications are web-based spaces where people can go to your document instead of your having to send it to them as an email attachment. Two advantages to using such applications are that you avoid the virus risks of sending file attachments back and forth, and you avoid the confusion of having multiple versions of your draft existing in different places. The following web-based applications are free and easy to use:

▶ Zoho Writer (http://writer.zoho.com)

▶ Google Docs (http://docs.google.com)

▶ Various storage spaces, such as Box (http://box.com), Dropbox (https://www.dropbox.com/), and Stixy (http://stixy.com)

Presenting Your Research Results

Your research does not benefit anyone unless you share your results, especially with those who are willing and able to act on those results. The goal of this DIY section is to help you think through how to present the results of your research to your intended audience. Your research might be presented in a variety of formats or media, depending on the most appropriate way to reach your audience with your message.

Developing an effective presentation of your research results is a critically important part of the research process. In this section, we introduce you to two ways in which you might present your research, depending on your rhetorical situation:

▶ **scientific reports**

▶ **scholarly arguments**

We also discuss ways you might consider presenting the results of your research through other media.

Common Features of Presentations of Research

Presentations of research might take the form of reports of information or persuasive arguments, and they can be presented in a variety of media. If you have followed the assignment sequence outlined in this book, you have developed a focused research question in your project proposal and you have identified the audience you would like to address in your final argument. Although presentations of research can vary depending on the rhetorical situation, several specific features should be present in any presentation of research, regardless of the medium or audience:

▶ **Claim or thesis.** Determine a defensible and reasonable position on your issue that is an answer to your research question.

▶ **Reasons.** Include specific reasons or sub-points that lead to the claim, main point, or thesis that is central to the presentation of your research.

▶ **Evidence.** Establish the validity of your reasons by providing compelling and persuasive evidence, chosen for your audience.

Additional Features Found in Some Presentations of Research

In presentations of research that are arguments, the following features might also be present:

▶ **Solution.** Some arguments that identify specific problems also propose solutions and show how a particular solution will address a problem.

▶ **Counterarguments.** Consider competing positions that you might need to address, and include arguments showing the weaknesses in these positions.

Types of Presentations of Research

As you consider how to present the results of your research, several formats or media could be appropriate depending on your rhetorical situation. If you are researching and writing for a class, you might be required to write an academic essay for the final presentation of your research. But research presentations can take other forms, and the same research can be presented in more than one way. For example, a researcher might develop an oral presentation to deliver to a live audience and then write an essay-based version as well. Or a research project might be delivered through several different media, creating a multimodal presentation.

The most important consideration is matching the presentation of your research to your audience, purpose, and topic—your rhetorical situation. Because you know your rhetorical situation, your first step is done. The second step is to know your options for presentation. Then think about which presentation method will reach your audience most effectively. The two types of reports of research discussed in this DIY section—scientific reports and scholarly arguments—are usually presented as text-based arguments, but the "Make It with Multiple Media" section offers other alternatives that you might consider.

Scientific Reports

Features of Scientific Reports

Depending on your rhetorical situation, you might need to follow specific organizational patterns in the reporting of your research. For example, if you conducted a primary research study in the sciences or social sciences, you might be expected to follow what is often called the **IMRAD** format in the organization of your essay (for more detailed information, see Chapter 5):

I = introduction

The introduction usually provides a review of relevant literature related to the study, demonstrates why the study is important, and presents the research question and/or hypothesis.

M = methodology

The methodology section describes the research methods used to investigate the research question or test the hypothesis. This section includes information about the participants involved in the study, the method of data collection, and the method of analysis.

R = results

The results section provides the data collected during the study.

A = analysis

The analysis section provides an interpretation of the data collected.

D = discussion

The discussion section, or conclusion, generally demonstrates how the data answer the research question, what the implications of the study are, and often what future research is recommended to follow up on the study. In addition, most scientific reports include an abstract, which is a brief summary of the study that appears at the beginning of the report.

Example of a Scientific Report

Erin Hunter, a freshman at North Carolina State University, conducted a pilot research study to investigate whether there is a relationship between the amount of time that students spend on Facebook and the grades that they receive in their courses. She reports the results of her research in IMRAD format, typical for an empirical study that conducts primary research. Keep in mind that research that involves collecting information from people is subject to IRB regulations (see Chapter 5 for more information). Erin formatted her report in APA style, which is appropriate for a study in the social sciences. All but her cover page is shown.

FACEBOOK AND ACADEMIC PERFORMANCE   1

Abstract

Social media has exponentially grown in the last decade which has led to the vast use of social networking sites. The aim of this study was to determine whether or not there is a relationship between the amount of time college students use Facebook, the fastest developing social network site of its kind, and how well they perform in their courses. Undergraduate students, both male and female, from North Carolina State University were asked to complete a short survey about Facebook, reporting their use of the social networking site in addition to how well they perform inside and outside of the classroom. The results obtained from this study supported the expected conclusion that there is an inverse correlation between the amount of time students spend on Facebook and their grades. Because the sample was limited to twenty students and the questionnaire contained flaws, the findings of this study are limited in their ability to provide researchers with an accurate account of how the target population would respond. The information gathered in this study may help researchers conduct future studies that will help them gain a better understanding of the roles that social media and networking play and their effects on daily life.

Effects of Facebook on Students' Academic Performance

Facebook. LinkedIn. Twitter. All are designed to provide users with the ability to connect with family, friends, organizations, and companies on a local as well as a global scale. The onset of the social networking era has given birth to newer, faster, and more efficient forms of communication. However, some believe individuals today are consumed by their need to constantly be connected to others. While Facebook by itself neither behooves nor harms anyone, it is students' overuse of such social networking services that concerns many teachers and parents. Oftentimes, students are caught checking their

> How do you know this? You could probably find some resources to support this point and make it more engaging as an introduction.

> You set up Facebook as an emerging variable in students' lives; however, do you set up a "problem" that students are not doing well in their classes? In other words, do you have to show a problem to justify this is worth studying; or is it always worthwhile to study how/why students might do better, or not, with their academics?

FACEBOOK AND ACADEMIC PERFORMANCE   2

Facebook pages rather than the pages within a textbook. Several questions concerning the use of Facebook come up when considering recent student performance levels: Do social networking sites such as Facebook have an effect on student's grades? If so, is there a negative or positive correlation associated with the two variables? Researchers are interested in discovering such information because it can tell us what kind of impact and to what degree social media has on our ability to complete certain tasks. The aim of this paper is to answer these questions via providing the results of a study conducted on a college campus. The goal of this study is to determine whether or not there is a connection between college students using Facebook on a regular basis and the outcome of their grades. My hypothesis is that there is an inverse relationship that exists between the amount of time students spend on Facebook and their grades in the classroom.

What is recent? Who has these concerns?

Who?

Do you have any references to other resources that study similar questions/concerns about social media conflicting with "more serious work"?

I'm excited to read the results!

Methods

This study was conducted using a survey to gather information about how often students use Facebook and how they are performing in their current classes. The questionnaire, located in Appendix A, was made up of a total of 10 multiple choice questions: 2 demographic questions and 8 others relating to Facebook or academic performance. The sample group consisted of 20 college students attending North Carolina State University. The study population was made up of 10 males and 10 females. There were a total of 11 freshmen, 8 sophomores, and 1 junior who participated in this study. Students were asked if they would like to take a short survey about Facebook and the majority of people questioned were willing to participate. The sample was a convenience sample for the purpose of a pilot survey, and the survey was administered at Avent Ferry Complex and included both residents and nonresidents of this site. The surveys were distributed to participants from the mid-afternoon to the evening.

Did you get IRB approval? (See Chapter 5.)

Good job trying for a balanced group of subjects with sex and lower class ranking; however, how might you have done a better job getting people from different times and parts of campus? If you had surveyed people in the library during midday, you might have gotten more upper class ranking participants.

FACEBOOK AND ACADEMIC PERFORMANCE   3

Participants did not take the survey together and were encouraged not to share or discuss their answers with anyone else. This
was done to reduce the chance of one person influencing the
answers of another.

Results

Because this study looks at how the use of Facebook affects
students' grades, the 20 participants' results can be divided into
2 main categories based on their responses to number 6 on the
questionnaire: "Overall, how are you currently performing in
your classes?" Only 6 (30%) people said they are making a high
A to a high B while the remaining 14 (70%) people said they are
averaging a low B to a low C. None of the 20 participants said
they are earning a D average or are currently failing a majority of their classes. The following analysis breaks down the
responses of both categories of students. The percentages
for these groups are also provided in Tables 1 and 2. For a
complete analysis of the results for each question, refer to
Appendix B.

Of the 6 students who said they were averaging high A's and
B's, 2 (33%) said they had a Facebook profile between 1 and 2
years. The other 4 (67%) students recorded as having a profile
for 3 or more years. Four (67%) of these students said they
use Facebook about once a day while the remaining 2 (33%)
admitted to checking Facebook more than 5 times a day. Two
(33%) students said they read other people's status and comments; however, 3 (50%) said they post a status themselves, only
1 (17%) said they mostly play games and take quizzes, and 0
students said they looked at other people's profiles. Five of these
6 students (83%) claimed they do not get onto Facebook during
classes and lectures, leaving only 17% (1 person) who said they
do use Facebook during class time. The opposite happened when
students were asked if they use Facebook while doing any homework assignments or studying; 83% said they do use Facebook
and only 17% do not when working.

> Which group of students are you referring back to, the high A's & B's, the students with newer accounts, or the students with older accounts? At this point in the paragraph you've introduced three different groups of students.

FACEBOOK AND ACADEMIC PERFORMANCE   4

Table 1

Response of Students Who Answered A (A+ to B+) for Number 6

Question	A	B	C	D
1	0%	0%	33%	67%
2	67%	0%	0%	33%
3	33%	50%	0%	17%
4	17%	83%	–	–
5	83%	17%	–	–

Out of the other 14 people who reported averaging low B's and C's, 1 person (17%) claimed to have had their Facebook profile for each "less than 6 months" and "6 months to 1 year." Five of the 14 (36%) said they have had a profile for 1 to 2 years, and most (7 or 50%) responded to having a Facebook for more than 3 years. Five of the 14 students (36%) said they check their Facebook about once a day while there were 3 participants (21%) for each of the following answers: "2 to 3," "3 to 4," and "more than 5 times a day." A majority (11 or 79%) said they spend most of their time reading other people's status and comments, and the remaining 3 (21%) reported as writing their own posts. Again, none of the participants claimed to search through other profiles. In this particular group, no one recorded as spending most of their time on Facebook playing games or taking quizzes. Similarly to those who said they make high A's and B's, most of the students who said they make low B's and C's (9 or 64%) claimed to not use Facebook during classes. The other 5 (36%) admitted to getting onto Facebook during class and lectures. Eight (57%) of these participants said they also use it while doing homework and other assignments, leaving the other 6 (43%) claiming they do not.

One can also look at the results of how the students feel they perform to correlate academic performance with the amount of time spent on Facebook. Seventy percent of the participants felt they do well on

> Again, I'm confused about who exactly you are discussing. When you revise this, you'll want to carefully distinguish between groups of students as you are discussing your data.

FACEBOOK AND ACADEMIC PERFORMANCE   5

Table 2

Response of Students Who Answered B (B- to C-) for Number 6

Question	A	B	C	D
1	7%	7%	36%	50%
2	36%	21%	21%	21%
3	79%	21%	0%	0%
4	36%	64%	-	-
5	57%	43%	-	-

> You use quotation marks around the answer wording at various points throughout the essay (especially this section). However, please note two things: 1) this is done inconsistently and 2) the wording within quotation marks does not always match the wording in the survey.

examinations while 30% believe they have room for improvement. Of the 14 students who said they do well, 9 (64%) have used Facebook for over 3 years and 33% (5 students) have used Facebook between 1 and 2 years. A majority, or 50% of these students, reported as checking Facebook only once a day. Three of the 14 (22%) use it 2 to 3 times a day, and there was a tie of 2 students (14% each) that said they use Facebook "4 to 5 times a day" and "more than 5 times a day." Eight (29%) said it is very easy for them to complete school work, 5 (36%) said it is somewhat easy, three (21%) said it is moderately difficult, and 2 (14%) said it is extremely difficult. For those 6 who felt they did not do as well on examinations, there was a tie of 33% each (2 people each) of those who have used Facebook for "1 to 2 years" and "over 3 years." There was also a tie of 17% (1 person each) of those who have used Facebook for "less than 6 months" and "6 months to a year." Half of these students (3 or 50%) claimed to use Facebook on an average of more than 5 times a day, 1 (17%) answered "4 to 5 times a day," and 2 (33%) said only once a day. Finally, 33% (2 students) said it is somewhat easy, 50% (3 of the 6 students) said they find it "moderately difficult" to complete school work, and only 17% (1 student) said it is extremely difficult. Table 3 shows the results of questions 1, 2, and 8 based on the participants' response to whether or not the participants feel they do well on examinations in the class.

FACEBOOK AND ACADEMIC PERFORMANCE   6

Table 3

Responses Based on Number 7

Yes; I do well on examinations	A	B	C	D
1	0%	0%	36%	64%
2	50%	22%	14%	14%
8	29%	36%	21%	14%
No; I do not do well on examinations				
1	17%	17%	33%	33%
2	33%	0%	17%	50%
8	0%	33%	50%	17%

Discussion

The findings of this study demonstrate that although the correlation is somewhat weaker than it was expected it to be, there is some relationship between the amount of time students spend on Facebook and their differing academic levels of performance. A majority of the students who said they are currently making high A's and B's reported only checking their Facebook profiles about once per day. Only 33% of these students said they use Facebook more than one time a day; however, 63% of those students who made low B's and C's responded to checking their profiles more than once a day. This supports the hypothesis that was made; it indicates that those who spend less time on Facebook receive higher grades than those who spend more time on Facebook. Both groups had a majority of partici-pants selecting "daily" for question number 1, but they differed on their responses to question number 2 greatly. Seventy-nine percent of those who made lower grades said they spent most of their time

FACEBOOK AND ACADEMIC PERFORMANCE   7

on Facebook reading other people's comments. Half (50%) of the students who made higher grades said they mainly post a status or comment, spending less time on Facebook reading what others have to say. Therefore, they may receive higher grades because the total amount of time they spend on Facebook is less than those who take the time to read other people's posts and comments.

Great use of a qualifier to hedge your analysis.

Because the question in this study is "Does Facebook affect student performance?" data were needed to determine how the use of Facebook affects students while they are in the classroom. Students were asked whether or not they use Facebook during classes and lectures, and surprisingly, 70% of the total sample population said no. Seventeen percent of the students who make high A's and B's admitted to using Facebook during class time. The other group had more than double that (36%) in students who claimed to use Facebook in class. This suggests that students who are tempted to use Facebook in class are more likely to make lower grades than those who do not get on Facebook during lectures. This might be due to their not being as focused on the material being taught and missing pertinent information that will help them succeed in the course. In addition to determining the amount of students using Facebook in class, data was needed to show the number of students who used Facebook while completing academic assignments outside of the classroom. There were an equal amount of students (83%) that make higher grades who said they do not get onto Facebook in class but they do use it while working on homework or studying. This information suggests that students are more likely to be distracted by the use of social media when they are working outside of the classroom.

Again, be more precise with which group you are referring to as "other."

In regards to how students perceive their academic performance, the data shows that those who spend less time on Facebook believe they make better grades and therefore are more content with their efforts than those who spend a significantly greater amount of time on Facebook. One piece of significant evidence is the fact that 50% of students who said they feel they do well claimed to check their Facebook daily, whereas the students who do not feel they do as well use Facebook more than five times a day. The same amount of students

FACEBOOK AND ACADEMIC PERFORMANCE   8

from this group (those who do not feel they perform as well) said they have a somewhat difficult time completing school work. Over half of the students who feel they do well on exams said they find it either very easy or somewhat easy to perform school work. Such statistical information demonstrates that Facebook not only affects students' grades, but also the perception of their own academic performance.

Perhaps the greatest limitation in this study was the number of participants surveyed. Only 20 students participated in this study, a number that hardly reflects the target population of those college students that use Facebook. While there was an even number of males and females that participated, a majority of the sample group consisted of college freshmen and sophomores; there was only 1 junior and no seniors or graduate students in this study. Such demographics also do not adequately represent the average college Facebook user. Another limitation in this study deals with how the questionnaire was written. In question number 2, the term "daily" was used as an indicator of how often students checked their Facebook. Because the frequency increased with each new answer choice, it was intended for students to understand that "daily" referred to one time. This was not as clear as it should have been, and, thus, provided some confusion among students. Many students saw this as their first answer choice and immediately selected it without looking at the rest of the answers. Also, the answers to this question were biased; it was assumed that those who have a Facebook profile check it at least once every day; this was not the case, though. One student specifically pointed this out since that person did not frequently use Facebook. If one person had this problem, others may have faced the same issue. Due to such limitations, the results of this study are not generalizable, but they indicate an interesting trend that could be explored further.

> How do you know what the average college Facebook user is? Where might you find demographics on Fb users?

> Did you pilot your survey instrument (aka, get a handful of students in the class to use it) so that you might have caught these errors in advance?

Conclusion

Several improvements can be made to this study in order to obtain more accurate results in the future. Researchers should survey a wider range of participants with a greater amount of diversity in their demographics; the larger a sample population is, the easier it

FACEBOOK AND ACADEMIC PERFORMANCE   9

is to correlate two variables. Also, researchers should include those students who do not use Facebook or any other type of social networking site to show how they perform in school compared to those students who do use such online networking services. Every question and answer choice used in the survey needs to be carefully reviewed so that the survey does not appear biased. Specifically, in question number 2, the term "daily" used for the first answer choice should be changed to "once a day." The frequency that students use Facebook should also be changed to encompass a broader time interval.

The significance that stems from this study is that there is a negative, or inverse, relationship between the amount of time a student spends on Facebook and how that student performs academically. The results of this study show that the more time students spend on social networking sites, such as Facebook, the more likely they are to receive lower grades and feel less satisfied with the efforts they are putting towards their education. These findings can assist those in the fields of social media and education find solutions to help those students who do not perform as well in school due to a lack of concentration caused by Facebook and other social networking outlets. This revelation may also lead researchers to question in what other ways do social media and social networking in today's society affect the level of human performance in completing various tasks in diverse environments. Researchers may ask if social media affects one's ability to perform efficiently in the workplace. If so, to what degree is it beneficial or detrimental to that individual or place of business? Answers to such questions, in addition to the findings of this study, have the potential to provide both academic and general audiences alike with a better understanding of the impact social media has on society as a whole.

Appendix A

Fall 2011 Survey for English 101 Empirical Study:

Please read ALL directions thoroughly. Do NOT put your name on this survey. Read each question carefully, and answer survey questions to the best of your knowledge. Do not share or discuss any questions or answers while taking this survey. Your participation is greatly appreciated.

FACEBOOK AND ACADEMIC PERFORMANCE   10

Please indicate the following demographic information.

Gender: M / F   Year of Study: F   S   Jr   Sr

Clearly circle your answers.

1. How long have you had a Facebook profile?

   a. less than 6 months   b. 6 months to a year

   c. 1 to 2 years   d. over 3 years

2. About how often do you use/check your Facebook?

   a. daily   b. 2 to 3 times a day

   c. 4 to 5 times a day   d. more than 5 times a day

3. What activity do you perform the most?

   a. read other people's status   b. post a status or comment
       and comments

   c. search other people's   d. play games and take quizzes
       profiles

4. Do you get onto Facebook during classes and lectures?

   a. yes   b. no

5. Do you frequently use Facebook while working on homework,
    a project, or studying?

   a. yes   b. no

6. Overall, how are you currently performing in your classes?

   a. A+ to B+   b. B– to C–

   c. D+ to D–   d. F

7. Would you say you do well on examinations?

   a. yes   b. no

8. How easy or difficult is it for you to get your school work done?

   a. very easily   b. somewhat easily

   c. moderately difficult   d. extremely difficult

Appendix B, which provides an analysis of every question given
by all 20 participants, is available online at the *Wadsworth Guide
to Research* site.

Discussion Questions

▶ After reading Erin's scientific report, what do you think are the advantages and disadvantages of using IMRAD format to report primary research?

▶ Erin wrote an abstract at the beginning of her scientific report. How well does that abstract capture the results of her study? What suggestions would you make to her if she were to revise?

▶ Erin uses tables to report data throughout the report. Why do you think she has used tables? What do they add to the reporting of her research? Can you think of any other visual representations of data that might work well for this report?

▶ The number of students surveyed is small, as the author mentions in her report, and they were selected by convenience. What are the limitations of the study? If she were going to conduct something that would be more generalizable, what might she do?

▶ In her Discussion and Conclusion, Erin analyzes the data she collected and offers possible interpretations. Were there any results you would have highlighted that Erin didn't discuss?

Scholarly Arguments

Most research projects assigned in school take the form of academic essays, usually based off the more formal scholarly arguments presented in academic journals. When writing an academic essay or scholarly argument, it is important to follow the formatting requirements of the citation style you are using for the essay, and the citation style should be chosen according to the requirements of your rhetorical situation. Chapter 11 can help you determine which citation style is most appropriate for your argument.

Features of Scholarly Arguments

Not all scholarly arguments have a format as prescribed as a scientific report, but you should investigate the expectations of your audience and the disciplinary community in which you are conducting your research. If you are not to follow a format such as IMRAD, then you will likely want to include analysis throughout your essay instead of relegating it to one section of the paper. Find out the conventions of your audience and discipline, and also ask specific questions of your instructor if you are writing for a class, or of another faculty member or professional who works and writes in that field. At the very least, academic audiences expect a clear introduction, a thorough analysis and discussion in the body of the essay, and a conclusion that brings closure to the research and/or argument.

Example of a Scholarly Argument

Elizabeth Vincent, a first-year writing student at Mesa Community College, wrote the following researched argument for her writing class. She includes outside resources to support the claims she makes in her argument, and her format follows that of a typical academic argument essay written in MLA format.

Vincent   1

Professor Rodrigo

ENG 103

23 April 2011

Childhood Obesity: Can Arizona Focus on Primary Prevention?

Childhood obesity is a national health epidemic with Arizona ranking among the highest for obese children ("Progress"). Childhood
obesity rates have started to increase greatly since the 1970's (Birch
and Ventura S74). There are many factors that contribute to childhood obesity. First, Americans have greater access to inexpensive
processed foods and also choose foods based on convenience.
Second, technological advances keep children sedentary rather
than outside and participating in physical activity. As a result,
obesity increases the risks for chronic health concerns, such as
heart disease, high blood pressure, and diabetes ("Progress"). In
other words, obesity leads to chronic and debilitating diseases which
will ultimately lower life expectancy (Wang and Veugelers 615).
A study published in 2010 by the *American Journal of Preventive
Medicine* named obesity the new leading cause of preventable death
(Freedhoff). Clearly, treating obesity after the problem is out of
control is no longer acceptable, and is not always effective. Prevention
programs can be an essential tool in decreasing the childhood
obesity statistic in Arizona and will only be successful if society
becomes motivated to get involved.

In general, obesity often presents itself in childhood and
doctors use the Body Mass Index (BMI) to assist in the diagnosis.
Typically obesity is indicated when a BMI is thirty or above. The
Mayo Clinic offers a free Body Mass Index calculator on their
website for children and adults (Mayo Clinic Staff). After individuals enter their weight, height, sex, and age the calculator will
display the BMI and indicate if the number is in the underweight,
normal, overweight, or obese category. In fact the Mayo Clinic
also offers suggestions based on the results of the calculations.
Suggestions include basic dietary recommendations and simple
exercises children can do to help achieve a healthy weight (Mayo
Clinic Staff). The internet can be a great place to start searching
for information on obesity prevention and obesity recovery. However, a nationwide prevention program is in place that can assist
individuals seeking additional tools, information, and motivation.

Margin annotations:

You might want to include some actual "startling" numbers here to grab and hold the reader's attention.

Only technology? What about parental fear of kids being abducted and/or hurt so that children are no longer just told to play outside or go to the park by themselves? What about the long hot months in Arizona; many people find it hard to exercise when it is difficult to go outside? All this to say, you could point to more than one reason that children do not "go play" as much. Certainly technology is a part of the equation, though.

After reading this introduction I'm unsure of whether or not you are arguing about the fact there is a childhood obesity problem or about how to solve it. Either way, it might help to provide a one sentence outline of the topics you'll be covering in your essay to help prepare the reader. Make sure the goal of your argument is clear.

Could you include a citation for this information? Depending on your audience, this might not be considered common knowledge, and some readers might be interested in reading more about BMI.

2   Vincent

In February of 2010, First Lady Michelle Obama launched the Let's Move! nationwide task force. The goal is to lower the childhood obesity rate to just five percent by the year 2030 (Whitehouse.gov, et al.). The initiative believes that every child has the right to a healthy lifestyle and recognizes that obesity is not an issue that will just disappear. The task force has designed action plans for many members of the community including parents, schools, mayors and local officials, community leaders, chefs, kids, and health care providers. Let's Move! has already started to make an impact in many lives all around the nation. Each action plan is simple to follow and is just five simple steps to success. Let's Move! presents the nation with the shocking statistic that one in three children are overweight or obese. With the prevalence of obesity increasing, one-third of all children born after 2000 will suffer from diabetes at some point in their lives. Therefore, Arizona should feel inspired to join the Let's Move! initiative and make a commitment to decreasing the childhood obesity statistic.

Parents can start transforming their family by making simple changes throughout the home. The Let's Move! task force offers tips to make modifications less difficult for children and family members. For example, people tend to snack on easily accessible items; to prevent children from making an unhealthy decision try placing a fruit bowl on the kitchen counter or the dining room table (Whitehouse.gov et al.). Also parents can rearrange the refrigerator and place healthier items in the front and at eye level. When kids go for a snack, the healthy items are the first choices they see. In other words, children may be more likely to make nutritious choices if they have easier access to fruits and vegetables, and less access to junk food. Another great idea for families is to plan weekly menus and have everyone participate in meal preparation. Once parents start making small changes to improve the overall health of their family they will be motivated to start larger transformations. For instance, parents can sit down with their children and establish reasonable exercise goals that the whole family can do together. Going to the gym every day for an hour is probably not a reasonable goal for most families so maybe parents and children should start with something simple. For example, parking further away at the grocery store and counting the steps as you walk to the door is a great way to get children involved in exercise (Whitehouse.gov et al.). Also, families should feel motivated to create their own exercise games and different ways to participate in physical activity.

Obviously, sedentary lifestyles have contributed to the childhood obesity epidemic. The Let's Move! tasks force explains that it is extremely important to reduce screen time and get children to be more active. With technological advances children almost never have to leave the house, and this has drastically reduced physical activity. Parents can set strict time limits for TV time, computer time, or even time for video games and make sure that children are spending more time being active (Whitehouse.gov et al.). Finally, parents really need to get involved in the school systems and understand what is happening with health programs that impact their children.

Children spend a significant amount of time at school. For this reason, Arizona school systems need to be dedicated to the health and well being of our children. The Let's Move! task force offers a number of suggestions to help school systems get involved. The most important step is for all Arizona schools to create a school health advisory council. Parents of obese children or anyone who wants to get involved can join the council and make a difference. The purpose of the advisory council is to help monitor health programs and also offer recommendations for modifications to crucial areas. First, vending machines can offer healthier options. Also, the advisory council can suggest that parents bring fruits and other healthy snacks to celebrate birthdays instead of cupcakes and other sweets (Whitehouse.gov et al.). Finally, the advisory council can recommend that physical activity never be used as punishment (Whitehouse.gov et al.). Let's Move! encourages schools to join the Healthier US Schools Challenge (HUSSC). Since many children may consume half of their daily calories at school, the HUSSC establishes rigorous criteria in food quality, participation in meal programs, physical activity opportunities, and nutrition education (Whitehouse.gov et al.). As a result, chefs can volunteer their time and make an impact on the nutrition program in school systems. For instance, chefs can create healthier menus and also teach administrators which foods offer the best nutritional values and may be the most cost effective to prepare. The news frequently mentions budget cuts and how Arizona schools will be significantly impacted. However, if members of the community get involved, physical activity and nutrition is an area Arizona children will not be denied.

4   Vincent

Nobody denies that childhood obesity is a serious problem in Arizona. On the other hand, many elected officials and community leaders are not motivated to take action. In January 2010, First Lady Michelle Obama challenged mayors nationwide to become a Let's Move! city or town (Whitehouse.gov et al.). Steps for signing up are simple. First, elected officials choose one area of importance to work on throughout a twelve-month period. Second, officials need to publicly make a commitment to inspire change. Finally, elected officials need to initiate an action plan. Let's Move! states that recognition could be awarded for some elected officials. For example, "Mayors from Let's Move cities and towns could be invited to participate in conference calls with White House and federal agency staff to share ideas, discuss barriers and celebrate progress" (Whitehouse.gov et al.). As of March 23, 2011, only seven Arizona cities have committed to making a change in childhood obesity. Participating Arizona cities include Casa Grande, Cottonwood, Flagstaff, Goodyear, Mesa, Phoenix, and Tucson. However, according to the Arizona government website Arizona has one hundred thirty-six incorporated cities and towns. As a result, several obese children are not receiving the assistance or education they so desperately require. Additionally, community leaders need to be encouraging mayors to participate in this exciting opportunity for our state and our children. In the meantime, community leaders and elected officials can do many other things to get involved. For instance, creating a newsletter with healthy tips for parents and children is a great way to get nutrition information out to the community. The community can even take the newsletter one step further and create a website that is easily accessible. Also, after-school activity programs would be a great way to get children motivated and interested in physical activity. Initiating after-school obesity prevention programs can help children take a more active and decisive role in their own nutritious lifestyle.

Children need at least sixty minutes of exercise every day (Whitehouse.gov et al.). The best part about being a kid is sixty minutes of physical activity is easy to achieve. Older children should start up an activity group with some friends to make exercise fun and less stressful. Also, friends can gather and make a plan for which activities they will do throughout the week, most of which can be

---

You are relying on this web site for a great deal of information. It might be helpful to differentiate between different pages if you are getting information from different parts of the Let's Move! web site.

I love that you are making this personal by making it regional. However, if you share information like a list of participants, you need to include a citation from where you read the list. Don't forget, every sentence that includes information from an outside resource needs some form of in-text citation.

How do you motivate people to go to the web site?

These are great suggestions; do you have data from other places that implemented these solutions and saw a decrease in the number of obese children?

Vincent   5

done at school. Great examples are taking a walk after lunch, jump roping, basketball, or really anything that sounds fun and gets everyone moving. In the same way, younger children can get physical activity at school and at home. Parents and children can even create games to make this process more exhilarating (Whitehouse.gov et al.). Along with exercise, Let's Move! encourages children to try new fruits and vegetables. Fruits and veggies provide many nutrients needed for kids to grow up healthy and also to maintain a healthy weight. Besides, fruit is sweet and can be substituted for candy so children should be encouraged to choose a piece of fruit when candy cravings occur. For children who are nervous about trying new foods, Let's Move! has a lot of tips. For example, incorporate vegetables into some of the foods you already enjoy to make them healthier and the transition less stressful (Whitehouse.gov et al.). Also, parents can encourage children to pick fun flavors of yogurt at the grocery store and freeze them to use as an ice cream substitute. Additionally, children need to drink a lot of water on a daily basis to stay healthy. This is one way kids can take an active role in their own health. For instance, children should be encouraged to choose water instead of sugary drinks in vending machines and at meal times. Children can also express their independence and motivation by decreasing their technology time. In other words, children should watch less TV and spend more time being active. If children insist on watching TV for long periods of time, perhaps exercises can be done at certain time intervals. For example, after thirty minutes of TV the TV gets turned off and a few sets of jumping jacks are done. Children should feel inspired to take more responsibility for their own lives and health.

> A lot of your argument is dependent on this one resource; do you have others that support it? There are medical journals that have research that would support things like the need to exercise sixty minutes a day and to increase fruit and vegetable consumption.

Health care providers have the opportunity to make a significant impact on Arizona's children with each visit (Whitehouse.gov et al.). That is, providers have the ability to assess and educate families on the importance of a healthy and active lifestyle. Additionally, health care providers should be encouraging families to make changes together. Let's Move! provides a printable prescription for healthier living that providers can give to patients. The prescriptions have an area that lists recommendations as well as an area where children can make goals. For instance, the recommendation for fruits and vegetables is five servings a day. Next, the provider discusses with the family a reasonable goal and writes that in the goal area for fruits

6   Vincent

and vegetables. After the goals have been established everyone will sign the prescription and it is a commitment to a healthier lifestyle. In fact, this is a great motivational tool for health care providers to have as a resource! All in all, doctor's visits can also be a great time for doctor, parent, and child to discuss appropriate dietary guidelines.

> You've already discussed better eating and more exercise. It feels like you are arranging your argument based on your resources (more like a review of literature) instead of based on categories or reasons. Might this information have been more useful earlier in the argument?

The United States Department of Agriculture (USDA) Center for Nutrition Policy and Promotion released new dietary guidelines for Americans on January 31, 2011. The new dietary guidelines are focused on balancing calories with physical activity. The USDA recommends that America increase healthy food choices. For example, individuals should increase their intake of fruits and vegetables, seafood, and whole grains. At the same time individuals also need to decrease the consumption of unhealthy food choices. Along with the diet and exercise recommendations the USDA also provides information to help individuals incorporate these guidelines into their everyday lives. Families should take advantage of this information. In fact, the USDA dietary guidelines are the resources used by many nutritionists to make recommendations.

Undoubtedly, Arizona can expect to encounter resistance when trying to motivate citizens to become involved. People will want to know how childhood obesity ultimately affects them and their families. Arizona needs to participate in preventing and lowering the state's childhood obesity statistics. Society should feel motivated to become involved, especially with the rising health care costs associated with obesity-related complications.

> These are great numbers; why not use these in the introduction to motivate readers? You can even start your essay with your refutation arguing why "everyone" should care.

According to the USDA, in 2010 thirty-two percent of all children are overweight or obese. In fact, an obese child is more likely to become an obese adult. As a result these children can expect to encounter many health concerns and lower life expectancy by as much as two to five years (Rahman, Cushing, and Jackson 49). Additionally, three hundred thousand Americans die each year from obesity-related complications (Greenblatt). Also, one hundred seventeen billion dollars are spent each year as a result of obesity (Greenblatt). Childhood obesity does not just affect individual families. Every single person in Arizona is affected. Therefore, if obesity rates continue to increase, health care costs can be expected to increase as well.

Vincent   7

In the light of the childhood obesity epidemic it is easy to see that primary prevention programs are essential to lowering the statistics in Arizona. Children need to be educated about the risks that arise when obesity is left untreated. In fact, prevention programs need to be implemented in Arizona school systems immediately. Additionally, everyone in the community needs to get involved. The ultimate goal in obesity prevention is to help children live healthy and productive lifestyles. Clearly primary prevention can turn this goal into a reality for many kids. Parents need to take a more active role in the nutrition requirements for their children. In the same way schools need to take the initiative and provide healthier food choices. Arizona mayors and other elected officials need to take the important first step and become a Let's Move! city or town. Additionally, children need to take more responsibility for their health. Finally, health care professionals need to remember that every encounter is a possible opportunity. With a strong support system, obesity percentages in Arizona can be lowered. However, ignoring childhood obesity is irresponsible and can no longer be tolerated.

If you had this scholarly, peer-reviewed article about "what works," why do most of the suggestions in your paper come from a web site? You could rely on the ethos of scholarly articles to support your argument more.

Works Cited

Birch, L. L., and A. K. Ventura. "Preventing Childhood Obesity: What Works?" *International Journal of Obesity* 33 (2009): S74–S81. *EBSCOhost*. Web. 14 April 2011.

Freedhoff, Yoni. "Obesity the New #1 Preventable Cause of Death—Now What?" *Weighty Matters*. 12 Jan. 2010. Web. 15 April 2011.

Greenblatt, Alan. Obesity epidemic. *CQ Researcher* 13.4 (2003). Web. 14 April 2011.

Mayo Clinic Staff. "Obesity. *Mayo Clinic.com*. Mayo, 1998–2012. Web. 14 April 2011.

"Progress in Obesity Fight." *AZCentral.com*. The Arizona Republic, 19 June 2010. Web. 14 April 2011.

Rahman, Tamanna, Rachel A. Cushing, and Richard J. Jackson. "Contributions of Built Environment to Childhood Obesity." *Mount Sinai Journal of Medicine* 78.1 (2011): 49–57. EBSCOhost. Web. 14 April 2011.

8   Vincent

United States Department of Agriculture Center for Nutrition Policy and Promotion. "Dietary Guidelines for Americans." *DietaryGuidelines.gov*. USDA, 31 Jan. 2011. Web. 14 April 2011.

Wang, F., and P. J. Veugelers. "Self-esteem and Cognitive Development in the Era of the Childhood Obesity Epidemic." *Obesity Reviews* 9.6 (2008): 615–623. *EBSCOhost*. Web. 15 April 2011.

Whitehouse.gov, et al. *Let's Move!—America's Move to Raise a Healthier Generation of Kids*. Whitehouse, 2011. Web. 12 April 2011.

Discussion Questions

▸ How well do you understand the controversy surrounding this issue after reading the essay?

▸ What is the author's position on the issue? Does she provide appropriate qualifiers to explain her position clearly? What suggestions would you make to the author?

▸ What reasons does the author provide to support her position? Are these reasons sufficient? Are they clearly developed? What suggestions would you make?

▸ What evidence does the author use to support her reasons? Are there pieces of evidence that are unclear? What missing evidence would you like to have seen her provide? In other words, are claims or reasons given that have insufficient evidence? What suggestions would you make?

Steps to Presenting Research Results

You will likely follow five major steps in presenting your research results: first, identifying your rhetorical situation; second, determining which presentation mode is appropriate; third, determining a reasonable answer to your research question and writing it as a clear claim; fourth, identifying reasons and evidence in support of your claim; and fifth, designing your argument.

Identifying Your Rhetorical Situation

The rhetorical situation that you find yourself writing for is inevitably going to guide the rest of the choices you make in the other four steps. Therefore, your first task is to recall and make any necessary revisions to your rhetorical situation. If you worked through the assignments in Part 1 of this text, you have already done a great deal of thinking about your rhetorical situation. You might try the following activities to refresh your thinking about your specific audience, purpose, topic, and your position as the author of your research:

▶ "Write: Analyze the Rhetorical Situation," on page 41 of Chapter 3
▶ "Write: Consider Audience and Purpose," on page 43 of Chapter 3
▶ "Write: Define the Rhetorical Situation," on page 168 of Chapter 8

Determining Which Presentation Mode Is Appropriate

Once you have spent time thinking about your rhetorical situation, you can consider what presentation mode will best reach your audience. Try working through the following activity to help you determine which presentation mode is most appropriate for your project.

As you consider the ways you might present the results of your research, take a few minutes to write your responses to the following questions. Use your responses to choose the best presentation mode for your research.

Purpose

▶ Are there requirements you must consider regarding the presentation of your research? If so, what are they?
▶ What will your presentation need to do in order to fulfill the original purpose of your research? Is there a presentation mode that will best meet those needs?

Audience

▶ What expectations does your audience have for the presentation of your research?
▶ What media will your audience have access to?
▶ What presentation form will reach your audience? What will they be most receptive to, and where would they be looking for your argument?
▶ When would your audience be interested in and/or open to hearing about your research? How would you reach your audience at that time?
▶ Who might be interested in your research that might not yet know about it? How would you reach that potential audience?

Topic

▶ What presentation format is most appropriate for your topic?
▶ What presentation format is most appropriate for the argument you are making about your topic?
▶ Are there aspects of your research that might be difficult to understand in an exclusively text-based presentation? How might you explain those parts of your research in a different way?

Author

▶ What media are you most familiar with? Is there a presentation format that you are unfamiliar with that you would like to learn more about?
▶ Would a combination of media present your research most effectively? Do you already know how to use them or could you enlist someone to help you use them?

Developing Your Claim

In a researched argument, your audience will immediately look for the claim, or thesis, that signals the position you are taking in your argument. Your claim needs to be a defensible one; in other words, you need to be able to support your claim with clear reasons and evidence. As you develop your claim, you might revisit some of the following activities:

▶ "Write: Create a Cluster Map," on page 170 of Chapter 8

▶ "Write: Draft a Thesis Statement," on page 173 of Chapter 8

Identifying Reasons and Finding Evidence

Your claim needs to be supported by clear reasons and convincing evidence. As you construct your argument, you might consider various ways of developing reasons for your position. Chapter 8 deals with the development of an argument in detail, and you might want to look at the following activities for specific direction as you identify reasons and find evidence in support of your claim:

▶ "Reflect: Should You Conduct Primary or Secondary Research?" on page 71 of Chapter 4

▶ "Write: Develop a List of Search Terms," on page 75 of Chapter 4

▶ "Write: Search the Library Catalog," on page 82 of Chapter 4

▶ "Write: Search for Resources in Periodicals," on page 84 of Chapter 4

▶ "Write: Search for a Variety of Resources," on page 88 of Chapter 4

▶ "Write: Take Detailed Notes on a Resource," on page 122 of Chapter 6

▶ "Write: Track Bibliographic Information," on page 126 of Chapter 6

▶ "Write: Develop Your Authorial Ethos," on page 177 of Chapter 8

▶ "Write: Develop Emotional Arguments," on page 178 of Chapter 8

▶ "Write: Understand Your Warrants," on page 182 of Chapter 8

▶ "Write: Develop Counterarguments," on page 183 of Chapter 8

▶ "Write: Construct an Argument," on page 183 of Chapter 8

Designing Your Argument

The medium and format you choose for presenting your research results will guide how you design that presentation. One way of thinking through an argument that is rather linear is to develop an outline. There are different types of outlines, and various degrees of detail can be included in those outlines. Instead of trying to produce your outline in one sitting, try building continuous layers of the outline.

1. Begin with an outline that has your claim (the answer to your research question) at the top of the page, and simply list the reasons for supporting that claim.
2. Next, list the pieces of evidence (individual units of information) that support your reasons. Be sure to include the basic citation information with each outside source.
3. Revise your outline by explaining how each reason connects to the claim (the logic of the reason).
4. Finally, explain how each piece of evidence connects to each reason (the logic of the evidence).

You will also want to include a compelling introduction that grabs your audience's attention and an effective conclusion that compels your audience to action. Try these activities to get started:

▶ "Write: Develop an Outline," on page 206 of Chapter 10

▶ "Write: Draft an Effective Introduction," on page 208 of Chapter 10

▶ "Write: Develop Closure," on page 209 of Chapter 10

▶ "Write: Identify Possible Frames," on page 210 of Chapter 10

Make It with Multiple Media: Multimodal Presentations

Depending on the nature of your research project, you might find that a presentation mode other than a text-based academic essay or scientific report would reach your audience most effectively. Keep in mind the multiple audiences and purposes that you might be addressing in this project. For example, a student writing about solutions to parking problems on campus might address her research to specific administrators on campus, but she might also be conducting the research for a class where she is addressing an audience of her teachers and classmates. One purpose of her research is to propose a solution for campus parking, but she has an additional purpose of completing the assignment for class credit. Each of these influences is a factor in her choice of how she presents her research.

Many research projects are best shared through a multimodal presentation that combines elements of several formats. For example, a blog entry might include a link to a video clip to emphasize a point. Or a slide presentation (such as one designed with PowerPoint) might include links to web pages, pictures, or other static images, or embedded animation, audio, and/or video. You could combine elements of any of the previously mentioned types of presentation to reach your audience.

The following list of possible presentation modes is not exhaustive. The categories outlined here might help you think of other possibilities, too; the important thing is to find the method that will reach your audience most effectively. You might consider presenting your research as:

❖ a newspaper article or piece in a periodical

❖ a slide show (using an application such as PowerPoint or Prezi)

❖ a poster

❖ an infographic

❖ a blog entry

❖ a contribution to an online resource, such as Wikipedia

❖ flyers

❖ pictures

❖ graphs or charts

- ❋ a video broadcast

- ❋ an oral presentation, talk, or speech

- ❋ an audio file uploaded to a web site

- ❋ a podcast (if the research is something you would like to incorporate into a serial, or syndicated, broadcast)

- ❋ a pamphlet or brochure

- ❋ an interactive web site

- ❋ a film/video presentation

Shelley Rodrigo, one of the authors of the text, was asked to present for an online conference. Because her audience was online, and because they were accessing her presentation at different times, she chose to create a video presentation that visitors to the conference's web site could watch at their convenience. She created a static, poster-style image of her talking points and then walked through various parts of the image in a screencast video.

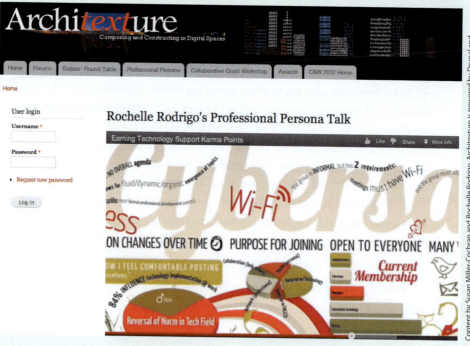

Formatting Your Research

DIY: **Writing a Rhetorical Analysis of Citations**

chapter 11

Understanding Citation Styles Rhetorically

Although in previous classes you may have only worked with one, maybe two, formatting and citation style guides, there are many to choose from. One thing to keep in mind when discussing formatting and citation styles is that you may hear people use the term "documentation" instead of "citation." The terms "citation" and "documentation" can be used interchangeably in most situations. When people refer to a "style guide," they're referring to one of the major citation styles used in academic writing. One of the primary goals of this chapter is to help you determine which style guide is appropriate to use in a given rhetorical situation.

we'll explore

▶ *formatting your document or project*

▶ *citing sources*

▶ *dealing with complications of citation in an age of digital distribution*

▶ *learning citation styles by constructing your own citations*

Research in Action

Author: Harper is currently enrolled in a Technology and Society class. She wants to go to graduate school to be a veterinarian.

Topic: Her Technology and Society instructor said she might research any topic about how a given technological advancement affects a particular group. When she has the opportunity to select her own research topics, she tries to connect them to her passion, helping animals. She remembers flipping through a classmate's issue of *Wired* magazine and seeing an article about prosthetics for animals; she loved the article's title, "Made Whole."

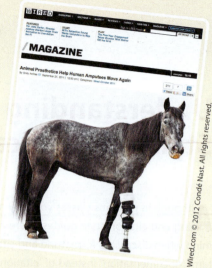

Audience: Since this project is an academic paper, Harper knows she needs to follow a citation style carefully. As she researches, reads, and take notes, she carefully documents bibliographic information like author, title, and other publication details.

Purpose: Harper understands a main function of a bibliographic citation is to get the reader back to the original resource; however, when she tracked down the same *Wired* article online by using the date of publication and issue number, she became confused. The images and information looked the same, but the title of the article online was different; instead of "Made Whole" it was "Animal Prosthetics Help Human Amputees Move Again." She also noticed that the online article had more content than the original print article did. Curious, Harper borrowed a friend's iPad to see how the article came up on the *Wired* mobile application. The article in the mobile application was titled "Made Whole," like the print version; however, it included all the same information as the Web version. Harper wondered, *were these three different versions of the same article, published in different media*?

Questions

1. Which resource should Harper cite? Why?

2. Which title should she use? Why?

3. In what situation(s) might you need to compare and contrast different versions of the same resource?

Four Popular Style Guides

Guidelines for formatting and citation have generally been given for alphanumeric texts printed on paper (such as manuscripts for essays, journal articles, and books). Formatting emerged to help printers interpret instructions for how to lay out, design, and print journals and books. Similarly, citation styles emerged to help readers understand what material is being quoted, paraphrased, or otherwise referred to and where readers can find that original material. Formatting and citation styles have begun to adapt to new kinds of texts beyond those printed on paper. Regardless of the medium, however, properly formatting and citing your documents is very important for meeting the needs and expectations of your readers. This book provides instruction for four popular style guides:

▶ *MLA Handbook for Writers of Research Papers* is the official style guide of the Modern Language Association of America, from whom the style takes its name. The Modern Language Association of America supports scholars who study the literature and culture of English and other languages. The MLA documentation style is generally used by language, literature, and other humanities scholars, and it would be most appropriate to use when writing about topics related to these disciplines, such as literature, language usage, art, and various types of media.

▶ *Publication Manual of the American Psychological Association* (**APA**) is the official style guide of the American Psychological Association. Obviously, the APA's style guidelines apply to those studying psychology; however, APA style is also used in many disciplines in or related to the social sciences.

▶ *The Chicago Manual of Style* (**CMS**) is the official style guide of the University of Chicago Press, from whom the style takes its name. History is one of the disciplines that most often uses CMS guidelines; however, CMS is used by a large number of academic presses dealing with several disciplines.

▶ *The CSE Manual for Authors, Editors, and Publishers* is the official style guide of the Council of Science Editors, from whom the style takes its name. CSE style is generally used by authors writing in the natural sciences as the generic formatting that they can then adapt to a specific journal's guidelines, and most of the disciplines in the natural sciences use a style guide that is at least loosely based on CSE guidelines.

Formatting Texts

Formatting refers to the layout, design, and presentation of material in any text, whether it is printed on paper, in digital format such as a web site, or a video. For example, if you visit the web sites of several different department stores, you will start to see similar layout and design conventions. Visitors to a particular store's web site—much like visitors to the brick-and-mortar store—expect to be greeted with familiar layout and design to help them easily navigate the store's merchandise. A written paper carries the same expectations for its layout and design: these elements make the content of a paper easier to navigate. For example, not only does printing your work with double-spacing make it easier for the reader's eyes to distinguish words on the page, it also leaves white space that your instructor may use to write comments on the paper to help as you continue revising.

Formatting guidelines are typically given for incorporating visual elements (such as charts, photographs, or other illustrations); spacing and margins; headers, footers, and page numbers; titles, title pages, and bylines; and section headers. While it is possible for you to memorize formatting conventions for a given style guide, it is generally not worth your time. While drafting papers, it is probably a good idea to use one-inch margins and double-spacing; however, you should always refer to the specific formatting guidelines of any assignment or the submission guidelines for a publication prior to making your last round of revisions.

Remember, formatting guidelines are not only relevant for essays printed on paper. If you are submitting projects in other media, you may be told to follow some formatting guidelines relevant to a particular medium. For example,

▶ For **presentation slides** you may be given guidelines on minimum or maximum size of text, how to cite images on the slides, and how to provide information found on traditional title pages and end-of-paper bibliographies.

▶ For **web sites** you may be given guidelines on what type and color of font to use, the arrangement of different groups of information on the page, and whether or not to include a site map.

▶ For **videos** you may be given guidelines on where and how to run credits, whether or not you need captioning, and in what type of computer file format to compress your final video.

techno tip

Format a Document

If you are using a standard word-processing program to write your paper, you can use its features to format your paper with minimal difficulty. Use the formatting choices to set the following options for your paper.

▶ Double-space your paper throughout. Set this option before you type any text so that your entire paper is double-spaced.

▶ Set your header to include the heading required by the citation style you are using (your last name and page number in the case of MLA). Word-processing programs can automatically insert the page number for you after your name, and you can set the document to skip numbering the first page.

▶ On the works cited or references page, use the ruler at the top of the screen to set a hanging indent for your citations (unless you are using CSE) so that you don't have to hit "Enter" and "Tab" at the end of each line.

If you need help setting up these functions in your word-processing program, try checking the official web site for your word-processing program (like Microsoft Office, OpenOffice Writer, or Google Docs), and check out video repositories like *YouTube* and *Vimeo* for formatting help.

Citing Sources

When you cite resources, you are leaving a trail of breadcrumbs, so to speak, to help your reader find his or her way back to the original resource you used. You're also pointing to the research and conversations that have been important in developing your thoughts on a particular issue. Although you may not see this very much in informal essays or news articles, providing citations for any resources you quote, paraphrase, or refer to is critically important and expected in academic writing. Keep in mind that, as we discussed in Part 1 of this book, research projects provide a way to participate in ongoing conversations about an issue. Because the conversation is ongoing, it's important to give reference points to your readers so they understand the context of the research you are doing.

Because many texts can be found in a variety of locations, it is important to record all of the bibliographic information while researching and taking notes, including the medium of publication, such as print, Web, etc. (For example, how many different editions of Shakespeare's work have you seen in your academic studies?) Because the Internet is a dynamic medium and changes can occur quickly, it might be wise to print, or otherwise save, copies of your source documents.

In-Text Citations

You must include an in-text citation for every individual reference to information from an outside resource, whether you are directly quoting that source or not. Usually those citations are included at the end of the sentence, unless the information cited is in the beginning or middle of the sentence and the end of the sentence is your interpretation or idea. Even if you are only summarizing or paraphrasing the resource, you still must include an in-text citation in the same sentence in which you present the material. Indeed, you might argue that it's even more important to include in-text citations when you're summarizing and paraphrasing since it would be more difficult for the reader to find the original source of the information.

In-text citations generally come in two styles, parenthetical or superscripted footnote and/or endnote. In Standard Academic English, parenthetical citations are generally considered a part of the sentence; therefore, the end-of-sentence punctuation is included after the in-text citation. For example, standard in-text citations in MLA format include the author's name and the page number in the citation, as the following example demonstrates:

> Science fiction films "self-consciously foreground their own radicality" of special effects (Freedman 307).

If you are using footnotes or endnotes as an in-text citation method, the superscript number needs to come at the end of the sentence, as is the case with CMS's notes and bibliography citation system (see Figure 11.1).

When using parenthetical citation, you can include some of the bibliographic information in the sentence itself. This can be a strategy for emphasizing the name of the author

Lorie and Rodrigo 18

Thomas Tierney theorizes how technology functions as a way to overcome the temporal and spatial limits of the body, using technology to promote the Cartesian mind/body split and even overcome death.[1] Obviously in these shows the technologies begin to also overcome the emotional and mental limits of being human. These technofetishized scenes in the *CSIs*, *Bones*, and *ReGenesis* also reenact typical Mulvey[2] moments, with the close-ups of the technology standing in for the close-ups of female body parts; both objectifying, disavowing, and displacing dangerously emotional humanity.

---

[1] Thomas F. Tierney, *The Value of Convenience: A Genealogy of Technical Culture.*
[2] Laura Mulvey, "Visual Pleasure and Narrative Cinema."

Figure 11.1   Superscript Numbers for In-Text Citations and Corresponding Numbered Footnotes Using CMS. Shortened Notes Used In-Text with Full Bibliography at the End of the Paper.

you are citing, or it can simply be a way to vary the sentence structure in your writing. The next example, in MLA format, uses the same short quotation from the Freedman work cited above and only needs to provide the page where the quotation was found because Freedman's name is included in the sentence itself:

Carl Freedman criticizes science fiction films for "self-consciously foreground[ing] their own radicality" of special effects (307).

For in-text citations that use footnotes or endnotes, mentioning some bibliographic information in the sentence does not change the way the citation is noted in text (with a superscript numeral) or the content of the note: you still provide full information in the note.

As early as 1997, Carl Freedman criticized science fiction films for "self-consciously foreground[ing] their own radicality" of special effects.[1]

Full Bibliographic Citations

In-text citations are the first, very small, bread crumbs on the citation trail. As seen in Figure 11.2, the in-text citations provide just enough information to get the reader from the quote, paraphrase, or summary in the text to the full bibliographic citation at the end of the document (if you are using the CMS notes and bibliography system, the notes may be at the bottom of the page).

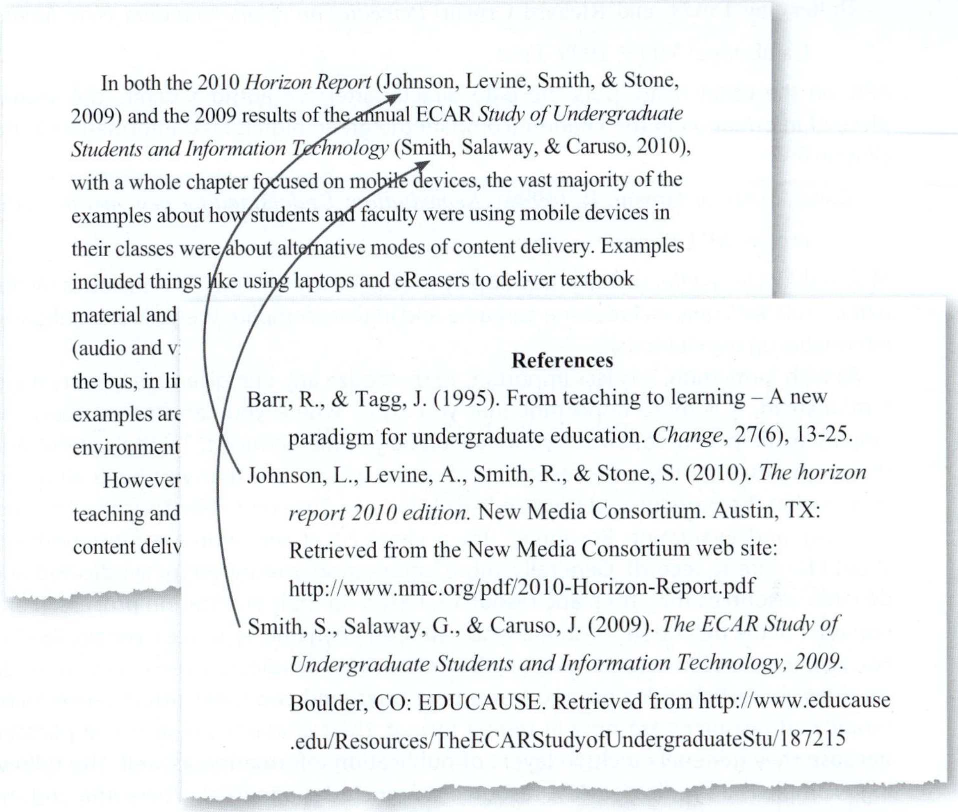

In both the 2010 *Horizon Report* (Johnson, Levine, Smith, & Stone, 2009) and the 2009 results of the annual ECAR *Study of Undergraduate Students and Information Technology* (Smith, Salaway, & Caruso, 2010), with a whole chapter focused on mobile devices, the vast majority of the examples about how students and faculty were using mobile devices in their classes were about alternative modes of content delivery. Examples included things like using laptops and eReasers to deliver textbook material and

(audio and v

the bus, in li

examples are

environment

However

teaching and

content deliv

References

Barr, R., & Tagg, J. (1995). From teaching to learning – A new
    paradigm for undergraduate education. *Change*, 27(6), 13-25.

Johnson, L., Levine, A., Smith, R., & Stone, S. (2010). *The horizon*
    report 2010 edition. New Media Consortium. Austin, TX:
    Retrieved from the New Media Consortium web site:
    http://www.nmc.org/pdf/2010-Horizon-Report.pdf

Smith, S., Salaway, G., & Caruso, J. (2009). *The ECAR Study of*
    Undergraduate Students and Information Technology, 2009.
    Boulder, CO: EDUCAUSE. Retrieved from http://www.educause
    .edu/Resources/TheECARStudyofUndergraduateStu/187215

Figure 11.2   Full Entries from the APA Style References Page Correspond to Parenthetical References in the Essay.

The various formatting and citation style guides title their full bibliographic pages differently:

    MLA: Works Cited

    APA: References

    CMS: Bibliography

    CSE: Cited References, References, or Literature Cited

As a rule of thumb, list on your bibliographic page only those resources cited in your paper, not resources that you found and read during your research process but did not refer to in the paper. Of course, your instructor or other audience may require that you list all works consulted, but you would use a separate title (Works Consulted) instead of Works Cited.

Although the information included in full bibliographic citations tends to be the same from one style guide to the next, the order and manner in which information is presented about the author(s), title, and publication vary widely. For example, MLA citations put the publication date at the end of the full bibliographic citation:

> Bolter, Jay David, and Richard Grusin. *Remediation: Understanding New Media.*
> Cambridge: MITP, 1999. Print.

APA, on the other hand, puts the date directly after the author's name, the second piece of information in the citation (compare the green highlighted information in the citations):

> Bolter, J. D., & Grusin, R. (1999). *Remediation*: *Understanding new media.* Cambridge: MIT Press.

MLA and APA also differ on how they display the author's first name. MLA includes the full name while APA only includes the surname and initials (compare the yellow highlighted information in the citations).

As with formatting, it is less important to memorize any one given citation style system; instead, it is more important that you know where you can find multiple examples to help you construct your full bibliographic citations. Taking careful and thorough notes during your research processes will ensure that you have all of the information the particular citation style calls for (see Chapter 6, "Rhetorically Reading, Tracking, and Evaluating Resources" for a checklist of the source information you should be sure to record). Generally, more information is required for syndicated and dynamic resources than for static resources, based on their publication process. (For a reminder of the definitions of static, syndicated, and dynamic resources, see pp. 78–79.) For example, multiple titles need to be tracked for syndicated resources (periodical titles and article titles or blog titles, post titles, and comment titles). Since many syndicated resources are now in digital format, their citations are also complicated because they generally include layers of publication information as well. The following example is a syndicated APA resource that includes a journal article title and the name of the journal as well:

> Norris, D., Bear, L., Leonard, J., Pugliese, L., & Lafrere, P. (2008, January/February).
> Action analytics: Measuring and improving performance that matters in higher
> education. *EDUCAUSE Review*, 43, 42–67. Retrieved from http://www.edu-
> cause.edu/ir/library/pdf/ERM0813.pdf

Compare the blue highlighted areas above with the dynamic resource example below, in CMS footnote/endnote style. In the wiki page example, there is the name of the article with the name of the web site as well.

> 23. Andrew Churches, "Bloom's Digital Taxonomy," *Educational Origami*, last
> modified October 1, 2010, accessed September 14, 2011, http://edorigami.wiki-
> spaces.com/page/history/Bloom%27s+Digital+Taxonomy.

Since dynamic resources change regularly, it is very important to include the exact date that you found, read, or interacted with the resource. For example, all of the green highlighted areas above are the original publication date (or the last modified date of the wiki page). The wiki page citation example includes the retrieval date as well.

write

Practice Citations

Use the following sample paragraph and its list of resources to practice inserting in-text citations and constructing properly formatted full bibliographic citations. The following steps will help you:

1. Identify which citation style you will use and refer to the appropriate chapter (that is, Chapter 12, 13, 14, or 15).

2. Identify where you need to include in-text citations; the sample paragraph contains direct quotes, paraphrases, and summaries.

3. Insert the in-text citations where they are required. Be sure to include the appropriate information for each type of in-text citation.

4. Finally, convert the resource information at the bottom of the text into an appropriately formatted bibliographic page.

Strauss concludes that "the moral is that unless we show faculty members how technology can meet their needs, they won't consider using it." While studying what community college faculty needed to incorporate technology into their instruction, Quick and Davies found faculty needed time, money, software, classroom computers (professor podium), department computer lab, and faculty technical support and training.

In discussing how to prepare college faculty for the incoming 'Net generation of students, Clayton-Pedersen and O'Neill claim that "much of the learning technology innovation in higher education has been focused on K–12 teacher preparation and development" and that "more focus needs to be placed on preparing existing faculty for the future 'Net Generation students who will populate the twenty-first century classroom." They continue that call for action in claiming that "faculty's understanding of the teaching and learning power of technology needs to be increased" and "tools need to be developed to help faculty integrate technology into the curriculum." Strauss, Quick and Davies, and Clayton-Pedersen and O'Neill demonstrate that faculty first needs blatant introductions to the new technologies themselves: what they are and what they can do.

Resources Referred to in the Text Above

Resource #1: Ebook

Authors: Alma R. Clayton-Pedersen and Nancy O'Neill

Article Title: Curricula Designed to Meet 21st Century Expectations

Book: Educating the Net Generation

Book Editor: Diana G. Oblinger and James L. Oblinger

Publisher: EDUCAUSE

Publisher location: Washington, DC

Copyright Date: 2005

>>>

>>>

Location of Resource: Web

Date Located: August 22, 2011

Resource #2: Journal Article

Authors: Don Quick and Timothy Gray Davies

Article Title: Community College Faculty Development: Bringing Technology into Instruction

Journal Title: Community College Journal of Research and Practice

Volume Number: 23

Issue Number: 4

Publication Date: 1999

Page Numbers: 641–653

Location of Resource: Library Stacks

Date Located: September 14, 2011

Resource #3: Online Magazine

Author: Howard Strauss

Article Title: Why Many Faculty Members Aren't Excited about Technology

Trade Magazine Title: The Chronicle of Higher Education

Publication Date: June 24, 2005

Location of Resource: Web

Date Located: December 31, 2011

Reproduced by permission of Rochelle Rodrigo.

Handling Citation Challenges in the Age of Digital Distribution

The emergence of digital media and the Internet have made citation more difficult, to say the least. Many traditionally written, alphanumeric texts are now available in a variety of locations and formats, sometimes making it difficult to share citation information, especially page numbers, when referring to quotations. For example, newspaper and magazine web sites simultaneously publish articles on the Web without any reference to the section or page numbers of the article in the traditional print version.

Similarly, many ereaders like the Amazon Kindle and the Nook from Barnes & Noble do not have page numbers. Many books on the Kindle do have section numbers, however. But is it useful to post a section number for a quotation if the reader of your text only has access to the traditional print version of the book with page numbers?

It has also become increasingly easy for individuals to self-publish to the Internet in a variety of media. Without editors and publishers to help streamline some of the formatting, some of these self-published resources make it very difficult to find basic publishing information. For example, we are used to looking on the back of title pages in books to find publisher information, but there is no similarly standard location for publication information in self-published resources.

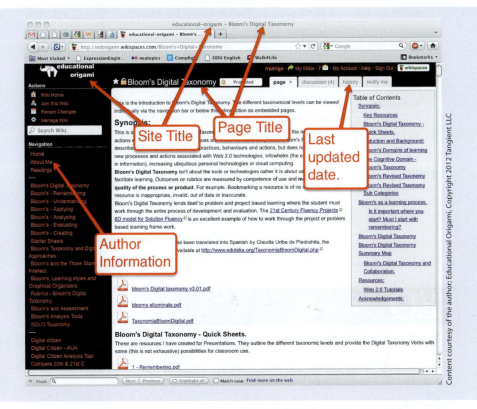

In your research you will likely encounter many new genres of texts (e.g., blogs, wikis, and podcasting) and many more hybrid mash-ups of multiple media and genres. The organizations that sponsor the different citation styles have been unable to keep up with all the new forms of texts and therefore do not always provide examples of full bibliographic citations for those sources. Often you will have to find one or two "official" citation examples that most resemble the type of resource you are citing, and then make up your own full bibliographic citation style doing your best to think like the style guide authors. For example, if you were doing research about the public reaction to the tenth anniversary of the 9/11 tragedies, you might want to refer to specific comments made by people on *Twitter* and *Facebook*. It would be difficult to find an example of a citation of *Twitter* or *Facebook* in the MLA or APA guides, however.

Many of these problems are avoided when you publish on the Internet. The ability to use hyperlinks when composing in digital texts is, like Figure 11.3, both less disruptive to the flow of text (no in-text citation) and more precise in citation (they link to the actual resource). Assuming you are producing a project that requires citation in one of the four traditional styles (MLA, APA, CMS, or CSE), however, you'll need to find a way to cite your sources without relying on hyperlinks. Let's consider an extended example using the Declaration of Independence as a resource that you need to incorporate into your project.

In both the 2010 *Horizon Report* (Johnson, Levine, Smith and Stone, 2010) and the 2009 results of the annual ECAR *Study of Undergraduate Students and Information Technology* (Smith, Salaway and Caruso, 2010), with a whole chapter focused on mobile devices, the vast majority of the examples about how students and faculty were using mobile devices in their classes were about alternative modes of content delivery. Examples included things like using laptops and eReasers to deliver textbook material and

(audio and v…

the bus, in li…

examples are…

environment…

However…

teaching and…

content deliv…

References

Barr, R., & Tagg, J. (1995). From Teaching to Learning – A New Paradigm for Undergraduate Education. *Change*, 27(6): 13-25.

Johnson, L., Levine, A., Smith, R. & Stone, S. (2010). *The Horizon Report 2010 Edition.* New Media Consortium. Austin, TX: The New Media Consortium. Retrieved from: http://www.nmc.org/pdf/2010-Horizon-Report.pdf

Smith, S., Salaway, G., & Caruso, J. (2009). *The ECAR Study of Undergraduate Students and Information Technology, 2009* Boulder, CO: EDUCAUSE. Retrieved from: http://www.educause.edu/Resources/TheECARStudyofUndergraduateStu/187215

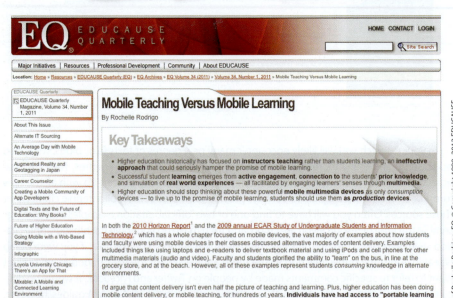

Figure 11.3 The Same Passage from an Essay, Shown in the Print Version (note separate References page) and in the Online, Hyperlinked Version (note that same citations are given as direct links).

There is the original document, held at the National Archives in Washington, DC; however, how many people really "read" that version of the document? There is generally a large number of people surrounding the document, and even if you get to it, the document is kept under glass and is faded due to its age.

For many people, the first time they read the Declaration of Independence was either in a book, probably a history or government textbook, or on the Web. In both of these locations, there can be both static images (photographs) of the original document as well as texts that just reproduce the words themselves, perhaps with each line numbered to help with reference. While the versions published in textbooks and at the National Archives web site are considered the most "official," these exist along with less official versions found as vacation pictures in *Flickr* and on various blogs, wikis, and other web sites.

As with everything else in this book, which versions of the text you choose to use and cite in your research project would be dependent on your research question, purpose, and audience. If your project is a textual analysis of the Declaration of Independence, it might help to refer to a version that has line numbers printed on it. If you were doing a project about the social popularity of the Declaration of Independence and how people interact with it, you might refer to lots of different personal photos posted on *Flickr*. And if you were composing this social popularity project for a traditional academic paper, you would have to use full in-text citations that might include odd "author" names from *Flickr* usernames.

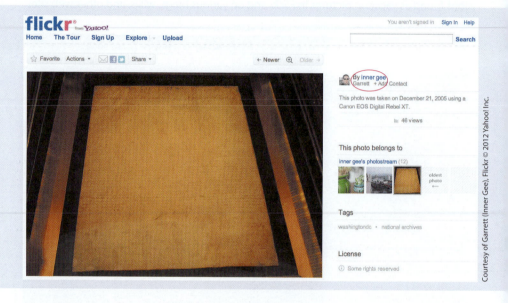

If you were composing a digital project published to the Web, however, you might just add a link to the actual *Flickr* page with the image on it. Who knows—on the social popularity project you might want to refer to a t-shirt that a cousin purchased from a street vendor in Philadelphia. Would you cite the shirt? If so, how? Would you cite the picture of your cousin on *Facebook*? If it were important to do so, how would you do it?

As this extended example with the Declaration of Independence demonstrates, digital media and the Internet allow for greater opportunities in research but also make that process more complicated. The next section will help you work through situations where you need to construct your own citation.

Learning Citation Styles by Constructing Your Own Citations

You may often find, even when you are using this book, that you cannot locate an example of how to cite the exact resource you are using. Whether you are citing a retweeted post on *Twitter* that someone has edited, or you are trying to cite the director's commentary that is voiced over in a film you are writing about, you will need to learn the skill of constructing your own citations.

There are three major steps for constructing your citation. **First, you must really understand the type of resource, taking the time to think about whether it is a static, syndicated, or dynamic text.** If you want to cite a web page you are using, you can find an example for how to do that. A web page is a simple static source. But imagine that you are using a web page and you want to cite the annotations that someone has made on that web page through a social bookmarking tool like Diigo. The nature of the resource has changed to something dynamic, and you will likely have difficulty finding an example of how to cite that particular resource.

> **Guide to Constructing a Citation for a Source Not Covered in the Style Guides**
> 1. Really understand the type of resource: static, syndicated, or dynamic.
> 2. Find the citation examples or models that most resemble the resource.
> 3. Mash-up existing examples.

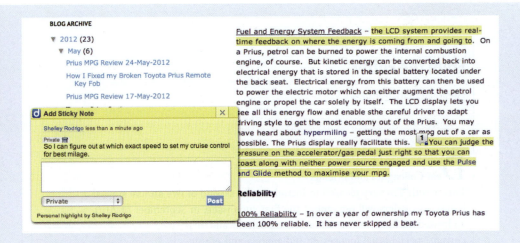

Second, you must find a few example citations that look and feel like your resource, based on your understanding of the resource. Imagine that you want to cite an editor's introduction to an issue of a journal article. A journal is syndicated, and there are plenty of examples of how to cite articles from journals. There are also examples for citing introductory materials to books, such as forewords. You can use these examples as models and take cues from them.

The **third step is to try to think like the citation system and mash-up known examples** to make a citation for your resource. Before trying to complete your mash-up, review a few different models based on the general citation type (static, syndicated, or dynamic) so you get a sense for how the citation style thinks. What kind of information comes first, second, third in citations? How are they punctuated? Then look closely at the two or three closely related examples you picked out and start trying to combine them based on your understanding of how the system works. If you wanted to cite an editor's introduction to an article in a journal, as we mentioned above, you might look at the citation example for a foreword to a book (using MLA style):

Gibson, William. "Geeks and Artboys." Foreword. *Multimedia: From Wagner to Virtual Reality*. Ed. Randall Packer and Ken Jordan. New York: Norton, 2001. xi–xiv. Print.

And an article in a journal:

Wan, Amy J. "In the Name of Citizenship: The Writing Classroom and the Promise of Citizenship." *College English* 74.1 (2011): 28–49. Print.

To come up with the citation of the editor's introduction:

Yancey, Kathleen Blake. "Beyond Blue Eyes." Editor's note. *College Composition and Communication* 63.1 (2011): 5–11. Web. 14 September 2011.

From the Editor

Beyond Blue Eyes

Dear Colleagues and Friends~~

This month, I'm very pleased to introduce the second of five annual special issues. As readers will remember, the first such issue, in September of 2010, addressed the future of rhetoric and composition, and this current special issue focuses on indigenous and ethnic rhetorics. In this introduction, I detail the contents of this special issue and, in addition, update the process of identifying poster page terms; announce the next special issue of *CCC*; and mark the departure of one *CCC* editorial assistant and the arrival of another.

Let me begin the introduction to the articles and the review essay by providing some background as to their selection. To compose this special issue, we announced a call for proposals, in this case defining indigenous and ethnic rhetorics capaciously and welcoming a diversity of approaches:

Let's try again with a movie director's commentary, such as one for the director's cut of the film *Alien*:

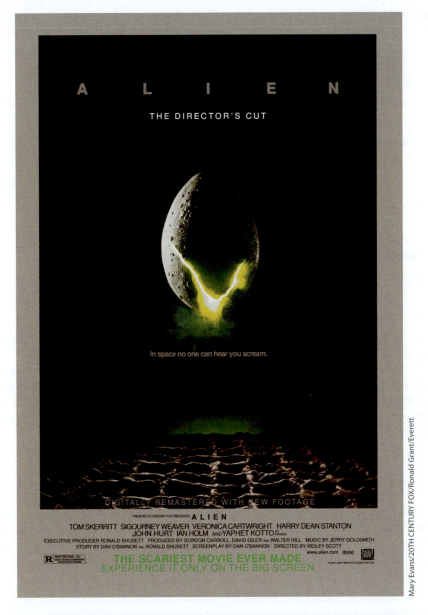

Mary Evans/20TH CENTURY FOX/Ronald Grant/Everett

In this case, there are multiple versions and sequels of the film *Alien* (originally released in 1979). Similarly, there are a variety of releases of DVD sets, especially after a new sequel is released. In this instance, we want to cite the director's commentary about one of the actor's screen tests, found on a specific box set. **First, is it static, syndicated, or dynamic?** A film is usually static. However, in 2003, as a part of a box set with three sequel films, Fox released a "director's cut" version of *Alien*. Although the director's cut of *Alien* is a newer edition of the film, it is still a static resource; it is not updated easily nor often. Similarly, the director's commentary attached to material provided in a specific box set is also a relatively static text; not easily or frequently updated.

Next, you need to find some example citations that look and feel like the resource. MLA, APA, and CMS all give examples of what a citation for a film should look like; however, they don't generally give examples of what a citation of different versions of the film should look like. In this case, consider looking at book citations for different editions or volumes.

MLA Film Example

Inception. Dir. Christopher Nolan. Perf. Leonardo DiCaprio, Joseph Gordon-Levitt,

and Ellen Page. Warner Bros. Pictures, 2010. Film.

MLA Book with Different Edition Example

O'Brien, Judith Grunert, Barbara J. Millis, and Margaret W. Cohen. *The Course*

Syllabus: A Learning-Centered Approach. 2nd ed. San Francisco: Wiley, 2008.

Print.

And since this is one film found within a box set, you might look at an example of a work within an anthology.

MLA Selection from an Edited Collection or Anthology

Peigin, Chen. "Magazines: An Industry in Transition." *New Media for a New China*.

Ed. James F. Scotton and William A. Hachten. West Sussex: Clackwell-Wiley,

2010. 74–82. Print.

If you need to cite the director's commentary specifically, you might also want to look at an example of a foreword or introduction.

Now you are ready to **think like the citation system and mash-up the examples.** First, you are citing the director's commentary, not the film itself, which means that your citation needs to emphasize the commentary. In this instance, the commentary is by Ridley Scott, the director. The rest of the citation should look like that of a specific edition of the film.

Scott, Ridley. "Director Commentary: Sigourney Weaver's Screen Test." *Alien*

Quadrilogy. Dir. Ridley Scott. Perf. Tom Skerritt, Sigourney Weaver,

John Hurt, and Michael Beane. 20th Century Fox, 2003. DVD.

The last question is about how to title the "Quadrilogy" box edition that includes *Alien* and three of its sequels. We think you could do it two ways—either treat "Quadrilogy" as a part of the title of the film (as above) or treat "Quadrilogy" as a listing of a separate or different edition, as below (it is separate from the title and is not italicized).

Scott, Ridley. "Director Commentary: Sigourney Weaver's Screen Test." *Alien*.

Quadrilogy. Dir. Ridley Scott. Perf. Tom Skerritt, Sigourney Weaver,

John Hurt, and Michael Beane. 20th Century Fox, 2003. DVD.

In scholarly publishing, this would be a moment when the author talks to the editor of the journal or press about which version to use. If this were for a paper in a class, you would want to show both versions to your instructor and get feedback on which version your instructor wants you to use.

write

Selecting Examples for a Citation Mash-Up

You have just read an example of how to mash-up a citation of a director's commentary of a film, a static resource. What if you were citing a director's commentary on a specific episode of a television show, a syndicated resource? Look at the chapter of the citation style you are using for a current writing project. What specific citation examples would you use as your point of reference in mashing up a citation for a director's commentary on a specific television episode? Why would you use them? What do you think would be tricky parts of the citation?

Choosing the Appropriate Style Guide

Like all of the other choices you've made in this book, choosing which formatting and citation style to use is highly rhetorical. Usually your decision is based on your reader's expectations.

Since scholars who use MLA style can be working from texts that are centuries old and are published in a variety of editions, the MLA citation style privileges the names of the author and the text; therefore, the last name of the author of the text is given in the in-text citations, but not the publication year. And on the works cited page, MLA's name for the bibliography at the end of the paper, the author's name and the title of the text come before any of the publication information. Most disciplines from the arts and humanities focus on research and analysis of a specific text and therefore use MLA style.

APA style is most appropriate to use when writing about topics related to disciplines such as psychology, justice studies, education, linguistics, and sociology. However, many of these disciplines have their own citation styles as well, like those of the Linguistic Society of America and the American Sociological Society. The scholars who developed APA style emphasize current data. And that preference makes sense; shouldn't a psychologist treating someone be working from the most current information? Therefore, the APA citation style gives the author's name and the copyright date of the text first in a citation. Both pieces of information appear in in-text citations as well as on the references page, which is the APA name for the list of resources at the end of the paper. If your project emphasizes timely data and secondary resources, you may want to use APA style.

CMS is known for being used by historians; however, it is also used by a variety of disciplines, journals, and presses. CMS has two basic citation systems that split themselves along disciplinary lines. The notes and bibliography system, which is our focus in Chapter 14, is primarily used by disciplines in the humanities and some social sciences, and the author-date system is primarily used by the sciences and other social sciences. The notes and bibliography system uses numbered footnotes (at the bottom of the page) for in-text citations or numbered endnotes (at the end of the chapter or article) for in-text citations and then has a bibliography at the end of the document with complete publication information. The notes and bibliography system is good to use when you don't want to disrupt the flow of your writing with a long, confusing in-text citation. A subtly raised superscript numeral signals the reader to go read more information about the resource at the bottom of the page or the end of the essay (see essay example in Chapter 14).

The CMS author-date system resembles the APA's style for in-text citations and bibliographies. If you are interested in using CMS, especially the author-date system, consult the most current edition of *The Chicago Manual of Style* for any larger questions not addressed in Chapter 14.

CSE style has three basic in-text citation systems and only one system for full bibliographies. Many journals in the hard sciences have their own specific citation systems; therefore, many authors usually draft their essays using CSE and then revise the citations based on the specific journal they submit the essay to for publication. Chapter 15 introduces all three in-text citation systems and gives examples of the full bibliographic entries as well.

While it's true that most undergraduate students find their instructors want them to use MLA or APA styles, the most important thing to know when selecting your citation style is audience expectation. If you are submitting to a teacher, what does he or she expect? If you are submitting to a journal, what are the submission guidelines for the journal?

chapter 12

MLA Formatting Guidelines

As mentioned in Chapter 11, the citation guidelines presented in the *MLA Handbook for Writers of Research Papers* (7th edition) include two functioning parts: the in-text citation that helps identify what piece of the text is being quoted, paraphrased, or summarized, and the full bibliographic citation at the end of the paper that helps the reader find the original resource being referenced.

In-Text Citations

MLA in-text citations require only the author's name and, if you are including a paraphrase or direct quote, a page number.

Quotations and Paraphrases

Standard in-text citations in MLA format include the author's name and the page number in the citation, as the following example demonstrates:

> Science fiction films "self-consciously foreground their own radicality" of special effects (Freedman 307).

If the source was written by more than one author, your in-text citation will include the names of both authors, like this:

> (Miller-Cochran and Rodrigo 252).

If the author's name is already mentioned in the sentence, you only need to include the page number from which the information or quotation came in the in-text citation. The next example uses the same short quotation from Freedman's work and only needs to provide the page where the quotation was found because Freedman's name is included in the sentence itself:

> Carl Freedman criticizes science fiction films for "self-consciously foreground[ing] their own radicality" of special effects (307).

The 2009 update of MLA does not explicitly address how to cite resources from ereaders that do not have page numbers. MLA does mention that if an electronic text has paragraph numbers, the author should reference those. Therefore, you might use chapter numbers in electronic books that do not have page numbers.

> In *The Future of Learning Institutions in a Digital Age*, Cathy N. Davidson and David T. Goldberg consider "self-learning" one of the ten principles "to rethinking the future of learning institutions" (chapter 2).

MLA does not suggest using "location numbers" like those referenced in an Amazon Kindle ereader. If you cannot reference a page, paragraph, or chapter number, just reference the work as a whole.

Long Quotations

In MLA style, quotations that are longer than four lines of your paper must be formatted as block quotations, which are indented one inch from the left margin. Because they are direct quotations, block quotes need an in-text citation that includes the author's name and the page number of the quotation.

Figure 12.1 shows a long quotation that includes the author's name in the introduction to the quote; however, at the end of the quote the in-text citation not only includes the page number but also an abbreviated title of the resource that gives enough information to find the resource in the works cited list. In this particular paper, the author uses more than one source by Schatz; therefore, to lead the reader to the correct bibliographic citation in the works cited list, the in-text reference also needs to include a portion of the

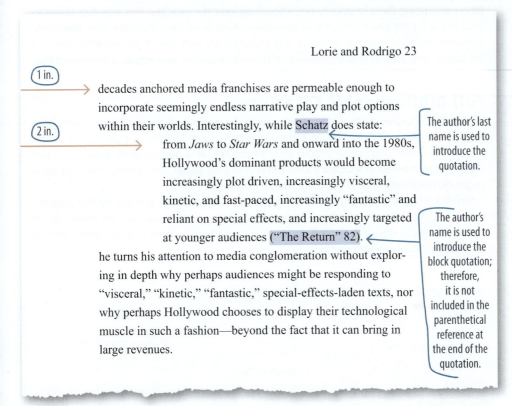

Lorie and Rodrigo 23

1 in.

2 in.

decades anchored media franchises are permeable enough to incorporate seemingly endless narrative play and plot options within their worlds. Interestingly, while Schatz does state:

> The author's last name is used to introduce the quotation.

from *Jaws* to *Star Wars* and onward into the 1980s, Hollywood's dominant products would become increasingly plot driven, increasingly visceral, kinetic, and fast-paced, increasingly "fantastic" and reliant on special effects, and increasingly targeted at younger audiences ("The Return" 82).

he turns his attention to media conglomeration without exploring in depth why perhaps audiences might be responding to "visceral," "kinetic," "fantastic," special-effects-laden texts, nor why perhaps Hollywood chooses to display their technological muscle in such a fashion—beyond the fact that it can bring in large revenues.

> The author's name is used to introduce the block quotation; therefore, it is not included in the parenthetical reference at the end of the quotation.

Figure 12.1   An Extended Quotation in MLA Style

resource's title. If only one resource by Schatz had been included in the paper, the in-text citation would have only included the page number, since Schatz's name is used to introduce the quote. Likewise, if no author had been listed for this resource, only the abbreviated version of the title would be used in the in-text citation (see the example below in "Summaries and Multiple Resources").

Summaries and Multiple Resources

If you are summarizing the main point of a resource and not referencing one particular part of the source, MLA style only requires that you provide enough information in an in-text citation to get the reader to the full bibliographic citation in the works cited list. In the following text example, the writer briefly refers to multiple texts within the same sentence. Notice, however, that these texts do not have authors; therefore, the writer's in-text citation includes the article title as the little bit of information that gets the reader to the correct entry in the works cited list.

Interestingly, even a mediocre film can open revenue streams for other outlets and media tie-ins, like *Van Helsing* (2004) did. Although the film only earned a reported $120 million domestic, short of its $160 million budget ("Top 250"; "Business Data"), it did extremely well in foreign markets (Groves), and its video game made *Electronic Gaming Monthly*'s Top 10 list for April 2004 ("Top 10 . . . April 2004").

When discussing films in papers you should include the year the film was first released after the first time you mention it in the paper; many films have the same title. Electronic resources are cited in text in the same way as hard-copy resources. If you have the name of the author, you include that information. If there is no author, you include a shortened title.

Full Bibliographic Citations

MLA format requires a list of resources used in the paper, and this list is provided under the heading "Works Cited." The list includes only the names of the resources cited in the paper. The works cited page should start at the top of a new page in your essay and should be numbered in sequence with the rest of your paper. Any additional works cited pages do not have a special heading but are paginated.

Entries in MLA works cited lists are presented in alphabetical order by the author's last name. If you have more than one text by the same author, alphabetize within those author entries by title of the text. If you have texts with no authors, incorporate them into the alphabetical list based on title.

Miller-Cochran 16

Works Cited

Bass, Frank. *The Associated Press Guide to Internet Research and Reporting*. Cambridge: Perseus, 2001. Print.

Evans, Ellen, and Jeanne Po. "A Break in the Transaction: Examining Students' Responses to Digital Texts." *Computers and Composition* 24.1 (2007): 56-73. *ScienceDirect*. Web. 15 July 2012.

Helms-Park, Rena, Pavlina Radia, and Paul Stapleton. "A Preliminary Assessment of Google Scholar as a Source of EAP Students' Research Materials." *Internet and Higher Education* 10 (2007): 65-76.

Kress, Gunther. *Literacy in the New Media Age*. London: Routledge, 2003. Print.

- - -. "Gains and Losses: New Forms of Texts, Knowledge, and Learning." *Computers and Composition* 22.1 (2005): 5-22. *ScienceDirect*. Web. 15 July 2012.

> When more than one source is listed from the same author, only list the author's name for the first listed source. Type three hyphens to represent the same author, followed by a period.

Figure 12.2   Example of First Page of the Works Cited List

Walker, Billie E. "Google No More: A Model for Successful

Research." *Teaching Professor* 20 (2006): 1-4. *EBSCOhost*.

Web. 3 Aug. 2012.

"Web 2.0 Tools and Reference Resources." *Baltimore County*

Public Schools Offices. The Baltimore County Public

Schools, 2009. Web. 11 July 2012.

If there is no author listed for your resource, incorporate it alphabetically based on the title.

Figure 12.2 Example of First Page of the Works Cited List *(continued)*

MLA full bibliographic citation style generally provides information in the following order:

1. Name of author
2. Title of text
3. Publication information (usually publisher's name, place [city] of publication, copyright date)
4. Medium of publication: Print, Web, CD, DVD, etc. (Additional information on resources may follow the medium of publication for certain resources.)

Periods are included after each major section of information. For example, a period is included after the name of the author(s), after the text's title, and after the complete publication information. If there is *no author* for the text, start with the text's title; however, remember that a government agency or a corporation can function as an author. With various online resources, you may have to look on other pages to find the author's name.

Similarly, you may have to search dynamic online resources for the last updated date as well (like the "history" page in wikis). If you cannot find a date or other publication information, you may use the following abbreviations:

- ▶ n.p. No place of publication given
- ▶ n.p. No publisher given
- ▶ n.d. No date of publication given

In MLA style, abbreviate all names of months except May, June, and July. For example, *October* is abbreviated to "Oct." and *January* to "Jan." MLA style also calls for the abbreviation of publishers' names. When the publisher is a university press, the phrase "University Press" is shortened to "UP."

The citation rules for static, syndicated, and dynamic resources all follow this general pattern, but each category has some unique characteristics. See Chapter 4 for the definitions of static, syndicated, and dynamic sources.

MLA Citation Examples

Static Resources

Static resources (e.g., books, films, and pieces of art) are generally easy to cite using MLA style. These citations usually include author, title, and publication information. The following examples indicate how to cite various types of static sources.

MLA-1, Printed Book with One Author

Balsamo, Anne. *Designing Culture: The Technological Imagination at Work.* Durham: Duke UP, 2011. Print.

MLA-1

MLA-2, Printed Book with One to Three Authors

Gane, Nicholas, and David Beer. *New Media: The Key Concepts.* New York: Berg, 2008. Print.

If there had been three authors, the first author's last name would be first, followed by the first name, then the coauthors with their first names followed by their last names (Story, Jonelle, Anne Kroening, and James Anderson.). List the authors in the same order as they are presented on the title page of the book.

MLA-2

MLA-3, Printed Book with Four or More Authors

Lister, Martin, Jon Dovey, Seth Giddings, Iain Grant, and Kieran Kelly. *New Media: A Critical Introduction.* 2nd ed. London: Routledge, 2009. Print.

Lister, Martin, et al. *New Media: A Critical Introduction.* 2nd ed. London: Routledge, 2009. Print.

If there are more than three authors, you can either include all of their names, or you can use only the first author's name and then write "et al.," which is Latin for "and others." Be careful not to use a period after "et" because it is an entire Latin word. The Latin abbreviation "al." (with a period) is an abbreviation for "alii" or "alia," which means "others."

MLA-3

MLA-4, Book with a Publisher's Imprint

Brookfield, Stephen D. *Becoming a Critically Reflective Teacher.* San Francisco: Jossey-Bass-Wiley, 1995. Print

Some publishers use an imprint, a separately titled subsection of the company, for certain types and series of books. If both the imprint and publisher name are made available on the title page, include both in your citation: the imprint name, a hyphen, then the publisher name. In this example, "Jossey-Bass" is the name of the imprint and "Wiley" is the name of the publisher.

MLA-4

author   title   publication information

MLA-5

MLA-5, Electronic Book

Electronic Book on the Web

Shakespeare, William. *The Taming of the Shrew*. Ed. Amanda Ballard.
Shakespeare Online. 1999–2003. Web. 27 Oct. 2011. <http://
www.shakespeare-online.com/plays/tamingscenes.html>.

MLA does not require that you include a URL; however, since there are so many
versions of Shakespeare's work online and a Google Search including "Shakespeare Online Taming of the Shrew" does not list this resource first, we include it
as an example of when you would provide a URL.

Electronic Book in Database

Whitman, Walt. *Leaves of Grass*. London: Trubner & Co., 1881.
Google Books. Web. 2 Nov. 2011.

For a full discussion of citing databases, see *"Techno Tip: MLA and Databases,"*
pages 279–280.

Electronic Book Downloaded for an Ereader

Ambrose, Susan A., Michael W. Bridges, Michele DiPietro, Marsha
C. Lovett, and Maria K. Norman. *How Learning Works: 7
Research-Based Principles for Smart Teaching*. San Francisco:
Jossey-Bass-Wiley, 2010. *Amazon*. Kindle eBook. 2 Nov. 2011.

For ebooks found on the Internet, use the word "Web" in the publication information part of the citation. For ebooks downloaded for an ereader through a
service such as Amazon's Kindle, it is more appropriate to note the ebook platform. In the above example, that platform is "Kindle eBook."

MLA-6

MLA-6, Selection from an Edited Collection or Anthology

Peigin, Chen. "Magazines: An Industry in Transition." *New Media
for a New China*. Ed. James F. Scotton and William A.
Hachten. West Sussex: Blackwell-Wiley, 2010. 74–82. Print.

Edited collections or anthologies have two layers of both authorial and title
information. There is the author of the specific essay or chapter that you are
citing. The specific essay or chapter title is presented in quotation marks. The
second title, the title of the edited collection or anthology, is presented in italics
(like the title of a regular book). The second layer of authorial information, the
editors who put together the edited collection or anthology, comes after the
title of the book. You also need to include page numbers for the specific portion
of the book you are referring to; they are presented after the copyright year.

MLA-7, Introduction, Preface, Foreword, or Afterword from a Book

Baynes, W. E. C. Introduction. *The Prince.* By Niccolo Machiavelli. Trans. Rufus Goodwin. Wellesley: Dante UP, 2003. 13–25. Print.

The citation styles for introductions, prefaces, forewords, and afterwords are basically the same. If you are using one of these types of ancillary materials as a resource, start your citation with the author of the ancillary material. If the ancillary material has a title, give it next in quotation marks, followed by the word for the type of ancillary material. Finally, provide the remainder of the book's citation, placing the author's name after the title of the book.

MLA-8, Book with a Translator

Machiavelli, Niccolo. *The Prince.* Trans. Rufus Goodwin. Wellesley: Dante UP, 2003. 13–25. Print.

Several different versions of *The Prince* exist, and the translator's role in the publishing process distinguishes one version from another.

MLA-9, Book with an Editor (Entire Anthology)

Giggings, Seth, and Martin Lister, eds. *The New Media and Technocultures Reader.* London: Routledge, 2011. Print.

If you are citing an entire edited collection, you need to identify the "authors" as "editors" by including "ed." (for one editor) or "eds." (for more than one editor) after their names.

MLA-10, Book in a Series

Crow, Angela. *Aging Literacies: Training and Development Challenges for Faculty.* Cresskill: Hampton, 2006. Print. New Dimensions in Computers and Composition.

If the book you are citing is part of a series, include the series name after the medium of publication at the end of the citation.

MLA-11, Book in an Edition Other Than the First

Cohen, Arthur, and Florence B. Brawer. *The American Community College.* 5th ed. San Francisco: Jossey-Bass-Wiley, 2008. Print.

MLA-12

When referring to books in multiple editions, use the language you find on the title page of the book. Therefore, if it says second or third edition, put the numbers in your citation. If it says "Revised" or "Abridged" put "Rev. ed." or "Abr. ed." in the citation. Similarly, if your book is the fifth in a multivolume work, just include "Vol. 5."

MLA-12, Book with a Title within the Title

Sammon, Paul M. *Future Noir: The Making of* Blade Runner.
New York: Harper Paperbacks-HarperCollins, 1996. Print.

The title of the film within the title of the book is neither italicized nor enclosed in quotation marks. If the title within the title is of a shorter work, like a story, poem, or song, you'll keep everything in italics and put quotation marks around the shorter work's title.

techno tip

MLA and Web Pages

For citation purposes, you generally treat a web page or web site as static, unless you know that it is dynamic (a wiki, for example) or syndicated (like a blog). (Note: Many web sites are now actually online databases and should be treated accordingly. See "Techno Tip: MLA and Databases," pages 278–280.) Static web page citations look a lot like citations from a chapter or article in a book: author, specific web page title, *overall web site title*, the person or company hosting the web site, copyright date, and media. However, MLA also asks that you include a date of access—the date you looked at and retrieved information from the web site.

Burton, Gideon O. "Invention." *Silva Rhetoricae*. Brigham Young U, 2007. Web. 8 Nov. 2011.

Web sites are generally easier to update than books; when you provide the date you accessed the site, you account for the fact that your reader may not find the exact same version of the web page that you found.

The author's name and the copyright or posted date are sometimes located somewhere on the web page. If not, try searching for an "about" page. Include the publisher or sponsor of the web site (or "n.p." if there is no publisher or sponsor), the date the page was posted, and the date you accessed it. Note that after the 2009 update of the *MLA Handbook for Writers of Research Papers*, MLA no longer recommends the inclusion of URLs (web addresses) in your works cited list unless the reader *probably cannot find a source without it or if your instructor requires them*. When used, type the URL after the medium of publication and a period, enclose the URL in angle brackets, and end the citation with a period (see MLA-26).

If a web page or book has no author's or editor's name, and you cannot find one by looking around the site, begin the citation with the title. When citing web pages you want to be able to distinguish between the title of the web page, *the title of the web site*, and the publisher or site sponsor.

"Box Office/Business for Melancholia." IMDB: The Internet Movie Database.
IMDB.com-Amazon.com, 1999–2011. Web. 2 Nov. 2011.

MLA-13

MLA-13, Web Page

Burton, Gideon O. "Invention." *Silva Rhetoricae.* Brigham Young U,
2007. Web. 8 Nov. 2011.

MLA-14

MLA-14, Web Page with No Author Listed

"Box Office/Business for *Melancholia.*" *IMDB: The Internet Movie
Database.* IMDB.com-Amazon.com, 1999–2011. Web. 2 Nov. 2011.

MLA-15

MLA-15, Government Publication

United States. Cong. House. *Stop Online Piracy Act.* US 112th
Congress. HR 3261. *THOMAS.* Lib. of Congress, 26 Oct. 2011.
Web. 2 Nov. 2011.

If you are citing multiple types of government publications, refer to more
detailed discussion of government publications in the *MLA Handbook* (7th edition, section 5.5.20, "A Government Publication"). Like government agencies,
corporations and other organizations can also be author resources. In those
cases, the school or corporation's name would be listed as the author of a
resource (see also MLA-41).

MLA-16

MLA-16, Online Scholarly Project

Haswell, Rich, and Glenn Blalock, eds. *CompPile: 1939–current.*
CompPile, 2004–2011. Web. 2 Nov. 2011.

When projects are hosted on educational servers, be sure to include the name
of the institution hosting the project. In this case, the project was originally
hosted by Texas A&M at Corpus Christi; however, the editors have now started
a nonprofit corporation to host and manage the site. All of this information is
available by carefully reading the web site, especially the "about" pages.

MLA-17

MLA-17, Published Interview

Cochran, Stacey. "How to Publish a Book: Literary Agent Interview—
Peter Riva." *How to Publish a Book.org.* 2011. Web. 29 Jan. 2011.

A published interview is like any other smaller text, essay, or chapter within a
larger body of work (see MLA-6). A personal or "live" interview, however, is considered a dynamic text (see MLA-46).

| author | title of web page and title of overall web site | date of access | web site publisher, copyright date, and media |

MLA-18, Published Letter

Adams, John. "Letter from John Adams to Abigail Adams." 28 August 1774. *Adams Family Papers: An Electronic Archive*. The Massachusetts Historical Society, 2003. Web.

A published letter is like any other smaller text, essay, or chapter within a larger body of work (see MLA-6); however, you do need to include the date of the letter immediately after the title (think of it as part of the title of the letter). A personal letter is considered a dynamic text (see MLA-47).

MLA-19, Conference Proceedings

VanTassel-Baska, Joyce, and Tamra Stambaugh, eds. *Overlooked Gems: A National Perspective on Low-Income Promising Learners. Proc. of the National Leadership Conference on Low-Income Promising Learners.* Apr. 2006. Williamsburg: Natl. Assn. for Gifted Children and Center for Gifted Educ., Coll. of William & Mary, 2007. *ERIC*. Web. 27 Oct. 2011.

Conference proceedings are like edited collections (MLA-6); however, the title is a little longer because it needs to include the detailed information about the conference. In this case, the conference proceeding has both its own title, "Overlooked Gems: . . .," as well as the description, "Proceedings of the. . . ." The proceedings were accessed through a database (for information on citing from databases, see "Techno Tip: MLA and Databases," pages. 279–280).

MLA-20, Paper Published in Conference Proceedings

Baldwin, Alexinia Y. "Untapped Potential for Excellence." *Overlooked Gems: A National Perspective on Low-Income Promising Learners. Proc. of the National Leadership Conference on Low-Income Promising Learners, Apr. 2006.* Ed. Joyce VanTassel-Baska and Tamra Stambaugh. Williamsburg: Natl. Assn. for Gifted Children and Center for Gifted Educ., Coll. of William & Mary, 2007. 23–25. *ERIC*. Web. 27 Oct. 2011.

Published papers in conference proceedings are like essays or chapters found in edited collections (MLA-6).

MLA-21, Dissertation

Applegarth, Risa. *Other Grounds: Popular Genres and the Rhetoric of Anthropology, 1900–1940.* Diss. U of North Carolina at Chapel Hill, 2009. *ProQuest Dissertations and Theses.* Web. 7 Nov. 2011.

The citation for a published dissertation (shown above) includes information on the degree-granting university. To cite an unpublished dissertation, include all of the information from the published dissertation up through the degree-granting institution and the year the dissertation was defended; in other words, everything but the publication information. If you are only citing the dissertation abstract, put the title in quotation marks rather than italics.

MLA-22, Report or White Paper

Voloudakis, John. "The Economic Downturn and the Future of Higher Education IT: Executive Appraisals." *ECAR Occasional Paper.* Boulder: EDUCAUSE, 2010. Web. 2 Nov. 2011.

Reports and white papers are generally either internal documents or one-time publications by companies or organizations.

MLA-23, Film

In general, film citations start with the title of the film and then move on to the director, key performers, the distribution company, the year of release, and the medium. Since many films are available in different versions and via different media, it's important to include those particulars in the citation. If you viewed the film on television, you would need to consider it a dynamic production since television stations generally edit scenes and may incorporate advertising as part of the screening (see live television example in MLA-36).

Film Screened in a Theater

Blade Runner. Dir. Ridley Scott. Perf. Harrison Ford, Rutger Hauer, and Sean Young. Warner Bros., 1982. Film.

Film on DVD

Blade Runner: The Director's Cut. Dir. Ridley Scott. Perf. Harrison Ford, Rutger Hauer, and Sean Young. Warner Bros., 1991. DVD.

This version of the film was not released before 1991; therefore, it does not include the original theatrical release date; instead, it includes the copyright date of the new version of the film. However, if this was a DVD of the original theatrical cut, the original release date would need to appear after the performers.

Film Extra in Special Collection

Scott, Ridley. "Introduction." *Blade Runner: The Final Cut.* Dir. Ridley
Scott. Perf. Harrison Ford, Rutger Hauer, and Sean Young.
Warner Bros. Pictures, 2007. DVD.

Film Viewed Streaming through the Internet

Blade Runner: Theatrical Cut. Dir. Ridley Scott. Perf. Harrison Ford,
Rutger Hauer, and Sean Young. Warner Bros., 1982. *Netflix.*
2 Nov. 2011

The first date in the citation is the year the film was released; the second date is
the date the film was accessed using the *Netflix* database.

Film in a Language Other Than English

Sin Dejar Huella [Without a Trace]. Dir. María Novaro. Perf. Aitana
Sánchez-Gijón, Tiaré Scanda, Jesús Ochoa, and Martín
Altomaro. 2000. Alta Films, 2001. DVD.

If you are citing a resource that is in a language other than English, cite the original title (in its original language) and then, if you desire, provide the translation
of the resource's title in brackets.

MLA-24, Screenplay

Clooney, George, and Grant Heslov. *Good Night, and Good Luck.:
The Screenplay and History behind the Landmark Movie.*
New York: Newmarket P, 2006. Print.

MLA-25, Sound Recordings

Like films (MLA-23), audio recordings may be accessed in a variety of locations
and media.

Song from an Album

Deep Purple. "Space Truckin." *Machine Head.* Warner Bros., 1972. CD.

According to the *MLA Handbook*, you may choose to cite the composer, conductor,
ensemble, or performer first, depending on the "desired emphasis" of your rhetorical
situation. In this case, we went with the name of the performer, the band Deep Purple.

Downloaded Song

Deep Purple. "Space Truckin." *Machine Head.* Warner Bros., 1972.
iTunes. Web. 3 Oct. 2011.

Material downloaded from resources like iTunes can be treated as material downloaded from a database (see "Techno Tip: MLA and Databases," pages 279–280).

Song Heard Streaming on the Web

Deep Purple. "Space Truckin." *Machine Head*. *Pandora*. Web. 3 Oct.
2011.

Although you may not have an easy time locating bibliographic information
about a song streaming on the Web, you are still responsible for providing it
in the citation. If you listened to "Space Truckin" on Pandora and were only
able to find out the name of the band and the album name and you needed
the names of the song writers/composers, you would need to do research to
find the other information. Most of it would be easily found on the Internet;
you would just want to cross-check information to make sure you found the
correct names, spellings, etc.

MLA-26, Art and Images

Like films (MLA-23), there are often many versions of a single work of art found
in different media—beyond the original piece usually housed in a museum or
someone's private collection. So that your reader knows exactly which version
you are referring to, it is important to include distinguishing details.

Work of Art

Wright, Frank Lloyd. *Fallingwater*. 1936–1939. Building. Western PA
Conservancy, Mill Run.

After the title of the piece, include the year(s) of production. Don't forget to
include the medium of composition and then the name of the institution or
individual that owns the work (think of that as the publisher or distributor) and
the city in which the work is housed.

Work of Art Reprinted in a Book

Wright, Frank Lloyd. *Kaufmann House (Fallingwater)*. 1936–1939. Western
PA Conservancy, Mill Run. *Gardner's Art through the Ages*.
12th ed. By Fred S. Kleiner and Christin J. Mamiya. Belmont:
Thomson-Wadsworth, 2005. 1017. Print.

In this case, the book refers to the artistic work by two titles; therefore,
we cited it as such. Otherwise the citation is very similar to an essay in an
edited collection; the entire citation for the artistic piece appears with
the follow-up information of the book, or collection, it appears in (see
MLA-6).

Work of Art or Image Found on the Web

Donovan, Brian. "Fallingwater—at home in nature." *Flickr*, 10 Sept.
2011. Web. 2 Nov. 2011. <http://www.flickr.com/
photos/58621196@N05/6134336955/>.

MLA-26

MLA-27, Map

Maps can be considered specialized works of art or images. The citation will probably look like a traditional article, book, or web site citation with the descriptive label "map."

Print Map

"Las Vegas, NV2." Map. *North America Road Atlas*. Skokie: Rand, 2006. 65. Print.

Digital Map

"LIDAR Map of New Orleans Flooding from Hurricane Katrina." Map. By GISuser. *Flickr*. 22 Jan. 2008. Web. 19 Jan. 2012.

If your map does list an author, the MLA style guide lists it after the title and before the publication information. Since this is both a map and something found on the Web, the citation includes both the descriptor "Map" after the title of the map as well as "Web" in reference to the form of media. If the map is found in a book, cite it as if it was an essay in an edited collection (MLA-6) and include "Print" at the end of the citation.

MLA-28, Sacred Text

Since most sacred texts do not formally list individual authors, start with the title of the text. When you alphabetize the entries in your works cited list, be sure to ignore any initial articles, "a," "an," or "the." Therefore, you would alphabetize the first entry under "h" for "Holy."

Sacred Text, Print

The Holy Bible, New International Version. Green Rapids: Zondervan, 1973. Print.

In this example, the title included the version of the Bible being used.

Sacred Text, Online

Cascading Bible. n.d. Web. 27 Oct. 2011. King James Vers.

Since the title did not include the version of the Bible being used, indicate the version after the title (as with editions and volume information).

MLA-29, Entry from a Dictionary, Thesaurus, Encyclopedia, or Almanac

You only need minimal publication information if the reference resource (dictionary, thesaurus, encyclopedia, etc.) is well known. If the reference is not well known, include all bibliographic and publication information as in a book or other online resource.

Entry from a Print Dictionary

"Eclecticism." *Webster's Third New International Dictionary of the English Language Unabridged*. 1993. Print.

Entry from an Online Encyclopedia

"Russian Revolution of 1917." *Encyclopedia Brittanica.* 1994–2011. Web.

2 Nov. 2011.

Syndicated Resources

Syndicated resources (e.g., journal and magazine articles, television shows, and blogs) are generally easy to cite using MLA style. These citations usually include author, title of the specific essay or episode, *title of the periodical published work* (e.g., name of the overall journal, television show, or blog), and publication information. The following examples indicate how to cite various types of syndicated sources.

MLA-30, Article in a Scholarly Journal

The current MLA guidelines no longer make a distinction between journals that are numbered continuously (e.g., Vol. 1 ends on page 208, Vol. 2 starts on page 209) or numbered separately; that is, each volume starts on page 1. No matter how the journal is paginated, the citation must contain volume *and* issue numbers if available. One exception is journals with issue numbers only; simply cite the issue number alone as if it was a volume number.

Article in a Printed Journal

Cambridge, Barbara. "Research and Policy: Antithetical or

Complementary?" *Writing Program Administration* 35.1

(2011): 135–47. Print.

Journal Article Accessed through a Database

Cohen, Paul. "Cowboys Die Hard: Real Men and Businessmen in the

Reagan-Era Blockbuster." *Film & History* 41.1 (2011): 71–81.

EBSCOhost. Web. 8 Nov. 2011.

Journal Article from Journal That Only Exists Online

Leston, Robert, Geoffrey Carter, and Sarah Arroyo. "The Chora of

the Twin Towers." *Enculturation* 10 (2011): n. pag. Web. 8 Nov. 2011.

In an online journal, there are no page numbers; however, we still need to include the date the article was accessed.

techno tip

MLA and Databases

In theory, an article from a scholarly journal would be the same whether it was found in print or in any one of several different databases. However, as demonstrated in the magazine example below (MLA-33), differences can arise. That being the case, MLA does request that you include the database name from which you are pulling any resource. Notice in the example below, the database title comes directly after the publication information of the print version. In other words, the database title, media or mode of access, and access date become a secondary layer of publication information.

>>>

>>> Cohen, Paul. "Cowboys Die Hard: Real Men and Businessmen in the Reagan-Era Blockbuster." *Film & History* 41.1 (2011): 71–81. EBSCOhost. Web. 8 Nov. 2011.

As mentioned in "Techno Tip: Databases, Microfilm, and Microfiche" in Chapter 4 (pages 84–85), scholarly databases are not the only databases you will be citing. Databases like *iTunes, Netflix, Hulu,* and *Amazon* provide access to various audio and visual media. *Google Books* has been slowly scanning hundreds of thousands of books and is now its own online book database. As above, the *Hulu* and *Google Books* examples below provide the database information as a secondary layer of publication information, listed after the primary citation.

"New York." *Glee*. Dir. Brad Falchuck. Perf. Cory Monteith and Lea Michele. 2011. 20th Century Fox, 2011. Hulu. Web. 8 Nov. 2011.

Whitman, Walt. *Leaves of Grass*. London: Trubner & Co., 1881. *Google Books.* Web. 2 Nov. 2011.

Finding ebooks for ereaders, like Amazon's Kindle (or Kindle Reading Applications) and Barnes & Noble's Nook, potentially becomes a little trickier. In these cases, the computer code used to translate the book into the appropriate ereader application is different. Therefore, we suggest that you provide which specific application database your are accessing, as in the Kindle example below.

Ambrose, Susan A., Michael W. Bridges, Michele DiPietro, Marsha C. Lovett, and Maria K. Norman. *How Learning Works: 7 Research-Based Principles for Smart Teaching*. San Francisco: Jossey-Bass-Wiley, 2010. Amazon. Kindle eBook. 2 Nov. 2011.

Although you may not know the fine details of how a given database works, do the best you can with our mash-up instructions (Chapter 11, pages 257–261) and talk to your friends and instructors.

MLA-31, Newspaper Article

Newspaper articles can generally be easily located in three forms of media: print, online at the newspaper's web site, and through a library database.

Printed Newspaper Article

Sisario, Ben. "Sirius's Move to Bypass a Royalty Payment Clearinghouse Causes an Uproar." *New York Times*. 7 Nov. 2011, New York ed.: B3. Print.

Newspaper Article Found Online

You can adapt the various journal and magazine article citations for online publications of the newspapers just by adding the site's sponsor, medium of publication (Web), and an access date. Follow with a URL if your instructor requires one. An article accessed online may not include page numbers.

Sisario, Ben. "Sirius's Move to Bypass a Royalty Payment Clearinghouse Causes an Uproar." *New York Times.* New York Times, 7 Nov. 2011. Web. 8 Nov. 11.

Newspaper Article Found in a Database

Articles found in databases should include all the original print information, as provided by the database, as well as the secondary layer of database name, media, and access date.

Sisario, Ben. "Sirius's Move to Bypass a Royalty Payment Clearinghouse Causes an Uproar." *New York Times* 7 Nov. 2011, late ed.: B3. *EBSCOhost.* Web. 8 Nov. 11.

Whereas in the Web version of the article cited above said that it came from the "New York edition," this database version said it came from the "late edition."

Newspaper Article Accessed through a Mobile Application

Sisario, Ben. "Sirius's Move to Bypass Royalty Agency Causes Uproar." *New York Times* 7 Nov. 2011. New York Times iPhone Mobile Application. 9 Nov. 2011.

Like the Wired example at the beginning of Chapter 11 (page 244), the title for the same article in the mobile application was slightly different from the print, online, and database versions. For publication information, we have added the name of the application (both the *New York Times* and *Wired* have their own applications; other mobile application readers like Pulse and Amazon Kindle have access to other periodicals).

MLA-32, Newspaper Editorial

"Swirl, Sniff, Sip, Check the Price." Editorial. *Los Angeles Times.* 19 Jan. 2008. Web. 22 Jan. 2012.

If there is no author listed, start with the name of the text you are citing. Include the term "Editorial" after the title. If this were found in a print newspaper, you would just include the publishing information required of a print citation.

MLA-33, Article in a Magazine

Magazines that publish every week or two weeks should include the full publication dates; magazines that publish monthly (or every two months) only need the month(s) and year. Do not give a volume or issue number, even if they are listed.

Printed Magazine Article

Levy, Steven. "Inside Google+." *Wired* Oct. 2011: 158–61. Print.

Magazine Article Found Online

Levy, Steven. "Inside Google Plus." *Wired* Oct. 2011. Web. 2 Dec. 2011.

MLA-32

MLA-33

You can adapt the various journal and magazine article citations for online publications of the journals just by adding the medium of publication (Web) and an access date. Follow with a URL if your instructor requires one. However, in this case (as in the one at the beginning of Chapter 11), if you look closely, you'll notice that the titles of the print and online versions are *not* the same. In short, pay close attention to whichever version you are citing.

Magazine Article Found in a Database

Levy, Steven. "Inside Google+." *Wired* Oct. 2011: 168–71. *EBSCOhost.*
Web. 8 Feb. 2012.

The database generally archives the print version of the article, not the Web-based version. Therefore, the title matches the print version.

Magazine Article Accessed through a Mobile Application

Levy, Steven. "Inside Google+." *Wired* Oct. 2011. iPad Mobile
Application. 2 Dec. 2011.

Since the computer coding involved for producing mobile applications in different platforms (Apple products versus Android/Google products versus Blackberry products, etc.) is different, we suggest that you specify which brand of device the application is running on.

Article That Skips Pages in a Monthly or Bimonthly Magazine

Gale, Doug. "Biometrics Revisited." *Campus Technology* Jan. 2008:
28+. Print.

When citing an article that skips pages, usually with advertising between content pages, you may include the inclusive page numbers if they are grouped together (13–21, 46–63); however, if the article is spread out over the entire periodical, usually with the concluding pages at the very end, just include the first page number and the plus symbol, +.

MLA-34, Article with a Quotation in the Title

Kahne, Joseph, and Kim Bailey. "The Role of Social Capital in Youth
Development: The Case of 'I Have a Dream' Programs."
Educational Evaluation and Policy Analysis 21.2 (1999): 321–43. Print.

MLA-35, Review

Sometimes reviews have their own title (like the book review below). If the review does not have its own title, just start with "Rev. of" and the title of the work under review. The first author listed is the person doing the review; the second author is the author of the text under review. You do not need publication information about the work under review (it is usually provided within the review itself); instead, you need to make sure you include publication information from the resource where the review is published.

Book Review

Drucker, Johanna. "Philosophy and Digital Humanities." Rev. of
      Humanities Computing, by Willard McCarty. *Digital Humanities*
      Quarterly 1.1 (2007): n. pag. Web. 18 Nov. 2011.

Game Review

Miller, Greg. "Batman: Arkham City Review." Rev. of *Batman:*
      Arkham City, by Rocksteady. *IGN*. 29 Nov. 2011. Web. 8 Dec. 2011.

MLA-36, Television

Like journals and magazines, television shows include individual pieces (episodes instead of articles). As mentioned above in the film examples, shows viewed on "live," or broadcast, TV need to be considered a dynamic production since television stations generally edit scenes and may incorporate advertising as part of the screening. However, once a television episode has been more formally "published" to DVD or to an online database like *Hulu* or *iTunes*, it should be considered a stable syndicated episode.

Broadcast of Television Episode (dynamic)

"New York." *Glee.* Dir. Brad Falchuck. Perf. Cory Monteith and Lea
      Michele. 2011. Fox. FOX10, Phoenix, 24 May 2011. Television.

Notice in a broadcast citation you need to include both the production company, in this case Fox, and the local channel name and number, in this case FOX10 (as well as the location).

Episode from a DVD

"New York." *Glee.* Dir. Brad Falchuck. Perf. Cory Monteith and Lea
      Michele. 2011. 20th Century Fox, 2011. DVD.

Although the production company is the same, please notice that they label it slightly differently in the two types of media ("Fox," for television broadcast and "20th Century Fox" for DVD publication and distribution).

Television Episode Downloaded from Database

"New York." *Glee.* Dir. Brad Falchuck. Perf. Cory Monteith and Lea
      Michele. 2011. 20th Century Fox, 2011. *iTunes*. Web. 8 Nov.
      2011.

Television Episode Streamed from Database

"New York." *Glee.* Dir. Brad Falchuck. Perf. Cory Monteith and Lea
      Michele. 2011. 20th Century Fox, 2011. *Hulu*. Web. 8 Nov.
      2011.

MLA-36

MLA-37

MLA-37, Blogs

Blogs, like periodicals and television shows, have overall titles and then specific articles, or "postings." Therefore, you might cite the entire blog web site, with all of its postings, an individual post, or a reader's comment to an individual post.

Entire Blog

Jenkins, Henry. *Confessions of an Aca-Fan: The Official Weblog of Henry Jenkins.* Web. 21 Jan. 2008.

Individual Blog Post

Jenkins, Henry. "Reconsidering Digital Immigrants. . . ." *Confessions of an Aca-Fan: The Official Weblog of Henry Jenkins.* 5 Dec. 2007. Web. 21 Jan. 2008.

Comment on a Specific Posting in a Blog

Marquard, Michelle. Comment on "Reconsidering Digital Immi grants. . . ." *Confessions of an Aca-Fan: The Official Weblog of Henry Jenkins.* By Henry Jenkins. 6 Dec. 2007. Web. 21 Jan. 2008.

A comment is like an entry in an anthology: you need the author and title of the individual entry as well as the editor, or in the case of blogs an author and title of the larger work. If the comment or reply of a weblog has its own title, use that; otherwise just call it a "comment on" or "reply to" the title of the original blog posting.

MLA-38

MLA-38, Podcast

Podcasts are just audio versions of blogs; cite them accordingly. However, since it is an audio file, you may want to alert your audience by including "Podcast" after the title.

Fogarty, Mignon. "'Ado' versus 'Adieu'." Podcast. *Grammar Girl: Quick and Dirty Tips for Better Writing.* Macmillan Holdings, 24 Oct. 2011. Web. 8 Nov. 2011.

MLA-39

MLA-39, Posting on *Twitter*

Lark, William. "Facebook 'pleased' . . ." Post. @*SocialNetworkTV.* 11 Nov. 2011. Web. 14 Nov. 2011.

Twitter is a microblog, a blog with a small entry space; therefore, you cite it like a blog. In this case, we made the title a shortened version of the full tweet (posting). Since individual Twitter posts have their own static, published, individual page URLs, they are more of a syndicated resource.

MLA-40, Online Video in User-Published Video Repository

If you were just posting an online video someone included on a web site, you would use some mash-up of a citation between film and a web page (see MLA-23 for ideas). If you were citing a video from a group of hosted videos by one company or organization, like *Hulu* or *TED*, you would use some mash-up of a citation between a film and a database. However, video repositories like *YouTube* and *Vimeo* are tricky. Technically *YouTube* and *Vimeo* are like blogs; individuals who post videos to *YouTube* have their own channel. Once you know that, it is easy to see that a *YouTube* posting is more like a blog, with a main channel title and individual postings (click on the name of the person who uploaded the video, circled in Figure 12.3, to see the channel page, which is shown in Figure 12.4).

Since *YouTube* also functions like an online database, we think it is important to include both *YouTube* (or *Vimeo*), in the title as well as the channel name.

YouTube Posting

Wesch, Michael. *A Vision of Students Today.* Online video. *YouTube: Digital Ethnography.* 12 Oct. 2007. Web. 21 Jan. 2008.

Video Reply to YouTube Posting

YouTube allows written replies to videos (which you would cite like a written reply to a blog post; see MLA-37) as well as video replies. A YouTube video reply might be cited one of two ways, depending on what you are emphasizing. If you are emphasizing the content of the video as it stands on its own,

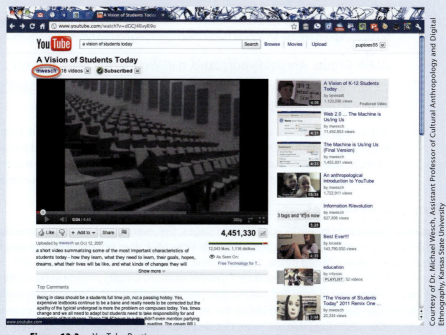

Figure 12.3   YouTube Posting.

Figure 12.4   YouTube Channel.

you would just cite it as another video at YouTube, with no reference to it also being a video reply. If you are commenting on the video as a reply to Wesch's original video, your citation would look more like a blog reply, as shown here.

Marino, Mark. *(Re)Visions of Students Today.* Video reply to online video of Michael Wesch. *YouTube: Digital Ethnography.* 19 Jan. 2008. Web. 21 Jan. 2011.

MLA-41, Annual Report

Annual reports are just syndicated reports or white papers. In other words, companies or organizations release an annual publication reporting certain types of information.

BMW Group. *Annual Report 2010.* n.d. Web. 8 Nov. 2011. <http://annual-report.bmwgroup.com/2010/gb/files/pdf/en/BMW_Group_AR2010.pdf>.

In this case, the author is a company. Some annual reports have titles; if it has a title, be sure to include "Annual Report" after the title. The report does not provide a specific publication date; therefore, we included "n.d." for no date. Since this document is not easy to find online, it is appropriate to include the URL in this citation.

Dynamic Resources

Dynamic resources (e.g., easily editable wiki pages, live events, and personal correspondence) are not necessarily easily cited, especially since MLA does not provide examples for some of the resources listed below. Since dynamic resources can change daily, all dynamic citations should include the access date. Dynamic citations usually include author, title of the text or event, and publication information that includes both the original publication or presentation date, and if found online the access date as well. Many dynamic citations include media descriptors that are more detailed than the traditional "print" or "Web" listings. The following examples indicate how to cite various types of dynamic sources.

MLA-42

MLA-42, Page from a Wiki

Churches, Andrew. "Bloom's Digital Taxonomy." *Educational*
Origami. 1 Oct. 2010. Web. 14 Nov. 2011. <http://edorigami
.wikispaces.com/Bloom%27s+Digital+Taxonomy>.

Most wiki pages have a "history" or "page history" link or tab that will allow you
to see the last time the page was updated. The information on that page should
help you determine if there is a primary author for the page or if there are a
multitude of authors (like most *Wikipedia* articles). For a resource that lists no
author or has a multitude of authors over time, treat the text as "no author" and
start with the title.

MLA-43

MLA-43, Public Address

Godin, Seth. "Invisible or Remarkable?" EDUCAUSE. Philadelphia
Convention Center, Philadelphia. 19 Oct. 2011. Keynote speech.

If there is no title, just skip to the meeting and sponsoring organization's
information (in this case, EDUCAUSE is in all capitals because that is how the
name of the organization is spelled). Your publication information includes
the name of the meeting, the name of the building, and the city. Be sure to
include an appropriate descriptive label (Address, Lecture, Keynote speech,
Reading, etc.).

MLA-44

MLA-44, Lecture Notes

Hellner, Nancy. "Three Waves of Feminism." Lecture notes. WST209:
Women and Film. Mesa Community College, Mesa. 29 Aug.
2009. Print.

The author is whoever produced the notes, not necessarily the person who
delivered the lecture. The title of the notes is probably the title of the lecture.
Include name and location of the lecture in the publication section. In this case
you have two identifications of media: the type of resource or text you are citing
as well as the media in which it was found. For example, these notes might just
as easily be found online and labeled "Web."

MLA-45

MLA-45, Live Performance

Vagina Monologues. By Eve Ensler. Dir. Felicia Davis. Perf. Malinda
Williams, Nicole Ari Parker, and Vanessa Williams. Herberger
Theater, Phoenix. 26 Apr. 2008. Performance.

 author   title   ▢ media descriptor   ▢ publication information   ▢ access date

A live performance entry looks a lot like a film entry (MLA-23). Start with the title of the performance, the names of the playwright and director, and the main performers. You also include the location of the performance in the publication information.

MLA-46, Live Personal Interview

Groom, Jim. Personal interview. 6 Sept. 2011.

Although a personal interview is considered primary research, MLA requires that you include an in-text and a full bibliographic citation to give readers the details of where and when you conducted the interview. What looks like the author in this instance is actually the title, the name of the person you interviewed. You then include the detailed descriptor and the date of the interview.

MLA-47, Personal Correspondence

If the letter or email is published as a part of a larger work, it is static; therefore, treat it like a section from a book. If it is not published elsewhere, treat it as a dynamic resource.

Personal Letter

Adams, Devon. Letter to the author. 19 Mar. 2011. MS.

In this case "Letter to the author" can function as the title as well as a detailed description. However, MS stands for "manuscript" (a work written by hand) and definitely represents the media. If the letter had been typed, the citation would have used "TS" for "typescript" (a work produced by a machine).

Email Message

Adams, Donna. "Nominate a STAR!" Message to Shelley Rodrigo. 13 Oct. 2011. E-mail.

The title of the email comes from the email's subject line.

MLA-48, Message Posted to a Discussion Group

Nielson, Chris. "Twitter and the Teen Brain." *Cyber Salon.* Online posting. 10 Nov. 2011. Web. 14 Nov. 2011.

Citing a post to a discussion group or board, listserv, or newsgroup is basically the same; you need an author, a title, a brief description of the type of text, the date of the original posting, and the typical online citation information, including date of access and web address (if needed).

MLA-49, Wall Message on *Facebook*

> Gierdowski, Dana Cockrum. *Kevin Brock's Facebook Page.* Wall
>   *Facebook* posting. 8 Nov. 2011. Web. 14 Nov. 2011. <https://
>   www.facebook.com/kevin.brock.359/posts/10100329849515839>.

A posting to an individual's wall on *Facebook* or *Google+* are very similar to a discussion board posting; therefore, you emulate the citation style as best you can. *Facebook* Wall postings now have permanent URLs; therefore, you should include the URL as part of your citation.

MLA-50, Video Game

Video games are tricky to cite. On the one hand, many games are mainly static: every player will access the same material in the same way. Other games, like *World of Warcraft*, are mostly dynamic. Everybody playing the game at the same time impacts your game experiences. Depending on what portion of the game, or game play, you are citing, you will have to decide whether it is static or dynamic.

Video Game on MP3 Player (static)

> *Sudoku.* Version 1.0.0. Video game for iPod. Redwood City: Electronic
>   Arts, 2007. Game.

Massive Multiplayer Online Role Playing Game (MMORPG, dynamic)

> *The World of Warcraft: The Burning Crusade.* Online video game.
>   Irvine: Blizzard Entertainment, 2007. Web. 22 Jan. 2008.

MLA Style: Some Common Errors

reflect

▶ Only include the authors' last names in the in-text parenthetical citations.

▶ No commas or other punctuation should appear in the in-text parenthetical citation.

▶ Confusion between the publication, release, or copyright date and the date of access.

▶ Spelled-out names of months. Except for May, June, and July, all months are abbreviated.

▶ Omission of the name of the institution in the citation of a web site hosted at an academic institution.

▶ Omission of the medium of publication, of delivery, or reception, etc. (print, Web, DVD, weblog, podcast, film, etc.).

Paper Formatting

MLA simplifies paper formatting so that students do not have to know how to use every tool in their word-processing programs.

Title Page

MLA style does not require a separate title page. Instead, in the upper left corner, on the first page of the paper, include the following information:

- your name
- instructor's name
- course title
- date

Spacing and Margins

MLA style requires that you double-space the entire document, including title page information, quotations, and the list of works cited. You do not need to include extra spaces (i.e., quadruple space) anywhere in the text. Set your top, left, and bottom margins for one inch. All paragraphs should be indented by one-half inch.

Headers and Page Numbers

In the upper right corner of each page, include a header with your last name and the page number. All pages in the paper should be consecutively numbered. The header is placed one-half inch from the top of the page and one inch from the right side of the page. Include the header on the first page and all subsequent pages.

Section Headings

If your paper is long enough and it includes coherent sections, and even subsections, you might consider including section headings in your paper. MLA does not prescribe specific guidelines for section headings. For each section use an Arabic numeral with a relevant title. Make sure that all of your section titles are syntactically parallel. In other words, if you start your first section title with a noun, start all of your section titles with nouns. For example, the following outline could represent section headings from a paper in MLA style. Ultimately, MLA emphasizes that section headings be concise, well-organized, and above all, consistent.

1. Technological Advancements
   a. Advancements in Visual Technologies
   b. Advancements in Production and Distribution
   c. Advancements in Interactive Technologies
2. Narrative Structure
3. Ideological Differences
4. Hollywood's Enterprises
   a. Vertical Integration
   b. Further Economic Trends
5. Conclusions

Visuals

MLA style divides visuals into two categories: tables and figures. Whenever you place visuals into your text, you must place them as close as possible to the paragraph referring to them.

Tables   If you are presenting numerical data in a table format, label the table with the word *Table* (not italicized), an Arabic numeral, and a title. The label and title are placed on top of the table as it appears in your text. If you are reprinting the table from an outside source, you must include the full bibliographic citation for the table directly under the table (not at the end of your paper in the works cited list).

Table 12.1

A Table in MLA Style with Appropriate Captions

Kairos in the Rhetorical Situation	Purpose	Audience	Author
Time	What has happened in the past or is happening in the present that motivates research and communication? What will happen in the future that will require research and communication?	What has happened in the past or is happening in the present that motivates this audience to care about the topic? What does the audience need to do in the future that motivates their reading/ learning about the topic?	What has happened in the author's past or is happening in the present or may happen in the author's future that motivates him or her to research and write?
Space	What persons, places, or things will be affected by the outcomes of this research?	What real-world things can the audience do to impact this issue based on the research and writing?	What resources does the author have to facilitate research, writing, and publishing on this topic?

Source: Miller-Cochran, Susan K., and Rochelle L. Rodrigo. "Kairos in the
Rhetorical Situation." *The Wadsworth Guide to Research*. 2nd ed. Boston:
Wadsworth, Cengage Learning, 2014. 291. Print.

Figures   MLA style refers to all other types of visuals such as charts, graphs, maps, and images as figures. Label each figure with the word *Figure* or the abbreviated *Fig.* (not italicized), an Arabic numeral, and a title. The label and title of a figure are placed below the visual as it appears in your text, along with a reference to the source of the figure if it came from an outside resource.

© Andia/Alamy

Fig 1. Digital Mapping. This film still from *Avatar* exemplifies how the advancements in digital facial mapping technologies improves the emotional appeal of CGI constructed characters. From *Avatar*. Dir. James Cameron. Perf. Sam Worthington, Zoe Saldana, and Sigourney Weaver. Twentieth-Century Fox, 2009. *Netflix*. 4 Feb. 2012.

Using an image in a text that discusses the importance of computer generated imagery (CGI) in the construction of the characters within the film *Avatar* (2009) would be similar to including a long quotation that describes the image. The image itself, in this instance, is a better representation of "CGI constructed characters." It would probably be better to directly "quote" by including the figure than to try to describe what the image looks like on the screen.

Sample Paper

Zack Hill

Professor Jacobs

English 423

7 December 2011

Religion and the Romantic Superhuman

  In the British Romantic period, much of the literature produced implored readers to re-evaluate their societal ideals in an "intellectual-revolutionary" manner, as several Romantic texts challenge readers to revise the way in which they viewed their world. One of the techniques, chiefly implemented in the Shelleys' writings— namely Mary Shelley's *Frankenstein* and Percy Shelley's *Prometheus Unbound*—is the "superhuman" character. This character is an entity that is ultimately human in nature, but becomes an exaggeration of the primal desires of those it is supposed to serve through extra-human means. Essentially, a superhuman is a character who is elevated within a text by a distinct ability. While the tradition of employing a "superhuman" character in a work of literature did not begin in the Romantic Period, the Shelleys adapt this archetype to the purpose of their literary works as a lens through which the topic of religion can be explored and problematized.

  Both of these narratives are overtly linked with Greek mythology, with the full title of Mary Shelley's novel, *Frankenstein; or, The Modern Prometheus*, and Percy Shelley's epic drama titled *Prometheus Unbound*. The Greek tradition of telling myths of the gods and goddesses they worshipped served a primitive purpose of explaining why the world works in the way that it does (e.g., the myth of Persephone and Hades explaining the reason for the change in seasons). One of the most prominent features of the mythological Greek gods is the fact that they are given the title of "gods," yet their personalities, strengths, and weaknesses are composed of exaggerated versions of the same aspects in humans (Habib). The Shelleys build on this tradition by including specific elements that echo the myth of Prometheus in their works or, in Percy's case, by expanding on the mythos completely.

Callout annotations:
- 1 in.
- 1 in.
- ½ in.
- 1 in.
- All regular double spacing; no extra spaces
- Indent paragraphs 1/2 in.
- Title is centered on the page.

Mary Shelley fleshes out the theme of the superhuman in her novel by making it tangible through the character of Victor Frankenstein. Although it can be argued that the monster is a superhuman character, it is Victor who best fits this particular definition of the term, as the monster is not human, but "[his] own species" (195), by his own definition. During the course of the novel, Victor is made superhuman by his knowledge and ability to reanimate life and becomes Creator, or Parent, to the monster. This makes him superhuman in relation to both the monster and subsequently to the world. This ability and knowledge essentially elevates him to the status of a God, a role which he is clearly not prepared to play, as the reader can observe even before the monster comes to life: Victor describes that he labored "With an anxiety that almost amounted to agony" (148). Victor's story not only echoes the Christian story of Creation, with God creating Adam from dust, but it also echoes popular Promethean mythology, with Prometheus crafting mankind from clay. The difference between these stories and *Frankenstein*—and what precisely causes tension within the text—is the fact that this superhuman-God casts his creation aside as quickly as it breathes its first breaths. With the abandonment of his creation as the catalyst for the rising action of the novel, Shelley, according to critic Harriet Hustis, "explores the ethics of a[…]creator's relationship to his progeny by questioning the extent to which he incurs an obligation for the well-being and happiness of that creation by virtue of the creative act itself" (Hustis, 846). This assertion, coupled with the lens of the superhuman, reveals one of the text's crucial questions: *What if God was, or is, like Victor Frankenstein?*

By juxtaposing Victor and the Christian God on a metaphoric level, the text becomes a questioning of Deistic beliefs, as Victor performs similarly to how Deists believe God has done with Man. This problematization of Deistic beliefs concerns itself largely with the supposition that if God created Man and left him to fend for himself, never interfering in the interests of his creation, he would lack a component essential to a "responsible" creator: pity. The absence of "[p]ity and the willingness to give another precedence over oneself (regardless of whether s/he 'deserves' it)" (Hustis, 849) in a creator conjures anxiety for the reader because the thought of

Hill 3

a pitiless, omnipotent being is truly horrifying, which Shelley aptly conveys through Victor. To this effect, Victor states "[he] compassionated [the monster], and sometimes felt a wish to console him; but when [he] looked upon him, when [he] saw the filthy mass that moved and talked, [his] own heart sickened, and [his] feelings were altered to those of horror and hatred" (Shelley, 99). Shelley quells the anxiety she has built in the novel through this juxtaposition by reminding the reader that, regardless of how closely Victor may resemble God, Victor is ultimately human—in the end, he is mortal.

Just as his wife constructed a narrative that is a derivation of the Promethean myth, *Prometheus Unbound* is an epic poem written in dramatic style about Greek Gods and Titans. While these figures are superhuman by definition, Demogorgon is the poem's focus for this analysis, as he is able to transcend even their power when he is provoked into action by Asia and Panthea. Throughout the course of the poetic drama, Shelley characterizes Jupiter (Zeus) as tyrannical, cruel, and torturous, not only in his treatment of Prometheus, but also in his nonchalant attitude towards humankind. The poem illustrates the latter point through the visions that the Furies give Prometheus when Jupiter sends them to torture Prometheus. His tyranny even extends to the act of rape through which Demogorgon was conceived. These elements build a unique tension towards Jupiter, who acts as a metaphor for the Christian God, which questions both the reality of his being and the necessity of it. As with *Frankenstein*, the reader can see fragments of Deistic theology woven into the poem as it faces the reader with the question of whether or not God cares about the suffering of humanity. The answer to the question, through Jupiter, suggests that God does not care, which drives Panthea and Asia to follow the Echoes and seek out Demogorgon, the "superhuman" of the text.

The very realm in which Demogorgon lives sets him up as the superhuman character of the text, as he abides behind a " . . . mighty portal,"

Like a volcano's meteor-breathing chasm,
Whence the oracular vapor is hurled up

Hill 4

Which lonely men drink wandering in their youth,
And call truth, virtue, love, genius, or joy,
That maddening wine of life . . . (2.3.2–7).

Not only is his place of residence indicative of his superhuman
status, but also his demeanor and manner of answering Asia and
Panthea's questions indicates that he is privileged to a higher level
of understanding concerning the hierarchy of the world. The women
believe that Demogorgon will provide them with the answers they
need to free Prometheus and set things right with Jupiter, which
he does; however, in the process, he creates three areas of tension
within the text (essentially whenever he appears in the text).

The tension he creates upon his first appearance in the text
revolves precisely around the fact that he speaks in the language
of equivocation, a tactic once employed by the Spanish Inquisi-
tion to implicate guilt. He references an unnamed "Almighty" and
"Merciful" God (1120), which confuses both Asia and Panthea,
largely because he will not reveal who this God is. His second
appearance creates a more proactive tension by his ascension to
Jupiter's threshold to drag him down into the abyss. His presence
perplexes Jupiter, as he asks, "Awful shape, what art thou? Speak!"
to which Demogorgon responds

Eternity. Demand no direct name.
Descend, and follow me down the abyss.
I am thy child, as thou wert Saturn's child,
Mightier than thee: and we must dwell together
Henceforth in darkness [. . .]
The tyranny of heaven none may retain. (3.52–57).

The threat of dragging God into the "darkness," or "Hell," in
Christian terms, for eternity is an act in and of itself that sparks
anxiety not only because of the possibility of the absence of God, but
also because of what critic Christopher Miller calls the "emptying
of Heaven" (Miller 588). He states that this emptying of Heaven
simultaneously "reclaimed by the choric voices of the Earth" which
"harmoniously" merges the realms of Heaven and Earth (589). This
implies that humans would be essentially on their own to traverse
through life, an implication that does not cause anxiety for humankind in the text because of how tyrannical Jupiter's rule was before

he was evicted; however, for the Protestant reader, this notion is preposterous.

Demogorgon's final appearance in the poetic drama causes the drama to close on an apprehensive note as he returns to the renewed Earth for his final departure with a cryptic message. This message alludes to how the world should be governed and the duality of that governance by stating that:

> Love, from its awful throne of patient power
> In the wise heart, from the last giddy hour
> Of dread endurance, from the slippery, steep,
> And narrow verge of crag-like agony, springs
> And folds over the world its healing wings. (4.557–561)

Love is, at the same time, a healing power and a power that can provoke feelings of agony. The former ability alludes to the traditional feel-good aspect of love and the latter presents a more judicious form of love—one that cuts swiftly and accurately against injustice.

The Shelleys use a version of the superhuman character in their narratives as a means of challenging their readers to redefine the way in which they view crucial social issues, specifically religion. Through Victor Frankenstein, Mary Shelley contrives the Promethean myth to explore Deist theology and expose the anxieties it provides its believers. In *Prometheus Unbound*, Jupiter, a metaphor for Christianity, has become cold and tyrannical, creating the need for Demogorgon to abolish theology by vacating the realm of Heaven of Jupiter's presence. These superhuman characters ultimately remind readers of the shortcomings and consequences of humanity, a notion which gives them the agency to instill a sense of anxiety in readers, especially for readers contemporary to the Shelleys' time period.

Hill 6

Works Cited

Habib, Imitaz. ENGL305. Old Dominion University, Norfolk. 13 April 2010. Classroom lecture.

Hustis, Harriet. "Responsible Creativity and the 'Modernity' of Mary Shelley's Prometheus." *Studies in English Literature, 1500–1900* 43.4 (2003): 845–58. *JSTOR*. Web. 1 Dec. 2011.

Miller, Christopher R. "Shelley's Uncertain Heaven." *ELH* 72.3 (2005): 577–603. *JSTOR*. Web. 1 Dec. 2011.

Shelley, Mary. *Frankenstein*. New York: Norton, 1996. Print.

Shelley, Percy Bysshe. "Prometheus Unbound: A Lyrical Drama in Four Acts." *The Complete Poetical Works of Percy Bysshe Shelley*. Boston: Houghton, 1901. *Bartleby.com*. Web. 24 Nov. 2011.

chapter 13

APA Formatting Guidelines

The American Psychological Association (6th edition) citation style guidelines include two functioning parts, the in-text citation that helps identify what piece of the text is being quoted, paraphrased, or summarized, and the full bibliographic citation at the end of the paper that helps the reader find the original resource being referenced. In this section, you will find explanations and examples of how to cite resources that you might use in your research, both in the text of your work (in-text citations) and at the end of your research (reference list).

In-Text Citations

APA in-text citations require the author's name, the copyright or publication date, and, if you are including a paraphrase or direct quote, a page number with the lowercase letter "p" and a period.

Quotations and Paraphrases

Standard in-text citations in APA format include the author's name, the date, and the page number in the citation.

> Science fiction films "self-consciously foreground their own radicality" of special effects (Freedman, 1997, p. 307).

If the resource was written by two authors, your in-text citation includes the names of both authors, connected by "&."

> (Miller-Cochran & Rodrigo, 2009, p. 294).

If the resource was written by three or more authors, your in-text citation will include all the author's names the first time you cite the resource, and any subsequent in-text citations can be shortened by using just the last name of the first author followed by "et al." (which in Latin means "and others"). Be careful not to use a period after "et" because it is an entire Latin word. The Latin abbreviation "al." (with a period) is an abbreviation for "alii" or "alia," which means "others."

> (Westman, Linton, Ahrik, Wahlen, & Leppert, 2007, p. 647).
>
> (Westman et al., 2007, p. 647).

If you choose to mention the author's name in the sentence, include the copyright or publication date right after the author's name in a set of parentheses. If the author's name and the date are already mentioned in the sentence, you only need to include the page number from which the information or quotation came in the in-text citation. The next example uses the same short quotation from Freedman's work and only needs to provide the page number where the quotation was found because Freedman's name and the date are included in the sentence itself:

> Freedman (1997) criticizes science fiction films for "self-consciously foreground[ing] their own radicality" of special effects (p. 307).

APA style calls for authors to be specific about identifying the location of direct quotations and paraphrases. Therefore, if you are citing from an electronic resource without page numbers, such as a web page or an ebook, APA requires that you identify the paragraph number your quotation comes from. To distinguish the citation from a normal page marker, introduce the paragraph number with "para."

> Introducing his blog posting about "live action" anime, Jenkins (2007) proclaims that this type of event could happen "only at MIT" (para. 1).

Long Quotations

In APA style, text quotations that are forty words or longer need to be presented in a block quote. Instead of using quotation marks to identify the text being directly quoted, block quotes indent the material so that it stands out on the page. Block quotations are set off one-half inch from the left margin (Figure 13.1). Because they are direct quotations, block quotes need an in-text citation that includes the author's name and the page number the quotation came from.

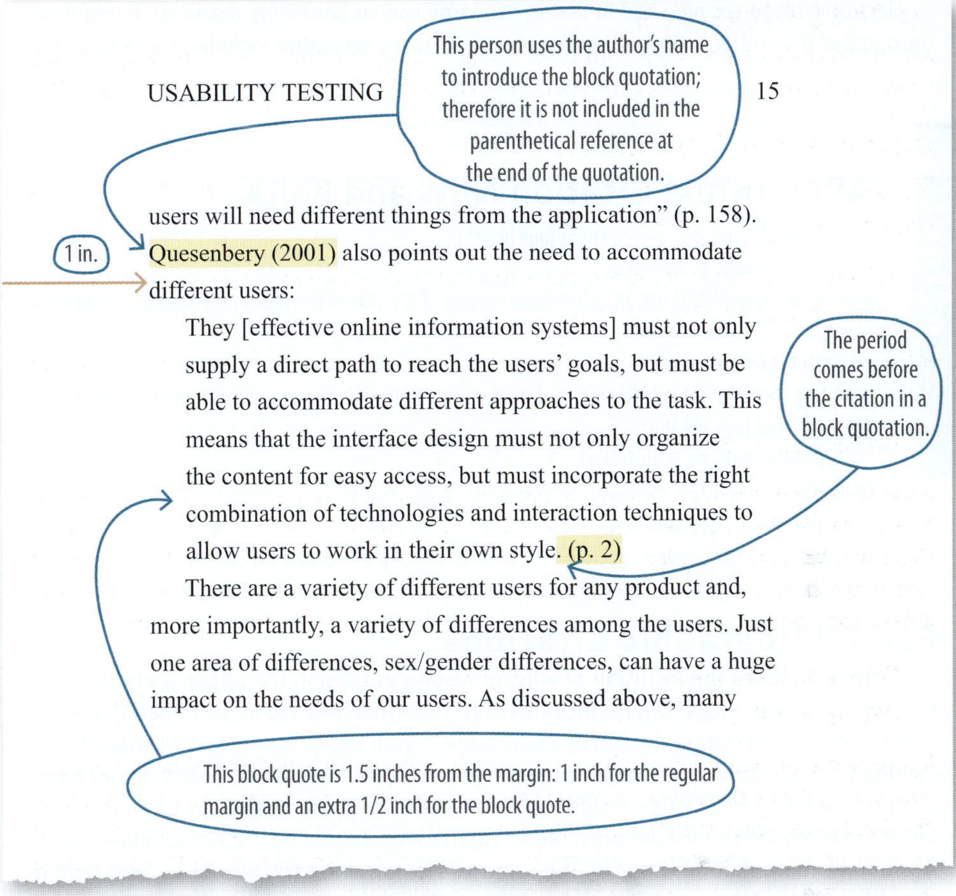

USABILITY TESTING

> This person uses the author's name to introduce the block quotation; therefore it is not included in the parenthetical reference at the end of the quotation.

15

users will need different things from the application" (p. 158).

1 in.

Quesenbery (2001) also points out the need to accommodate different users:

> They [effective online information systems] must not only supply a direct path to reach the users' goals, but must be able to accommodate different approaches to the task. This means that the interface design must not only organize the content for easy access, but must incorporate the right combination of technologies and interaction techniques to allow users to work in their own style. (p. 2)
>
> There are a variety of different users for any product and, more importantly, a variety of differences among the users. Just one area of differences, sex/gender differences, can have a huge impact on the needs of our users. As discussed above, many

> The period comes before the citation in a block quotation.

> This block quote is 1.5 inches from the margin: 1 inch for the regular margin and an extra 1/2 inch for the block quote.

Figure 13.1   An Extended Quotation in APA Style.[1]

Summaries and Multiple Resources

If you are summarizing the main point of a resource and not referencing one particular part of the source, APA style only requires that you provide enough information in an in-text citation to get the reader to the full bibliographic citation in the reference list, which is usually just the author's last name and the resource's copyright or publication date. In the following example, the writer briefly refers to multiple texts within the same sentence.

Notice that the resources are listed in alphabetical order by the author's last name, not in numerical order by the publication date.

During the 1980s and early 1990s, *Computers and Composition* published many articles discussing methods and criteria for evaluating and choosing instructional software packages (Condon, 1992; Eiler, 1992; Hepler, 1992; Kemp, 1992; Redmond, Lawrence, & Villani, 1985; Taylor, 1992; Wahlstrom, 1985).[2]

1. Bowie, Jennifer. "Beyond the Universal: The Universe of Users Approach to User-Centered Design." In *Rhetorically Rethinking Usability*. Ed. Susan Miller-Cochran and Rochelle Rodrigo. Cresskill, NJ: Hampton Press, 2009. Reproduced by permission.
2. Cahill, Lisa, and Rochelle Rodrigo. "Educational Usability in Online Writing Courses." In *Rhetorically Rethinking Usability*. Ed. Susan Miller-Cochran and Rochelle Rodrigo. Cresskill, NJ: Hampton Press, 2009. Reproduced by permission.

Electronic resources are cited in text in the same way as hard-copy resources. If you have the name of the author, include that information. If there is no author, include a shortened title.

APA: In-Text Citation Nuts and Bolts

In APA format, typical in-text citations look like this:

(Author, date, p. number)

If no author is available, use an abbreviated version of the title of the source. The citation would look like this:

(Title, date, p. number)

If no page number is available (e.g., a digital resource), include the paragraph number instead. The citation would look like this:

(Author, date, para. number)

Or like this:

(Title, date, para. number)

Full Bibliographic Citations

APA format requires the inclusion of a list of resources used in the paper, and this list is referred to as "references." This list includes only the resources cited in the paper. The references page should start at the top of a new page in your essay; however, it will need to be included in your continuous page numbering. Subsequent references pages do not have a special heading but simply include APA-formatted page numbers and running head. Entries in the reference list are presented in alphabetical order by the author's last name. If you have more than one text by the same author, organize the entries by year (and if they have the same year, alphabetize within those author entries by title of the text). If you have texts with no authors, incorporate them into the alphabetical list based on title.

Entries in a reference list should have a hanging indent, a format that looks a bit like an upside-down paragraph. The first line of the citation is left-justified, with no indent. Then all subsequent lines have a half-inch indentation. The examples in Figure 13.2 demonstrate how the hanging indent looks on the page.

APA full bibliographic citation style generally provides information in the following order:

1. Name of author (only including initials for author's first and middle names)
2. Copyright or publication year (in parentheses)
3. Title of text (only the first word and proper names are capitalized except for periodical titles)
4. Other publication information (usually the location or online location where you found the resource, including the city *and* state or the city and country, as well as the publisher's name)

Periods are included after each major section of information. For example, a period is included after the name of the author(s), the date, the title of the text, and the complete publication information. If there is *no author* for the text, start with the text's title; however, remember that a government agency or a corporation can function as an author. With some online resources, you may have to look on other pages besides the

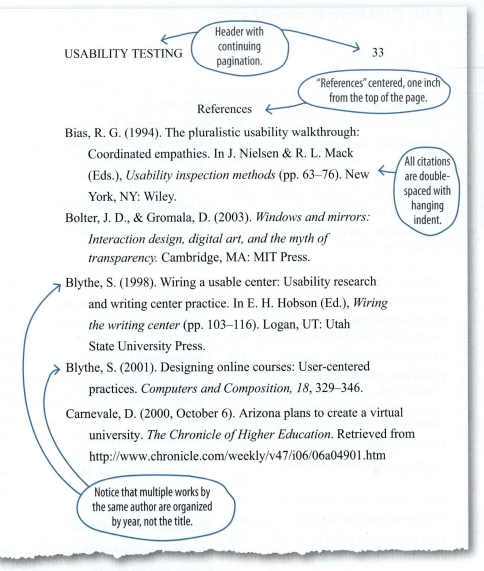

Figure 13.2   The First Page of the References in APA Style.[3]

homepage to find the author's name. Similarly, you may have to search dynamic online resources for the last updated date (like the "history" page in wikis). If you cannot find a date, include "n.d." within parentheses.

The citation rules for static, periodic, and dynamic resources all follow this general pattern, but each category has some unique characteristics. (For definitions of static, syndicated, and dynamic resources, see Chapter 4.)

3. Bowie, Jennifer. "Beyond the Universal: The Universe of Users Approach to User-Centered Design." In *Rhetorically Rethinking Usability*. Ed. Susan Miller-Cochran and Rochelle Rodrigo. Cresskill, NJ: Hampton Press, 2009. Reproduced by permission.

APA Citation Examples

For more examples of APA citations go to the English CourseMate for this text at cengagebrain.com

Static Resources

Static resources (e.g., books, films, and government documents) are generally easy to cite using APA style. These citations usually include author, title, and publication information. The following examples indicate how to cite various types of static sources.

APA-1

APA-1, Printed Book with One Author

Balsamo, A. (2011). *Designing culture: The technological imagination at work.* Durham, NC: Duke University Press.

APA-2

APA-2, Printed Book with Two Authors

Bolter, J. D., & Grusin, R. (1999). *Remediation: Understanding new media.* Cambridge, MA: MIT Press.

Notice that between the authors' names, the ampersand, the "&" symbol, is used instead of "and."

APA-3

APA-3, Printed Book with Three or More Authors

Lister, M., Dovey, J., Giddings, S., Grant, I., & Kelly, K. (2009). *New media: A critical introduction* (2nd ed.). London, England: Routledge.

Include the names of up to seven authors. If there are more than seven authors, include the first six, then three ellipsis points (periods) and the last author's name.

APA-4

APA-4, Electronic Book

Electronic Book on the Web

Shakespeare, W. (1999–2003). *The taming of the shrew.* A. Ballard (Ed.). Retrieved from http://www.shakespeare-online.com/ (Original work published 1593–1594)

Since this is an electronic version of a republished book, APA suggests that you include the original publication date at the end of the citation.

Electronic Book in Database

Whitman, W. (1881). *Leaves of grass.* Retrieved from http://books .google.com/books

Electronic Book Downloaded for an Ereader

Ambrose, S. A., Bridges, M. W., DiPietro, M., Lovett, M. C., & Norman, M. K. (2010). *How learning works: 7 research-based principles for smart teaching* [Amazon Kindle Reader version]. Retrieved from http://www.amazon.com/

In all three cases, traditional book publication information is replaced with electronic retrieval information. Notice with ereaders the APA guidelines suggest including the type of reader or format.

 author   title   publication information

APA-5

APA-5, Selection from an Edited Collection or Anthology

> Peigin, C. (2010). Magazines: An industry in transition. In J. F. Scotton & W. A. Hachten (Eds.), *New media for a new China* (pp. 74–82). West Sussex, England: Blackwell.

Edited collections or anthologies have two layers of both authorial and title information. There is the author of the specific essay or chapter that you are citing. The specific essay or chapter title is presented in the same font style with capital letters for only the first word in the title and proper nouns. The second title, the title of the edited collection or anthology, is presented in italics (like the title of a regular book). The second layer of authorial information, the editors who put together the edited collection or anthology, comes before the title of the book. You also need to include page numbers for the specific portion of the book you are referring to; they are presented after the title of the book.

APA-6

APA-6, Introduction, Preface, Foreword, or Afterword from a Book

> Baynes, W. E. C. (2003). Introduction. In N. Machiavelli, *The prince* (R. Goodwin, Trans.) (pp. 13–25). Wellesley, MA: Dante University Press.

The citation styles for introductions, prefaces, forewords, and afterwords are basically the same as a resource from an edited collection or anthology (APA-5). If you are using one of these types of ancillary materials as a resource, start your citation with the author of the ancillary material. If the ancillary material has a title, use it, or put the title as a word that represents the material (i.e., preface, foreword, etc.) before the remainder of the book's citation.

APA-7

APA-7, Book with a Translator

> Machiavelli, N. (2003). *The prince* (R. Goodwin, Trans.). Wellesley, MA: Dante University Press.

Several different versions of *The Prince* exist, and the translator's role in the publishing process distinguishes one version from another.

APA-8

APA-8, Book with an Editor (Entire Anthology)

> Giggings, S., & Lister, M., (Eds.). (2011). *The new media and technocultures reader.* London, England: Routledge.

If you are citing an entire edited collection, you need to identify the "authors" as "editors" by including "Ed." (for one editor) or "Eds." (for more than one editor) within parentheses after their names.

APA-9

APA-9, Book in a Series

Crow, A. (2006). *Aging literacies: Training and development challenges for faculty.* In G. E. Hawisher & C. Selfe (Series Eds.), *New Dimensions in Computers and Composition.* Cresskill, NJ: Hampton Press.

APA-10

APA-10, Book in an Edition Other Than the First

Cohen, A., & Brawer, F. B. (2008). *The American community college.* (5th ed.). San Francisco, CA: Jossey-Bass-Wiley.

When referring to books in multiple editions, use the language you find on the title page of the book. Therefore, if it says second or third edition, put the numbers in your citation. If it says "Revised" or "Abridged" put "Rev. ed." or "Abr. ed." in the citation. Similarly, if your book is the fifth in a multivolume work, just include "Vol. 5."

APA-11

APA-11, Book with a Title within the Title

Sammon, P. M. (1989). *Future noir: The making of* Blade Runner. New York, NY: Harper Paperbacks-HarperCollins.

The title of the film within the title of the book is neither italicized nor enclosed in quotation marks. If the title within the title is of a shorter work, like a story, poem, or song, you'll keep everything in italics and put quotation marks around the title (see APA-30).

techno tip

APA and Web Pages

For citation purposes, treat a web page or web site as static, unless you know that it is dynamic (a wiki, for example) or syndicated (like a blog). (Note: Many web sites are now actually online databases and should be treated accordingly. See "Techno Tip: APA and Databases," page 314.) Static web page citations look a lot like citations from a chapter or article in a book: author, specific web page title, *overall web site title,* the date of publication and retrieval location (URL with no concluding punctuation). APA style does not ask that you include date of access (the date you looked at and retrieved information from the web site) unless the web page clearly changes over time (like a wiki).

Burton, G. O. 2011). Invention. *Silva rhetoricae.* Retrieved from http://rhetoric.byu.edu/

>>>

The author's name and the copyright or posted date are sometimes located somewhere on the web page; if not, try searching for an "about" page. If the specific page within the web site is easy to find, you only need to include the web site homepage; however, if it is difficult to find, include the full URL. Type the URL after "Retrieved from" and do not include a period after the URL.

If a web page or book has no author's or editor's name, and you cannot find one by looking around the site, begin the citation with the title. Use italics to distinguish between the title of the web page and *the title of the web site.*

Box office/business for *Melancholia.* (1999–2011). *IMDb.* Retrieved from http://www .imdb.com/

APA-12, Web Page

Burton, G. O. (2011). Invention. *Silva rhetoricae.* Retrieved from http://rhetoric.byu.edu/

APA-13, Web Page with No Author Listed

Box office/business for *Melancholia.* (1999–2011). *IMDb.* Retrieved from http://www.imdb.com/

APA-14, Government Publication

U.S. Health and Human Services. (2011, June 27). *Open government progress report.* Retrieved from http://www.hhs.gov/open/ plan/june2011progressreport /opengov_progreport20110627.pdf

The sixth edition of the APA style guidelines also provides very detailed instructions for different types of legal documents. If you are working with a variety of legal documents, be sure to reference Appendix 7.1 in the APA style guide. Like government agencies, corporations and other organizations can also be authors of resources. In those cases, the school or corporation's name would be listed as the author of a resource (also see APA-37).

APA-15, Published Interview

Cochran, S. (2011, January 20). How to publish a book: Literary agent interview—Peter Riva. *How to publish a book.* Retrieved from http://howtopublishabook.org/2011.01.01_arch.html

A published interview is like any other smaller text, essay, or chapter within a larger body of work (see APA-5). A personal or "live" interview, however, is considered primary data that you collect and only cite in text. Interviews may also be "published" in online archives or databases (see "Techno Tip: APA and Databases," page 314).

APA-16, Published Letter

Adams, A. (1774, August 28). [Letter to Abigail Adams]. *Adams family papers: An electronic archive.* Retrieved from http://www .masshist.org/digitaladams/aea/

A published letter is like any other smaller text, essay, or chapter within a larger body of work (see APA-5); however, you do need to include the full date of the letter. The brackets in this example indicate that the words do not appear on the letter itself, but are a description. A personal letter is considered a primary resource and is only cited in text. According to APA, the name of the archive should *not* be italicized; however, since this archive is also a web site, we decided to italicize it.

APA-17, Conference Proceedings

VanTassel-Baska, J., & Stambaugh, T. (Eds.) (2007). Overlooked gems: A national perspective on low-income promising learners. *Proceedings of the National Leadership Conference on Low-Income Promising Learners.* Williamsburg, VA: National Association for Gifted Children and the Center for Gifted Education, College of William & Mary. Retrieved from http:// www.eric.ed.gov (ED494579)

APA treats *regularly published* conference proceedings as if they were periodicals. Most professional conferences occur yearly; therefore, if they have regularly printed proceedings, it would be considered a syndicated resource. If the conference does not regularly print proceedings, the resulting entry resembles a book with a layered title and long publication information. After the author and copyright date, the entry includes the title of the proceedings and then the conference title. In this instance, the publication information is long because two organizations copublished the proceedings. Since ERIC includes a reference number for every entry, it is helpful for your reader to include the entry within the bibliographic citation.

APA-18, Paper Published in Conference Proceedings

Baldwin, Alexinia Y. (2007). Untapped potential for excellence. In J. VanTassel-Baska & T. Stambaugh (Eds.), Overlooked gems: A national perspective on low-income promising learners.

Proceedings of the National Leadership Conference on Low-Income Promising Learners (pp. 23–25). Williamsburg, VA: National Association for Gifted Children and the Center for Gifted Education, College of William & Mary. Retrieved from http://www.eric.ed.gov (ED494579)

Full bibliographic entries for papers published in conference proceedings are exactly like edited collections (APA-5). You just need to add the paper's author, title, and page numbers to the full conference proceedings bibliographic entry.

APA-19, Published Dissertation

Todorovska, V. (2000). *E-mail as an emerging rhetorical space in the workplace.* Retrieved from ProQuest Digital Dissertations. (AAT 9965414)

Most dissertations are published through UMI, which is now accessed through the electronic database by ProQuest. If you accessed the dissertation by this method, then you need to include the document's access number.

To cite an unpublished dissertation, include all of the information from the published dissertation up through the degree title. You then add "Unpublished doctoral dissertation" in parentheses, followed by a period and then the name of the institution and location.

APA-20, Report or White Paper

Voloudakis, J. (2010). *The economic downturn and the future of higher education IT: Executive appraisals.* (ECAR Occasional Paper). Retrieved from http://net.educause.edu/ir/library/pdf/ECP1001.pdf

Reports and white papers are generally either internal documents or one-time publications, many times with companies, organizations, committees, and/or task forces as the authoring group.

APA-21, Film

In general, film citations start with the producer and director of the film, then move on to the year, title, country of origin, and then the studio. Most of this information is then appropriately labeled with parentheticals. You will probably need to use the Internet Movie Database (http://www.imdb.com/) to identify all of the information you need for a complete citation. Since many films are available in different versions and via different media, it's important to include those particulars in the citation. If you viewed the film on television, you would need to consider it a dynamic production since television stations generally edit scenes and may incorporate advertising as part of the screening (see live television example, APA-32).

Film Screened in a Theater

Deeley, M. (Producer), & Scott, R. (Director). (1982). *Blade runner* [Motion picture]. United States: Warner Bros.

Film on DVD

Deeley, M. (Producer), & Scott, R. (Director). (1991). *Blade runner: The director's cut* [DVD]. United States: Warner Bros.

Film Extra in Special Collection

Scott, Ridley. (2007). Introduction. In C. de Lauzirika (Producer) & R. Scott, *Blade runner: The final cut* [DVD]. United States: Warner Bros. Pictures.

A film extra, like deleted scenes or an actor's commentary, is treated like a section from an edited collection (APA-5).

Film Viewed Streaming through the Internet

Deeley, M. (Producer), & Scott, R. (Director). (1982). *Blade runner: Theatrical cut* [Motion picture]. Retrieved from Netflix.

APA-22, Sound Recordings

Like films (APA-21), audio recordings may be accessed in a variety of locations and media. Although you may not have an easy time locating bibliographic information about a song, you are still responsible for providing it in the citation. If you only know the name of the band and the album name and you need the names of the song writers/composers, you would need to do research to find the other information. Most of it can be easily found on the Internet; you just want to cross-check information to make sure you found the correct names, spellings, etc.

Song from an Album with Same Writer and Recording Artists

Gillan, I., Blackmore, R., Glover, R., Lord, J., & Paice, I. (1972). Space truckin. On *Machine head* [CD]. Burbank, CA: Warner Bros.

Like traditional texts, with music recordings you start with the writer and then the copyright year. As with an edited collection (APA-5), you include both the title of the song and the title of the album along with the medium of the recording (CD, record, cassette, etc.).

Song from an Album with Different Writer and Recording Artists

Bonham, J., Jones, J. P., Page, J., & Plant, R. (1969). Whole lotta love [Recorded by T. Turner]. On *Tina Turner: The collected recordings* [Digital recording]. Retrieved from iTunes. (1994).

Although the band members from Led Zeppelin were the original writers/composers for the song "Whole Lotta Love," the recording being cited is Tina Turner's cover of the song. The first date represents the copyright date and the second date represents the recording date.

Downloaded Song

Gillan, I., Blackmore, R., Glover, R., Lord, J., & Paice, I. (1972). Space truckin. On *Machine head* [Digital recording]. Retrieved from iTunes.

Material downloaded from resources like iTunes can be treated as material downloaded from a database (see "Techno Tip: APA and Databases," page 314).

Song Heard Streaming on the Web

Gillan, I., Blackmore, R., Glover, R., Lord, J., & Paice, I. (1972). Space truckin. On *Machine head* [Digital recording]. Retrieved from Pandora.

APA-23, Map

The citation will probably look like a traditional article, book, or web site citation with the description of the type of map.

Print Map

Las Vegas, NV2 [Road map]. (2006). In *North America road atlas* (p. 65). Skokie, IL: Rand.

If the map is found in a book, cite it as if it were an essay in an edited collection (APA-5).

Digital Map

GISuser (Cartographer). (2005). LIDAR map of New Orleans flooding from Hurricane Katrina [Topographic map]. Retrieved from http://www.flickr.com/photos/gisuser/43339456

APA-24, Sacred Text

Since most sacred texts do not formally list individual authors, start with the title of the text. When you alphabetize the entries in your works cited list, be sure to ignore any initial articles, "a," "an," or "the." Therefore, you would alphabetize the first entry under "h" for "Holy."

Sacred Text, Print

The Holy Bible, New International Version. (1973). Grand Rapids, MI: Zondervan.

In this example, the title included the version of the Bible being used.

Sacred Text, Online

Cascading Bible (King James Version). (n.d.). Retrieved from http://
www.verselink.org

Since the title did not include the version of the Bible being used, indicate the version after the title (as with editions and volume information).

APA-25, Entry from a Dictionary, Thesaurus, Encyclopedia, or Almanac

Entry from a Print Dictionary

Eclecticism. (1993). In *Webster's third new international dictionary
of the English language unabridged.* Springfield, MA:
Merriam-Webster.

The above entry is like a selection from an edited collection (APA-5) without an author. Please note that many specialized reference resources have authors for individual entries.

Entry from an Online Encyclopedia

Russian Revolution of 1917. (1994–2011). In *Encyclopedia Brittanica.*
Retrieved from http://www.britannica.com/

Syndicated Resources

Syndicated resources are a little more complicated because there are usually multiple titles involved. These citations usually include author, title of the specific essay or episode, *title of the periodical published work* (e.g., name of the overall journal, television show, or blog), and publication information. The following examples indicate how to cite various types of syndicated sources.

APA-26, Article in a Scholarly Journal

The current APA guidelines makes a distinction between journals that are numbered continuously (e.g., Vol. 1 ends on page 208, Vol. 2 starts on page 209) or numbered separately (that is, each volume starts on page 1). Only if the journal pagination starts over in each issue must the citation contain volume *and* issue numbers if available.

Article in a Printed Journal with Separate Pagination

Cambridge, B. (2011). Research and policy: Antithetical or
complementary? *Writing Program Administration,
35*(1), 135–147.

Article in a Printed Journal with Continued Pagination

Yancey, K. B. (2004). A line for Wendy. *College English, 66*, 581–584.

Journal Article with Separate Pagination Accessed through a Database

Cohen, P. (2011). Cowboys die hard: Real men and businessmen in the Reagan-era blockbuster. *Film & History*, 41(1), 71–81. doi: 10.1353/flm.2011.0024

See "Techno Tip: APA and Databases" for help with citing materials found through databases.

Journal Article from Journal That Only Exists Online

Leston, R., Carter, G., & Arroyo, S. (2011). The chora of the Twin Towers. *Enculturation*, 10. Retrieved from http://enculturation.gmu.edu/

In some online journals, there are no page numbers.

techno tip

APA and Databases

In theory, an article from a scholarly journal would be the same whether it was found in print or in any one of a couple of different databases. However, as demonstrated in the magazine example below (APA-29), differences can arise. For the various resources you find in library databases (usually journals and other periodicals), you will need to look up the Digital Object Identifier (DOI). Finding the DOI can be tricky; consider asking a librarian for help.

Cohen, P. (2011). Cowboys die hard: Real men and businessmen in the Reagan-era blockbuster. *Film & History*, 41(1), 71–81. doi: 10.1353/flm.2011.0024

If you cannot find the DOI, you can provide a link to the homepage of the journal or periodical (not the URL of the library database).

Yancey, K. B. (2004). A line for Wendy. *College English*, 66, 581–584. Retrieved from http://www.ncte.org/journals/ce

As mentioned in "Techno Tip: Databases, Microfilm, and Microfiche" in Chapter 4 (pages 84–85), scholarly databases are not the only databases you might be citing. Databases like *iTunes, Netflix, Hulu*, and *Amazon* provide access to various audio and visual media. *Google Books* has been slowly scanning hundreds of thousands of books and is now its own online book database. As above, the *iTunes* and *Google Books* examples below provide the database information as a secondary layer of publication information, listed after the primary citation.

Murphy, R., & Falchuk, B. (Writers). Falchuk, B. (Director). (2011). New York, NY [iTunes download]. In I. Brennan (Executive producer), *Glee*. Retrieved from http://www.apple.com/itunes/store

Whitman, W. (1881). *Leaves of grass*. Retrieved from http://books.google.com/books

Although you may not know the fine details of how a given database works, do the best you can with our mash-up instructions (Chapter 11, pages 256–261) and talk to your friends and instructors.

APA-27, Newspaper Article

Newspaper articles can generally be easily located in three forms of media: print, online at the newspaper's web site, and accessed through a library database.

Printed Newspaper Article

Sisario, B. (2001, November 7). Sirius's move to bypass a royalty payment clearinghouse causes an uproar. *The New York Times*, p. B3.

Newspaper Article Found Online

You can adapt the various journal and magazine article citations for online publications of the newspapers by just adding the retrieval information (the URL). An article accessed online may not include page numbers.

Sisario, B. (2001, November 7). Sirius's move to bypass a royalty payment clearinghouse causes an uproar. *The New York Times*. Retrieved from http://www.nytimes.com/

Since the web site says a "version of this article appeared in print" you could use the edition information, or recognizing that "version" may imply some changes, solely cite the web site as the exact source you read and cited.

Newspaper Article Found in a Database

Since newspapers do not usually have DOIs, most newspaper citations from articles found in a database will look a lot like those from a web site; both will reference the publication's web site.

Sisario, B. (2001, November 7). Sirius's move to bypass a royalty payment clearinghouse causes an uproar. *The New York Times*, p. B3. Retrieved from http://www.nytimes.com/

Newspaper Article Accessed through a Mobile Application

Sisario, B. (2001, November 7). Sirius's move to bypass a royalty agency causes an uproar. *The New York Times* [iPhone NY Times mobile application]. Retrieved from http://itunes.apple.com/

Like the *Wired* example at the beginning of Chapter 11 (page 244), the title for the same article in the mobile application was slightly different from the print, online, and database versions. For publication information, we have added the name of the application (both the *New York Times* and *Wired* have their own applications, and other mobile application readers like Pulse and Amazon Kindle have access to other periodicals).

APA-28, Newspaper Editorial

Swirl, sniff, sip, check the price [Editorial]. (2008, January 19). *Los Angeles Times*. Retrieved from http://www.latimes.com/

If there is no author listed, start with the name of the text you are citing. After the title, include the term "Editorial" in brackets. If this were found in a print newspaper, you would just include the publishing information required of a print citation.

APA-29, Article in a Magazine

Magazines that publish every week or two weeks should include the full publication dates; magazines that publish monthly (or every two months) only need the month(s) and year. Since most magazines restart page numbering for every issue, you will generally include both the volume and issue numbers within the citation.

Printed Magazine Article

Levy, S. (2011, October). Inside Google+. *Wired*, *19*(10), 158–161.

Magazine Article Found Online

Levy, S. (2011, October). Inside Google Plus. *Wired*, *19*(10). Retrieved
    from http://www.wired.com/magazine/

You can adapt the various journal and magazine article citations for online publications of the journals by just adding the retrieval information and dropping the page numbers. In this case, if you look closely, you'll notice that the titles of the print and online versions are *not* the same. In short, pay close attention to whichever version you are citing.

Magazine Article Found in a Database

Levy, S. (2011, October). Inside Google+. *Wired*, *19*(10), 158–161.
    Retrieved from http://www.wired.com/magazine/

The database generally archives the print version of the article, not the web-based version. Therefore, the title matches the print version. However, since magazines, like newspapers, don't generally have DOI numbers, the citation will reference the web site.

Magazine Article Accessed through a Mobile Application

Levy, S. (2011, October). Inside Google+. *Wired* [iPad wired mobile
    application], *19*(10). Retrieved from http://itunes.apple.com/

Since the computer coding involved for producing mobile applications in different platforms (Apple products versus Android/Google products versus Blackberry product, etc.) is different, we suggest that you specify which brand of device the application is running on.

Article That Skips Pages in a Monthly or Bimonthly Magazine

Gale, D. (2008, January 1). Biometrics revisited. *Campus technology*,
    21(5), 28, 30–31, 46.

When citing an article that skips pages, usually with advertising between content pages, you may include the inclusive page numbers if they're grouped together (13–21, 46–63); however, if the article is spread out over the entire periodical, usually with the concluding pages at the very end, be sure to document every page.

APA-30, Article with a Quotation in the Title

Kahne, J., & Bailey, K. (1999). The role of social capital in youth development: The case of "I have a dream" programs. *Educational Evaluation and Policy Analysis*, 21, 321–343.

Use quotation marks around the quotation in the title.

APA-31, Review

The major difference between reviews and regular periodical publications is that you need to include the detailed information about the title and author of the text under review within brackets after the title of the review.

Book Review

Drucker, J. (2007). Philosophy and digital humanities [Review of the book *Humanities Computing*, by W. McCarty]. *Digital Humanities Quarterly*, 1(1). Retrieved from http://www.digitalhumanities.org/

Game Review

Miller, G. (2011, November 29). Batman: Arkham City review. [Review of the game *Batman: Arkham City* for PlayStation 3 by Rocksteady]. *IGN*. Retrieved from http://www.ign.com/

Acknowledging that video games are developed for different environments, we believe it is important to include both the version of the game, in this case for PlayStation 3, as well as the name of the company that "authored" it.

APA-32, Television

Like journals and magazines, television shows include individual pieces (episodes instead of articles). As mentioned above in the film examples, shows viewed on "live," or broadcast, TV need to be considered a dynamic production since television stations generally edit scenes and may incorporate advertising as part of the screening. However, once a television episode has been more formally "published" to DVD or to an online database like *Hulu* or *iTunes*, it should be considered a stable syndicated episode. According to APA, episodic radio and television entries use the same format as a chapter from an edited collection

(APA-5) with the scriptwriter and director in the author's position and the producer in the editor's position. You can usually find all of the required information at the Internet Movie Database (http://www.imdb.com/).

Broadcast of Television Episode (dynamic)

Murphy, R., & Falchuk, B. (Writers). Falchuk, B. (Director). (2011). New York [Broadcast television series episode]. In I. Brennan (Executive producer), *Glee.* Los Angeles, CA: Fox Broadcasting.

You usually need to search the production company's web site to find the broadcast location.

Episode from a DVD

Murphy, R., & Falchuk, B. (Writers). Falchuk, B. (Director). (2011). New York. In I. Brennan (Executive producer), *Glee* [DVD]. Los Angeles, CA: 20th Century Fox.

Notice in this instance the parenthetical descriptor of the medium used to deliver the episode shifted from being associated with the episode's name to the DVD box set name. Although the production company is the same, note that they label it slightly differently in the different media ("Fox," for television broadcast and "20th Century Fox" for DVD publication and distribution).

Television Episode Downloaded from Database

Murphy, R., & Falchuk, B. (Writers). Falchuk, B. (Director). (2011). New York [iTunes download]. In I. Brennan (Executive producer), *Glee.* Retrieved from http://www.apple.com/itunes/store

In this instance, we are stating we downloaded one specific episode from iTunes. If we had downloaded the entire season, the "[iTunes download]" would come after the title of the show, *Glee.*

Television Episode Streamed from Database

Murphy, R., & Falchuk, B. (Writers). Falchuk, B. (Director). (2011). New York [Hulu streaming video]. In I. Brennan (Executive producer), *Glee.* Retrieved from http://www.hulu.com/

APA-33, Blogs

Blogs, like periodicals and television shows, have overall titles and then specific articles, or "postings." Therefore, you might cite the entire blog web site, with all of its postings, an individual post, or a reader's comment to an individual post.

Entire Blog

Jenkins, H. (2006–2008). *Confessions of an aca-fan: The official weblog of Henry Jenkins* [Web log message]. Retrieved from http://henryjenkins.org/

An entire blog site is cited the same as an entire web site.

Individual Blog Post

Jenkins, H. (2007, December 5). Reconsidering digital immigrants. . . . [Web log message]. Retrieved from http://henryjenkins.org/

Although APA could treat an individual entry more like a traditional syndicated resource with the layering of two names, the individual entry, and the overall blog title, they have chosen to ignore the overall blog title when citing an individual entry. In this case, the blog does a good job archiving blog entries in an easy-to-search manner; therefore, we only used the overall blog site URL. If the blog did not have an easy-to-use archive or search function, you would want to include the long URL to the specific blog entry.

Comment on a Specific Posting in a Blog

Marquard, M. (2007, December 6). Re: Reconsidering digital immigrants . . . [Web log message]. Retrieved from http://henryjenkins.org/2007/12/reconsidering_digital_immigran.html

APA uses *Web log message* for both *blog post* and *blog comment*. If the comment has its own title, use that; otherwise, just write "Re:" before the title of the original blog posting. Since you are referring to a reply to an individual blog post, we suggest you include the detailed URL.

APA-34, Podcast

Podcasts are just audio versions of blogs; cite them accordingly.

Fogarty, M. (Producer). (2008, January 11). Yo *as a pronoun* [Audio podcast]. Retrieved from http://grammar.quickanddirtytips.com/

APA-35, Posting on *Twitter*

seejakenap. (2012, May 12). "it's exciting" "it's not your fault" "don't be afraid to make connections" "be prepared to adapt" final thoughts of #notbootcamp [Twitter post]. Retrieved from https://twitter.com/seejakenap/status/ 206051434519740416

Twitter is a microblog, a blog with a small entry space; therefore, you cite it like a blog. Since individual *Twitter* posts have their own static, published, individual page URL, they are more of a syndicated resource. APA suggests you use the actual *Twitter* handle/username as the author, not the name associated with the account. APA also suggests that you always self-archive various social media postings in case they are not retrievable in the next couple of years.

APA-36, Online Video in User-Published Video Repository

If you were just posting an online video someone included on a web site, you would use some mash-up of a citation between film and a web page (see APA-21 for ideas). If you were citing a video from a group of hosted videos by one company or organization, like Hulu or TED, you would use some mash-up of a citation between a film and a database. However, video repositories like *YouTube* and *Vimeo* are tricky. Technically *YouTube* and *Vimeo* are like a blog; individuals who post videos to *YouTube* have their own channel. Once you know that, it is easy to see that a *YouTube* posting is more like a blog, with a main channel title and individual postings (click on the name of the person who uploaded the video to see the channel page, as shown in Figures 12.3 and 12.4 on pages 285–286).

YouTube Posting

Wesch, M. (2007, October 12). *A vision of students today* [Video file]. Retrieved from http://www.youtube.com/watch?v=dGCJ46vyR9o

Video Reply to *YouTube* Posting

YouTube allows written replies to videos (which you would cite like a written reply to a blog post, see APA-33) as well as video replies. Either way, the APA style citation looks the same.

Marino, M. (2008, January 19). (Re)visions of students today. [Video file]. Retrieved from http://www.youtube.com/watch?v=Ln6WUy29fAA&watch_response

APA-37, Annual Report

Annual reports are just syndicated reports or white papers. In other words, companies or organizations release an annual publication reporting certain types of information.

BMW Group. (n.d.). *Annual Report 2010.* Retrieved from http://annual-report.bmwgroup.com/2010/gb/files/pdf/en/BMW_Group_AR2010.pdf

In this case, the author is a company. Some annual reports have titles; if it has a title, be sure to include "Annual report" after the title. The report does not provide a specific publication date; therefore, we included "n.d." for no date.

Dynamic Resources

Since dynamic resources shift every time you use them, it is critical to cite the date you found, read, or interacted with the resource. APA style does not always ask for the access, or "retrieval" date; however, if you think it is appropriate to include the retrieval date, talk to your instructor or publication editor. APA considers a lot of dynamic resources as primary research (interviews, for example). The APA style calls for citation of the primary resources in the text of your document but not in the reference list.

APA-38

APA-38, Page from a Wiki

Churches, A. (2010, October 1). Bloom's digital taxonomy. In *Educational Origami*. Retrieved November 14, 2011, from http:// edorigami.wikispaces.com/Bloom%27s+Digital +Taxonomy

Most wiki pages have a "history" or "page history" link or tab that will allow you to see the last time the page was updated; use that as the "copyright" date. That same page should give you a sense of whether there is a primary author for the page or there are a multitude of authors (like most Wikipedia articles). For a resource that lists no author or has a multitude of authors over time, treat the text as "no author" and start with the title.

APA-39

APA-39, Public Address

Godin, S. (2011, October). Invisible or remarkable? Keynote address presented at the EDUCAUSE annual convention, Philadelphia, PA.

If there is no title, just skip to the meeting and sponsoring organization's information (in this case, EDUCAUSE is in all capitals because that is how the name of the organization is spelled). Your publication information includes the name of the meeting and the city. Be sure to include an appropriate descriptive label (Address, Lecture, Keynote speech, Reading, Poster session, etc.).

APA-40

APA-40, Message Posted to a Discussion Group

Nielson, C. (2011, November 11). Twitter and the teen brain [Online forum comment]. Retrieved from https://groups.google.com/ forum/?fromgroups#!searchin/cybersalon/Twitter$20and $20the$20teen$20brain$20%5B/cybersalon/4YzEgtEANyo/ co5gkE7Z5iIJ

Citing a post to a discussion group or board, listserv, or newsgroup is basically the same; you need an author, a title, a brief description of the type of text, typical online citation including the URL.

APA-41

APA-41, Wall Message on *Facebook*

Miller-Cochran, S. (2012, May 23). A question, not rhetorical: Is
it possible to be a WPA and live anxiety-free? Or at least
anxiety-level-low? If so, what's your secret? [Facebook
update]. Retrieved from http://www.facebook.com/miller
.cochran/posts/10150805988447056

If the posting is long, APA style guidelines suggest that you condense the content. APA also suggests you self-archive your posts for future reference.

APA-42

APA-42, Video Game

Video games are tricky to cite. On the one hand, many games are mainly static: every player will access the same material in the same way. Other games, like World of Warcraft, are mostly dynamic. Everybody playing the game at the same time impacts your game experiences. Depending on what portion of the game, or game play, you are citing, you will have to decide whether it is static or dynamic.

Video Game on MP3 Player (static)

Electronic Arts. (2007). *Sudoku* (Version 1.0.0.) [Video game for iPod].
Redwood City, CA: Electronic Arts.

Massive Multiplayer Online Role Playing Game (MMORPG, dynamic)

Blizzard Entertainment. (2007). *The world of warcraft: The burning
crusade* [Online video game]. Irvine, CA: Blizzard Entertainment.
Game portal located at http://www.worldofwarcraft.com/
burningcrusade

Paper Formatting

The APA style guidelines specify details for formatting papers, but they also include details for preparing and submitting various types of articles for publication. Check with your instructor to see if he or she wants you to follow all of the APA guidelines.

Title Page

APA style requires a title page (see page 325). Centered, and in the middle of the page, you need to include:

▶ the paper's title
▶ your name
▶ your institutional affiliation

APA style also requires running headers that are shortened versions of the title. You introduce this "running head" in the upper left corner of the title page as well as in the upper right corner with the page number.

Spacing and Margins

APA style requires that you double-space the entire document, including title page information, quotations, and the list of references. You do not need to include extra spaces (i.e., quadruple space) anywhere in the text. Set your top, left, right, and bottom margins for one inch. All paragraphs should be indented by one-half inch.

Headers and Page Numbers

In the upper left corner of each page, include the same page header that was introduced on the title page. The page number should appear in the upper right corner, as on the title page. All pages in the paper should be consecutively numbered (the title page is page 1).

Section Headings

If your paper is long enough and it includes coherent sections, and even subsections, you might consider including section headings in your paper. APA prescribes specific guidelines for section headings. If you have two levels of headings, center the first or highest level, and then format the second level flush left and in italics (see the following example). Make sure that all section titles are syntactically parallel. In other words, if you start your first section title with a noun, start all of your section titles with nouns. For example, the following outline could represent section headings from a paper in APA style.

Technological Advancements

Advancements in Visual Technologies
Advancements in Production and Distribution
Advancements in Interactive Technologies

Narrative Structure
Ideological Differences
Hollywood's Enterprises

Vertical Integration
Further Economic Trends

Conclusions

If you are using more layers or levels of headings, refer to the *Publication Manual of the American Psychological Association*. APA provides guidelines for up to five levels of headings.

Visuals

APA style divides visuals into two categories: tables and figures. Whenever you place visuals into your text, you must place them as close as possible to the paragraph referring to them.

Figures APA style refers to all other types of visuals like charts, graphs, drawings, and images as figures. You should label each figure with the word *Figure* and an Arabic numeral in italics. The label and caption of a figure are placed below the visual as it appears in your text, along with a reference to the source of the figure if it came from an outside resource.

Figure 13.3 shows an example of an APA-style figure. In this linguistics paper about how specific words function in a sentence, it is critical to provide sentence diagrams to show how the words work in a sentence. The figure helps the reader to understand the argument being made in the text.

INDONESIAN INFLECTION PHRASE   9

Mungkin saya bisa menolong anda?

Perhaps I can help you

"Might I be able to help you?"

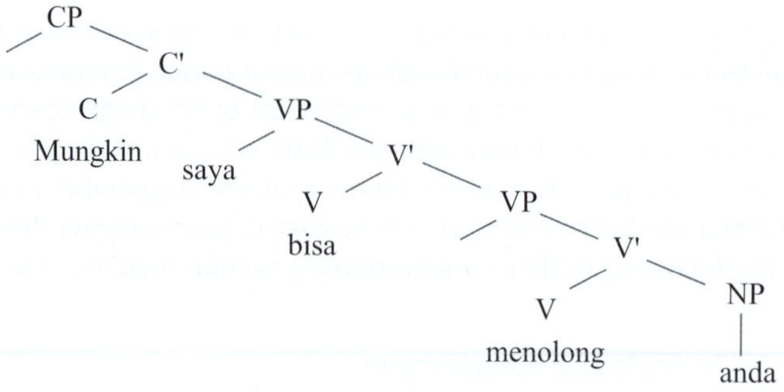

CP

C'

C
Mungkin

VP

saya

V'

VP

V
bisa

V'

NP

V
menolong

anda

Figure 6. When mungkin is in the C position, the modal cannot move there.

Indonesian does have a specific order for auxiliaries, however, and that makes the complete dismissal of the IP problematic.

Figure 13.3   A Figure in a Paper Using APA Style.[4]

_____

4. Adapted from Heck, S. K. "Does Indonesian Have an Inflection Phrase?" In Arizona State University Working Papers in Language 1, 1999. Reproduced by permission of the author.

Tables If you are presenting numerical data in a table format, you should label the table with the word *Table*, an Arabic numeral, and a title. The label and title are placed above the table as it appears in your text. If you are reprinting the table from an outside source, you must include the full bibliographic citation for the table directly under the table (not at the end of your paper in the list of references).

Table 5

Instructors' Responses to Question 1[5]

	Presemester survey	Postsemester survey Web-based	Postsemester survey face-to-face
Laura	4	3	3
Ann	4	3	2

Sample Paper

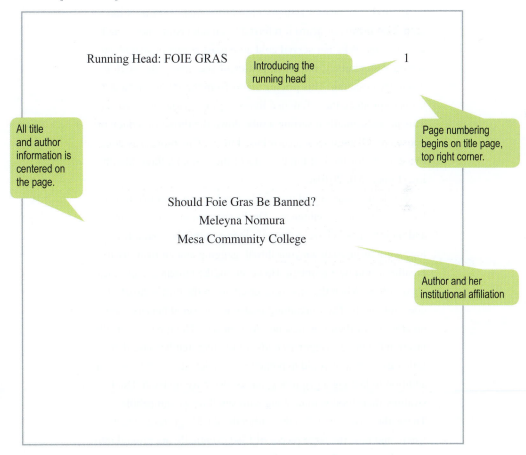

Running Head: FOIE GRAS   1

Introducing the running head

All title and author information is centered on the page.

Page numbering begins on title page, top right corner.

Should Foie Gras Be Banned?
Meleyna Nomura
Mesa Community College

Author and her institutional affiliation

---

5. Adaption from Miller, S. K. "Teaching Writing at a Distance: Exploring Instructional Decisions and Learning Perceptions." Diss. Arizona State U, 2002. Reproduced by permission of the author.

FOIE GRAS   2

Foie gras has always been identified as an item of luxury. While the fattened duck liver has enjoyed centuries of high class worship, it has recently found itself under scrutiny as a highly unethical product. For those of you that don't know how foie gras is produced, it is made by force-feeding either ducks or geese until the liver reaches close to 10% of the animal's total body weight (Lopez-Alt, 2010). Whether or not you find this to be an inhumane process, comparing foie gras to methods widely practiced across the meat industry shows that food politics should be prioritized elsewhere. Until the entire food production industry changes, it is unreasonable to target foie gras as a product to be banned.

Even if you haven't actually tasted foie gras, you might have seen it on menus or heard it referred to on television shows such as *Top Chef.* Whether served cold atop toast points or seared and served with chutney, the accompaniment you always see with it is a hefty price tag. This pricing stems from the intensive care it takes to produce these fattened livers, a process known as *gavage.* This process entails inserting a tube down the throat of a duck or goose and filling it with a corn-based meal. This process is done twice a day for the last three weeks of the animal's three-month life (Lopez-Alt, 2010).

While this may sound incredibly cruel, it is too simple to just label the practice as inhumane. Ducks are obviously not people, and their bodies behave differently than a human's would. If a tube were inserted down your throat, gagging and an inability to breathe would be a problem. However, unlike humans, ducks lack a gag reflex. When the tube is inserted down the bird's throat, it does not feel it. Their breathing is also not affected because they breathe out of their tongues, not their throats. The tube is typically inserted for three to eight seconds for feeding, but because there is little discomfort, it could hypothetically be left in much longer. In addition to lacking a gag reflex, ducks also have no teeth. Ducks swallow their food whole, along with small rocks and pebbles. These abrasives act as "teeth" within the duck's gizzard, which is where and how the large pieces of food eventually are ground into digestible pieces (Lopez-Alt, 2010).

FOIE GRAS   3

A more accurate comparison would be to compare duck feedings to cattle in a concentrated animal feed organization, or CAFO. While technically not force-fed, the animals have little else to do as there is such a small amount of space to move around. The bigger problem with this system is that these animals are raised almost entirely on corn, which cows are not biologically designed to eat. A cow's natural diet is grass, and when corn is introduced to its system, it suffers from numerous health issues because the animal is unable to digest corn properly. As a result, feedlot cattle are pumped with antibiotics—in fact, most of the antibiotics sold in the United States end up in animal feed. This grain-based diet also adds more weight to the animals than grass would, and an animal with a higher fat percentage yields a steak higher in fat. While foie gras is hardly heart healthy, it is also eaten on rare occasion by few, never by most. For much of America, dinner without meat is not dinner at all (Pollan, 2006).

What also must be considered is the type of duck being used for foie gras production. A Moulard duck is a cross between a male Muscovy and a female Pekin. This is important, as using this hybrid breed creates an animal ideal for foie gras production. Pekin ducks were originally a migratory animal. What this means is that before the animal's annual flight south, it would gorge itself on huge amounts of food in preparation for the long flight ahead—essentially a biological form of *gavage*. The Pekin duck is also a very friendly bird, and they naturally live in close quarters with fellow Pekins. Muscovies, however, do not migrate. What you get when you cross the two breeds is an animal that does not migrate, yet still has the natural tendency to gorge itself, and naturally groups itself in close quarters. All three American foie gras farms use Moulards exclusively (Lopez-Alt, 2010).

One of the most important aspects of foie gras farming is to look at the treatment and handling of the animals. At La Belle Farms in upstate New York, the birds are not kept in cages, but in a shed where the animals are free to roam around (Lopez-Alt, 2010). Their access to the outdoors is limited to prevent infection in the animals, as they are kept antibiotic free. Typically, American foie gras farms also have systems in place to encourage gentle handling of the animals. Gentle handling of the birds decreases chances of bruised livers, meaning a higher market value. The increase in price is passed on to the animal handlers—the greater number of high-end livers produced, the more the worker is paid. Such policies are unheard of in typical poultry farms.

In comparison, the average egg-laying chicken is confined to a cage so small that the animal will typically begin eating her cage mates. To help alleviate this issue, hens are often de-beaked to prevent them from pecking others around them. Hens also are commonly so stressed that they will rub themselves bald against the wire of the cage. As such, egg farms see a mortality rate of about 10% (Pollan, 2006). La Belle has a mortality rate of about 1% of their animals (Lopez-Alt, 2010).

What about all the photographs and videos floating around the internet of ducks confined to cages, vomit and cornmeal crusted to their beaks ("About")? Surely there is some truth to them—and in fact, there is. Just as there are reputable purveyors, there are ones that abuse the animals. This is true about meat product from foie gras to lamb shanks. If these photos and stories ("About") are concerning, educating yourself on the provenance of everything on your plate would be the responsible thing to do. Foie gras is often targeted because it is a specialized product, but most factory-farmed meat that America eats has endured no better a life.

This targeted prejudice is exemplified in the city of Chicago's ban on the sale of foie gras in April of 2006, reported by Vettel (2008). In the four months it took for the bill to go into effect, restaurants in the area reported a surge in foie gras sales. Once the ban was officially in place, restaurants performed tricks, such as attaching a hefty price to a green salad, claiming that "the foie gras torchon is on us." A visit from the Health Department resulted in no action—no citation, warning, nothing. Chicago's own mayor has been quoted, saying that the ban is "the silliest thing we've ever done" (Vettel, 2008). As a result of political backlash accompanied by lack of enforcement, the bill was repealed two years later (Vettel, 2008).

A slightly more logical approach came from California in September of 2004. Governor Arnold Schwarzenegger gave foie gras producers seven years to "evolve and perfect a humane way for a duck to consume grain to increase the size of its liver through

FOIE GRAS 5

natural processes," which means eliminating *gavage*. If within this time period, a new method can be developed, the ban, which eliminates not just the sale, but production, will not go into effect. Sonoma Foie Gras is a California-based farm and plans on using the seven years to prove that "foie gras production is safe and proper" ("California," 2004).

But, what constitutes "safe and proper"? If, like Governor Schwarzenegger, you believe *gavage* to be harmful, look to Spain. Since 1812, Pateria de Sousa has been quietly producing what can be considered to be truly ethical foie gras. Eduardo Sousa's geese are kept on 30 acres of quiet Spanish land where they live as nature truly intended. Figs, olives, and other indigenous plants and herbs are made readily available for the animals to gorge themselves as they are biologically inclined to do (Barber, 2008). The biggest problem with this method is that because the process follows a biological clock rather than a man-made one, the product is created in extremely limited quantities, as the animals are only slaughtered once a year. Sousa is also notorious for not selling his product to culinary professionals, "because chefs don't deserve my foie gras" (Barber, 2008). Chef and sustainable food aficionado Dan Barber has worked with Sousa to replicate the process at his New York Blue Stone Farms, but so far has failed at his attempts (Abend, 2009).

Even with all of this evidence, it is difficult to say whether or not foie gras is ethical to eat. Like all food products, it comes down to a personal choice. Eliminating it from one's diet would be quite easy for most, as there presumably are fewer people who have consumed it than those who have not. However, if some feel that foie gras is indeed unethical, they should consider questioning the rest of their diet. Until the government decides to take a hard look at the humanity, the ethics, and the sustainability of the entire commercial food industry, American foie gras should not be a target of political debate.

FOIE GRAS   6

                              References

Abend, L. (2009, August 12). Can ethical foie gras happen in
    America? *Time*. Retrieved from http://www.time.com/

About foie gras. (n.d.). *nofoiegras.org.* Retrieved
    from http://nofoiegras.org/about.html

Barber, D. (2008, November). Dan Barber's foie gras parable
    [Video file]. *TED* Retrieved from http://www.ted.com/
    talks/dan_barber_s_surprising_foie_gras_parable.html

California bans foie-gras force-feeding. (2004, September 30).
    Fox News Retrieved from http://www.foxnews.com/story/
    0,2933,134074,00.html

Lopez-Alt, J. K. (2010, December 16). The physiology of foie:
    Why foie gras is not unethical [Web log message]. *Serious
    Eats* Retrieved from http://www.seriouseats.com/2010/12/
    the-physiology-of-foie-why-foie-gras-is-not-u.html

Pollan, M. (2006). *The omnivore's dilemma: a natural
    history of four meals.* New York: Penguin Press.

Vettel, P. (2008, May 18). Hold the jokes the rest of yous:
    Foie gras back on menus. *Chicago Tribune*. Retrieved
    from http://www.chicagotribune.com

chapter 14

CMS Formatting Guidelines

*T*he *Chicago Manual of Style* (CMS) is the official style guide of the University of Chicago Press, from whom the style takes its name. CMS has two basic citation systems that split themselves along disciplinary lines. The notes and bibliography system, which we focus on in this chapter, is primarily used by disciplines in the humanities and some social sciences, and the author-date system is primarily used by the sciences and other social sciences. For in-text citations the notes and bibliography system uses numbered footnotes at the bottom of the page or numbered endnotes that appear at the end of the chapter or article with a bibliography at the end of the document that gives complete publication information. The CMS author-date system resembles APA's style for in-text citations and bibliographies. If you are interested in using CMS, especially the author-date system, consult *The Chicago Manual of Style*, 16th edition, for any questions not addressed in this chapter.

If you are using the notes and bibliography system, you need to know how to cite a source in note format as well as how to cite the source as a bibliographic reference. In note format you might have a shortened citation (if there is a full bibliography at the end of the paper) or a full citation (if there is not a bibliography at the end of the paper). All of the example citations in this chapter include a sample of the complete CMS footnote or endnote (which corresponds to superscript numbers placed within the paper) as well as the full bibliographic entry that would appear at the end of the paper.

Complete Footnote

1. Don Tapscott, *Growing Up Digital: The Rise of the Net Generation* (New York: McGraw-Hill, 1997), 123–24.

Complete Full Bibliographic Citation

Tapscott, Don. *Growing Up Digital: The Rise of the Net Generation*. New York: McGraw-Hill, 1997.

In-Text Citations

Rodrigo, Rochelle. "Technofetishized TV: CSI, Bones, and ReGenesis as Science Fiction Television?" FlowTV, vol. 7, 16 Nov. 2007. Web. <http://flowtv.org/2007/11/technofetishized-tv-csi-bones-and-regenisisas-science-fiction-television/>. Reproduced by permission of the author.

Lorie and Rodrigo 18

In *A Genealogy of Technical Culture: The Value of Convenience*, Thomas Tierney theorizes how technology functions as a way to overcome the temporal and spatial limits of the body, using technology to promote the Cartesian mind/body split and even overcome death.[1] Obviously in these shows the technologies begin to also overcome the emotional and mental limits of being human. These technofetishized scenes in the *CSI*s, *Bones*, and *ReGenesis* also reenact typical Mulvey moments,[2] with the close-ups of the technology standing in for the close-ups of female body parts; both objectifying, disavowing, and displacing dangerously emotional humanity. In many of these episodes female characters conduct the scientific analyses seeking the truth. The women who play these roles have their "Hollywood beautiful" bodies erased by the lab coat wardrobes they wear; nothing must distract the viewer from focusing on the beautiful infallible technology.

In the same 2000 article that Sawyer claimed science fiction will have to change, he also argued that "The days when you could tell the public that a microwave oven would replace the traditional stove are long gone; we all know that new technologies aren't going to live up to the hype."[3] Maybe Sawyer is focusing on the public that reads science fiction, because the "we" in this statement clearly are not the primary viewers of the various technofetishized murder/mystery dramas. In these shows the technologies do live up to the hype. They are not emotionally fallible humans; they can remain "objective" to find "the truth" so that "justice" prevails.

[1] Tierney, *A Genealogy of Technical Culture*.
[2] Mulvey, "Visual Pleasure and Narrative Cinema."
[3] Sawyer, "The Profession of Science Fiction, 54: The Future Is Already Here," 11.

Figure 14.1   Superscript Numbers for In-Text Citations and Corresponding Numbered Footnotes Using CMS. Shortened Notes, with Author's Last Name, Used in Text with Full Bibliography at the End of the Paper.

You must include an in-text citation in every sentence that includes information from an outside resource. Even if you are only summarizing or paraphrasing the resource, you must include an in-text citation in the same sentence in which you present the material. The in-text citation usually appears at the end of the sentence, but it could also appear at the end of a clause or after the mention of an author's name. CMS in-text citations require a superscript Arabic numeral in the text, which should follow any punctuation (except a dash) with no spacing before it. A corresponding footnote (or endnote) with the same number should appear at the bottom of the page (or the end of the chapter or article), containing the bibliographic information (Figure 14.1). If the paper includes a full bibliography (see Figure 14.2) at the end, the citations in the notes can be concise. However, if there is a not a full bibliography, the notes must include a full citation. If you cite the source more than once, subsequent citations can be condensed.

Quotations and Paraphrases

Standard condensed notes in CMS format include the author's name, the title of the work, and the page or paragraph number of the material being cited. Use the condensed note style when you are just including the note to cite a text and will be including a full bibliography at the end of the paper. If you are not including a full bibliography at the end of the paper, make sure your notes include the complete citation information.

Quoted Text with Footnote Reference

Science fiction films "self-consciously foreground their own radicality" of special effects.[8]

Resident Franchise 23

Bibliography

Mulvey, Laura. "Visual Pleasure and Narrative
    Cinema." *Screen* 16, no. 3 (1975): 6–18.

Sawyer, Robert J. "The Profession of Science Fiction, 54:
    The Future Is Already Here." *Foundation: The
    International Review of Science Fiction* 80 (2000): 5–18.

Tierney, Thomas F. *A Genealogy of Technical
    Culture: The Value of Convenience.* Albany:
    State University of New York Press, 1993.

Figure 14.2   Example of Bibliography Page in CMS Format.

Condensed Footnote

8. Freedman, "Kubrick's *2001* and the Possibility of a Science-Fiction Cinema," 307.

Complete Footnote

8. Carl Freedman, "Kubrick's 2001 and the Possibility of a Science-Fiction Cinema,"
Science-Fiction Studies 25, no. 2 (1998): 307.

Complete Full Bibliographic Citation

Freedman, Carl. "Kubrick's 2001 and the Possibility of a Science-Fiction Cinema."
Science-Fiction Studies 25, no. 2 (1998): 300–318.

When incorporating short quotations or paraphrases, you can include some of the bibliographic information in the sentence itself. This strategy can be a way to emphasize the name of the author you are citing, highlight the date in which the resource was originally published, or vary the sentence structure in your writing. You may also include this type of a discussion in the note itself. If your next in-text citation is of the same resource, you need to give it another note number; however, the note itself can say "ibid."

Quoted Text with Footnote Reference[*]

Science fiction films "self-consciously foreground their own radicality" of special effects.[8] However, it is Freedman's act of disavowing the overt display of technological prowess[9] that best exemplifies Bolter's and Grusin's concept of immediacy: "if immediacy is promoted by removing the programmer/creator from the image, it can also be promoted by involving the viewer more intimately in the image."[10]

Condensed Footnotes

8. Freedman, "Kubrick's 2001 and the Possibility of a Science-Fiction Cinema," 307.

9. Ibid., 312.

10. Bolter and Grusin, *Remediation*, 28.

You should be as specific as possible about identifying the location of direct quotations and paraphrases. Therefore, if you are citing from an electronic resource without page numbers, like a web page, CMS asks that you include in the note a "descriptive locator" such as a section subhead.

Quoted Text with Footnote Reference

Levine claims that the presentation software Slide "has a good library of templates, backgrounds, [and] effects."[32]

Condensed Footnote

32. Levine, "The Fifty Tools," in the "Slideshow Tools" section.

---

* Rodrigo, Rochelle. "Technofetishized TV: CSI, Bones, and ReGenesis as Science Fiction Television?" *FlowTV*, vol. 7, 16 Nov. 2007. Web. <http://flowtv.org/2007/11/technofetishized-tv-csi-bones-and-regenisis-as-science-fiction-television/>. Reproduced by permission of the author.

Long Quotations

In CMS, text quotations longer than one hundred words, or longer than eight lines, need to be presented in a block quote (Figure 14.3). Instead of using quotation marks to identify the text being directly quoted, block quotes indent the material one-half inch from the left margin so that it stands out on the page. Because they are direct quotations, block quotes need an in-text citation as well; therefore, they'll have a superscript number at the end.

Summaries and Multiple Resources

If you are summarizing the main point of a resource and not referencing one particular part of the source, CMS only requires that you provide the superscript footnote number as the in-text citation and enough bibliographic information in the footnote to get the reader to the entry in the bibliography, which usually includes only the names of the author(s) and the resource. In the following example, the writer refers to multiple texts within the same sentence. Notice that in the condensed footnote

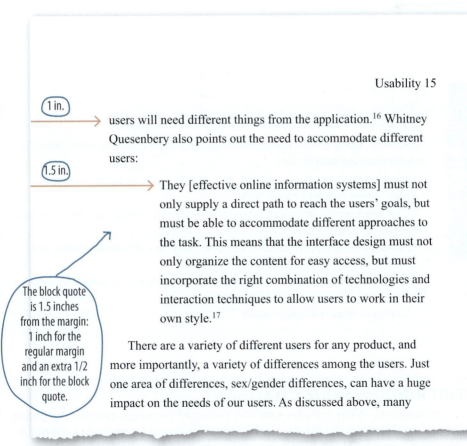

Usability 15

1 in.

users will need different things from the application.[16] Whitney Quesenbery also points out the need to accommodate different users:

1.5 in.

> They [effective online information systems] must not only supply a direct path to reach the users' goals, but must be able to accommodate different approaches to the task. This means that the interface design must not only organize the content for easy access, but must incorporate the right combination of technologies and interaction techniques to allow users to work in their own style.[17]

The block quote is 1.5 inches from the margin: 1 inch for the regular margin and an extra 1/2 inch for the block quote.

There are a variety of different users for any product, and more importantly, a variety of differences among the users. Just one area of differences, sex/gender differences, can have a huge impact on the needs of our users. As discussed above, many

Figure 14.3   An Extended Quotation in CMS Style.

the resources are listed in alphabetical order by the author's last name, the order in which they would appear in the bibliography.

Text with Multiple Footnoted References

During the 1980s and early 1990s, *Computers and Composition* published many articles discussing methods and criteria for evaluating and choosing instructional software packages.[6]

Condensed Footnote

6. Condon, "Selecting Computer Software for Writing Instruction"; Eiler, "Perspectives on Software"; Hepler, "Things to Consider When Evaluating Software"; Kemp, "Who Programmed This?"; Redmond, Lawrence, and Villani, "User-Friendly Software"; Taylor, "Evaluating Software"; and Wahlstrom, "What Does User-Friendly Mean Anyway?"

Electronic resources are cited in the notes in the same way as hard-copy resources. If you have the name of the author, include that information. If there is no author, include a shortened title.

reflect

CMS: In-Text Citation Nuts and Bolts

In CMS format, typical in-text citations include a superscript number that refers to a condensed footnote or endnote that looks like this:

Number of in-text reference. Author, *Title* (in italics, may be a shortened version), page number (just the numeral itself).

If no author is available, use an abbreviated version of the title of the source. The notation would look like this:

Number of in-text reference. *Title* (in italics, may be a shortened version), page number (just the numeral itself).

If no page number is available (e.g., a digital resource), include some textual marker like a subhead. The citation would look like this:

Number of in-text reference. Author, *Title*, "Subhead."

Full Bibliographic Citations

The bibliography often includes only the names of resources cited in the paper, not resources that you found and read during your research process but did not include in the paper. CMS style does permit you to include particularly useful sources you did not cite in your paper, however. (As with all writing situations, audience expectations should be your guide.) The bibliography page should start with the word "Bibliography" centered at the top of a new page in your essay, and it should also be included in your continuous page numbering. Subsequent bibliography pages do not need to include the word "Bibliography," but should be paginated. Entries in bibliographies are presented in alphabetical order by the author's last name. If you have more than one text by the same author, alphabetize those entries by title of the text, and include three dashed lines for the author's name in the subsequent entries. If you have texts with no authors, incorporate them into the alphabetical list based on title (see Figure 14.4).

Entries in a bibliography should have a hanging indent, a format that looks a bit like an upside-down paragraph. The first line of the citation is left-justified, with no indent. Then all subsequent lines have a half-inch indentation. The examples in Figure 14.4 demonstrate how the hanging indent looks on the page.

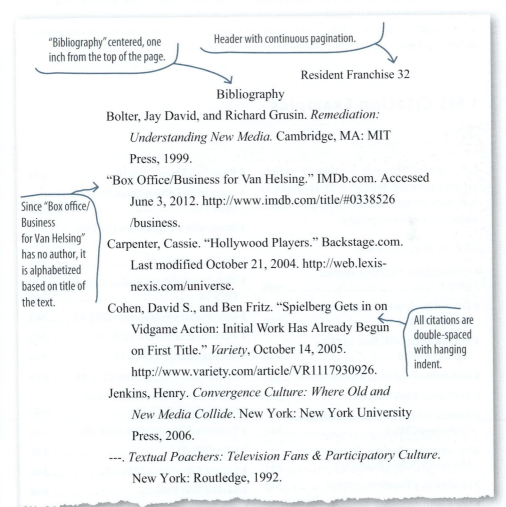

Figure 14.4   The First Page of the Bibliography in a CMS-Formatted Paper.

CMS full bibliographic style generally provides information in the following order:

1. Name of author (spell out the entire name)
2. Title of resource (major words start with capital letters)
3. Publication information (usually including publisher's name and location and the copyright date; if the city of publication might be confused with another city, include the state or country within the citation)

Periods are included after each major section of information. For example, a period is included after the name of the author(s), after the text's title, and after the complete publication information. If there is no author for the text, start with the title of the text; however, remember that government agencies and corporations can function as authors. With some online resources you may have to look on other pages besides the homepage to find the name of the author.

Similarly, you may have to search online resources for the date of the last update (like the "history" page in wikis). If you can't find a date, you may provide the date on which you accessed the resource instead.

The citation rules for static, syndicated, and dynamic resources all follow this general pattern, but each category has some unique characteristics.

CMS Citation Examples

 For more examples of CMS citations go to the English CourseMate for this text at cengagebrain.com.

Each citation example includes a sample for an extended footnote or endnote as well as a complete entry that you would include in the bibliography.

Static Resources

Syndicated Resources

Dynamic Resource

Static Resources

Static resources (e.g., books, films, and government documents) are generally easy to cite using CMS style. These citations usually include author, title, and publication information. The following examples indicate how to cite various types of static sources.

CMS-1, Printed Book with One Author

1. Anne Balsamo, *Designing Culture: The Technological Imagination at Work* (Durham: Duke University Press, 2011).

Balsamo, Anne. *Designing Culture: The Technological Imagination at Work*. Durham: Duke University Press, 2011.

CMS-2, Printed Book with Two to Three Authors

2. Nicholas Gane and David Beer, *New Media: The Key Concepts* (New York: Berg, 2008).

Gane, Nicholas, and David Beer. *New Media: The Key Concepts*. New York: Berg, 2008.

With more than one author, only the first author's name is presented last-name first. If there had been three authors, the first author's last name would be first, followed by the first name, then the coauthors with their first names followed by their last names (Story, Jonelle, Anne Kroening, and James Anderson.). Put the authors in the same order as they are presented on the title page of the book.

author   title   publication information

CMS-3, Printed Book with Four or More Authors

3. Martin Lister et al., *New Media: A Critical Introduction,* 2nd ed. (London: Routledge, 2009).

Lister, Martin, Jon Dovey, Seth Giddings, Iain Grant, and Kieran Kelly. *New Media: A Critical Introduction.* 2nd ed. London: Routledge, 2009.

For resources with four to ten authors, include all names in the bibliography and in the note only include the first author and "et al." Be careful not to use a period after "et" because it is an entire Latin word. The Latin abbreviation "al." (with a period) is an abbreviation for "alii" or "alia," which means "others."

CMS-4, Book with a Publisher's Imprint

4. Stephen D. Brookfield, *Becoming a Critically Reflective Teacher* (San Francisco: Jossey-Bass, 1995).

Brookfield, Stephen D. *Becoming a Critically Reflective Teacher.* San Francisco: Jossey-Bass, 1995.

Some publishers use an imprint, a separately titled subsection of the company, for certain types and series of books. If both the imprint and publisher name are made available on the title page, you only need include the imprint name, not the publisher's name. In this example, "Jossey-Bass" is the name of the imprint and "Wiley" is the name of the publisher.

CMS-5, Electronic Book

Electronic Book on the Web

34. William Shakespeare, *The Taming of the Shrew,* ed. Amanda Ballard, last modified December 8, 2011, http://www .shakespeare-online.com/plays/tamingscenes.html.

Shakespeare, William. *The Taming of the Shrew,* ed. Amanda Ballard. Last modified December 8, 2011. http://www.shakespeare-online.com/plays/tamingscenes.html.

Electronic Book in Database

35. Herman Melville, *Moby Dick* (Charleston, SC: Forgotten Books, 2008), http://books.google.com/.

Melville, Herman. *Moby Dick.* Charleston, SC: Forgotten Books, 2008. http://books.google.com/.

In this instance, the URL for the specific *Google Books* title is too long to accurately type from a written document without making errors. Since the search feature at *Google Books* works well, we have only included the URL to the *Google Books* homepage.

Electronic Book Downloaded for an Ereader

36. Susan A. Ambrose, Michael W. Bridges, Michele DiPietro, Marsha C. Lovett, and Maria K. Norman, *How Learning Works: 7 Research-Based Principles for Smart Teaching* (San Francisco, CA: Jossey-Bass, 2010, Kindle edition).

Ambrose, Susan A., Michael W. Bridges, Michele DiPietro, Marsha C. Lovett, and Maria K. Norman. *How Learning Works: 7 Research-Based Principles for Smart Teaching*. San Francisco, CA: Jossey-Bass, 2010. Kindle edition.

For ebooks downloaded for an ereader through a service such as Amazon's Kindle, it is more appropriate to note the ebook edition. In the above example, that platform is "Kindle edition."

CMS-6, Selection from an Edited Collection or Anthology

6. Chen Peigin, "Magazines: An Industry in Transition," in *New Media for a New China*, eds. James F. Scotton and William A. Hachten (West Sussex: Blackwell, 2010), 79.

Peigin, Chen. "Magazines: An Industry in Transition." In *New Media for a New China*, edited by James F. Scotton and William A. Hachten, 74–82. West Sussex: Blackwell, 2010.

Edited collections or anthologies have two layers of both authorial and title information. There is the author of the specific essay or chapter that you are citing. The specific essay or chapter title is presented in quotation marks. The second title, the title of the edited collection or anthology, is presented in italics (like the title of a regular book). The second layer of authorial information, the editors who put together the edited collection or anthology, comes after the title of the book. You also need to include page numbers for the specific portion of the book you are referring to; they are presented after the editor's name; notice that the page cited in the endnote comes after the publication information.

CMS-7, Introduction, Preface, Foreword, or Afterword from a Book

7. W. E. C. Baynes, introduction to *The Prince*, by Niccolo Machiavelli, trans. Rufus Goodwin (Wellesley: Dante University Press, 2003).

CMS-6

CMS-7

Baynes, W. E. C. Introduction to *The Prince*, by Niccolo Machiavelli. Translated by Rufus Goodwin, 13–25. Wellesley: Dante University Press, 2003.

The citation styles for introductions, prefaces, forewords, and afterwords are basically the same. If you are using one of these types of ancillary materials as a resource, start your citation with the author of the ancillary material. If the ancillary material has a title, give it next in quotation marks, followed by the word for the type of ancillary material. Finally, provide the remainder of the book's citation, placing the author's name after the title of the book.

CMS-8, Book with a Translator

8. Niccolo Machiavelli, *The Prince*, trans. Rufus Goodwin (Wellesley: Dante University Press, 2003).

Machiavelli, Niccolo. *The Prince*. Translated by Rufus Goodwin. Wellesley: Dante University Press, 2003.

Several different versions of *The Prince* exist, and the translator's role in the publishing process distinguishes one version from another.

CMS-9, Book with an Editor (Entire Anthology)

9. Seth Giggings and Martin Lister, eds., *The New Media and Technocultures Reader* (London: Routledge, 2011).

Giggings, Seth, and Martin Lister, eds. *The New Media and Technocultures Reader*. London: Routledge, 2011.

If you are citing an entire edited collection, you need to identify the "authors" as "editors" by including "ed." (for one editor) or "eds." (for more than one editor) after their names.

CMS-10, Book in a Series

10. Angela Crow, *Aging Literacies: Training and Development Challenges for Faculty*, New Dimensions in Computers and Composition (Cresskill, NJ: Hampton, 2006).

Crow, Angela. *Aging Literacies: Training and Development Challenges for Faculty*. New Dimensions in Computers and Composition. Cresskill, NJ: Hampton, 2006.

If the book you are citing is part of a series, include the series name after the title of publication.

CMS-11, Book in an Edition Other Than the First

11. Arthur Cohen and Florence B. Brawer, *The American Community College*, 5th ed. (San Francisco: Jossey-Bass, 2008).

Cohen, Arthur, and Florence B. Brawer. *The American Community College*. 5th ed. San Francisco: Jossey-Bass, 2008.

When referring to books in multiple editions, use the language you find on the title page of the book. Therefore, if it says second or third edition, put the numbers in your citation. If it says "Revised" or "Abridged" put "rev. ed." or "abr. ed." in the citation. Similarly, if your book is the fifth in a multivolume work, just include "vol. 5."

CMS-12, Book with a Title within the Title

12. Paul M. Sammon, *Future Noir: The Making of* Blade Runner (New York: Harper Paperbacks, 1996).

Sammon, Paul M. *Future Noir: The Making of* Blade Runner. New York: Harper Paperbacks, 1996.

The title of the film within the title of the book is neither italicized nor enclosed in quotation marks. If the title within the title is of a shorter work, like a story, poem, or song, you'll keep everything in italics and put quotation marks around the shorter work's title.

CMS and Web Pages

For citation purposes, you generally treat a web page or web site as static, unless you know that it is dynamic (a wiki, for example) or syndicated (like a blog). (Note: Many web sites are now actually online databases and should be treated accordingly. See "Techno Tip: CMS and Databases," page 350.) Static web page citations look a lot like book citations: author, specific web page title, owner or sponsor of the site, copyright date or last modified date, and URL (with a period as closing punctuation). CMS states you should include an access date if there is no publication or last modified date.

37. Gideon O. Burton, "Invention," Brigham Young University, accessed June 4, 2012, http://rhetoric.byu.edu/canons/invention.htm.

Burton, Gideon O. "Invention." Brigham Young University. Accessed June 4, 2012. http://rhetoric.byu.edu/canons/invention.htm.

The author's name and the copyright or posted date are sometimes located somewhere on the web page. If a web page or book has no author's or editor's name, and you cannot find one by looking around the site, begin the citation with the title.

>>>

>>>

38. "Box Office/Business for Melancholia," IMDb.com, 1999–2012, http://www.imdb.com/title/tt1527186/business.

"Box Office/Business for Melancholia." IMDb.com. 1999–2012. http://www.imdb.com/title/tt1527186/business.

CMS-13, Web Page

13. Gideon O. Burton, "Invention," Brigham Young University, accessed June 4, 2012, http://rhetoric.byu.edu/canons/invention.htm.

Burton, Gideon O. "Invention." Brigham Young University. Accessed June 4, 2012. http://rhetoric.byu.edu/canons/invention.htm.

CMS-14, Web Page with No Author Listed

14. "Box Office/Business for Melancholia," IMDb.com, 1999–2012, http://www.imdb.com/title/tt1527186/business.

"Box Office/Business for Melancholia." IMDb.com. 1999–2012. http://www.imdb.com/title/tt1527186/business.

CMS-15, Government Publication

15. Stop Online Piracy Act, H.R. 3261, 112th Cong. (2011), THOMAS, http://thomas.loc.gov/cgi-bin/query/z?c112:H.R.3261:.

Stop Online Piracy Act. H.R. 3261. 112th Congress, 2011. THOMAS. http://thomas.loc.gov/cgi-bin/query/z?c112:H.R.3261:.

"H.R." stands for "House of Representatives" and "3261" represents the document number. If you are citing multiple types of government publications, refer to more detailed discussion of government publications in the *Chicago Manual of Style* (sixteenth edition, Legal and Public Documents, page 769). Like government agencies, corporations and other organizations can also author resources. In those cases, the school or corporation's name would be listed as the author of a resource (also see CMS-30, Review).

CMS-16, Published Interview

16. "How to Publish a Book: Literary Agent Interview—Peter Riva," by Stacey Cochran, last modified January 1, 2011, http://howtopublishabook.org/2011.01.01_arch.html.

Riva, Peter. "How to Publish a Book: Literary Agent Interview—Peter Riva." By Stacey Cochran. Last modified January 1, 2011. http://howtopublishabook.org/2011.01.01_arch.html.

A published interview is like any other smaller text, essay, or chapter within a larger body of work (see CMS-6); however, note that the person interviewed is treated like the author and the interviewer is treated more like an editor (see CMS-9). A personal or "live" interview, however, is considered a dynamic text (see CMS-36).

CMS-17, Published Letter

17. John Adams to Abigail Adams, 28 August 1774, *Adams Family Papers: An Electronic Archive,* ed. Massachusetts Historical Society, accessed June 4, 2012, http://www.masshist.org/digitaladams/aea/cfm/doc.cfm?id=L17740828ja.

Adams, John. John Adams to Abigail Adams, 28 August 1774. *Adams Family Papers: An Electronic Archive*, ed. Massachusetts Historical Society. Accessed June 4, 2012. http://www.masshist.org/digitaladams/aea/cfm/doc.cfm?id=L17740828ja.

A published letter is like any other smaller text, essay, or chapter within a larger body of work (see CMS-6). However, "title" the letter with the author's name first and then the recipient's name, a comma, then the date. A personal letter is considered primary research and is just mentioned within the actual text of the research paper or in a note.

CMS-18, Conference Proceedings

18. Joyce VanTassel-Baska and Tamra Stambaugh, eds., *Overlooked Gems: A National Perspective on Low-Income Promising Learners* (Williamsburg: Natl. Assn. for Gifted Children and Center for Gifted Educ., Coll. of William & Mary, 2007), http://www.eric.ed.gov/PDFS/ED494579.pdf.

VanTassel-Baska, Joyce, and Tamra Stambaugh, eds. *Overlooked Gems: A National Perspective on Low-Income Promising Learners.* Williamsburg: Natl. Assn. for Gifted Children and Center for Gifted Educ., Coll. of William & Mary, 2007. http://www.eric.ed.gov/PDFS/ED494579.pdf.

Conference proceedings are like edited collections (CMS-6).

CMS-19, Paper Published in Conference Proceedings

19. Alexinia Y. Baldwin, "Untapped Potential for Excellence," in *Overlooked Gems: A National Perspective on Low-Income Promising Learners,* eds. Joyce VanTassel-Baska and Tamra Stambaugh (Williamsburg: Natl. Assn. for Gifted Children and Center for Gifted Educ., Coll. of William & Mary, 2007), http://www.eric.ed.gov/PDFS/ED494579.pdf.

Baldwin, Alexinia Y. "Untapped Potential for Excellence." In *Overlooked Gems: A National Perspective on Low-Income Promising Learners*, eds. Joyce VanTassel-Baska and Tamra Stambaugh, 23–25. Williamsburg: Natl. Assn. for Gifted Children and Center for Gifted Educ., Coll. of William & Mary, 2007. http://www.eric.ed.gov/PDFS/ED494579.pdf.

Published papers in conference proceedings are like essays or chapters found in edited collections (CMS-6).

CMS-20, Published Dissertation

20. Risa Applegarth, *Other Grounds: Popular Genres and the Rhetoric of Anthropology, 1900–1940* (PhD diss., University of North Carolina at Chapel Hill, 2009), ProQuest (AAT 3366302).

Applegarth, Risa. *Other Grounds: Popular Genres and the Rhetoric of Anthropology, 1900–1940.* PhD diss. University of North Carolina at Chapel Hill, 2009. ProQuest (AAT 3366302).

The citation for a published dissertation (shown above) includes information on the degree-granting university. To cite an unpublished dissertation, put the title of the work in quotation marks.

CMS-21, Film

In general, film citations start with the title of the film and then move on to the director, the descriptor, the distribution company, the year of release, and the medium. Since many films are available in different versions and via different media, it's important to include those particulars in the citation. If you viewed the film on television, you would need to consider it a dynamic production since television stations generally edit scenes and may incorporate advertising as part of the screening (see live television example, CMS-31).

Film Screened in a Theater

39. Blade Runner, directed by Ridley Scott (Warner Bros., 1982), Film.

Blade Runner. Directed by Ridley Scott. Warner Bros., 1982. Film.

Film on DVD

40. *Blade Runner: The Director's Cut*, directed by Ridley Scott (Warner Bros., 1991), DVD.

Blade Runner: The Director's Cut. Directed by Ridley Scott. Warner Bros., 1991. DVD.

This version of the film was not released before 1991; therefore, it does not include the original theatrical release date; instead, it includes the copyright date of the new version of the film. If this was a DVD of the original theatrical cut, you would include the copyright of the DVD version.

Film Extra in Special Collection

41. Ridley Scott, "Introduction, *Blade Runner: The Final Cut*," on disc 1 of *Harrison Ford: Blade Runner* (Five-Disc Ultimate Collector's Edition), directed by Ridley Scott (Warner Bros. Pictures, 2007), DVD.

Scott, Ridley. "Introduction, *Blade* Runner: The Final Cut." Disc 1. *Harrison Ford: Blade Runner*, Five-Disc Ultimate Collector's Edition. Directed by Ridley Scott. Warner Bros. Pictures, 2007. DVD.

Film Viewed Streaming through the Internet

42. *Blade Runner: Theatrical Cut*, Directed by Ridley Scott (1982; Warner Bros.), Netflix, accessed June 3, 2012, http://movies .netflix.com/.

Blade Runner: Theatrical Cut. Directed by Ridley Scott. (1982). Warner Bros. Netflix. Accessed June 3, 2012. http://movies.netflix.com/.

CMS-22

CMS-22, Sound Recordings

Like films (CMS-21), audio recordings may be accessed in a variety of locations and media.

Song from an Album

43. Deep Purple, "Space Truckin," *Machine Head* (Warner Bros., 1972), compact disc.

Deep Purple. "Space Truckin." *Machine Head*. Warner Bros., 1972. Compact disc.

Downloaded Song

44. Deep Purple, "Space Truckin," *Machine Head* (Warner Bros., 1972), iTunes, http://www.apple.com/itunes/.

Deep Purple. "Space Truckin." *Machine Head*. Warner Bros., 1972. iTunes. http://www.apple.com/itunes/.

Material downloaded from resources like *iTunes* can be treated as material downloaded from a database (see "Techno Tip: CMS and Databases," page 350).

Song Heard Streaming on the Web

45. Deep Purple, "Space Truckin," *Machine Head* (Pandora, accessed October 3, 2011, http://www.pandora.com/).

Deep Purple. "Space Truckin." *Machine Head*. Pandora. Accessed October 3, 2011. http://www.pandora.com/.

CMS-23

CMS-23, Sacred Text

CMS does not generally include sacred texts in the bibliography. It only includes the appropriate citation information in the footnote or endnote.

23. Isaiah. 38:9–15 (King James Version).

CMS-24

CMS-24, Entry from a Dictionary, Thesaurus, Encyclopedia, or Almanac

In CMS you generally include well-known reference citations in the footnote or endnote (without publication information); "s.v." stands for *sub verbo*, meaning "under the word."

Entry from a Print Dictionary

46. *Webster's Third New International Dictionary of the English Language Unabridged*, 3rd ed., s.v. "eclecticism."

Entry from an Online Dictionary

> 47. *Merriam-Webster*, s.v. "eclecticism," accessed June 4, 2012, http://www.merriam-webster.com/dictionary/eclecticism.

Entry from an Online Encyclopedia

> 48. *Encyclopedia Britannica*, s.v. "Russian Revolution of 1917," accessed June 4, 2012, http://www.britannica.com/ EBchecked /topic/513907/Russian-Revolution-of-1917.

Syndicated Resources

Syndicated resources (e.g., journal and magazine articles, television shows, and blogs) are generally easy to cite using CMS style. These citations usually include author, title of the specific essay or episode, *title of the periodical published work* (e.g., name of the overall journal, television show, or blog), and publication information. The following examples indicate how to cite various types of syndicated sources.

CMS-25, Article in a Scholarly Journal

The current CMS guidelines request that you include both volume and issue number within the citation.

Article in a Printed Journal

> 49. Barbara Cambridge, "Research and Policy: Antithetical or Complementary?" *Writing Program Administration* 35, no.1 (2011): 135–47.

Cambridge, Barbara. "Research and Policy: Antithetical or Complemen tary?" *Writing Program Administration* 35, no.1 (2011): 135–47.

Journal Article Accessed through a Database

> 50. Paul Cohen, "Cowboys Die Hard: Real Men and Businessmen in the Reagan-Era Blockbuster," *Film & History* 41, no. 1 (2011): 71–81, doi: 10.1353/flm.2011.0024 .

Cohen, Paul. "Cowboys Die Hard: Real Men and Businessmen in the Reagan-Era Blockbuster." *Film & History* 41, no. 1 (2011): 71–81. doi: 10.1353/flm.2011.0024.

Journal Article from Journal That Only Exists Online

> 51. Robert Leston, Geoffrey Carter, and Sarah Arroyo, "The Chora of the Twin Towers," *Enculturation* 10 (2011), http://enculturation .gmu.edu/the-chora-of-the-twin-towers.

CMS-25

> Leston, Robert, Geoffrey Carter, and Sarah Arroyo. "The Chora of
> the Twin Towers." *Enculturation* 10 (2011). http://enculturation
> .gmu.edu/the-chora-of-the-twin-towers.

As an online journal, there are no page numbers.

techno tip

CMS and Databases

In theory, an article from a scholarly journal would be the same whether it was found in print or in any one of a couple of different databases. However, as demonstrated in the magazine example below (CMS-28), differences can arise. For the various resources you find in library databases (usually journals and other periodicals), you will need to look up the Digital Object Identifier (DOI). Finding the DOI can be tricky; consider asking a librarian for help.

> 50. Paul Cohen, "Cowboys Die Hard: Real Men and Businessmen in the Reagan-Era
> Blockbuster," *Film & History* 41, no. 1 (2011): 71–81, doi: 10.1353/flm.2011.0024.

> Cohen, Paul. "Cowboys Die Hard: Real Men and Businessmen in the Reagan-Era
> Blockbuster." *Film & History* 41, no. 1 (2011): 71–81. doi: 10.1353/flm.2011.0024.

If you cannot find the DOI, you can provide a URL (try looking for a shortened or "stable" URL to use).

> 52. Jeanne Marie Rose, "Writing Time: Composing in an Accelerated World," *Pedagogy*
> 12, no. 1 (2012): 45–67, http://muse.jhu.edu/journals/ped/summary/v012
> /12.1.rose.html.

> Rose, Jeanne Marie. "Writing Time: Composing in an Accelerated World." *Peda-*
> *gogy* 12, no. 1 (2012): 45–67. http://muse.jhu.edu/journals/ped/summary/v012
> /12.1.rose.html.

As mentioned in "Techno Tip: Databases, Microfilm and Microfiche" in Chapter 4 (page 84), scholarly databases are not the only databases you will be citing. Databases like *iTunes, Netflix, Hulu*, and *Amazon* provide access to various audio and visual media. *Google Books* has been slowly scanning hundreds of thousands of books and is now its own online book database. Like the journal examples above, the *Hulu* and *Google* Books examples below provide the database information as a secondary layer of publication information, listed after the primary citation.

> 66. Ian Brennan, "New York," *Glee*, season 2, episode 22, directed by Brad Fal-
> chuck, aired May 24, 2011 (Los Angeles: 20th Century Fox), Hulu, accessed Novem-
> ber 8, 2011, http://www.hulu.com/glee.

> Brennan, Ian. "New York." *Glee*, season 2, episode 22. Directed by Brad Falchuck.
> Aired May 24, 2011. Los Angeles: 20th Century Fox. Hulu. Accessed November 8,
> 2011. http://www.hulu.com/glee.

Electronic Book in Database

> 35. Herman Melville, *Moby Dick* (Charleston, SC: Forgotten Books, 2008), http://
> books.google.com/.

Melville, Herman. *Moby Dick.* Charleston, SC: Forgotten Books, 2008. http://books
.google.com/.

In this instance, the URL for the specific *Google Books* title is too long for a person to accurately type from a written document without making errors. Since the search feature at *Google Books* works well, we have only included the URL to the *Google Books* homepage.

Finding ebooks for ereaders like Amazon's Kindle (or Kindle Application) and Barnes & Noble's Nook potentially becomes a little trickier. In these cases, the computer code used to translate the book into the appropriate ereader application is different. Therefore, we suggest that you mention the specific application database you are accessing, as in the Kindle example below.

36. Susan A. Ambrose, Michael W. Bridges, Michele DiPietro, Marsha C. Lovett, and Maria K. Norman, *How Learning Works: 7 Research-Based Principles for Smart Teaching* (San Francisco, CA: Jossey-Bass, 2010, Kindle edition).

Ambrose, Susan A., Michael W. Bridges, Michele DiPietro, Marsha C. Lovett, and Maria K. Norman. *How Learning Works: 7 Research-Based Principles for Smart Teaching.* San Francisco, CA: Jossey-Bass, 2010. Kindle edition.

Although you may not know the fine details of how a given database works, do the best you can with our mash-up instructions (Chapter 11, page 256) and talk to your friends and instructors.

CMS-26, Newspaper Article

Newspaper articles can generally be easily located in three forms of media: in print, online at the newspaper's web site, and through a library database. CMS suggests that newspaper items usually be referenced in text or in the notes. However, we have still provided an example of how different types of newspaper articles might look in the bibliography. CMS recognizes that most newspapers have numerous editions and versions; therefore, you do not need to include a reference to a specific page.

Printed Newspaper Article

53. Ben Sisario, "Sirius's Move to Bypass a Royalty Payment Clearing- house Causes an Uproar," *New York Times*, New York edition, November 7, 2011.

Sisario, Ben. "Sirius's Move to Bypass a Royalty Payment Clearing house Causes an Uproar." *New York Times*, New York edition. November 7, 2011.

Newspaper Article Found Online

You can adapt the various journal and magazine article citations for online publications of the newspapers just by adding the URL.

54. Ben Sisario, "Sirius's Move to Bypass a Royalty Payment Clearinghouse Causes an Uproar," *New York Times*, New York edition, November 7, 2011, http://www.nytimes.com/2011/11/07/business /media/siriuss-move-to-bypass-royalty-agency-causes-uproar.html?_r=1.

Sisario, Ben. "Sirius's Move to Bypass a Royalty Payment
   Clearinghouse Causes an Uproar." *New York Times*, New
   York edition. November 7, 2011. http://www.nytimes
   .com/2011/11/07/business/media/siriuss-move-to-bypass
   -royalty-agency-causes-uproar.html?_r=1.

Newspaper Article Found in a Database

55. Ben Sisario, "Sirius's Move to Bypass a Royalty Payment Clearinghouse Causes an Uproar," *New York Times,* Late edition, November 7, 2011, http://www.nytimes.com/.

Sisario, Ben. "Sirius's Move to Bypass a Royalty Payment Clearinghouse
   Causes an Uproar." *New York Times*, Late edition.
   November 7, 2011. http://www.nytimes.com/.

Whereas the web version of the article cited above said that it came from the "New York edition," this database version said it came from the "Late edition." The database gave the general URL for the *New York Times* as the article's URL. The *New York Times* web site search engine works well enough to easily find the article with the title and author.

Newspaper Article Accessed through a Mobile Application

56. Ben Sisario, "Sirius's Move to Bypass Royalty Agency Causes Uproar," *New York Times*, November 7, 2011, *New York Times* iPhone mobile application.

Sisario, Ben. "Sirius's Move to Bypass Royalty Agency Causes
   Uproar." *New York Times*. November 7, 2011. *New York Times*
   iPhone mobile application.

Like the *Wired* example at the beginning of Chapter 11 (page 244), the title for the same article in the mobile application was slightly different from the print, online, and database versions. For publication information, we have added the name of the application (both the *New York Times* and *Wired* have their own applications; other mobile application readers like *Pulse* and *Amazon Kindle* have access to other periodicals).

CMS-27, Newspaper Editorial

27. "The Price Is Right," editorial, *Los Angeles Times*, January 19, 2009, http://articles.latimes.com/2008/jan/19/opinion/ ed-wine19.

"The Price is Right." Editorial. *Los Angeles Times*. January 19, 2009. http://articles.latimes.com/2008/jan/19/opinion/ed-wine19.

If there is no author listed, start with the name of the text you are citing. Include the term "Editorial" after the title. If this were found in a print newspaper, you would just include the publishing information required of a print citation.

CMS-28, Article in a Magazine

Magazines, even if they have a volume and issue number, are usually cited by date only. Since most articles in magazines are separated by advertisements, CMS does not require that you include page numbers unless you are quoting a specific page; you would then include the page number in the note.

Printed Magazine Article

57. Steven Levy, "Inside Google+," *Wired*, October 2011.

Levy, Steven. "Inside Google+." *Wired*. October 2011.

Magazine Article Found Online

58. Steven Levy, "Inside Google Plus," *Wired*, October 2011, http://www.wired.com/magazine/2011/09/ff_google_horowitz/all/1.

Levy, Steven. "Inside Google Plus." *Wired*. October 2011, http://www.wired.com/magazine/2011/09/ff_google_horowitz/all/1.

You can adapt the various journal and magazine article citations for online publications of the journals by just adding the URL. In this case (as mentioned at the beginning of Chapter 11), if you look closely, you'll notice that the titles of the print and online versions are not the same. In short, pay close attention to whichever version you are citing.

Magazine Article Found in a Database

59. Steven Levy, "Inside Google+," Wired, October 2011, http://search.ebscohost.com.proxy.lib.odu.edu/login.aspx?direct=true&db=iih&AN=67665467&site=ehost-live.

Levy, Steven. "Inside Google+." *Wired*. October 2011. http://search.ebscohost.com.proxy.lib.odu.edu/login.aspx?direct=true&db=iih&AN=67665467&site=ehost-live.

The database generally archives the print version of the article, not the web-based version. Therefore, the title matches the print version. In this instance, there is no getting around the long, complicated URL. *Wired* does not have a doi; therefore, to cite the database article, which is different from the online version, you must cite the database's URL.

Magazine Article Accessed through a Mobile Application

60. Steven Levy, "Inside Google+," *Wired*, October 2011, *Wired* iPad mobile application.

Levy, Steven. "Inside Google+." *Wired*. October 2011. *Wired* iPad mobile application.

Since the computer coding involved for producing mobile applications in different platforms (Apple products versus Android/Google products versus Blackberry products, etc.) is different, we suggest that you specify which brand of device the application is running on.

CMS-29, Article with a Quotation in the Title

Since the article title is already surrounded by double quotation marks, a quotation within the title would simply use single quotation marks.

29. Joseph Kahne and Kim Bailey, "The Role of Social Capital in Youth Development: The Case of 'I Have a Dream' Programs," *Educational Evaluation and Policy Analysis* 21, no. 2 (1999).

Kahne, Joseph, and Kim Bailey. "The Role of Social Capital in Youth Development: The Case of 'I Have a Dream' Programs." *Educational Evaluation and Policy Analysis* 21, no. 2 (1999): 321–43.

CMS-30, Review

Sometimes reviews have their own title (like the book review below) or just start with "Review of" and the title of the work under review. The first author listed is the person doing the review; the second author is the author of the text under review. You do not need publication information about the work under review (it is usually provided within the review itself); instead, you need to make sure you include publication information from the resource where the review is published.

Book Review

61. Johanna Drucker, "Philosophy and Digital Humanities," review of *Humanities Computing*, by Willard McCarty, *Digital Humanities Quarterly* 1, no.1 (2007), http://www.digitalhumanities.org /dhq/vol/1/1/000001/000001.html.

Drucker, Johanna. "Philosophy and Digital Humanities." Review of *Humanities Computing*, by Willard McCarty. *Digital Humanities Quarterly* 1, no.1 (2007). http://www.digitalhumanities.org /dhq/vol/1/1/000001/000001.html.

Game Review

62. Greg Miller, "Batman: Arkham City Review," review of *Batman: Arkham City*, by Rocksteady, *IGN*, November 29, 2011, http:// ps3.ign.com/articles/119/1199705p1.html.

Miller, Greg. "Batman: Arkham City Review." Review of *Batman: Arkham City*, by Rocksteady. *IGN*. November 29, 2011. http:// ps3.ign.com/articles/119/1199705p1.html.

In this instance, the company "Rocksteady" is functioning as the author, or producer, of the text being reviewed.

CMS-31, Television

Like journals and magazines, television shows include individual pieces (episodes instead of articles). As mentioned above in the film examples, shows viewed on "live," or broadcast, TV need to be considered a dynamic production since television stations generally edit scenes and may incorporate advertising as part of the screening. However, once a television episode has been more formally "published" to DVD or to an online database like *Hulu* or *iTunes*, it should be considered a stable syndicated episode. CMS expects you to include both the name of the producer—we suggest using the executive producer—and the director of the episode. You will probably need to look everything up at IMDb.com.

Broadcast of Television Episode (dynamic)

63. Ian Brennan, "New York," *Glee*, season 2, episode 22, directed by Brad Falchuck, aired May 24, 2011 (Los Angeles: Fox), accessed May 24, 2011, FOX10, Phoenix.

Brennan, Ian. "New York." *Glee*, season 2, episode 22. Directed by Brad Falchuck. Aired May 24, 2011. Los Angeles: Fox. Accessed May 24, 2011, FOX10, Phoenix.

Notice in a broadcast citation you need to include both the production company, in this case Fox, and the local channel name and number, in this case FOX10 (as well as the location). Even if you watched the episode at a later date (so the second date would be different), CMS requires that you keep the original air date.

Episode from a DVD

> 64. Ian Brennan, "New York," *Glee*, season 2, episode 22, directed by Brad Falchuck, aired May 24, 2011 (Los Angeles: 20th Century Fox), DVD.

> Brennan, Ian. "New York." *Glee*, season 2, episode 22. Directed by Brad Falchuck. Aired May 24, 2011. Los Angeles: 20th Century Fox. DVD.

Although the production company is the same, please notice that they label it slightly differently in the different media ("Fox" for television broadcast and "20th Century Fox" for DVD publication and distribution). CMS requires that you still include the original airing date for the episode.

Television Episode Downloaded from Database

> 65. Ian Brennan, "New York," *Glee*, season 2, episode 22, directed by Brad Falchuck, aired May 24, 2011 (Los Angeles: 20th Century Fox), iTunes, http://www.apple.com/itunes/.

> Brennan, Ian. "New York." *Glee*, season 2, episode 22. Directed by Brad Falchuck. Aired May 24, 2011. Los Angeles: 20th Century Fox. iTunes. http://www.apple.com/itunes/.

Television Episode Streamed from Database

> 66. Ian Brennan, "New York," *Glee*, season 2, episode 22, directed by Brad Falchuck, aired May 24, 2011 (Los Angeles: 20th Century Fox), Hulu, accessed November 8, 2011, http://www.hulu. com/glee.

> Brennan, Ian. "New York." *Glee*, season 2, episode 22. Directed by Brad Falchuck. Aired May 24, 2011. Los Angeles: 20th Century Fox. Hulu. Accessed November 8, 2011. http://www.hulu.com /glee.

CMS-32, Blogs

Blogs, like periodicals and television shows, have overall titles and then specific articles, or "postings."

Individual Blog Post

> 67. Henry Jenkins, "Reconsidering Digital Immigrants . . .," *Confessions of an Aca-Fan: The Official Weblog of Henry Jenkins* (blog), December 5, 2007, http://henryjenkins .org/2007/12 /reconsidering_digital_immigran.html.

Jenkins, Henry. "Reconsidering Digital Immigrants . . ." *Confessions of an Aca-Fan: The Official Weblog of Henry Jenkins* (blog). December 5, 2007. http://henryjenkins .org/2007/12 /reconsidering_digital_immigran.html.

Comment on a Specific Posting in a Blog

68. Charles Nelson, May 29, 2011 (3:33 p.m.), comment on Clay Spinuzzi, "Reading :: Flow," *Spinuzzi* (blog), May 29, 2011, http://spinuzzi.blogspot.com/2012/05/reading-flow.html.

Nelson, Charles, May 29, 2011 (3:33 p.m.). Comment on Clay Spinuzzi, "Reading :: Flow." *Spinuzzi* (blog). May 29, 2011. http:// spinuzzi.blogspot.com/2012/05/reading-flow.html.

A comment is like an entry in an anthology: you need the author and title of the individual entry as well as the editor, or in the case of blogs an author, and title of the larger work. If the comment or reply of a weblog has its own title, use that; otherwise just call it a "comment on" the title of the original blog posting.

CMS-33, Podcast

Podcasts are just audio versions of blogs; cite them accordingly. However, since it is an audio file, you may want to alert your audience by including "podcast audio" after the title.

33. Mignon Fogarty, "'Ado' versus 'Adieu'," *Grammar Girl: Quick and Dirty Tips for Better Writing*, podcast audio, October 24, 2011, http://grammar.quickanddirtytips.com/ado-versus-adieu.aspx.

Fogarty, Mignon. "'Ado' versus 'Adieu'." *Grammar Girl: Quick and Dirty Tips for Better Writing*. Podcast audio. October 24, 2011. http://grammar.quickanddirtytips.com/ado-versus-adieu.aspx.

Dynamic Resources

Dynamic resources (e.g., easily editable wiki pages, live events, and personal correspondence) are not necessarily easily cited, especially since CMS does not provide examples for some of the resources listed below. Many dynamic resources, like personal correspondence, are usually solely referenced in the text or in a note and are not included in the bibliography. Since dynamic resources can change daily, all dynamic citations should include the access date. Dynamic citations usually include author, title of the text or event, and publication information that includes both the original publication/presentation date or last modified date, and if found online, the access date as well. Many dynamic citations include detailed media descriptors

CMS-34, Page from a Wiki

34. Andrew Churches, "Bloom's Digital Taxonomy," last modified October 1, 2010, accessed November 14, 2011, http://edorigami .wikispaces.com/Bloom%27s+Digital+Taxonomy.

Churches, Andrew. "Bloom's Digital Taxonomy." Last modified October 1, 2010. Accessed November 14, 2011. http://edorigami .wikispaces.com/Bloom%27s+Digital+Taxonomy.

Most wiki pages have a "history" or "page history" link or tab that will allow you to see the last time the page was updated. That same page should give you a sense of whether there is a primary author for the page or if there are a multitude of authors (like most *Wikipedia* articles). For a resource that lists no author or has a multitude of authors over time, treat the text as "no author" and start with the title.

CMS-35, Public Address

35. Seth Godin, "Invisible or Remarkable?" (keynote presentation at the annual EDUCAUSE conference, Philadelphia, October 19, 2011).

Godin, Seth. "Invisible or Remarkable?" Keynote presentation at the annual EDUCAUSE conference, Philadelphia, October 19, 2011.

If there is no title, just skip to the meeting and sponsoring organization's information (in this case, EDUCAUSE is in all capitals because that is how the name of the organization is spelled). Your publication information includes the name of the meeting, city, and the date. Be sure to include an appropriate descriptive label (Address, Lecture, Keynote speech, Reading, etc.).

CMS-36, Unpublished Interview

Since CMS more or less considers unpublished interviews as primary research, they suggest you only include citations within the actual research paper or in the notes (not in the bibliography).

36. Jim Groom [instructor designer of MOOC course], in discussion with author, September 6, 2011.

Although a personal interview is considered primary research, CMS requires that you include an in-text and a full bibliographic citation to give readers the details of where and when you conducted the interview. What looks like the author in

author   title   publication information   access date   media descriptor   modified date this instance is actually the title, the name of the person you interviewed. You then include the detailed descriptor about the author (within brackets) and the date of the interview.

CMS-37, Personal Correspondence

If the letter or email is published as a part of a larger work, it is static; therefore, treat it like a section from a book (see CMS-6). If it is not published elsewhere, treat it as a dynamic resource.

Personal Letter

> 69. Devon Adams, letter to the author, March 19, 2011.

In this case "letter to the author" can function both as the title and as a detailed description.

Email Message

> 70. Donna Adams, "Nominate a STAR!" email message to author, October 13, 2011.

If there is a title, include it with commas between the author and "email message to the author." The title of the email comes from the email's subject line.

CMS-38, Message Posted to a Discussion Group

CMS suggests that citations of discussions for mailing lists and discussion groups be limited to the text or notes.

> 38. Chris Nielson, "Twitter and the Teen Brain," to CyberSalon mailing list, November 10, 2011, https://groups.google.com /forum/?fromgroups#!searchin/cybersalon/Twitter$20and $20the$20teen$20brain$20%5B/cybersalon/4YzEgtEANyo /co5gkE7Z5iIJ.

If there is a title, include it with commas between the author and the name of the mailing list.

CMS Style: Some Common Errors

reflect

▶ Long notes. If you include a full bibliography at the end of the paper, notes only need minimal citation information (author's name, shortened name of the text, and a page number for a direct quote).

▶ The first name goes first in the note; the author's last name is first in the bibliography.

▶ Periods separate elements in the bibliography; elements in the notes should be separated by commas.

>>>

>>>

- Confusion of publication or release and copyright dates.

- Abbreviated names of months; all month names should be spelled out entirely.

- Omission of a word or phrase that describes the type of resource that is not a written document (e.g., media or modality, DVD, weblog, podcast, etc.).

Paper Formatting

CMS includes formatting guidelines that are specifically for formal manuscript preparation and submission. In other words, the guidelines are primarily for academic writing that is being submitted for publication in places like scholarly journals. Kate L. Turabian's *A Manual for Writers of Research Papers, Theses, and Dissertations* (7th ed., Chicago: University of Chicago Press, 2007), is based on CMS and provides formatting guidelines for college-level writing. Except as noted, the guidelines below come from CMS; the others are from Turabian's *Manual*, otherwise referred to as Turabian style. Check with your instructor to see if he or she wants you to use all of the following guidelines.

Title Page

The CMS guidelines for title pages are specifically for book manuscript preparation and submission. Turabian style is used for course papers, and it calls for the full title of the paper, the name of the author, the course title, and the date. The paper title is in all caps; each line on the title page is centered.

Spacing and Margins CMS requires that you double-space the entire document (see Figure 14.1 on page 332), including the footnotes or endnotes, quotations, and the bibliography at the end of the paper. You do not need to include extra spaces (i.e., quadruple space) anywhere in the text. Set your top, left, and bottom margins for at least one inch. All paragraphs should be indented by one-half inch.

Headers and Page Numbers According to Turabian style, you should include at least the page number in the upper right corner of each page. However, your instructor may also request the author's last name or a shortened version of the title of the paper (see Figure 14.1 on page 332). All pages in the paper should be consecutively numbered. The header is placed one-half inch from the top of the page and one inch from the right side of the page. You do not need to include the header and page number on the title page of your paper.

Section Headings If your paper is long enough and it includes coherent sections, and even subsections, you might consider including section headings in your paper. Turabian style does not provide specific formatting guidelines for sections; just be consistent. Make sure that all of your section titles are parallel in both syntax and format. In other words, if you start your first section title with a noun, start all of your section titles with nouns. And if the first level of subheads is in bold type, all of the first-level subheads must be bold. If the second level of subheads is in italics, all of the second-level subheads must be in italics. For example, the following outline represents section headings from a paper using CMS.

> **Technological Advancements**
> *Advancements in Visual Technologies*
> *Advancements in Production and Distribution*
> *Advancements in Interactive Technologies*
> **Narrative Structure**
> **Ideological Differences**
> **Hollywood's Enterprises**
> *Vertical Integration*
> *Further Economic Trends*
> **Conclusions**

Visuals

CMS divides visuals into two categories: tables and figures. Whenever you place visuals in your text, you must place them as close as possible to the paragraph referring to them.

Tables If you are presenting numerical data in a table format, you should label the table with the word *Table*, an Arabic number, and a title. The label and title are placed on top of the table as it appears in your text. According to Turabian style, table titles should use an initial capital only. If you are reprinting the table from an outside source, you must include complete bibliographic information for the table directly under the table (not at the end of your paper in the bibliography).

Table 5   Instructors' responses to question 1[*]

Instructor	Presemester survey (level of emphasis on outcome during course)	Postsemester survey (student competence at end of course), web-based	Postsemester survey (student competence at end of course), face-to-face
Laura	4	3	3
Ann	4	3	2

---

[*] Adaption from Miller, S. K. "Teaching at a Distance: Exploring Instructional Decisions and Learning Perceptions. Diss. 2002. Reproduced by permission of the author.

Figures According to CMS, all other types of visuals, like charts, graphs, drawings, and images, are treated as figures. According to Turabian, you should label each figure with the word *Figure* and an Arabic number (see Figure 14.5). The label and caption of a figure are placed below the visual as it appears in your text, along with a reference to the source of the figure if it came from an outside resource.

INDONESIAN INFLECTION   9

Mungkin saya bisa menolong anda?

Perhaps I can help you

"Might I be able to help you?"

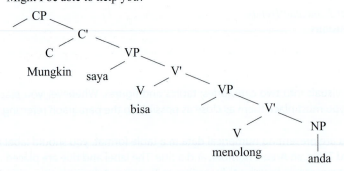

Figure 6. When mungkin is in the C position, the modal cannot move there.

This structural evidence indicates that modals in Indonesian reside in the V position, and that Indonesian contains only root but not epistemic modals. Indonesian does have a specific order for auxiliaries, however, and that makes the complete dismissal of the IP problematic.

Figure 14.5   A Figure in a CMS-Formatted Paper.[*]

---

[*] Adapted from Heck, S. K. "Does Indonesian Have an Inflection Phrase?" *Arizona State University Working Papers in Language* 1. 1999. Reproduced by permission of the author.

chapter 15

CSE Formatting Guidelines

*S*cientific Style and Format: The CSE Manual for Authors, Editors, and Publishers (7th edition), is the official style guide of the Council of Science Editors (CSE), from whom the style takes its name. CSE has three basic in-text citation systems and only one system for full bibliographic entries. This section provides explanations and examples of how to cite resources that you might use in your research, both in the text of your work (in-text citations) and at the end of your research (cited references).

In-Text Citations

You must include an in-text citation in every sentence that includes information from an outside resource. Even if you are only summarizing or paraphrasing the resource, you must include an in-text citation in the same sentence in which you present the material. CSE uses three systems for in-text citations:

- name-year
- citation-sequence
- citation-name

Name-Year In-Text Citation Method

The name-year in-text citation method is similar to the APA citation method. Insert the author's last name and the copyright year in parentheses at the end of the resource you are referencing; this information refers to the full reference that appears in alphabetic order in a cited references list at the end of the paper. Unlike APA style, CSE does not require a comma between the author's last name and the copyright year.

> If pus under pressure is found at the time of aspiration, surgical evacuation of the abscess should be performed, because an abscess will prevent adequate penetration of antibiotics into the infected tissue (Nade 1983). If the process is diagnosed within 1 or 2 days of the start of the disease before an abscess has formed, antibiotic treatment alone is successful in curing the infections in approximately 90 percent of cases (Cole et al. 1982).

To see additional examples of the name-year system for parenthetical references, see the "In-Text Citations" section of Chapter 13 on APA citation style guidelines. These examples work for both APA and CSE styles.

Citation-Sequence In-Text Citation Method

The citation-sequence in-text citation method is a lot like the notes and bibliography citation system used in CMS style. Insert a superscript Arabic number after the phrase or sentence that you are citing, after any punctuation, and with no space before the superscript. Entries in your cited references list have the same numbers as the corresponding in-text citations. If you need to refer to a resource again, use the number originally assigned to it.

> If pus under pressure is found at the time of aspiration, surgical evacuation of the abscess should be performed, because an abscess will prevent adequate penetration of antibiotics into the infected tissue.[36] If the process is diagnosed within 1 or 2 days of the start of the disease before an abscess has formed, antibiotic treatment alone is successful in curing the infections in approximately 90 percent of cases.[37]

Citation-Name In-Text Citation Method

The citation-name sequence also uses superscript numbers as in-text citation markers; however, the references are numbered in alphabetical order on the reference list. Therefore, after completing the final draft of the paper, compile the complete publication data of all the resources you cited in the paper and list them in alphabetical order. Once they are in order, number them by author's last name. For example, "Adams" might be number 1; "Ashbeck," number 2; "Cochran," number 3; and "Zimmerman" would be the last number in the sequence. Like the citation-sequence method, no matter how many times you refer to a resource in the paper, the in-text superscript citation number is the same. In the following example, where the first text reference is to Nade and the second is to Cole, the Nade reference has a higher number because, even though it occurs earlier in the paper, it comes later in the alphabet.

> If pus under pressure is found at the time of aspiration, surgical evacuation of the abscess should be performed, because an abscess will prevent adequate penetration of antibiotics into the infected tissue.[28] If the process is diagnosed within 1 or 2 days of the start of the disease before an abscess has formed, antibiotic treatment alone is successful in curing the infections in approximately 90 percent of cases.[4]

Long Quotations

In CSE style, long quotations need to be presented in a block quote. Instead of using quotation marks to identify the text being quoted, block quotes indent the material so that it stands out on the page. Block quotations are usually set one-half inch from the left margin. Because they are direct quotations, block quotes need an in-text citation as well.

Summaries and Multiple Resources

If you are summarizing the main point of a resource and not referencing one particular part of the source, CSE style requires that you provide the appropriate in-text citation as well as the appropriate full bibliographic citation in the cited references list.

Full Bibliographic Citations

CSE format requires the inclusion of a list of resources used in the paper, and this list is referred to as the "Cited References," "References," or "Literature Cited." This list includes only the names of resources cited in the paper, not resources that you found and read during your research process but did not include in the paper. The cited references page should start at the top of a new page in your essay, and it should also be included in your continuous page numbering. Subsequent cited references pages do not have a special heading but simply have CSE-formatted page numbers. References are presented in the order dictated by the in-text citation system you choose to follow. If you are using the name-year method for in-text citation, your entries in the reference list should be alphabetized and use a hanging indent (the first line of the resource is flush left and subsequent lines are indented five spaces). If you are using the citation-sequence or the citation-name methods for in-text citation, your entries in the reference list should be listed in numerical order with the numbers followed by a period and a space before each name that begins the entry. All lines of the reference should be aligned with the left margin; if you use endnotes, the citations should have a hanging indent so that the numbers stand alone (see Figure 15.1). In the citation-name method, alphabetize your list of resources prior to numbering. If you have more than one text by the same author, be sure to write out the author's name each time and organize by publication year. If you have texts with no authors, incorporate them into an alphabetically organized reference list based on title. CSE style requires that the cited references list include the page numbers, if available, on which the quotation or paraphrase appears in the resource.

Online Research 16

Cited References

1. Hunt TJ, Hunt B. Research and authority in an online world: who knows? who decides? English Journal 2006;95:89–92.

2. Hewson C, Yule P, Laurent D, Vogel C. Internet research methods: a practical guide for the social and behavioural sciences. Thousand Oaks (CA): Sage; 2003.

3. Evans E, Po J. A break in the transaction: examining students' responses to digital texts. Computers and Composition 2007;24(1):56–73.

4. Bass F. The Associated Press guide to internet research and reporting. Cambridge (MA): Perseus; 2001.

5. Tardy C. Expressions of disciplinarity and individuality in a multimodal genre. Computers and Composition 2005;22(3):319–36.

6. Lunsford A. Writing, technologies, and the fifth canon. Computers and Composition 2006;23(2):169–77.

7. Kress G. Gains and losses: new forms of texts, knowledge, and learning. Computers and Composition 2005;22(1):5–22.

8. Walker BE. Google no more: a model for successful research. Teaching Professor 2006;20:1–4.

9. Helms-Park R, Radia P, Stepleton P. A preliminary assessment of Google Scholar as a source of EAP students' research materials. Internet and Higher Education 2007;10:65–76.

10. Bruckman AS. Student research and the internet. Communications of the ACM 2005;48:35–7.

Figure 15.1   A Complete References Page Using CSE Style.

The examples you'll see in this chapter are formatted in the citation-sequence system. To convert these examples to the name-year method, delete the number preceding the citation and move the copyright year of the resource directly after the author's last name. CSE citation-sequence references generally provide information in the following order:

1. Name of author (last name and initials without space or periods separating them; with multiple authors there is no "and" before the last author listed)
2. Title of text (capitalize only the first word and proper names and do not italicize or underline the title)
3. Publication information (usually including publisher's name and location and the publication date)
4. If your resource is anything besides a traditional book or journal article, like a film or audio file—or even a special type of traditional text like an editorial or a dissertation—use a content or medium designator after the title. Insert the designation in brackets before the end of title punctuation.

Periods are included after each major section of information. For example, a period is included after the name of the author(s), the title of the text, and the complete publication information. If there is no author for the text, start with the title of the text; however, remember that government agencies and corporations can function as an author. With various online resources you may have to look on other pages besides the homepage to find the name of the author.

Similarly, you may have to search online resources for the date of the last update (like the "history" page in wikis). If you can't find a date, or other publication information, you may put the phrase "date unknown" within square brackets. The citation rules for static, syndicated, and dynamic resources all follow this general pattern, but each category has some unique characteristics.

CSE Citation Examples

> For more examples of CSE citations go to the English CourseMate for this text at cengagebrain.com.

Static Resources

Static resources (e.g., books, films, and government documents) are generally easy to cite using CSE style. These citations usually include author, title, and publication information. The following examples indicate how to cite various types of static sources.

CSE-1, Book with One Author

1. Galison P. Image and logic: a material culture of microphysics. Chicago: University of Chicago Press; 1997.

CSE-2, Book with Two Authors

2. Foreman JK, Stockwell PB. Automatic chemical analysis. Chichester (UK): E. Horwood; 1975.

Notice there is no "and" between the two authors; it is just a list of names. If there are more authors, the citation would appear similar to example CSE-2 but with the additional authors' last names and first initials included.

CSE-3, Electronic Book

3. Ambrose SA, Bridges M, DiPietro M, Lovett MC, Norman MK. How learning works: 7 research-based principles for smart teaching. [Amazon Kindle Reader version]. San Francisco: Jossey-Bass-Wiley, 2010. (2010). Available from: http://www .amazon.com/

After the basic bibliographic information, you need to include a brief description of the type of text; in this case we thought identifying the type of ereader was important. You then need to include where it is "Available from" (as with other digital texts).

CSE-4, Selection from an Edited Collection or Anthology

4. Fell DA, Thomas S, Poolman MG. Modeling metabolic pathways and analyzing control. In: Bryant JA, Burrell MM, Kruger NJ, editors. Plant carbohydrate biochemistry. Oxford (UK): BIOS Scientific; 1999. p. 17–28.

If you are citing an introduction, preface, foreword, or afterword, treat it like a section from a book.

☐ author   ☐ title   ☐ publication information

CSE-5

CSE-5, Book in an Edition Other Than First

5. Mohapatra RN, Palash BP. Massive neutrinos in physics and astrophysics. 3rd ed. River Edge (NJ): World Scientific; 2004.

When referring to books or other media in multiple editions, use the language you find on the document's title page. Therefore, if it says second or third edition, put the number in your citation. If it says "Revised" or "Abridged," put "Rev ed." or "Abr ed." in the citation. Similarly, if the book is the fifth in a multivolume work, include "Vol. 5."

CSE-6

CSE-6, Book in a Series

6. Agricultural Research Council (UK). Methods for the detection of the viruses of certain diseases in animals and animal products. Brussels: Commission of the European Communities; 1976. (Information on agriculture; no. 16).

Notice there is an organization as the author.

CSE-7

CSE-7, Book with a Translator

7. Trinh XT. Chaos and harmony: perspectives on scientific revolutions of the twentieth century. Reisinger A, translator. New York: Oxford University Press; 2001.

According to CSE, you do not need to include the information about a translator unless it is relevant to what you are writing about.

---

techno tip

CSE and Web Pages

In CSE the citation for a web site should include traditional information like author, title, publisher, and publication date; however, CSE also wants both the URL as well as a last date modified and date cited. If you can find an original publication date, that is what you would give for the publication; if not, list the last date modified. The last date modified is the date noted on the web site as the last time the web page changed. The date cited is when you specifically accessed the web page.

35. Centers for Disease Control and Prevention. Autism spectrum disorders: screening and diagnosis [Internet]. Atlanta (GA): Department of Health and Human Services; c2010 [modified 2010 May 13; cited 2012 Jun 2]. Available from: http://www.cdc.gov/ncbddd/autism/screening.html

CSE-8, Web Site

8. Kang K. Graduate enrollment in science and engineering grew substantially in the past decade but slowed in 2010 [Internet]. Arlington (VA): National Science Foundation, National Center for Science and Engineering Statistics; 2012 [modified 2012 May; cited 2012 Jun 2]. Available from: http://www.nsf.gov/statistics/infbrief/nsf12317/?org=NSF

CSE-9, Conference Proceedings

9. Watson J, Beswick K, editors. Mathematics: essential research, essential practice (vol. 1). Proceedings of the 30th annual conference of the Mathematics Education Research Group of Australasia; 2007 Jul 2–6; Tasmania, Australia [Internet]. Adelaide (Australia): MERGA [cited 2012 Jun 2]. Available from: http://www.eric.ed.gov/PDFS/ED503746.pdf

If the proceedings has a title, provide the title; if not, just start the title with "Proceedings of. " Then include the conference dates and location. CSE treats conference proceedings like books; therefore, if you are citing the entire proceedings, treat it like an edited book. If you are citing a particular section of the proceedings, cite it as a work in an anthology or edited collection.

CSE-10, Published Dissertation

10. Amir A. Industry technology roadmapping of nonwoven medical textiles [master's thesis]. Raleigh (NC): North Carolina State University; 2006 Nov.

The bracketed descriptor can state dissertation.

CSE-11, Film

11. Wakabayashi M, Yaskin K, editors; Cohen D, Tarantino L, producers. Life after people [digital video disc]. Los Angeles: Flight 33 Productions; 2008. 1 digital video disc: 94 min., sound, color.

When citing audiovisual material, CSE includes a lot of descriptive information. Consider using the Internet Movie Database (http://www.imdb.com) to find the names of editors and producers, information about the production and distribution companies, as well as the other details required by the citation.

CSE-12, Government Web Site

12. Centers for Disease Control and Prevention [Internet]. Atlanta
(GA): Department of Health and Human Services; c2008
[modified 2008 Mar 14; cited 2008 Mar 16]. Available from:
http://www.cdc.gov

Syndicated Resources

Syndicated resources are a little more complicated to cite in CSE style because there are
usually multiple titles involved: author of the work, title of the work, title of the journal or
newspaper that the work was published in, and publication information. Since many syndicated resources are now found in digital format, their citations are further complicated
because they generally include layers of digital publication information as well.

CSE-13, Article in a Scholarly Journal

The current CSE guidelines make a distinction between journals that are numbered continuously (e.g., Vol. 1 ends on page 208, Vol. 2 starts on page 209) or
numbered separately; that is, each volume starts on page 1. Only if the journal
pagination starts over in each issue must the citation contain volume *and* issue
numbers if available. Check several issues of journals you are citing to see which
format they follow and then use the appropriate format for your cited references
list. Use common journal title acronyms (e.g., JAMA for JAMA: The Journal of the
American Medical Association) or abbreviate journal titles when possible; for
example:

▶ Journal = J
▶ Medical = Med
▶ Hospital = Hosp

Article in a Printed Journal with Continued Pagination

36. Azawi OI. Postpartum uterine infection in cattle. Animal Reprod
Sci. 2008;105(3–4):187–208.

In this case "Science" has been abbreviated to "Sci." Note that no punctuation
follows the abbreviation; however, the citation style does include a period after
the journal title. The publication year is followed by a semicolon, no space, the
volume number, and the issue numbers of the journal in parentheses. Notice
there is no space between the colon and the page numbers.

Article in a Printed Journal with Separate Pagination

37. Quick D, Davies GD. Community college faculty development:
bringing technology into instruction. Community College J
Research and Practice. 1999;23:641–653.

| author | title | title of journal or newspaper | publication information | date cited |

Journal Article Accessed through a Database with Separate Pagination

38. Cohen P. Cowboys die hard: real men and businessmen in the Reagan-era blockbuster. Film & History [Internet]. 2011 [cited 2012 Jun 2]; 41: 71–81. Available from: http://muse.jhu.edu.ezproxy1.lib.asu.edu/journals/film_and_history/v041/41.1.cohen.html

Journal Article from Journal That Only Exists Online

39. Leston R, Carter G, Arroyo S. The chora of the Twin Towers. Enculturation [Internet]. 2011 [cited 2012 Jun 2] ; 10. Available from: http://enculturation.gmu.edu/the-chora-of-the-twin-towers

techno tip

CSE and Databases

CSE treats journals from databases as it does web pages on the Internet in that a modified date is not required. You will include the bracketed cited information after the year of publication and before the location associated with the print version of the article. Therefore, like a resource on a web site, you include the full URL of the database.

38. Cohen P. Cowboys die hard: real men and businessmen in the Reagan-era blockbuster. Film & History [Internet]. 2011 [cited 2012 Jun 2]; 41:71–81. Available from: http://muse.jhu.edu.ezproxy1.lib.asu.edu/journals/film_and_history/v041/41.1.cohen.html

CSE-14

CSE-14, Newspaper Article

Newspaper articles can generally be easily located in three forms of media: in print, online at the newspaper's web site, and through a library database. Newspaper entries look exactly like journal article entries, except you do not abbreviate a newspaper title. You also replace volume number with section information and add column information.

Printed Newspaper Article

40. Horgan D. College students seeing green as the way to go. USA Today. 2008 Mar 13; Sect. D: 8 (col. 2).

Newspaper Article Found Online

41. Brown E. White dwarf star measurements bring Milky Way into focus. Los Angeles Times [Internet]. 2012 May 30 [modified 2012 May 30; cited 2012 Jun 2]; Science. Available from: http://www.latimes.com/news/science/la-sci-milky-way-age-20120531,0,6600765.story

Newspaper Article Found in a Database

42. Brown E. Bringing star ages into sharper focus. Los Angeles Times (Home Ed.) [Internet]. 2012 May 31 [cited 2012 Jun 2]; Part A:15. Available from: http://www.lexisnexis.com.proxy. lib.odu.edu/hottopics/ lnacademic/?verb=sr&csi=8006

Like the *Wired* example at the beginning of Chapter 11 (page 244), the title for the same article on a web site is different from the title of the database version.

CSE-15, Newspaper Editorial

15. O'Cleireacain C. D.C.'s big sewer dig: why the whole region should pitch in [editorial]. Washington Post [Internet]. 2012 Jun 1. [modified 2012 Jun 1; cited 2012 Jun 2]. Available from: http://www. washingtonpost.com/opinions/dcs-big-sewer-dig-why-the-whole-region-should-pitch-in/2012/06/01/gJQAhu4l7U_story.html

CSE-16, Article in a Magazine

Treat magazine articles the same as journal articles.

Printed Magazine Article

43. Jacobs B. Corporate cannabis. Utne 2005 May-Jun:26–27.

Magazine Article Found Online

44. Pain E. Playing well with industry. Science [Internet]. 2008 Mar 14 [cited 2008 Mar 16]; 319(5869): 1548–1551. Available from: http://www.sciencemag.org/cgi/content/full/319/5869/1548

CSE-17, Blogs

Blogs, like periodicals and television shows, have overall titles and then specific articles, or "postings." Therefore, you might cite the entire blog web site, with all of its postings, an individual post, or a reader's comment to an individual post.

Individual Blog Post

45. Latter J. Support or sponsor "evolution research" [blog post on the Internet]. 2006 Jul 17 [cited 2008 Mar 17]. Available from: http://evolutiontest.blogspot.com/2006/07/support-or-sponsor-evolution-research.html

CSE-15

CSE-16

CSE-17

Comment on a Specific Posting in a Blog

46. Adams D. Reply to "cyber salon, the reality" [reply to blog post on the Internet]. 2008 Mar 9 [cited 2008 Mar 17]. Available from: http://www.committedtechnofile.com/index.php/application/comments/cyber_salon_the_reality

Dynamic Resources

Since dynamic resources change regularly, it is very important to include the exact date that you accessed the resource. CSE considers personal correspondence (e.g., letters, email, and live interviews) as primary research that you would describe in the text. No citation is required for primary research resources.

CSE-18, Page from a Wiki

19. Classrooms for the future: CFF science, life_science [wiki on the Internet]. [modified 2012 Jan 16; cited 2012 Jun 2]. Available from: http://cffscience.wikispaces.com/Life_Science

Notice there is no author listed. If you cannot find an author for your resource, then start with the title of the resource. Most wiki pages have a "history" or "page history" link or tab that will allow you to see the last time the page was updated.

CSE Style: Some Common Errors

reflect

▶ Entries in your cited references list fail to correspond to citations or are in the wrong format. The style of the cited references list is dictated by the in-text citation style you use.

▶ Punctuation in the author's name. The author's first initial is not separated from the last name with punctuation. The author's initials have no periods after them (except after the last one, which is the end of the category "author" in the entry).

▶ Confusion of publication or release and copyright dates.

▶ Spelled-out names of months. Most month names are condensed to three letters.

▶ Omission of a word or phrase that describes the type of resource that is not a written document (e.g., media or mode of access, DVD, weblog, podcast, etc.).

Paper Formatting

CSE's formatting guidelines are formal journal and book publication guidelines. Check with your instructor to see if he or she wants you to follow all of the following guidelines.

Title Page

The CSE style guidelines for journal article title pages specifically ask for the article title, the authors' names, the authors' affiliations, an abstract of the article, and the initial page number. For a course paper, you may want to change "author affiliation" to the names of the instructor and course for which you are submitting the paper. Your instructor may ask for the submission date as well. If there is enough room on the page, feel free to begin the text of your paper on the title page. You will need to check with your professor for specific guidelines on how to format a title page for your course paper.

Spacing and Margins

Your instructor will probably require that you double-space the entire document, including any footnotes you might have and the cited references list at the end of the paper. You do not need to include extra spaces (i.e., quadruple space) anywhere in the text. Set your top, left, and bottom margins for at least one inch. All paragraphs should be indented by one-half inch.

Headers and Page Numbers

CSE does not give specific page header and numbering guidelines for paper submissions. However, in the upper right corner of each page, you should include a running header with either a shortened version of your title or your last name and the page number. All pages in the paper should be consecutively numbered. The header is placed one-half inch from the top of the page and one inch from the right side of the page. You do not need to include the header and page number on the title page of your paper.

Section Headings

If your paper is long enough and it includes coherent sections, and even subsections, you might consider including section headings in your paper. Make sure that all of your section titles are parallel in both syntax and format. In other words, if you start your first section title with a noun, start all of your section titles with nouns. And if the first level of subheads is in bold type, all of the first-level subheads should be bold. If the second level of subheads is in italics, all of the second-level subheads must be in italics. CSE also calls for subheads that are concise and which fairly represent the importance of the material.

Writing a Rhetorical Analysis of Citations

One of our goals in the *Wadsworth Guide to Research* is to help you understand the rhetorical situation surrounding everything you write and how that context influences the development of a text. In the first three parts of the book, we ask you to think about the rhetorical situation of the research you are conducting, and, in this section, we ask you to extend that rhetorically critical eye to the ways you are documenting the research you have conducted—namely, how you cite resources.

In this DIY, we build on Chapter 11's coverage of the rhetorical situation of documentation styles such as MLA, APA, CMS, and CSE. So that you can gain practice thinking about and analyzing the rhetorical situation of citations themselves, this DIY introduces you to:

- **analyzing citation practices in a scholarly article**
- **constructing your own citation**

Common Features of a Rhetorical Analysis

A rhetorical analysis identifies the various elements of the rhetorical situation (topic, purpose, audience, and author) and then discusses how different rhetorical strategies support the elements of the rhetorical situation. This is true whether you are analyzing a scholarly article, an advertisement, or a piece of art.

▶ **Rhetorical Reading.** As discussed in Chapter 6, a rhetorical analysis needs to identify the various elements of the rhetorical situation of the text you are analyzing. Specifically, you should identify the topic, purpose, audience, and author and then provide evidence to justify your claim. The evidence needs to come from within the text, and possibly from other resources outside of the text.

▶ **Strategy Analysis.** Identify rhetorical strategies within the text that support the wants and needs of the different elements of the rhetorical situation. Rhetorical strategies might include things like different types of appeals (see Chapter 8's discussion of ethos, pathos, logos), types of evidence (see Chapter 8), arrangement patterns (see Chapter 10), and word choice, style, and tone.

Additional Features Found in Some Rhetorical Analyses

▶ **Focused Rhetorical Strategy.** Some rhetorical analyses may focus solely on one type of rhetorical strategy. For example, a rhetorical analysis of a peer reviewed article from a medical journal might focus on the rhetorical strategy of using passive voice as a way to emphasize the process of the scientific experiment and erase any bias that an individual researcher might have on the experiment process.

▶ **Focused Rhetorical Element.** Some rhetorical analyses may focus solely on how various rhetorical strategies support a specific element of the rhetorical situation. For example, a rhetorical analysis of a prescription drug advertisement in a women's magazine might focus on how the advertisement targets women of a specific age range and socioeconomic status.

Two Ways to Analyze Citations Rhetorically

The following sections can help you understand citation practices better by closely examining citations within scholarly writing and by constructing your own citation of a source without an existing model.

Analyzing Citation Practices in a Scholarly Article

A rhetorical analysis that examines citation practices in a scholarly article is a rhetorical analysis focusing on a specific rhetorical strategy. Conducting rhetorical analyses of citation practices of a given text will help you to understand more deeply how a citation style functions within an argument. Knowing how citations work can help you identify which citation style you should follow in your own projects or discipline. Analyzing citations rhetorically can also help you write your own project, especially if you are required to make up a citation for an unusual resource or provide citations in a multimedia project.

Features of a Rhetorical Analysis of Citation Practices

As with any rhetorical analysis, you must first identify the various rhetorical elements of the given text. Depending on the audience of the rhetorical analysis, you may need to spend more or less time providing evidence to support what you identify as a specific topic, purpose, audience, and author. Citations are generally a convention to help the audience identify and locate the original resource mentioned in the text. Therefore, in a rhetorical analysis of citation practices, it is important to spend time identifying a very specific audience to understand and analyze their wants and needs as readers.

In a citation analysis, pay attention to both in-text citations as well as full bibliographic citations. The analysis should take into account (1) the content included in the citation, (2) the location and format of the citation, and (3) the surrounding context of the in-text portion of the citation. (See Chapter 11 for more information on how in-text and full bibliographic citations work together.)

Example of a Rhetorical Analysis of Citation Practices

Sharon Salyer, Amanda David, Keya Murphy, and Mae Gree

Professor Rodrigo

ENGL439

March 20, 2012

Citation Roots: A Rhetorical Analysis of

Citation Practices in Jennifer Bowie's

"Rhetorical Roots and Media Future"

The author, Jennifer L. Bowie, created this podcast for college computer writing teachers. She addresses how the five canons of rhetoric are pertinent to new media texts. As she explains, "I address how podcasting may be used in classrooms to help students rethink the 'old' writing concepts we have been teaching, such as the five canons and audience, tone, purpose, and context, in new ways and consider how students may bring the lessons they learned from podcasting back to their print text writing" (3). The purpose of the series is to explore how podcasting fits into a computer writing class: "The most interesting aspect of podcasting, especially from an educational standpoint, is the time- and location-shifted aspects of the texts. People may listen anytime, anywhere—they are not chained to a specific time or place" (5).

Although the predominant method of delivering this article is audio, through a podcast, Bowie does a good job of citing her information. Any information that she did not create on her own and what she has gathered from other sources needs to be cited.

This information needs to be cited because you cannot use or build upon someone else's work without giving them credit. (This is done to avoid plagiarism and copyright infringement.) Within her works she needed to cite: student papers, interviews, and music. Specifically, Bowie cites her information in the following ways:

- **Within the podcasts:** She read excerpts from student papers and cited individual student's names.
- **At the end of the transcripts:** She listed inactive hyperlinks to web sites and sources of information she used.
- **On the web page** where the podcasts and transcript can be accessed: She listed active hyperlinks to the same web pages and information that is in the transcript.

The citations work for this article because they are cleanly presented, simple to read and understand, and accurate so that the reader may access the original source being referenced. The citations are also in several places: in the transcript, in the podcast, and on the web site. Users are able to view the resources from several different locations. To be more precise about which student was being cited, she could have spoken the individual student podcast clips citations instead of just stating that they were "used with permission."

In a final demonstration of rhetorical citation savvy, Bowie also directly states her creative commons licensing of her podcast in the audio; therefore it also appears in the transcript.

Work Cited

Bowie, Jennifer. "Rhetorical Roots and Media Future: How Podcasting Fits into the Computers and Writing Classroom." *Kairos*. Web. 28 Feb. 2012. <http://www.technorhetoric.net/16.2/topoi/ bowie/index.html>.

Discussion Questions

▶ In what ways is the rhetorical situation for citation in Bowie's text complex? How might the student authors better articulate those complexities?

▶ How do the authors analyze the citations? What "traditional" aspects of citations might the authors have spent more time analyzing?

▶ Based on the topic of Bowie's text, what citation style should she use? Why? What style would the readers of her text most likely expect?

▶ What citation style do the authors of this analysis use for their citation analysis? Why do you think they chose that citation style?

Steps to Developing a Rhetorical Analysis of Citation Practices

For this assignment your task is to analyze rhetorically how the citations function within a given text to support the rhetorical elements: topic, purpose, audience, and author. Regardless of what type of scholarly text you analyze, you should include the following features:

▶ Introduction to the text you are analyzing and discussion of why it is important to understand the citation practices used in the text

▶ Descriptions labeling each rhetorical element as well as evidence supporting your label

▶ Descriptions identifying each rhetorical strategy as well as discussion of how that strategy supports the rhetorical elements

You will likely follow four major steps in completing your rhetorical analysis of citation practices:

1. Select the text you will be analyzing
2. Identify the elements of the rhetorical situation
3. Locate and analyze in-text citations
4. Locate and analyze full bibliographic citations

Identifying your Text

If the text you will be analyzing is not already assigned, your first task is to identify a text to analyze. You will want to think of your rhetorical situation in completing this activity. What will you be learning from the rhetorical analysis of citation style and why is it important to learn it? In most cases, you will be analyzing the citation patterns in a specific discipline so that you better understand the discipline's writing patterns. If you are responsible for identifying the text you will be analyzing, be prepared to propose two or three options. Also be sure to carefully track where you found each text so that you can easily find it again.

Here are some additional activities to try as you search for a text:

▶ "Write: Identify Kairos," on page 39 of Chapter 3

▶ "Write: Analyze the Rhetorical Situation," on page 41 of Chapter 3

▶ "Write: Discover Disciplinary Patterns and Conventions," on page 14 of Chapter 1

▶ "Write: Develop a List of Search Terms," on page 75 of Chapter 4

▶ "Write: Search the Library Catalog," on page 82 of Chapter 4

▶ "Write: Search for Resources in Periodicals," on page 84 of Chapter 4

▶ "Write: Search for a Variety of Resources," on page 88 of Chapter 4

Identifying the Rhetorical Elements

Before analyzing how the citations function within the text, you need to first identify the rhetorical elements of the text: topic, purpose, audience, and author. To be able to precisely identify these elements, you will probably need to read the text numerous times.

Here are some additional activities to try as you identify the rhetorical elements in your text:

- ▶ "Write: Situate a Resource Rhetorically," on page 116 of Chapter 6
- ▶ "Write: Annotate a Resource," on page 118 of Chapter 6
- ▶ "Write: Take Detailed Notes on a Resource," on page 122 of Chapter 6

Analyze In-Text Citations

As you begin your analysis, you might want to start with the in-text citations; however, that is not required. Here are some resources to help you analyze your in-text citations:

- ▶ "Integration of Resources into Your Arguments," on page 137 of Chapter 7
- ▶ "In-text Citations," on page 247 of Chapter 11

Analyze Full Bibliographic Citations

Finally, you want to be sure to also analyze the full bibliographic citations. Here are some resources that might help:

- ▶ "Integration of Resources into Your Arguments," on page 137 of Chapter 7
- ▶ "Full Bibliographic Citations," on page 248 of Chapter 11

Constructing a New Citation

The skill of constructing full bibliographic citations for resources that do not have an exact model in either textbooks or the citation style guide is no longer optional for college students. We guarantee that you will need to do this during your college career if you are carefully documenting your work and giving credit to the sources you have consulted. We also know that by constructing citations you will better understand how and why the citation style is organized and presented in a specific manner.

Features of Constructing a New Citation

As described in "Learning Citation Styles by Constructing Your Own Citations" (page 256), you must first carefully understand the type of resource you are citing so that you can find models that best resemble the types of resources most like your text. You will also need to understand some of the reasons for how and why the citation style you are using presents bibliographic information in the manner outlined in the style guide. You then need to combine the elements from the sample citations to make your own. In a project where you not only have to make the citation, but where you also have to describe how and why you constructed the citation in the manner you chose, you will need to carefully describe the reasons for your choices.

Example of Constructing a New Citation

Zoe Fraser

Professor Miller-Cochran

ENG 101

25 September 2012

National Geographic Explorer Application for Android

Cengage Learning offers a free downloadable application for Android tablets titled *National Geographic Explorer*. The free version of the app offers limited information on various geologic and earth science topics. Although the resource is downloadable and could be easily updated, it appears to be static, more like a book. It is edited by *National Geographic*, but there is no evidence that the information has undergone peer review. The resource most resembles an encyclopedia such as *Britannica Online* (http://www.britannica.com/, a web site). The resource is different from *Britannica Online*, however, because it is a downloadable app that would reside on a mobile device, and it comes in multiple versions (a free version and a subscription version, which includes more information).

In APA style, static, edited resources such as encyclopedias are generally cited with the editor's name first, then the year of publication in parentheses, the title of the encyclopedia in italics, the edition and volume numbers in parentheses, and the publication city and publisher at the end. The site http://www.easybib.com lists this example:

Taparia, N. (Ed.). (2000). Columbia encyclopedia (2nd ed., Vols. 1–45). Chicago: Columbia Press.

The *National Geographic Explorer* does not appear to have multiple volumes and editions, however, and it is a digital resource. The closest example I could find of a digital resource downloaded onto a mobile device was an ebook. The sixth edition of the *Publication Manual of the American Psychological Association* (2010) lists the following example of a cited electronic version of a print book (which would be a book that can be accessed in multiple versions, like the information in the *National Geographic Explorer*):

Schiraldi, G. R. (2001). *The post-traumatic stress disorder sourcebook: A guide to healing, recovery, and growth* [Adobe Digital Editions version]. doi:10.1036/0071393722

The unique element of this citation that seems relevant is that the version is included in brackets after the title of the resource. There is no DOI available for the downloadable app of *National Geographic Explorer*, so I don't believe that would be useful. Rather, the best location information could be found from knowing where the app was retrieved from. The second ebook example in the APA guide does not list a DOI, but instead has this at the end of the citation:

Retrieved from http://www.ebookstore.tandf.co.uk/html/index.asp

Based on this example, I believe I would list the place from which I downloaded the app instead of a DOI.

I constructed a citation for my resource by piecing together the prior examples. My citation looks like this:

Mayor, M. (2012). *National Geographic Explorer* [Free down-loadable version for Android]. Retrieved from Android Play Store.

I constructed it this way because the author should be listed first, followed by the year. The title of the resource is clear, and I listed which version of the resource I accessed, including that it was the free version. This information is important because a subscription version is also available. I also listed the place from which I down-loaded the app.

Discussion Questions

▶ Are there other examples or models that you think the author of the preceding citation could have used to help construct the citation?

▶ On page 385, take a look at an image of the "title page" of the resource, as viewed on an Android device. Notice that the image of the title page does not list the author's name. Where would you look for that information? What would you do if you could not find it (or other important elements of the citation)?

▶ If you were constructing a citation from another style—MLA, CMS, CSE, or something else—where would you find examples to cite? What references would you use as authorities on the citation style?

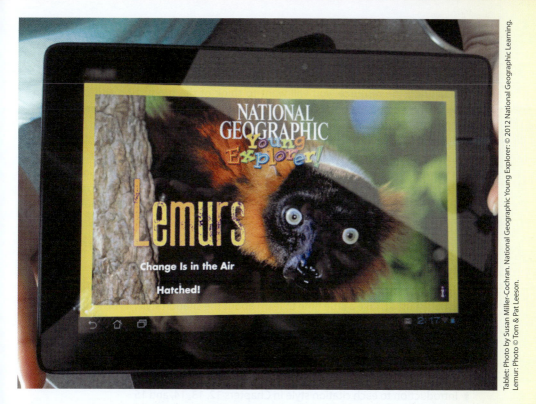

Tablet: Photo by Susan Miller-Cochran. National Geographic Young Explorer: © 2012 National Geographic Learning. Lemur: Photo © Tom & Pat Leeson.

Steps to Constructing a New Citation

For this assignment your task is to construct a new full bibliographic citation for a resource that does not have a model in this textbook or in the citation guide. Regardless of what type of text you construct a citation for, include the following features:

▶ Introduction of the resource you are constructing the citation for, along with a discussion of what type of resource it is (static, syndicated, dynamic, edited, peer reviewed, and/or self-published) and what types of recognizable resources it resembles.

▶ Brief description of the citation style guide you are using to construct the citation with a discussion of how and why the style presents bibliographic information to meet the needs of the purpose and audience.

▶ Presentation of the example full bibliographic entries you will be referencing.

▶ Presentation of your newly constructed full bibliographic entry.

▶ Discussion of how and why you presented the bibliographic entry in the manner you chose, with references to models from the textbook or style guide as evidence.

You will likely follow five major steps in your construction of a new citation:

1. Analyze the resource for which you will be constructing the bibliographic citation
2. Analyze the citation style you will be using to construct the citation
3. Identify model citations that are similar to the resource you are citing
4. Construct your citation
5. Reflect on how and why you constructed the citation in the manner you chose

Analyzing Your Resource

If the resource for which you will be constructing a full bibliographic citation is not already assigned to you, your first task is to identify a resource. We suggest you have fun and be creative. Some of our favorite creative resources are skywriting, outdoor advertisements, and body art.

In analyzing the resource, you will want to think of the production and publication process of the text. Once published is it easily republished (more or less static or dynamic)? Can someone find another copy of it (mass—usually static—publishing or one-time dynamic publishing)? Is the resource part of a series that publishes regularly (more syndicated)? Does the resource have an editor or is it self-published? Was it somehow peer reviewed or crowd-sourced? List the types of more "normal" scholarly resources that your resource resembles and discuss how and why the resources are similar to yours, and how they are different. Here are some resources to help you analyze your resource:

- ▶ "Types of Resources," on page 78 of Chapter 4
- ▶ "Learning Citation Styles by Constructing Your Own Citations," on page 256 of Chapter 11

Analyzing the Citation Style

To help you construct your new citation, it is helpful to understand the citation style guide you are using. Take a little time to learn about the citation style, its history, what disciplines use it, and how various publication elements are listed in an individual citation. Here are some resources to help you analyze your citation style:

- ▶ Introduction to citation styles in "Choosing the Appropriate Style Guide" on page 261 of Chapter 11
- ▶ Introduction to each citation style in Chapters 12, 13, 14, and 15
- ▶ Introduction and About sections in the actual citation style guides

Identifying Example Citations

Now you are ready to find example citations that will help you construct your own. Here are some resources to help you find example citations:

- ▶ The individual citation style chapter in Chapters 12, 13, 14, and 15
- ▶ The individual citation style guide

Constructing Your New Citation

Finally, you are ready to construct your own citation. As you make decisions about how and why you are presenting information, be sure to take notes so you can reference them later. Here is a resource that might help:

- ▶ "Learning Citation Styles by Constructing Your Own Citations," on page 256 of Chapter 11

Reflecting on the Construction of Your New Citation

In a project that asks you to critically construct a full bibliographic citation, you need to justify your decisions. Discuss what aspects of each sample citation you combined to construct your new citation. Describe how and why these aspects and examples were appropriate and mention any minor changes you may have made.

Here is a resource that might help:

- ▶ "Learning Citation Styles by Constructing Your Own Citations," on page 256 of Chapter 11

Make It with Multiple Media:
Screencapture Video

When rhetorically analyzing or constructing citations, it is sometimes easier to visually show what you are discussing instead of (or in addition to) trying to write about it. There are a variety of free screen capture applications that allow you to take pictures or make a video of what you are doing on your computer screen. When analyzing citations in an article you can highlight or otherwise annotate sections of the text while you are shooting a video and talking about the analysis. Similarly, when discussing how and why you constructed a citation in a particular way, you can visually highlight, compare, and contrast citation examples with your new citation during a screen captured video.

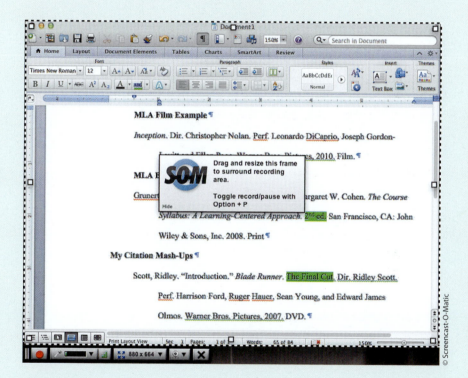

Some free screen capture applications include:

* Jing: http://jingproject.com
* Screencast-O-Matic: http://www.screencast-o-matic.com/
* CamStudio: http://camstudio.org/

Answers to Part 4: Formatting Your Research

Answers to Writing Activity, page 251: Practice Citations

MODERN LANGUAGE ASSOCIATION (MLA)

Strauss concludes that "the moral is that unless we show faculty members how technology can meet their needs, they won't consider using it." While studying what community college faculty needed to incorporate technology into their instruction, Quick and Davies found that faculty needed time, money, software, classroom computers (professor podium), department computer lab, and faculty technical support and training. In discussing how to prepare college faculty for the incoming Net generation of students, Clayton-Pedersen and O'Neill claim that "much of the learning technology innovation in higher education has been focused on K–12 teacher preparation and development" and that "more focus needs to be placed on preparing existing faculty for the future Net Generation students who will populate the twenty-first century classroom" (9.5). They continue that call for action in claiming that "faculty's understanding of the teaching and learning power of technology needs to be increased" and "tools need to be developed to help faculty integrate technology into the curriculum" (9.2). Strauss, Quick and Davies, and Clayton-Pedersen and O'Neill demonstrate that faculty first need blatant introductions to the new technologies themselves: what they are and what they can do.

Comments

▶ The Strauss quotation does not need anything more than what is already there (the last name of the author) since it is an electronic source and there are no page numbers.

▶ The reference to Quick and Davies summarizes their entire article; therefore, it is not necessary to include a page number. However, if this were reporting very specific information from a specific page or two of the text, you would be required to include page numbers.

▶ The first two Clayton-Pedersen and O'Neill quotes come from the same page; therefore, you need to include the page reference only at the end of the sentence. When the quotes come from different pages, you need to include a different page number (within parentheses) after each quotation. And although the bibliographic citation makes this resource "look" like an electronic text without page numbers, it is an ebook and therefore has specific page numbers that you could reference. The "9.5" and "9.2" references reflect the way that this book is numbered. As an ebook, each chapter starts the page numbering over at 1. The "9.5" numbering scheme takes into account that this is the fifth page of the ninth chapter. Finally, notice that the period has been moved from within the quotation to after the citation. Citations are considered a part of the sentence and therefore need to come before the end-of-sentence punctuation.

Works Cited Entries

Works Cited

Clayton-Pedersen, Alma R., and Nancy O'Neill. "Curricula Designed to Meet Twenty-first-Century Expectations." *Educating the Net Generation*. Ed. Diana G. Oblinger and James L. Oblinger. Washington, DC: EDUCAUSE, 2005. Web. 22 Aug. 2011.

Quick, Don, and Timothy Gray Davies. "Community College Faculty Development: Bringing Technology into Instruction." *Community College Journal of Research and Practice* 23.4 (1999): 641–53. Print.

Strauss, Howard. "Why Many Faculty Members Aren't Excited about Technology." *The Chronicle of Higher Education* 24 June 2005. Web. 31 Dec. 2011.

AMERICAN PSYCHOLOGICAL ASSOCIATION (APA)

Strauss concludes that "the moral is that unless we show faculty members how technology can meet their needs, they won't consider using it" (2005, para. 20). While studying what community college faculty needed to incorporate technology into their instruction, Quick and Davies (1999) found that faculty needed time, money, software, classroom computers (professor podium), department computer lab, and faculty technical support and training. In discussing how to prepare college faculty for the incoming Net generation of students, Clayton-Pedersen and O'Neill (2005) claim that "much of the learning technology innovation in higher education has been focused on K–12 teacher preparation and development" and that "more focus needs to be placed on preparing existing faculty for the future Net Generation students who will populate the twenty-first century classroom" (p. 9.5). They continue that call for action in claiming that "faculty's understanding of the teaching and learning power of technology needs to be increased" and "tools need to be developed to help faculty integrate technology into the curriculum" (p. 9.2). Strauss, Quick and Davies, and Clayton-Pedersen and O'Neill demonstrate that faculty first need blatant introductions to the new technologies themselves: what they are and what they can do.

Comments

▶ In citing an electronic resource without page numbering, APA requires that you count the paragraphs in the text and cite the quotation with the paragraph number. In this citation, you could have also put the publication year within parentheses directly after the author's last name and then left the paragraph number portion of the citation after the quotation (as with the Clayton-Pedersen example). Finally, notice that the period has been moved from within the quotation to after the citation. Citations are considered a part of the sentence and therefore need to come before the end-of-sentence punctuation.

▶ The reference to Quick and Davies summarizes their entire article; therefore, it is not necessary to include a page number. However, if this were reporting very specific information from a specific page or two of the text, you would be required to include page numbers. Unlike MLA, APA still requires that you include the publication year.

▶ The first two Clayton-Pedersen and O'Neill quotes come from the same page; therefore, you need to include the page reference only at the end of the sentence. If the quotes had come from different pages, you would have needed to include a different page number (within parentheses) after each quotation. And although the bibliographic citation makes this resource "look" like an electronic text without page numbers, it is an ebook and therefore has specific page numbers you could reference. The "9.5" and "9.2" references are due to the way that this book is numbered. In an ebook, each chapter starts the page numbering over at 1. The "9.5" numbering scheme takes into account that this is the fifth page of the ninth chapter.

▶ Notice that in the last sentence you do not need to put the publication years after mentioning the authors' names. Once you've mentioned the author's name and publication year in your paper, you do not need to mention the publication year again.

References Entries

References

Clayton-Pedersen, A. R., & O'Neill, N. (2005). Curricula designed to meet twenty-first-century expectations. In D. G. Oblinger, & J. L. Oblinger (Eds.), *Educating the Net generation* (chap. 9). Washington, DC: EDUCAUSE. Retrieved from http://www.educause.edu/ir/library/pdf/pub7101.pdf

Quick, D., & Davies, T. G. (1999). Community college faculty development: Bringing technology into instruction. *Community College Journal of Research and Practice, 23*, 641–653.

Strauss, H. (2005, June 24). Why many faculty members aren't excited about technology. *The Chronicle of Higher Education, 51*(42). Retrieved from http://chronicle.com/weekly/v51/i42/42b03001.htm

THE CHICAGO MANUAL OF STYLE (CMS)

Strauss concludes that "the moral is that unless we show faculty members how technology can meet their needs, they won't consider using it."[1] While studying what community college faculty needed to incorporate technology into their instruction, Quick and Davies found that faculty needed time, money, software, classroom computers (professor podium), department computer lab, and faculty technical support and training.[2] In discussing how to prepare college faculty for the incoming Net generation of students, Clayton-Pedersen and O'Neill claim that "much of the learning technology innovation in higher education has been focused on K–12 teacher preparation and development" and that "more focus needs to be placed on preparing existing faculty for the future Net Generation students who will populate the twenty-first century classroom."[3] They continue that call for action in claiming that "faculty's understanding of the teaching and learning power of technology needs to be increased" and "tools need to be developed to help faculty integrate technology into the curriculum."[4] Strauss, Quick and Davies, and Clayton-Pedersen and O'Neill demonstrate that faculty first need blatant introductions to the new technologies themselves: what they are and what they can do.

Bibliography Entries

Condensed Footnote

Notes

1. Howard Strauss, "Why Many Faculty Members Aren't Excited," Faculty members believe the technology will hurt them, paragraph 20.

2. Don Quick and Timothy Gray Davies, "Community College Faculty Development"

3. Alma R. Clayton-Pederson and Nancy O'Neill, "Curricula Designed," 9.5.

4. Ibid, 9.2

Complete Footnote

Notes

1.   Howard Strauss, "Why Many Faculty Members Aren't Excited about Technology," *The Chronicle of Higher Education,* June 24, 2005, http://chronicle.com/article/Why-Many-Faculty-Members/3167/, paragraph 20.

2.   Don Quick and Timothy Gray Davies, "Community College Faculty Development: Bringing Technology into Instruction," *Community College Journal of Research and Practice* 23, no. 4 (1999): 641–53.

3.   Alma R. Clayton-Pedersen and Nancy O'Neill, "Curricula Designed to Meet Twenty-first-Century Expectations," *Educating the Net Generation*, ed. Diana G. Oblinger and James L. Oblinger (Washington, DC: EDUCAUSE, 2005), accessed August 14, 2012, http://www.educause.edu/ir/library/pdf/pub7101.pdf, 9.5.

4. Ibid, 9.2

Complete Full Bibliography

Bibliography

Clayton-Pedersen, Alma R., and Nancy O'Neill. "Curricula Designed to Meet Twenty-first-Century Expectations." *Educating the Net Generation*, edited by Diana G. Oblinger and James L. Oblinger. Washington, DC: Educause, 2005. Accessed August 14, 2012. http://www.educause.edu/ir/library/pdf/pub7101 .pdf.

Quick, Don, and Timothy Gray Davies. "Community College Faculty Development: Bringing Technology into Instruction." *Community College Journal of Research and Practice* 23, no. 4 (1999): 641–53.

Strauss, Howard. "Why Many Faculty Members Aren't Excited about Technology." *The Chronicle of Higher Education.* June 24, 2005. http://chronicle.com/article /Why-Many-Faculty-Members/3167/.

Comments

▶ As seen with the Strauss example, *Chicago* style asks that you include some type of textual marker, like a subhead, to help readers find the direct quote. Notice that the superscript numbers are put after the end-of-sentence punctuation.

▶ The reference to Quick and Davies summarizes their entire article; therefore, it is not necessary to include a page number. However, if this were reporting very specific information from a specific page or two of the text, you would be required to include page numbers.

▶ The first two Clayton-Pedersen and O'Neill quotes come from the same page; therefore, you need to include the page reference only at the end of the sentence. If the quotes had come from different pages, you would have needed to include a different superscript number after each quotation (and if you wanted to keep them both within the same sentence, you would include the first superscript number within the sentence). Once you are citing the same source, you may use "ibid." in the condensed footnotes area. Although the bibliographic citation makes this resource "look" like an electronic text without page numbers, it is an ebook and therefore has specific page numbers you could reference. The "9.5" reference is due to the way that this book is numbered. As an ebook, each chapter starts the page numbering over at one. The "9.5" and "9.2" references are due to the way that this book is numbered. In an ebook, each chapter starts the page numbering over at 1. The "9.5" numbering scheme takes into account that this is the fifth page of the ninth chapter.

Index